Decentralization and Local
Governance in Developing
Countries

Decentralization and Local Governance in Developing Countries

A Comparative Perspective

Edited by Pranab Bardhan and
Dilip Mookherjee

The MIT Press
Cambridge, Massachusetts
London, England

MIT Press books may be purchased at special quantity discounts for business or sales promotional use. For information, please e-mail ⟨special_sales@mitpress.mit.edu.⟩.

This book was set in Palatino on 3B2 by Asco Typesetters, Hong Kong, and was printed and bound in the United States of America.

Library of Congress Cataloging-in-Publication Data

Decentralization and local governance in developing countries : a comparative perspective/edited by Pranab Bardhan and Dilip Mookherjee.
    p. cm.
Includes bibliographical references and index.
ISBN-10 0-262-02600-7—ISBN-13 978-0-262-02600-0 (hc : alk. paper)
ISBN-10 0-262-52454-6—ISBN-13 978-0-262-52454-4 (pbk. : alk. paper)
1. Decentralization in government—Developing countries. 2. Local government—Developing countries. 3. Developing countries—Politics and government.
4. Comparative government. I. Bardhan, Pranab K. II. Mookherjee, Dilip.

JF60.D43   2006
320.809172′4—dc22   2005058425

10 9 8 7 6 5 4 3 2

Contents

Preface

This book emerged from our growing awareness that social scientists know relatively little about a contemporary trend to devolve political and economic power to local governments throughout the developing world. While some academic studies of the impact of decentralization in particular contexts have appeared recently, a comparative perspective on this institutional transformation has not been available. We therefore organized a conference and invited experts involved in development as academics or policy practitioners from a number of different countries that have embarked on significant devolution initiatives to describe these experiences in some detail. The May 2003 conference was funded by the MacArthur Foundation Network on Inequality and Economic Performance and was hosted by the Suntory Toyota International Centre for Economics and Related Disciplines (STICERD) at the London School of Economics. We are grateful to the MacArthur Foundation and STICERD for their generous support. In particular, we would like to thank Sam Bowles of the Macarthur Foundation Network on Inequality and Economic Performance for his encouragement and Tim Besley and Kate Perry of STICERD for being such gracious hosts.

Special acknowledgments are due to the discussants of the papers presented at the conference: Oriana Bandiera, Robin Burgess, Bhaskar Dutta, Maitreesh Ghatak, Geeta Kingdon, James Manor, Paul Seabright, and Chengang Xu, whose comments generated useful discussion and helped the authors revise their chapters. Patricia Meirelles and Catherine Rodriguez provided substantial research assistance to us in our writing the introductory chapter and with the editing and preparation of the entire manuscript. Without their help, this book would not have been possible.

Pranab Bardhan and Dilip Mookherjee

Decentralization and Local Governance in Developing Countries

1   The Rise of Local Governments: An Overview

Pranab Bardhan and
Dilip Mookherjee

Introduction

The last two decades of the twentieth century witnessed a significant rise in the scope of local democracy throughout the developing world, with increasing devolution of political, economic, and administrative authority to local governments. Along with privatization and deregulation, this shift represents a substantial reduction in the authority of national governments over economic policy. The phenomenon is geographically widespread, occurring simultaneously in Latin America, Africa, Asia, and Eastern Europe. The earliest changes were initiated in the 1970s, picked up momentum in the 1980s, and accelerated after 1990.

The purpose of this volume is to describe this institutional transformation in comparative perspective: its historical origins, the underlying motives of the principal agents initiating the changes, the details of the devolution of rights and responsibilities to local governments, and the dimensions of the likely impact of this transformation. The principal objectives are to describe the political context of decentralization, consider how this context shaped the way that decentralization evolved, and examine the potential equity and efficiency effects that might be realized. We view this as a necessary first step to an evaluation of the overall impact of decentralization on development. Whatever evidence exists concerning impact in the chosen countries is reported in the studies, but these reports fall short of providing a rigorous impact assessment. The institutional description of the process should instead help identify the issues, contexts, and problems that more detailed impact analyses will need to address in future research.

Eight countries were chosen from three different continents (Bolivia and Brazil from Latin America, South Africa and Uganda from Africa, and China, India, Indonesia, and Pakistan from Asia). These countries have witnessed significant recent shifts toward decentralization or transformations in the nature of decentralization. Table 1.1 provides some broad summary statistics concerning their size, per capita income, indicators of poverty, and quality of life. Together they represent a population of approximately 2.8 billion, concentrated among poor and middle-income countries, accounting for more than half of all people in the world in these two categories. The majority of countries are poor: excluding Brazil and South Africa, per capita incomes range between $1,100 and $3,300 (1999 U.S. dollars using purchasing-power parity). The Asian countries tend to be more populated, poorer, less literate, less urban, and have less access to sanitation. Four Asian countries were included partly to make the study more representative in terms of population size. The countries vary considerably in historical and political contexts and the nature of decentralization. The case studies aim to present a perspective that stresses political and economic aspects of the decentralization in equal measure. Table 1.2 profiles the seven selected regions.

The first part of this chapter presents a conceptual framework for classifying and evaluating these diverse decentralization experiments and identifies the issues addressed by the case studies. The second part presents a brief summary of the main findings of each country case study. The third part appraises the diverse country experiences using a comparative perspective.

Our main focus here is on decentralization of political authority to local governments and on democracy at a level lower than states or provinces. This distinction is meaningful in countries of medium size or large enough size that state, regional, or provincial governments form an intermediate tier between national and local governments. In such contexts, our main interest is in devolution and democracy at district, county, municipal, or village levels rather than at the state or regional levels. In small countries where there are principally two tiers of government—the national and local—the issue is the allocation of powers and functioning of local governments. In others with at least three important tiers, we are interested in the bottom tier rather than the relation between the top two tiers. This distinguishes our enquiry from Rodden, Eskeland, and Litvack (2003), for instance, who provide a comparative perspective on how fiscal decentralization affects regional, provincial, or state governments within different federated systems across a broad spectrum of developed and developing countries.

Table 1.1
Profiles of selected countries

	Population (million, 2002)[a]	GDP per Capita (U.S. dollars PPP, 2002)[b]	Percentage below $1 a Day (survey year in parentheses)[c]	Life Expectancy at Birth (years, 2002)[b]	Percentage of Adult Literacy[b]	Percentage of Population Urban[c]	Percentage of Urban Population with Access to Sanitation[c]
China	1,281	4,580	18.5 (1998)	70.9	90.9	32	58
India	1,048	2,670	44.2 (1997)	63.7	61.3	28	46
Pakistan	145	1,940	31.0 (1996)	60.8	41.5	36	53
Indonesia	212	3,230	15.2 (1999)	66.6	87.9	40	73
South Africa	44	10,070	11.5 (1993)	48.8	86.0	52	79
Uganda	23	1,390	36.7 (1992)	45.7	69.9	14	75
Bolivia	9	2,460	11.3 (1990)	63.7	86.7	62	77
Brazil	174	7,770	5.1 (1997)	68.0	86.4	81	74

a. World Bank (2004).
b. United Nations (2004).
c. World Bank (2000).

Table 1.2
Profile of selected regions

	Population (millions, 2002)[a]	GDP per Capita (U.S. dollars PPP, 2002)[b]	Life Expectancy at Birth (years, 2002)[b]	Percentage of Adult Literacy[b]
East Asia and Pacific	1,838	4,768	69.8	90.3
South Asia	1,401	2,658	63.2	57.6
Sub-Saharan Africa	688	1,620	46.3	63.2
Latin America and Caribbean	527	7,223	70.5	88.6
World	6,201	7,804	66.9	—
Low-income countries	2,495	2,149	59.1	63.6
Middle-income countries	2,742	5,908	70.0	89.7

a. World Bank (2004).
b. United Nations (2004).

Conceptual Framework

From the standpoint of politics, decentralization is typically viewed as an important element of participatory democracy that allows citizens to have an opportunity to communicate their preferences and views to elected officials who are subsequently rendered accountable for their performance to citizens. Apart from actual outcomes in terms of policies, their detailed implementation, and their impact on economic well-being, popular participation is valued for its own sake for a variety of reasons. It can promote a sense of autonomy in citizens, enhance social order by promoting the legitimacy of the state, and limit pressures for separatism by diverse regions or ethnic groups.

In terms of relevant normative economic criteria, local public goods should be provided according to the preferences of residents, with conflicts between preferences of different groups settled according to welfare weights that correspond to their respective demographic weights and relative needs. In utilitarian terms, this is represented by a social-welfare function that aggregates utilities of different citizens. Distortions in the political mechanism correspond to deviations of weights implicit in actual policy choices from normative welfare weights—in other words, where certain groups receive special treatment not commensurate with their demographic significance or urgency of need. More often than not, it takes the form of an antipoor bias and sometimes discrimination against specific regions, ethnic, or religious groups in favor of special-interest groups. The sources of these distortions have received much attention from scholars of politics and political economy. In the contexts of functioning democracies, these include the following:

• An inability of voters to communicate intensities of preference;

• Asymmetries in turnout and awareness of voters and in the abilities of different parties to mobilize voters;

• The presence of interest groups and various means available to them to influence policy choices;

• The difficulties faced by candidates or elected officials in committing to long-term policy positions;

• The absence of stable political parties;

• Instabilities resulting from coalitional politics;

• An unevenness or a lack of effective political competition;

• Multidimensional policy issues;

• A lack of coordination among voters;

• Party ideologies that deviate from popular preferences;

• An absence of free and fair elections;

• Incumbency advantages.

In other contexts involving lack of effective political contestability, policies reflect the preferences of those in power. Added to these problems of political incentives are problems of incentives of bureaucrats appointed by politicians to implement public policies: corruption, inappropriate selection and monitoring of projects, and lack of responsiveness to citizen needs.

In practical economic terms, the purpose of widening the scope and fairness of a democracy is to promote twin objectives of accountability and responsiveness of policy concerning delivery of local public goods and services to citizens. *Accountability* can be defined in terms of either the nature of the political process or the outcomes induced. The former definition is the more commonly used, especially by political scientists. In their recent book *Democracy, Accountability, and Representation*, A. Przeworski, S. C. Stokes, and B. Manin (1999, p. 10) define accountability thus: "Governments are 'accountable' if citizens can discern representative from unrepresentative governments and can sanction them appropriately, retaining in office those who perform well and ousting from office those who do not." While this definition pertains to democracies, accountability may exist even in nondemocracies if officials respond to pressure exerted directly or indirectly by citizen groups. The political definition of *accountability* can therefore be modified as "the ability of citizens to put effective pressure on officials who deviate from the expressed wishes of a majority among them." Such deviations can take the form of violations of distributive justice resulting in cases where the actual policy weights accorded to disparate citizen groups are seriously misaligned with their welfare weights reflecting demographic size or relative need.

This leads to an alternative definition of accountability in terms of induced outcomes rather than the process, in what would constitute a revealed-preference approach popular among economists. Lack of accountability in economic terms corresponds to outcomes that reflect implicit policy weights that deviate substantially from welfare weights. In other words, chosen policies exhibit systematic bias in favor of some groups at the expense of others, which cannot be justified by their demographic size or intensity of need. The notion thus includes criteria of distributive justice (vertical and horizontal equity) between different citizen groups. Insofar as government officials constitute one relevant citizen group, accountability also includes minimization of corruption and inefficient rent-seeking by government officials. In more practical terms, lack of accountability corresponds to situations where policy makers exhibit a systematic antipoor bias—for example, are captured by (regional, landed, or corporate) elites or wealthy special-interest groups—or where elected officials engage in corruption at the expense of ordinary citizens. It includes in particular an assessment of distribution of resources *within* communities—how the poor are treated relative to the nonpoor within the same community or how effective government is in catering to the needs of local citizens relative to the resources earmarked for this purpose.

The notion of *responsiveness* requires policies to be flexible with respect to heterogeneous or time-varying community needs. Here the primary component is the relative treatment of different communities with distinct characteristics or the treatment of a given community that changes its composition or needs over time. In the context of fiscal decentralization, the traditional literature in economics on fiscal federalism has stressed this particular aspect, while presuming the absence of any accountability problems.[1] If heterogeneous communities have distinct preferences for local public goods and services, economic efficiency requires a pattern of provision of such goods and services that caters to these diverse needs. The traditional theory of federalism is based on the assumption that centralized governments are incapable of achieving such differentiation, owing either to the high costs of communicating information concerning local preferences to a central government or an inability of the central government to process such information and utilize it in its decision making concerning delivery of local public goods. The argument in favor of decentralization of government is that local government officials are likely to be better informed about preferences of local citizens and thus exhibit greater responsiveness to heterogeneous needs. Traditional free-rider problems in communicating preferences for public goods can be overcome in addition if citizens are mobile and able to vote with their feet in the manner hypothesized by Tiebout (1956). The disadvantage of decentralization is that it is vulnerable to problems of coordination of decision making across different communities (owing to intercommunity externalities or spillovers) or to losses of scale economies. The optimal design of decentralization according to this theory requires trading off the incentive advantages and coordination disadvantages. This approach recommends that the responsibility for providing local public goods—subject to spatially heterogeneous preferences, low intercommunity spillovers, or economies of scale—should be devolved to local governments. Conversely, if preferences for some good are homogeneous across communities, there is no reason to delegate the delivery of that good to local government.

A particular problem arises with respect to assignment of taxation responsibilities. Responsiveness of local public spending (for example, with respect to heterogeneous preferences between private and public goods across diverse communities) requires each community to be able to set its own tax policies. But this typically gives rise to coordination problems: agents can choose their locations strategically, inducing governments to engage in a race to the bottom to attract wealthy individuals and corporations. Moreover, national governments typically have a mandate to redistribute across different regions, especially when agglomeration externalities cause economic growth to be sharply concentrated in a few regions within the country. For these reasons, the bulk of the country's revenues accrues to the national government, which are then distributed across different regions by an intergovernmental system of top-down fiscal transfers. Full economic efficiency cannot be realized by any such arrangement, then, as these intergovernmental transfer mechanisms are subject to problems of asymmetric information, moral hazard, and limited ability of national governments to commit to a formula-bound scheme of fiscal transfers.

One possible manifestation of these problems is the soft budget constraint wherein local governments tend to overspend, expecting that their deficits will eventually be filled by the national governments, funded out of tax revenues raised from other communities in the federation. Alternatively, if the national government does not respond to requests for supplementary transfers sought by local governments on the grounds of special needs that are difficult to verify, transfers (and hence local public expenditures) end up insufficiently responsive to local need. This can result in underinvestment in local infrastructure and widespread complaints of unfunded mandates (wherein the expenditure responsibilities of local governments are not matched by revenues devolved).

As elaborated elsewhere (Bardhan, 2002; Bardhan and Mookherjee, 2003, 2004; Mookherjee, 2004; Seabright, 1996; Tommasi and Weinschelbaum, 1999), the traditional theory of fiscal federalism does not address the dimension of accountability that appears to have been important in the recent experience of developing countries. A key concern with traditional centralized mechanisms of economic policy and regulation in the developing world has been their vulnerability to corruption and bureaucratic inefficiency, resulting in problems such as cost padding, service diversion, limited access, and high prices charged especially to the poor.[2] The 2004 *World Development Report*, for instance, starts with the following argument for decentralization:

Too often, services fail poor people—in access, in quantity, and in quality. But there are strong examples where services do work, which means governments and citizens can do better. Putting poor people at the center of service provision enables them to monitor and discipline service providers, amplifies their voice in policymaking, and strengthens the incentives for providers to serve the poor. (World Bank, 2004)

Such accountability problems can justify the devolution of service delivery to elected local governments, even if preferences for those do not manifest any significant heterogeneity across local communities. Provided the preconditions for a functioning local democracy exist, competitive pressures associated with winning local elections could induce greater accountability among service providers.

Nevertheless, decentralization is unlikely to be a universal panacea for problems of accountability. As stressed by constitution designers such as James Madison (see, e.g., Hamilton, Madison, and Jay, 1937) or more recently by scholars such as Tendler (1997) or Crook and Manor (1998), to achieve its purpose local democracy requires a significant set of prerequisites that often are lacking in developing countries. These include an educated and politically aware citizenry, an absence of high inequality in economic or social status that inhibits political participation of the poor or of minorities, a prevalence of law and order, the conduct of free and fair elections according to a constitutional setting that prevents excessive advantage to incumbents, effective competition between political candidates or parties with long-term interests, the presence of reliable information channels to citizens (for example, from an active, independent media), and the presence of oversight mechanisms both formal (legislatures, judiciary, independent auditors) and informal (such as civil society organizations). These problems may well be more acute at the level of local governments, in which case local democracy may be more vulnerable than a centralized system to problems of low accountability. Whether these problems are more acute at the level of the national or local government in general is far from obvious, however, as we have discussed at length elsewhere (Bardhan and Mookherjee, 1998, 2000).

Economic analyses stress a number of additional potential pitfalls of decentralization, including some discussed by the traditional literature on fiscal federalism. In Bardhan and Mookherjee (1998), for instance, a model of delivery of infrastructure services is presented in which the following conditions are shown to be sufficient for decentralization to achieve welfare-optimal outcomes: a functioning local democracy (this is stressed by political scholars and explained above); adequate fiscal autonomy for local governments, wherein they can raise revenues from local sources with the same level of administrative and economic efficiency as the central government; the absence of intercommunity externalities in service provision; and administrative and technical expertise in local and national government officials (in particular, equal access to information and bargaining power with the service producers they procure from).[3] In addition, each of these conditions is also necessary for decentralization to produce superior outcomes relative to that of a corrupt central bureaucracy, in the following sense: *if any one of these conditions is not satisfied, then the outcome of decentralization can be inferior to that of a corrupt and inefficient central bureaucracy.*

This suggests that the impact of decentralization will depend both on the context where it is implemented (particularly political traditions pertaining to the functioning of local democracy) and on the way it is designed and implemented. There cannot be any general presumption that decentralization will improve public-service delivery or represent the interests of the poor better. Instead, one should expect the outcomes to be context and design specific. As the case studies reveal, there is enormous heterogeneity in both these respects across regions, countries, and continents. The main task of research on decentralization, then, is to study the nature and sources of heterogeneity and identify how they affect the nature of resulting outcomes. This information is key to future policy makers, who would want to predict the impact of a given decentralization design and in the light of that information select between different designs.

While context can be taken as given at least in the short run, the design of decentralization may itself depend on the context, depending on the motives of the principal actors initiating and implementing the decentralization. For this reason, the political economy of decentralization is important: before appraising any given decentralization or comparing experiences of two different countries or regions that have decentralized to differing degrees or in different ways, one needs to understand why the decentralizations were designed the way they were. In econometric terminology, if the design of the decentralization is endogenous, one cannot treat it as an independent cause of differential outcomes observed. The extent or nature of decentralization may simply be a proxy for deeper underlying factors, in which case misleading inferences of its impact could be drawn if these factors are excluded or unobserved from the analysis.

To implement the research agenda described above, we need to define the key elements of context and design and the relevant avenues of impact that can potentially be observed or measured for purposes of evaluation. We now proceed to describe specific dimensions for each of these.

Dimensions of Impact

The principal economic dimensions of government accountability and responsiveness can be classified into intra- and intercommunity targeting. *Intracommunity targeting* includes both the representation of interests of different groups of citizens within a given community relative to one another and the delivery of services to the community as a whole relative to costs or the fiscal burdens imposed (thus including the effect of corruption). This corresponds to the criterion of accountability. How are the interests of the poor or of minority groups represented relative to other citizens within the community? This can be measured by the targeting of public services and fiscal burdens across different groups of citizens within given communities or the extent to which the composition of local public goods responds to the preferences of poor or minority groups. It is more difficult to measure corruption. One approach is to use citizen surveys concerning corruption. The other is to measure the effects on citizen welfare, the cost-effectiveness of services delivered, or the proportion of government expenditures accounted by salaries and administrative expenses of government officials.

Intercommunity targeting includes the allocation of fiscal resources or specific public services *across* different communities, corresponding to the criterion of responsiveness. This incorporates considerations both of interregional equity and the extent to which community resources are responsive to variations in community need.

Dimensions of Context
Here the main issue concerns the functioning of local democracy. This can be gauged by patterns of political participation of different citizen groups (such as election turnout, attendance in community meetings, complaints or suggestions filed, contributions of time or money to election campaigns, civic organizations, civic events pertaining to local politics, or involvement in and influence of civic organizations in local politics). However, these pertain mainly to the behavior of local agents, who may respond endogenously to decentralization. If most citizens perceive that their participation will have little or no impact on the local government or if local government does not have much authority over service delivery or fiscal resources, then with little at stake they might decide not to engage in any local political activity. In such cases, one might erroneously infer that decentralization was ineffective because of lack of a functioning local democracy, owing to a classic case of reverse causality: the low levels of political participation may themselves be the result of a poorly designed and ineffective decentralization. Moreover, patterns of political participation prior to decentralization may be a poor predictor of the patterns that might be induced subsequent to it.

For these reasons, it is better to rely instead on characteristics of communities, which are less mutable at least in the short run and which are likely to be important determinants of political participation. These include the distribution of literacy and education, economic and social status within the community, the existence of media or other reliable sources of information flow to citizens concerning actions of public officials, active civil society organizations, and traditions of civic engagement. There is considerable literature on how such characteristics affect patterns of social and political participation, including Delli Carpini and Keeter (1996) and Rosenstone and Hansen (1993) in the context of the United States; Gaviria, Panizzi, and Seddon (2002) in the context of a number of Latin American countries; and Putnam (1993) for Italy. Nevertheless, there is a relative paucity of such studies for developing countries (see, however, Crook and Manor, 1998, for an interesting study of patterns of political participation at the local level in states in South Asia and Africa). To the extent that political participation is viewed as an end in itself, the effect of decentralization on participation needs to be addressed.

Historical traditions of voter loyalty can also affect the extent to which local political space is effectively contestable: some regions have a tradition of domination by a single party or elite group, while others may involve active competition between different political rivals. The distribution of voter loyalties or of capacity to engage in electoral mobilization between different contestants can also affect the potential for effective political competition. Measures of political contestability, however, could be endogenous with respect to the decentralization process, so the underlying characteristics of the community that affect the potential for contestability need to be selected rather than simply the actual levels of competition observed.

Dimensions of Design
Dimensions of design include the following:

• *Constitutional authority*   Do the local governments have an independent authority enshrined in the constitution, or do they exist at the mercy of upper-level governments?

• *Electoral process*   Are elections to executive or legislative bodies mandated by law to occur periodically? Are key officials elected directly or indirectly? Is there any restriction on electoral contestants or on electoral mobilization efforts? Are political parties freely allowed to participate? Are there adequate safeguards to ensure the conduct of free and fair elections, including the use of secret ballots and the absence of intimidation of voters, manipulation of voter lists, or the electoral machinery?

• *Range of expenditure and management responsibilities devolved* What are the precise decisions devolved to local government? Do they include local infrastructure such as sanitation, water, irrigation, roads, and public buildings; primary education and health clinics; and local welfare programs such as pensions, housing, and special benefits for the disabled or the poor? Can the local government decide on the allocation of fiscal resources across these areas and across citizens or localities within the community? What other spending responsibilities are devolved? Is there significant ambiguity in allocation of responsibility across different tiers of the government? Are there likely to be significant intercommunity spillovers? Do the responsibilities include investment of new facilities, management, or maintenance of existing facilities? What autonomy does the local government have over the hiring, firing, and paying of personnel?

• *Financial devolution* To what extent can the local government raise resources either through local taxes, user fees, or borrowing? What is the extent of autonomy accorded to them over such decisions—for example, what proportion of local government budgets are self-financed, and who sets local tax rates or user-fee schedules? How are fiscal transfers from upper-level governments determined, and how much scope is given to local governments to affect these transfers via processes of decentralized budgeting or planning? Are the transfers formula-bound or subject to political discretion of upper-level government officials or negotiation between upper and lower levels?

• *Authority and competence of local officials* Is the decentralization both de jure and de facto? Or do decisions continue to be taken by upper levels of government? How has the balance of actual control rights shifted from central bureaucrats to elected local government officials? How do their administrative and technical skills compare?

• *Information and oversight mechanisms* Are local citizens and leaders likely to be sufficiently well informed? This includes having information concerning the value of different services and having information concerning the other party. Do citizens have access to information concerning local government budgets or the actions of the government officials? Are local government officials subject to oversight of citizen oversight committees or upper-level governments? Conversely, are there channels or forums allowing citizens to communicate their priorities and concerns to elected officials? Many of these are affected by the design of the decentralization, while some of them are context variables reflecting underlying community characteristics.

Political Economy of Decentralization

In some contexts, decentralization may be implemented via a comprehensive constitutional amendment in a relatively uniform fashion through different regions of a country. In others, the mandated change may have left many important details of implementation unspecified or may have devolved the implementation to existing national or regional governments. In that case, the timing and design of the decentralization is likely to vary from one region to the next, depending on the motives and capacities of key protagonists in the transition process. If so, understanding the political economy of the decentralization is important to evaluating its impact. A well-designed decentralization in one region may just be a manifestation of a responsive and accountable local leadership, in which case one risks attributing to the decentralization some of the associated differences in government performance with those of other regions. Insofar as the design of the decentralization is an endogenous outcome of the context, with some important features of the latter unobserved and thus not controlled for, it is important to understand why the decentralization was designed or timed the way it was. Assessing the impact of the decentralization as a causal factor then requires identification of suitable instruments that predict the decentralization yet do not have an independent direct impact on the impact variables. Sources of randomness of the design or implementation of the reform, which are uncorrelated with relevant context variables that have a direct effect on the impact variables, are then needed. This renders the task of impact assessment challenging and difficult.

Besides, the political economy of the decentralization presents questions that are intriguing and important in their own right: What persuaded a national or provincial government to voluntarily relinquish some of its own power to lower levels? What were the original sources or causes of the decentralization process?

Addressing these questions requires a rich historical description of experiences of countries embarking on decentralization, one of the main purposes of this volume. This is a domain in which political historians rather than economists have expertise. Nevertheless, it is useful to list the possible motivations for decentralization that the country experts were asked to address:

• *Political pressures (P)* Parties or politicians or dictators at the national level face threats to their own authority (competition either from other centralized parties or from rising regional parties) or seek to preempt future threats by enhancing their own legitimacy by widening political participation of citizens and improving social service delivery.

• *External shocks or crises (S)* Some shocks force drastic changes in policy-making institutions (including pressure from multilateral institutions as loan conditionality).

• *Ideology (I)* Various groups can be disillusioned with previous centralized development patterns or with the prevailing orthodoxy among multilateral agencies, policy makers, social scientists, or popular opinion in favor of decentralization and local decision making. A new party or candidate might emerge at the national or provincial level with an ideology predisposed in favor of redistribution or local democracy.

• *Other hidden agendas (O)* Other hidden agendas might include a conservative agenda of reducing social spending by devolving responsibilities for social-sector spending to local governments while not raising their fiscal base.

Specifically, the writer of each country case study was asked to discuss the following issues:

• The historical context in which decentralization arose (including assessment of problems inherent in the preceding regime),

• A positive political economy question (Why did the centralized state agree to devolve its powers, and how this affected subsequent design—the role of factors P, S, and I and others?),

• Other dimensions of context with an important bearing on how well local democracy is expected to function,

• The design of the decentralization (authorities and responsibilities transferred and accompanying political reforms), and

• The impact expected or observed so far on targeting and service delivery and econometric problems likely to arise in impact assessment.

Summary of Country Case Studies

There is no obvious way to classify the country case studies. We select some relevant elements of the relevant historical and political *context*. Later we categorize the cases according to their *design* and discuss how design was related to the context. The first category of countries experienced a singular transition from a more centralized regime to one with greater devolution of political, administrative, or economic power to local governments. These include Brazil, Indonesia, Bolivia, India, and Uganda. The second category includes countries such as Pakistan and China in which recent decentralization episodes have represented one phase of a longer pattern of alternation between more and less centralized modes of governance. South Africa represents a unique case of transition from one form of decentralization to another.

Singular Transition from Centralized to Decentralized Governance

Within this category, one can differentiate further by other aspects of context. The first subcategory consists of countries such as Brazil and Indonesia in which the transition to decentralization was part of a wider transition to democracy from dictatorship at the national level. In these countries, greater devolution was a natural corollary of dispersing political and economic power more widely in the society. The second subcategory includes countries such as Bolivia and India that remained democracies throughout at the national level, where the transition reflected a widely shared dissatisfaction with the previous centralized mode of governance, allied with rising political competition at the national level (owing to the rise of competing national or regional parties). The third category includes Uganda, which was a nondemocracy both before and after the transition to decentralization. Here the decentralization was an instrument of consolidation of power of a new military government.

Brazil Gianpaolo Baiocchi (chapter 2) describes the motivation for decentralization reform in Brazil during the late 1980s by a mixture of internal and external factors. Internally, the country was transiting back to democracy after a twenty-year military regime. Traditionally, Brazilian provinces and municipalities have been strong, and the transition back to democracy created the opportunity for the regional elites to regain their power. Concomitantly, the 1980s was a period in which poverty and exclusion in the cities increased a lot, owing to poor economic performance of the country as a whole. The austere structural adjustment policy preached by the International Monetary Fund (IMF) was felt mostly in urban services. Numerous neighborhood associations and urban associations were created, giving rise to a series of social movements that could arise only because of the democratization process and that demanded better local governance. On the external front, the debt crisis of the 1980s gave international agencies (such as the IMF and World Bank) with fiscal austerity concerns, the reason to pressure harder for the transfers of government responsibilities. To comply with international lending agencies, the center was encouraged to transfer social-services responsibilities to the local levels. Ideology also played a role in the reforms. There was a consensus in Latin America in the 1980s that argued that a less centralized government would be less bureaucratic, more efficient, and more responsive. The 1988 constitution was thus influenced by pressures from a wide range of groups such as regional elites, social movements, and international agencies.

Baiocchi describes four main transformations in the assignment of power rendered by the 1988 constitution. Local governments were given greater political autonomy (achieving the same status as provinces), were given greater fiscal autonomy from the union, became responsible for social service delivery and became "free to implement channels of direct popular participation into public affairs." The share of local governments in tax revenues rose from 11 to 13 percent between 1987 and 1991, while their spending responsibilities rose from 11 to 16 percent (of total government spending) over the same period. Fiscal problems in the early 1990s led to some degree of recentralization in 1994 with curbs on fiscal transfers to states and on public spending. While the degree of fiscal autonomy of local governments was high by international standards, the dependence of poorer municipalities on transfers exceeded 90 percent.

Baiocchi thereafter turns to assess the impacts of decentralization. Indicators of public education increased in the country as a whole since the late 1980s, and the disparity between regions has decreased. Health indicators show an improvement in infant mortality and life expectancy but an increase in interregional disparities. Disparities in size of government budgets between small and large municipalities and between backward and less backward regions have also increased.

The most striking achievement of the Brazilian decentralization pertains to patterns of popular participation in certain regions. Baiocchi argues that the decentralization created an opportunity for local governments to introduce democratic innovations such as participatory budgeting. Most of these democratic innovations were carried out by Worker's Party administrations. Baiocchi describes in detail the experience with participative budgeting (PB) of Porto Alegre, which subsequently improved public-service delivery substantially (as gauged by school enrollments or sanitation services). However, PB practices diffused unevenly, were confined mainly to areas that were relatively better off, and had an active civil society.

Indonesia   Bert Hoffman and Kai Kaiser (chapter 3) provide an overview of the decentralization process in Indonesia. The big-bang decentralization in Indonesia took place in 2001 after the fall of Suharto in 1998 as a natural component of the subsequent resurgence of democracy. Decentralization had been a recurrent topic in Indonesian history, and the 2001 reform was not the first attempt. From 1966 to 1998, Indonesia experienced a highly centralized regime characterized by high levels of corruption and low bureaucratic efficiency. Hoffman and Kaiser also argue that decentralization was a political choice made by President Habibie, Suharto's successor, with the intention of sustaining himself in power and also keeping the country from disintegrating. The new president had to award regions some autonomy to get the support of regional representatives in parliament and attenuate separatist tendencies. Decentralization was also a strategy to bypass provinces that had been the center of regional unrest, and there was a sense that local governments would be easier to control.

The decentralization was defined by laws 22 and 25, which devolved to provincial and local governments a wide range of powers and fiscal resources. These included all but a few functions retained by the center such as defense, national security, foreign policy, monetary policy, finance, development planning, justice, and police. Local governments became responsible for the delivery of health, education, infrastructure, and environmental services. The provinces were given a minor role. The new fiscal framework replaced the earlier system with earmarked grants with one of general allocation grants, the bulk of which are formula based. These grants constituted over 95 percent of local government budgets. Two-thirds of all civil servants were transferred from the central to the local governments. The local governments had to cope with the expenses of these servants but had no autonomy to hire or fire them. Despite the dimensions of the reform and the speed in which it was implemented, there was no major disruption in the provision of any of these services.

The local governments, however, are subject to limits on their political authority. The central government can annul local laws and regulations if they conflict with national ones. The head of district-level governments can be dismissed by regional legislatures. Hoffman and Kaiser find in a sample of 128 regions (out of 400 in the country) that 6 percent of heads were actually dismissed in this fashion. While there was no allowance for regional parties nominally, such parties are beginning to emerge gradually.

Hoffman and Kaiser assess the effectiveness of local accountability mechanisms, using the new Governance and Decentralization Survey. They construct indicators of local governance based on citizen perceptions of governance quality, including corruption and public-service provision. The agents interviewed included households, nongovernmental organizations, and local government officials. Significant improvements in service deliveries were reported, and satisfaction ratings of locally supplied services were higher than for centrally supplied services. Nevertheless, high levels of corruption continued to be reported at both district and local village levels, especially in recruitment and personnel. Perceptions of corruption and governance quality were positively correlated with ethnic and political fragmentation but uncorrelated with local per capita income, inequality, poverty, or education levels.

Bolivia   The Bolivian experience with decentralization is described in chapter 4 by Jean-Paul Faguet. He starts by documenting the origins of the big-bang decentralization that occurred in 1994. Following the 1952 revolution, Bolivia had evolved a highly centralized state that aimed to create a modern industrial and egalitarian society. Monopolized by the Nationalist Revolutionary Movement, it pursued a development policy based on import substitution and industrialization, implemented by a "national chain of cascading authority emanating from the capital." There was little scope for governance at the local level and considerable inequality in the distribution of public spending between the main cities and the rest of the country. The impetus for change came from the lack of economic progress since the late 1970s and the resulting social unrest. Ethnic-based political parties began to challenge the ruling party in its key rural bases, motivating the party to recapture its rural constituencies. The new decentralization law was developed by a few technocrats in the ruling party in secrecy and was initially the object of ridicule and opposition throughout the country.

Yet as Faguet explains, it had a dramatic effect on the pattern of governance and resource allocation. The devolution included fiscal measures (that doubled local revenues from approximately 10 to 20 percent of their spending and introduced formula bound interregional transfers), transferred responsibility for services in education, health, irrigation, roads, sports, and culture to local governments, created oversight committees over local governments, created a large number of new municipalities, and expanded new ones. Faguet then cites other papers by him that use quantitative analyses to conclude that decentralization shifted resources to poorer districts and made investments more responsive to local needs. The composition of public investment shifted from production and infrastructure to social services and human-capital formation.

Thereafter, Faguet turns to a qualitative analysis in which he describes the local institutions and the political setting of two local governments (Baures and Guayaramerin) with dramatically differing patterns of local governance. The author conducted a series of systematic interviews in both municipalities to gather the qualitative information necessary for this exercise. Based on this, he constructs a conceptual framework of local government that explains why local government performance varied so much between the two locations. In this framework, the dynamic of the local government is dictated by three sets of interactions between political parties, local government institutions, civil society, and economic groups. One is a political market, in which political parties interact with voters exchanging promises and ideas for votes. The second one links political parties with interest groups via campaign contributions in exchange for influence over policies. The third concerns the relationship of civil society with government. The author concludes that good governance is the outcome when these three interactions counterbalance each other and none dominates the other.

India   In chapter 5, Shubham Chaudhuri describes the gradual process of decentralization to local governments in India, especially the effect of constitutional amendments in 1993 and 1994. This followed a period where the central government encouraged state governments to initiate decentralization on a voluntary basis, setting up an expert committee in 1957 that made detailed recommendations for setting up a three-tier system of local government. Only a few states made any effort to implement such a system in the 1970s and 1980s, with the notable exception of West Bengal (whose experience constitutes a separate case study). The 1993 and 1994 constitutional amendments mandated direct elections to three tiers of local government, with reservations for women and low-caste groups, and devolved powers principally over local infrastructure and welfare schemes. Also mandated were biannual village meetings (where local government budgets and accounts were presented and discussed) and appointment of state finance commissions (which would recommend division of fiscal resources between the state and local governments). The detailed implementation of this mandate was left to the concerned state governments.

The stated objectives of the decentralization were to correct the defects in the traditional system wherein delivery of public services was in the hands of state appointed bureaucrats, with limited accountability to local citizens. The underlying political compulsions were however not transparent: Chaudhuri speculates that the Congress-dominated national government was seeking to consolidate its power in response to rising competition from political parties at both national and regional levels.

Chaudhuri's judgment was that the reform was incremental rather than radical, aimed principally at remedying shortcomings of the previous regime. He documents the slow and uneven pattern of implementation of the constitutional mandate across different states. The extent of genuine functional or fiscal devolution is low on average, with state bureaucrats continuing to retain control over public-service programs in all but three or four states. While regular elections have been held by and large, village meetings were marked by widespread participation in only a few states. Indices of devolution were uncorrelated at the state level with ten indicators of economic performance and human development, after controlling for state and year dummies. Chaudhuri nevertheless speculates that the reform has set in motion a learning process in local democracy, with new coalitions of local government representatives emerging as a force even in national politics.

West Bengal   One of the Indian states that implemented decentralization more thoroughly than others is West Bengal, whose experience we describe in chapter 6. The decentralization in West Bengal dates back to 1977 with the adoption of a three-tier system of local government whose officials at every tier were directly elected, with mandatory elections every five years since 1978. In contrast to other Indian states, the Left Front government substantially increased the authority of local governments at the expense of the state bureaucracy. The responsibilities transferred included administration of local infrastructure and welfare programs but excluded primary education and health services, which remained under the jurisdiction of relevant departments of state government. In the 1990s, local governments also became responsible for the administration of Shishu Shiksha Kendras, an alternative to the primary schools run by the state education department. Reservations of local government positions for women and low-caste minorities were introduced via a number of amendments during the 1990s. Furthermore, the amendments mandated twice yearly meetings of the village council. The extent of financial devolution was limited: local taxes accounted for less than 4 percent of local government budgets, with employment grants accounting for 60 percent and grants tied to specific projects for 25 percent.

The chapter subsequently reviews empirical evidence concerning patterns of participation and targeting of resources. Approximately two-thirds of local government positions were secured by landless, marginal, and small landowners, compared with a demographic weight of 96 percent, implying that the poor constituted a majority but were nevertheless underrepresented. As for women and low-caste groups, the seat reservations implemented in the 1990s ensured proportional representation. The consequence was that women's participation in village council meetings increased, as did the filing of complaints and requests to the local government. Participation in the village council meetings shows a pattern similar to those of local government positions: the majority of attendants were small and landless, but medium and large landowners were overrepresented.

The evidence on resource allocation indicates that the village governments exhibited considerable accountability and responsiveness. Seat reservation for women for local government chair positions caused a statistically significant shift in public spending from informal education centers to drinking-water facilities and road maintenance. This result is consistent with the reports on women's complaints on village assembly meetings. In terms of targeting patterns within villages, welfare programs (such as the distribution of agricultural minikits and subsidized credit and employment programs) showed that the bulk of the resources flowed to poorer sections. There is evidence of disproportionate influence yielded by medium and large landowners, however, especially over intervillage allocations. The absence of formula-bound allocations indicated that greater poverty, literacy, and proportion of low-caste residents were negatively correlated with the extent of resources flowing into the village.

Uganda Omar Azfar, Jeffrey Livingston, and Patrick Meagher (chapter 7) start by describing the context of the decentralization reforms in Uganda. These were initiated the victory of the guerilla movement, the National Resistance Movement (NRM), which was led by General Museveni in the mid-1980s. To consolidate their power and help administer the national territory, the guerrilla movement established local resistance councils, a common tactic among revolutionary movements. A hierarchy was established linking them to the district and the district to the center. They were subsequently converted into elected bodies with partyless elections. The councils became organs of state administrative control and provided a forum for local political participation. The state party then tried to accommodate various political forces into the movement. The local governments thus allowed the NRM to mobilize popular participation to offset the influence of old political parties, traditional chiefs, and major ethnic separatist groups. They were thus important instruments of consolidation of power, widening the legitimacy of the NRM and restoring stability and security to Uganda. The devolution of resources for public services and administration was necessary to achieve these outcomes. Azfar, Livingston, and Meagher claim that the reform enabled the NRM party to "abstract from challenges of multipartyism and federalism and focus on economic liberalization."

The devolution of responsibilities to the local governments was accomplished gradually. In 1987, the resistance councils were formalized, and the 1993 Decentralization Act consolidated their powers. The general framework for decentralization was set up in the 1995 constitution, with further details specified by the 1997 Local Government Act. District councils are elected in nonparty elections once every four years, with executive authority vested in the district chair, who is directly elected. These bodies do not have the power to impose local taxes without the approval of Parliament; indeed, the Parliament retains the right to take them over. Azfar, Livingston, and Meagher describe the powerful pressure on local governments to conform to the priorities of the NRM, which has a structure that parallels the elected government councils at every level.

Responsibilities devolved to the local governments include primary education and health services, and local infrastructure. There is supervision and monitoring across successive levels and also by civil servants appointed by the president. On the fiscal side, the local bodies have some ability to set local taxes and fees but are reliant on most part on fiscal grants based on formula-based allocations of tax revenues. The transfers combine conditional, unconditional, and equalization grants. Numerous constraints accompany the use of funds, in addition to delays in disbursements. Their fiscal autonomy is further compromised by large wage bills for personnel that they have little control over.

The extent of de facto decentralization often falls short of the de jure devolution: the health sector continues to be quite centralized. Numerous efforts to curb corruption and inefficiency in deliveries have been made, which have been more successful in the education sector (with the setting up of school-management committees involving parents and greater transparency in fiscal transfers) and less successful in the health sector. It is quite likely that health services have not improved much with the decentralization for this and other reasons. District governments do not have much freedom concerning salaries and staff decisions, drugs are still delivered by the central government, and hospital funding is based on the number of beds giving local politicians the incentive to build new hospitals instead of managing them efficiently. Moreover, the health sector is marked by externalities and limited awareness of the value of preventive procedures: immunization coverage after decentralization is lower than expected. The impact on the education sector seems more positive. The universal primary education program abolished school fees, increased education funding, and allowed families to choose among public schools. Primary enrollment increased, the budget share on education spending increased, and there was greater transparency in the use of funds. The impacts in terms of school quality are less clear.

Azfar, Livingston, and Meagher also assess the functioning of local democracy to identify the potential for the decentralization to enhance accountability. They use data gathered in a survey of households and public officials from different government levels conducted in spring 2000. Levels of political participation were high: turnouts in elections exceeded 80 percent, and more than half of surveyed households had placed specific requests with the local administration. However, information flows between citizens and elected officials were poor. District officials' perceptions of citizen priorities over public spending were uncorrelated with the latter; the situation was only slightly better at the subdistrict level. Citizens relied predominantly on community leaders rather than the media for information about local politics; the former source was negatively correlated with likelihood of receiving news of corruption (after controlling for household and community characteristics). Based on this and evidence of low citizen mobility and limited political competition, their overall assessment is that the preconditions for decentralization to have an effective impact are largely absent in Uganda.

Periodic Alternation between More and Less Decentralized Governance

This category includes Pakistan and China. In Pakistan's case, alternation between greater and less devolution to local governments corresponded with alternation between dictatorship and democracy at the national level. Similar to the Ugandan experience, decentralization to local governments was used as an instrument of consolidation of power by a military government over traditional political parties and regional powers. China, on the other hand, has not experienced any multiparty democracy at the national level. Here the nature of the decentralization was primarily administrative and economic in nature, utilized by the Chinese Communist Party to create strong economic incentives for development at the local level, while restricting the political power of local governments. Alternation between more and less centralized regimes has corresponded—much as in a large multidivisional corporation—to the severity of problems of duplication and lack of coordination inherent in decentralized modes of governance, relative to their benefits in terms of stimulating economic incentives. Only recently has China begun to experiment with elections for positions in local government, but it has placed severe curbs on the independent power of these officials over Communist Party officials. On the other hand, the Chinese experience is unique with regard to the extensive role played by local governments in promoting the development of local businesses and production enterprises.

Pakistan The historical context of the 2000 and 2001 decentralization reforms introduced by General Musharraf in Pakistan is described in chapter 8 by Ali Cheema, Asim Ijaz Khwaja, and Adnan Qadir. They briefly analyze the pre- and postindependence period followed by a description of two previous decentralization reforms, one under General Zia and the other under General Ayub. Local governments were originally introduced by the British colonial government. Although the British government maintained political and financial control in the hands of a nonrepresentative bureaucracy, it used local governments to develop loyal landowning elites to create an indigenous rural client base for the nonrepresentative center. In the postindependence period, the subsequent military regimes maintained the same approach. General Ayub Khan dissolved all higher-tier elected governments and established local governments as the only representative tier of government. Ayub's 1962 presidential constitution assigned an electoral function to local governments by declaring the 80,000 local government basic democrats as the electoral college for the election of the president in the transition to his model of controlled democracy. As in the British system, the urban and rural division favoring rural areas was maintained since these formed the main source of support for the regime.

In the subsequent period of democracy under President Bhutto in the 1970s, the importance of these local governments began to wane. With the restoration of a military government under General Zia, however, there was a revival in their role. As in the General Ayub period, local governments had no independent constitutional authority, and during the martial law period they were subservient to provincial governments headed by military officers. General Zia also continued to insist on partyless elections, despite the emergence of mass-based political parties in the 1970s. Some of the bias in favor of rural governments was lessened during the Zia regime, but Cheema, Khwaja, and Qadir document large disparities between rural and urban areas in both revenues and expenditures.

The intervening period of democracy at the national level between 1988 and 1998 again witnessed a decline in the importance of local governments. There was a conflict between provincial and local governments as alternative patronage machines, and all local bodies were suspended between 1993 and 1998. Democracy was accompanied by an increasing trend toward centralization. The Pakistan experience establishes that there is in general no connection between local and national democracy and that the two can be negatively correlated. Cheema, Khwaja, and Qadir argue that local governments in Pakistan have been "enacted by nonrepresentative regimes to legitimize their control over the state through the creation of a localized patronage structure of collaborative politicians."

Consistent with this pattern, local governments were revitalized with the return of military rule under General Musharraf in 1998. The motives were to secure legitimacy for his regime, coopt regional elites, reduce the authority of provincial governments, and manipulate interregional allocations. The reforms made provincial bureaucrats subordinate to elected nazims of district-level governments, transferred the vast majority of public services (including primary education and health, land and agricultural tax collection, agricultural extension, farm water management, roads and buildings, and municipal services) to the district governments, introduced rule-based fiscal transfers (which reduced urban-rural disparities, and gave greater weights for backward districts), and introduced reservations for peasants and women in these elected bodies. District governments remain severely restricted in their fiscal autonomy, with limited local revenue bases and high levels of "establishment charges" that they have no control over. In conclusion, the authors raise questions about the sustainability of the reforms owing to the time-bound constitutional protection of the local governments and emerging conflicts between provincial and district levels on the one hand and between the deconcentrated central bureaucracy and elected local government officials on the other.

Chapter 9, by Philip E. Keefer, Ambar Narayan, and Tara Vishwanath, assesses the likely impact of decentralization in Pakistan. They start by arguing that prior to the 2001 and 2002 devolution, the political incentives faced by the central government drove them to provide narrow, targeted goods and services at the expense of broader public goods. Different types of evidence are presented to support this claim. The first is the nature of policy failures in health and education. Statistics for the 1990s show that Pakistan lagged behind most of the countries in the South Asian region with respect to infant mortality. There were considerable disjunctions between quantity and quality of educational services. While government officials put more emphasis on school construction, primary gross enrollment rates have not changed much, and teachers' absenteeism shows deterioration. Documentation of legislator activities, such as declarations of legislators about their concern for pleasing their constituents, is the second piece of evidence that the provisions to decentralize were narrowly targeted.

Finally, Keefer, Narayan, and Vishwanath summarize econometric evidence that political competition prior to devolution spurred politicians to provide boys' schools but did not lead politicians to improve school quality or to construct girls' schools. They argue that many differences (in political and electoral institutions between central and local governments; in incentives of politicians to respond to special interests, including feudal lords; in the credibility of political competitors; in the horizons of political officials; and in the extent to which devolution is authentic) influence whether public-good provision will improve and corruption decline under devolution. In general, they find mixed results and little reason to believe that the dynamics of political competition that led central-government officials to provide low-quality public services are substantially different in the newly created local governments.

China   Justin Yifu Lin, Ran Tao, and Mingxing Liu (chapter 10) describe recent decentralization initiatives in China as part of a fundamental set of market-oriented reforms initiated since the late 1970s as a response to production inefficiency of enterprises and people's communes owing to a lack of incentives for workers and farmers. Decentralization was not a new initiative in the Chinese system. From the late 1950s until the late 1970s, decentralization had been experienced in the planned economy in the form of cyclic alternation between waves of centralization and decentralization. As a whole, the economy exhibited an exceptionally high degree of centralization of the productive and fiscal systems in the country, with most production organized in state-owned centrally managed enterprises whose accounts were not separated from the fiscal system.

Following the death of Mao Tse Tung, the late 1970s witnessed substantial market-oriented reforms, which included a program of administrative and fiscal decentralization, including awarding de facto control rights over production to households, awarding state-owned enterprises to managers, and entrusting local government leaders with various contractual responsibility systems. This increased the role of local governments in economic management: functions such as investment approval, entry regulation, and resource allocation were transferred to them. Local-government officials managed township and village enterprises (TVEs), which witnessed substantial growth during the 1980s and early 1990s. Coastal provinces were allowed to set up special economic zones, set up foreign trade corporations, set local tax rates, and provide special fiscal privileges. Fiscal relations with local governments were amended in successive reforms in 1980, 1982, 1988, and 1994. The reforms in the 1980s generally increased the fiscal autonomy of local governments and strengthened their incentives to generate higher local revenues by allowing them to retain the bulk of their revenues (including TVE surpluses) above an amount remitted to the center. Consequently, local governments were motivated to play a key role in local economic development. The 1994 reform, on the other hand, achieved some measure of recentralization, raising the revenue share of the central government from 35 to 60 percent, while at the same time raising fiscal transfers in a way that preserved the regional allocation of funds. The role of the TVEs was weakened in the late 1990s as market-based developments have rendered the role of governments managers less important.

Assessing the reforms, Lin, Tao, and Liu conclude that the positive impact of these developments was limited mainly to coastal provinces. The system achieved little interregional redistribution, with local governments in more backward, inland, and rural areas hamstrung by limited fiscal resources. The local governments are charged with the responsibility to provide local infrastructure and social services and to implement various central programs of grain procurement, birth control, and compulsory education. The limited revenue base implies that many of the mandated responsibilities of local governments are effectively unfunded, forcing them to impose coercive levies on local residents and allowing them to expand the scale of the local bureaucracy. The authors report results of an econometric analysis that verifies the hypothesis that more high-level governments mandates led to higher levels of rural taxation and higher local expenditures. Further, given the centralized political system, longstanding bureaucratic traditions, and the absence of electoral accountability to local citizens, government officials were held more responsible to upper-level governments than to the people of their own localities. Complaints of corruption and rent-seeking by local government officials are common.

There is evidence of some recent enhancement of local accountability based on the increasing mobility of workers and firms and the holding of direct elections for village committees since 1998. The elected members of these village committees hold an ambiguous and delicate relation with the nonelected party functionaries and local-government officials, with the latter having formal authority over the village committees. Despite this, the village committees appear to make local residents more likely to lodge complaints, to make local governments more likely to lower local tax burdens, and to improve transparency of administration. It remains to be seen how far the government will tolerate or encourage the growth of a genuinely participative local democracy.

Transition from One Form of Decentralization to Another
Finally, we come to the case of South Africa, which experienced a
major shift in its pattern of local governance in the mid-1990s as part
of a wider shift from apartheid to a genuine democracy at the national
level. In contrast to Brazil or Indonesia, the system prevailing before
cannot be described as more centralized than the one that followed:
it was simply a different form of decentralization and was used as
an instrument of central control and racial division by the apartheid
regime.

South Africa   Martin Wittenberg (chapter 11) first explains the nature of the pre-1994 regime. Three different systems of governance
emerged: a system of national, provincial, and municipal government
that applied to white South Africans; a system that controlled the black
South Africans outside the reserves; and a system within the black
reserves. This system served two ends. It scattered the opposition, creating different regional and ethnic interests that prevented the growth
of South African nationalism. It was also a strategic renouncement
of power over parts of political space to satisfy political aspirations of
the black majority. Besides the inhumane conditions that apartheid
brought to black people, the policies induced corruption at every government level and brought economic crises in the reserves and all urban areas. There was lack of an appropriate economic base for the
Bantustan (the system of reserves), and the barrier imposed to migration to the urban areas culminated in violence. The Soweto riots in
1976 illustrated the unsustainable situation reached by the system.
During the period 1982 to 1994, the state acknowledged the necessity
to review its policy and began some reforms, such as abolition of provincial legislatures and establishment of planning regions and regional
services councils. The idea behind these reforms was to give additional
groups of blacks a stake in the system to preserve the divided system.
Yet as Wittenberg explains, no white community was willing to be sacrificed for the general interest. The entire system collapsed by 1994.
    The new decentralization program was circumscribed by the 1996
constitution and came into being in 2000. Wittenberg explains that the
constitutional status of these local-level governments was important
since these would prevent the abuses by the central government that
had occurred in the past. In the new democratic system of decentralization, South Africa is organized in a four-tier system of governance
in which national and provincial governments are the upper tiers and

the district councils and municipalities the lower ones. The national government is in charge of the security and the economic policy of the country; provinces are the major providers of social services such as education, health, and transfer payments. Districts and municipalities overlap in their obligations of the provision water and sewerage reticulation, electricity, and other services. A certain recentralizing tendency arose from the rationalization of approximately 800 transitional councils to 231 municipalities formally institutionalized by the 1996 constitution. In the fiscal aspects, the system also underwent a significant reform. Resources are now divided in a more equitable and less arbitrary way according to a sharing formula, although the vertical division of resources between provincial and local levels is decided by consultative process. Lower-tier governments are also allowed to gather resources from regional services council levies and property taxes. The balance of authority and finances is held by provincial rather than local governments in accordance with the priorities of the African National Congress.

Wittenberg argues that the reforms have been broadly redistributive, owing to equalization components in the formula for horizontal allocation of unconditional grants across local governments. Improved intercommunity targeting appears to be reducing poverty and interracial inequality. In other respects, the evidence is mixed. For instance, although popular participation for blacks is now possible, the lively civic movement that was present in the early 1990s has ceased to exist. As for the supposed reduction in corruption due to the greater accountability of the politicians toward their constituents, there still exist serious service ethics problems that can be traced back to the apartheid system. Local governments are experiencing imbalances between finances and needs. However, Wittenberg stresses that this reflects a more fundamental problem throughout contemporary South Africa— a lack of enough resources in the system as a whole to meet the basic needs of all the citizens.

Decentralization Design: A Comparative Perspective

From the descriptions in the previous section, it is evident that decentralized systems vary greatly across different countries. In this section, we describe and categorize the different aspects of design using a comparative perspective. We then examine whether and how design was affected by context.

Classification of Types of Decentralization

The design and nature of implementation have varied in many ways: comprehensive or piecemeal, uniform or uneven throughout different regions of the country, and gradual evolution or big-bang reform. Approaches depended to some extent on context: small countries such as Bolivia tended to introduce comprehensive, uniform big-bang decentralizations, while large countries such as Brazil and India decentralized in a nonuniform and gradual manner. The extent and nature of devolution (such as whether local governments have been awarded independent constitutional authority, whether they are directly elected by citizens, whether parties are allowed in local elections, whether they have reasonable degrees of financial and administrative autonomy) depend considerably on the motives for the decentralization (whether upper-level governments are democratically elected and whether the reforms have been motivated to widen or narrow the scope for democracy more widely).

Tables 1.3 through 1.5 list the main features of the kind of decentralization in the different countries, according to the underlying motives of the principal actors involved and the nature of the devolution. The entries are based on our assessment following the country descriptions. While it is oversimplified and crude, it helps communicate some of the main aspects in a comparative light.

Table 1.3 indicates that the dominant motive for decentralization in a majority of cases was the challenge to the incumbent at the national level—either actual or latent—posed by competing political forces or regional interests. The only exceptions to this were China and South Africa. In general, decentralization was a concession to regional interests or an instrument for securing legitimacy of the national government or for quelling separatist tendencies. This applied to democracies as well as nondemocracies. A second reason for decentralization was that it accompanied a transition in the national political system: toward democracy in Brazil, Indonesia, and South Africa and toward nondemocracy in Pakistan and Uganda. It was less common for decentralization to be strongly motivated by external crises, pressure from multilateral institutions, or ideological considerations: only in the case of Brazil and South Africa did these play some role.

Table 1.4 describes the nature of political decentralization in different countries. In the majority of cases, decentralization was a gradual process where local governments inherited an independent constitutional authority with mandated regular elections. The record has been mixed

Table 1.3
Motives for decentralization

	Transition toward or away from Democracy (at national level)		Transition within Democracy (at national level)	Response of Incumbent (at national level) to Competitive Pressure	Changes in Ideology Concerning	External Shocks/Financial Crises	
	Transition to Democracy	Transition to Dictatorship/One-Party Rule	Changes in Party in Power at National Level	Incumbent Threatened by Another Political Party or Regional Interests	Redistribution or Social Services Provision	Crises-Induced Reform	Multilateral Institution Pressure
Bolivia (1995)	N	N	N	Y	N	N	N
Indonesia (2001)	Y	N	Y	Y	N	N	N
Pakistan (2000)	N	Y	N	Y	N	N	N
Uganda (1987–2004)	N	Y	N	Y	N	N	N
China (1978)	N	N	N	N	N	N	N
Brazil (1988)	Y	N	Y	Y	Y	Y	N
India (1994)	N	N	N	Y	N	N	Y
West Bengal (1978)	N	N	N	Y	Y	N	N
South Africa (2000)	Y	N	Y	N	Y	N	N

Table 1.4
Nature of political decentralization

	Uniform[a]	Big-Bang[b]	Independent Constitutional Authority[c]	Local Elections		
				Direct[d]	Parties Allowed[e]	Regular[f]
Bolivia	Y	Y	Y	N	Y	Y
Indonesia	Y	Y	Y	N	Y	Y
Pakistan[g]	Y	Y	N	N	N	Y
Uganda	—[h]	N	Y	Y	N	Y
China	N	N	N	N	N	N
Brazil	N	N	Y	Y	Y	Y
India	N	N	Y	Y	Y	Y
South Africa (post-1994)	Y	N	Y	Y	Y	Y

a. The legal framework underlying the reform was geographically homogeneous across the country.
b. The legal changes happened within one to one and a half years.
c. The reform granted local governments constitutional authority and therefore cannot be dismissed at will of higher-level governments.
d. The chief executive official of local government is directly elected by local citizens rather than by representatives of these citizens.
e. Political parties are allowed in local government elections.
f. Elections carried out according to a mandated timetable.
g. Here some qualifications are necessary: there were some regional variations, and local governments had independent constitutional authority during some phases.
h. No information available.

with respect to whether local government officials are directly elected or whether political parties are allowed: nondemocracies tend not to allow independent political parties to participate. Table 1.5 describes the nature of devolution in economic terms. In general, there has been little devolution of finances or authority over personnel; most of the responsibilities transferred have involved the administration of local infrastructure, welfare programs, education, and health services. Fiscal decentralization has been associated with a hard rather than soft budget constraint, with complaints of unfunded mandates of local governments far more frequent than problems of fiscal instability or macroeconomic indiscipline. Fiscal transfers received by local governments have generally tended to be formula-bound rather than based on political discretion or negotiation between upper and lower tiers. In some contexts (such as Brazil, Bolivia, and South Africa), this appears to have improved interregional equity considerably.

Table 1.5
Nature of economic decentralization

	Finances				Responsibility Transferred				
	Financial Autonomy[a]	Formula-Based Transfer[b]	Hard Budget Constraint and Unfunded Mandates[c]	Soft Budget Constraint and Financial Indiscretion[d]	Primary Education and Health	Local Infrastructure[e]	Welfare Program	Authority over Hiring/Firing of Personnel	Authority over Personnel Pay
Bolivia	Y	Y	N	—[f]	Y	Y	Y	—[f]	—[f]
Indonesia	N	Y	—[f]	—[f]	Y	Y	Y	N	N
Pakistan	N	Y	Y	N	Y	Y	N	N	N
Uganda	—[f]	Y	—[f]	—[f]	Y	Y	—[f]	N	N
China	Y	Y	Y	N	Y	Y	Y	Y	N
Brazil	Y	Y	Y	N	Y	Y	Y	—[f]	—[f]
India	N	N	Y	N	N	Y	Y	N	N
South Africa (post-1994)	Y	Y	Y	N	N	Y	Y	Y	Y

a. If at least 10 percent of local government expenditure is raised by local government taxes.

b. Fiscal transfers to local government are determined by explicit formula.

c. Prior expenditure by higher-level government on responsibilities transferred exceeded the increase in income of local government, local revenue, and fiscal transfers.

d. Local governments frequently incur fiscal deficit, due mostly to an increase in personnel spending, in expectation of a bailout by some higher-level government.

e. If local governments after decentralization are responsible for one or more of the following items: local roads, water, sanitation, irrigation, and town planning.

f. No information available.

The different kinds of decentralization can be classified into three types of design:

• *Type A*   Comprehensive big-bang political-cum-economic devolution (Bolivia, Indonesia, and post-1994 South Africa),

• *Type B*   Comprehensive political devolution and partial and uneven economic devolution (Brazil and India), and

• *Type C*   Limited political devolution with more significant administrative and economic devolution (China, Pakistan, Uganda, and pre-1994 South Africa).

The type of design is affected by the context within which the decentralization arose. Democracies at the national level tend to be of either type A or B, while nondemocracies tend to be of type C. However, within each of these categories, the connection between context and design is less straightforward. It is easier for a small country such as Bolivia to embark on a comprehensive big-bang decentralization, compared with countries of the size and heterogeneity of Brazil or India. But on the other hand, Indonesia is also large and heterogeneous, but it nevertheless experienced a type A comprehensive devolution. Nor can the explanation lie in whether the country in question is experiencing a transition in political regime toward democracy at the national level, since this was the case with Indonesia and Brazil, which nevertheless experienced different kinds of decentralization.

One possible explanation of whether a country undergoes a type A or type B process is the balance of power between the national government and regional interests at the time the decentralization was initiated. In Brazil and India, regional elites or parties exercised strong power, thus retaining significant control over the process. Indonesia in contrast was emerging from over three decades of military dictatorship, in which disparate regional and ethnic interests had long remained dormant, so the national government under President Habibie was able to pass a uniform, national decentralization measure on its own (partly to neutralize threats from dormant regional powers). Similarly, in 1994 the political space was dominated by the African National Congress in South Africa, enabling a comprehensive and uniform system to be instituted throughout the country.

Within democracies, the absence of independent regional powers seems to be a precondition for a type A comprehensive devolution to occur. We now describe each of the three types of decentralization in more detail.

Type A Decentralization: Bolivia and Indonesia Bolivia and Indonesia embarked on a type A decentralization—a comprehensive big-bang decentralization that was implemented simultaneously throughout the entire country. The motives in the two cases differed. In Bolivia, the reform was introduced by the long entrenched MNR in the face of rising political competition from ethnic-based populist groups to legitimize and consolidate its power among its rural constituents. In Indonesia, reform followed the transition to democracy following the collapse of the Soeharto regime and weakening of the power of the central government compared with regional interests. In both cases, the previous centralized regime had been associated with high inequality in interregional allocation of funds, poor service delivery, and high levels of corruption. External pressures or ideological considerations played relatively little role in the transition. In both cases, the decentralization was both political and economic, with local governments provided political authority independent of upper levels, regular elections with political parties, and devolution of responsibility over most local social services (including primary education, health, infrastructure, and welfare). Local governments have been transferred substantial funds—over 20 percent of total government expenditure in Bolivia and 30 percent in Indonesia. Transfers are largely formula-bound, greatly reducing the scope for political discretion at upper levels of government.

Type B Decentralization: Brazil and India Brazil and India are large democracies characterized by a high degree of heterogeneity and inequality across regions and across levels of economic well-being. Regional governments form an important intermediate tier between national and local governments. Regions of these countries are larger than many other countries in the world in terms of population or area. The extent and nature of their type B decentralization is ultimately chosen by each region independently, resulting in a gradual and uneven pattern across the country that is subject to significant learning and diffusion. The result is considerable heterogeneity in the extent and nature of responsibilities transferred, the fiscal and administrative capacity of local governments, and the planning and budgeting systems. In either case, there are a few examples of locations within each country where decentralization has significantly affected patterns of representation and service delivery. In most others, progress has been moderate or insignificant. Both countries have created directly elected local governments that have independent constitutional authority and that allow local parties allowed to compete.

Nevertheless, there are important differences between the Brazilian and Indian patterns. Local governments in Brazil have substantially greater fiscal authority and autonomy. Indian local governments are devolved significantly less spending or allocational responsibilities: it is the only country in this study where local governments have no jurisdiction over the administration of primary education and health. In most Indian regions, the devolution of administrative responsibility over most infrastructure and welfare programs has been de jure rather then de facto, with state bureaucracies continuing to retain their power over these programs.

In terms of motivation to implement the reforms, there were also different factors at work. In Brazil, the reform represented part of a transition to democracy that followed two decades of military rule and in which regional elites were beginning to reassert themselves. The Indian reform was part of an ongoing democracy, though one where the national government was gradually losing power at the expense of regional and other national parties. Development of a rural constituency at the local level was a key motivating factor in India in the competition between central parties and newly emerging regional or leftist parties. Ideology, economic crises, and external pressure from multilateral institutions played a role to some extent in Brazil, unlike India (with the exception of a few states in India where leftist parties acquired power). Nevertheless, both countries shared similar failures in social-service delivery from centralized economic administration over the previous two or three decades, with a frustrating lack of progress in reducing poverty and limiting social exclusion.

Type C Decentralization: Pakistan, Uganda, and China   In Pakistan, Uganda, China, a type C decentralization has been employed as an instrument of consolidating and legitimizing a nondemocratic political power at the national level. Pakistan and Uganda represent examples of military dictatorships that utilize local governments as a way of neutralizing the potential for political opposition from regional or ethnic groups, according to a divide-and-rule strategy dating back to British colonial rulers.

China is a substantially larger country characterized by a long tradition of centralized political power monopolized by a single ruler or one party. There are some notable contrasts in the Chinese decentralization with all other countries studied here, representing a combination of more extensive economic decentralization with near absence of local democracy. Local governments have represented the bottom tier of intertwined vertical hierarchies of government and party in the Chinese system: the former are not popularly elected, have no independent constitutional authority, and are accountable principally to upper-level government officials and party functionaries. Only recently has there appeared some form of local democracy in the form of locally elected village councils, but they have no executive power and are separate from the local governments. On the other hand, Chinese local governments have played a more significant role in economic development, especially with respect to management of township and village enterprises. Moreover, the transition in 1978 was accompanied by a massive transfer of land to individual peasant farmers, inducing relatively low levels of inequality within rural communities.

The common feature of these decentralizations is that local governments are essentially subordinate to the dominant power at the national level, are elected (if at all) in partyless elections, have no independent or limited constitutional authority or protection, and can be dismissed or neutralized by higher levels of government. Similar to other countries, they rely principally on grants devolved from upper levels and are assigned the role of delivering a wide range of local services, including primary education, health, infrastructure, and welfare. They differ in the degree to which local government officials are popularly elected and in the authority of these elected officials compared with state bureaucrats. Pakistan represents one extreme, where state bureaucrats have become subordinate to elected district officials at least at the de jure level. China represents the other extreme, with local government officials not elected and subordinated to upper-level government officials. In contrast to type B decentralizations, which are uniform with respect to the extent of political decentralization but nonuniform with respect to the extent of economic decentralization, type C decentralizations are nonuniform with respect to political decentralization and more uniform with respect to economic decentralization. Type A decentralizations are uniform in both dimensions.

Common to all three forms of decentralization is the feature that local governments typically have limited authority over the personnel they hire, especially with respect to pay and service conditions. Salaries of the personnel represent a significant part of their costs they have limited control over. The bulk of their expenditures (over

70 percent) are in the form of fiscal transfers received from upper-level governments. This gives rise to classic principal and agent problems, with each local government vying with others to receive more fiscal transfers by demonstrating exceptional need or manipulating processes of political bargaining. In most cases, their spending mandates were not comfortably covered by the devolved funds, giving rise to considerable fiscal strain. The outcome of the vertical agency problem was more frequently that of an unfunded mandate rather than fiscal indiscipline at the local level wrought by a soft budget constraint.

South Africa: Transition from Nondemocratic Decentralization to Democratic Decentralization   The experience of South Africa can be viewed as a transition from a nondemocratic type C to a democratic type of decentralization intermediate between types A and B, as part of the process of transition out of an apartheid regime. Despite being similar to Brazil and India in terms of geographical size, heterogeneity, and inequality, its decentralization was more even than type B, though not quite as big-bang as type A. The nature of the decentralization was thorough in both political and economic dimensions, more similar to type A in this respect. Local governments have independent constitutional authority, are elected directly with political parties allowed to participate, and receive formula-bound transfers (with respect to interregional allocations) that appear to have increased interregional equity considerably. They are, however, subordinated to the power of the ANC exercised principally at the provincial level, but this power is based on a genuine democracy at the national level.

Assessment of Likely Impact

As explained earlier, the impact of decentralization on intracommunity and on intercommunity service allocations needs to be evaluated. These two criteria broadly correspond to normative goals of, respectively, citizen accountability and responsiveness to heterogeneous need. Intracommunity allocations need to be based ultimately on evidence from surveys of living standards of households or individuals classified by socioeconomic status. These surveys are more reliable than reported perceptions of service delivery or evidence based on the composition of public expenditures at the local level. Even if such data were to be available, a number of challenging econometric problems would have to be confronted. Valuation of public goods such as infrastructure (roads, sanitation, irrigation, public transport) to any given household is intrinsically more challenging than valuation of private goods (transfers, welfare benefits). For instance, to value a new road one has to estimate changes in the amount of travel time for any given household, associated changes in occupational or cropping patterns induced by proximity to relevant markets, and changes in the valuation of housing owned.

Endogeneity of the degree and nature of decentralization is another key problem: a cross-sectional analysis that examined correlations of these with welfare impact on different socioeconomic categories would risk confusing the impact of greater decentralization with underlying unobserved community characteristics that were associated with it. Only in countries such as Brazil or India with spatially uneven patterns of decentralization would such an analysis be feasible, but in such contexts it is evident that the voluntary nature of local decentralization initiatives was such that communities less backward and characterized by more progressive involvement of civil society, patterns of political awareness or literacy of citizens, or greater redistributive ideology tended to embark on more thoroughgoing decentralizations. Most of these community attributes would also be likely to be directly correlated with patterns of targeting of resources in favor of the poor. Separating out the role of the decentralization from these community characteristics would require careful and clever isolation of independent sources of variation.

Comparing outcomes before and after the decentralization may get around some of these problems. But this would require the decentralization to occur at a particular point of time—which would apply only to big-bang decentralizations—when other confounding changes were not taking place simultaneously. The validity of the assessment would also be based on the assumption that the effects of the decentralization would be realized immediately rather than gradually over time. The former problem could be addressed by a difference-of-difference strategy of comparing changes in locations that decentralized with those which did not. But even this approach requires a number of strong assumptions (for example, that the timing of decentralization in any given location was random and uncorrelated with community characteristics that directly impact targeting).

With few exceptions, studies based on household-specific data on delivery of services are rare. The exceptions include Galasso and Ravallion (2005), who find that a decentralized educational subsidy program in Bangladesh was better targeted within than across communities, and research described in our chapter on West Bengal (chapter 6). Other papers examine the composition of public expenditures either across regions or spending categories. Jean-Paul Faguet (in chapter 4) reports that decentralization in Bolivia was associated with large increases in the share of social spending and in the share of poorer regions compared with wealthier regions and with a correlation between the changes and measures of need. Impressive increases in local infrastructure services provided and educational enrolments in Porto Alegre, Brazil, have been reported by Santos (1998), which suggests that public spending became responsive to the needs of poorer citizens. Chattopadhyay and Duflo (2004) identify the effects of randomized reservations of local government positions for women in two Indian states (West Bengal and Rajasthan) and find significant effects on the allocation of expenditures between roads, drinking water, and local education centers, which they argue is consistent with greater representation of women's interests. All these studies are based on a few regions' decisions to embark on a more thorough decentralization than others and on assumptions concerning correlation between composition of public spending and welfare of different categories of local citizens. They indicate that decentralization if properly implemented can significantly benefit distributive equity and service delivery. But the unevenness of the extent and nature of decentralization in countries such as Brazil and India indicates that this potential might remain unexploited in many regions. Moreover, given the wide disparity between different types of decentralization, the implications of findings for one type (such as types A or B based on studies in Bolivia, Brazil, and India) for others (such as type C, where local governments are considerably less subject to accountability pressures from local residents) are of limited value. An alternative approach to evaluating the potential significance of decentralization in promoting accountability would be to appraise how well local democracy functions or is likely to function. In type C decentralizations, there are severe limits on local democracy, so the resulting accountability improvement with respect to local citizens is likely to be modest. In the other types, there is considerable heterogeneity. Much of this heterogeneity concerns aspects of the community that cannot be influenced by the formal design of the decentralization. The available evidence suggests that it makes a considerable difference to the impact.

   This point is especially salient in Faguet's comparison of the communities of Baures and of Guayaramerin in Bolivia, where the extent and nature of the formal decentralization was similar and yet had dissimilar impacts owing to differences in the local political economy. One community was characterized by stronger traditions of political participation of citizens, functioning of civil society institutions, and substantially less socioeconomic inequality. Our study of targeting in West Bengal found that intraregional and interregional allocations were correlated with local inequality and literacy in the way that a typical model of political capture would predict. The effect was substantially more pronounced in interregional allocations and less in intraregional targeting, perhaps owing to greater transparency of intracommunity targeting processes.

In the context of other countries, assessments of the functioning of local democracy were based on more impressionistic evidence. In Indonesia, perceptions of corruption remain high following decentralization, though service improvements have been reported. In Pakistan, Philip E. Keefer, Ambar Narayan, and Tara Vishwanath (in chapter 9) express the judgment that capture by local landed elites is unlikely to be significant. But other aspects of the mode of decentralization are likely to limit accountability pressures on elected officials, such as indirect election of the district Nazim, lack of credibility of political competitors, and a continued tradition of provision of narrowly targeted benefits rather than broad-based public services. In the Ugandan context, Omar Azfar, Jeffrey Livingston, and Patrick Meagher (chapter 7) likewise express pessimism on the prospect that local democracy (or citizen mobility) will provide enough pressure on elected officials, owing to the poor quality of information flows in local communities. They also report a number of potential problems inherent in the decentralization design, stemming from overlapping and poorly defined jurisdictions between different tiers of government, de jure rather than de facto decentralization in many instances, and poor performance in the health sector. Despite this, the Ugandan context exhibits high rates of voter turnout in local elections and some evidence of successful outcomes in the education sector with greater involvement of citizens in school management and efforts to reduce leakages in the flow of funds. The Chinese context involves virtually no local democracy; only recently is there any evidence of some local accountability pressures on government officials as a result of increasing citizen mobility and elected village councils. Overall, in all of these countries the impressionistic evidence available so far suggests only limited accountability improvements. But this needs to be qualified until firmer empirical evidence based on household living standards becomes available. Moreover, the effects may become stronger as time passes. Many of these decentralization efforts are still recent, with possible scope from learning from past experience and neighboring regions.

This is a point stressed particularly in Gianpaolo Baiochhi's chapter (chapter 2), whose evaluation of the Brazilian decentralization is that it represented primarily "an opportunity for democratic innovation." While it has allowed only a few "islands of efficiency" so far, there is evidence of learning and social diffusion. The participative budgeting process of Porto Alegre has been attempted by over one hundred municipalities with varying success. Differences in success seem to correspond to how representative and thriving the pattern of local democracy is, which in turn is positively correlated with socioeconomic indicators of the community. Decentralization may thus lead to increasing interregional inequality, reflecting differences in administrative and fiscal capacity of different regions and greater proneness to capture by local elites. The gap between backward and forward regions may thus be heightened considerably: backward regions could fall behind compared with the past, while a few areas of the country take advantage of the opportunity for democratic innovation and surge ahead. Whether this will be a temporary or permanent phenomenon is hard to foresee.

General Lessons

The papers in this volume communicate the rich variety of decentralization experiences across different countries. In this chapter, we classify these into a few types in terms of both context and design and then explore the different designs in terms of the contexts and political motivation.

Classifying by context, the type A decentralization experienced by Bolivia and Indonesia involved devolution of both political and economic authority to a substantive degree in a uniform fashion. The type B decentralization experienced by Brazil and India represented a uniform political devolution but an uneven economic devolution that has been diffusing slowly through a heterogeneous set of regional contexts.

In contrast to these two types, which correspond to the spread and deepening of democracy in the broad sense of encouraging popular participation and accountability of elected governments, the type C decentralization experienced in Pakistan, Uganda, and China corresponds to consolidation of nondemocratic power at the national level. The experiences of Pakistan and Uganda over the past decades clearly illustrate how decentralization has been an instrument used by military governments to preempt regional or ethnically based political oppositions. Hence there is no general presumption that decentralization and democracy (broadly defined) go hand in hand. In type C kinds of decentralization, administrative and economic decentralization has been more significant. Of all countries, the Chinese case involves the most far-reaching role of local governments in development of local productive enterprises.

Finally, South Africa represents a transition from a type C to a type A decentralization as part of the transition out of the apartheid regime beginning in 1994.

The designs of the decentralizations were related to the historical and political contexts within which they arose. Types A and B correspond to countries that are democratic at the national level. Here decentralization has corresponded to greater political devolution to a set of local governments with independent constitutional authority and thus to a widening of the scope of democracy from national to local levels. Some of these were a natural part of a transition to democracy, as in Brazil, Indonesia, and South Africa. Others occurred within the context of an ongoing democracy, such as Bolivia and India. Whether the decentralization has been comprehensive and uniform (type A) or piecemeal, gradual, and uneven (type B) seems to be related to the balance of power between regional powers and the national government at the time the decentralization was initiated. If regional governments or elites exerted significant power, they had significant room and ability to control the process within their respective regions, resulting in a type B pattern.[4]

What motivated national governments to voluntarily relinquish their own authority to local governments? In some cases (Brazil, Indonesia, and South Africa), decentralization formed part of a transition from a nondemocracy to a democracy in the society at large, hence representing a natural diffusion of power over political and economic decisions. In ongoing democracies such as Bolivia and India, they occurred as incumbents at the national level faced challenges to their own authority from rising regional powers and other political parties. They sought to restore some of their own credibility in the wake of the disappointing performance of the previous centralized mode of governance and to cultivate new channels of patronage to counter the threat from new adversaries. Finally, type C decentralizations represented a way of consolidating the power of the national government: little political authority has been devolved, and the main purpose has been to improve economic incentives or administrative efficiency.

Some common features recur across different kinds of decentralization, with regard to the nature of economic and administrative devolution. Responsibilities transferred have consisted primarily of administration of local infrastructure, welfare, and social services. Financial devolution has been largely conspicuous by its absence, with most local governments relying overwhelmingly on fiscal transfers from higher-level governments. Hard rather than soft budget-constraint problems dominate. This is in contrast to fiscal decentralization to regional, provincial, or state governments in various developing countries (see, e.g., the studies in Rodden, Eskeland, and Litvack, 2003). Decentralization to local governments has not tended to increase the overall scale of government spending or to allow much flexibility with respect to variation in the scale of local need. In this aspect of responsiveness, there was probably little improvement (or cause for concern) relative to more centralized governance modes.

Regarding impact of the decentralizations on other dimensions of responsiveness, such as interregional equity (or intercommunity targeting), type A decentralizations appear to have achieved significant improvement. The evidence is not so clear for the other types of decentralization. This is explained by the combination of the following two facts. First, the general lack of local autonomy over revenue rising implies that the scale of resources available to local governments has been determined primarily by fiscal transfers received from higher-level governments. Second, in a type A decentralization that is mandated by a nationally uniform, comprehensive reform linking the national government with local governments that have independent constitutional authority, fiscal transfers tend to be determined by transparent formulas incorporating demographic size and needs. Compared with previous patterns of interregional resource transfers reflecting political discretion or negotiation, this results in considerable improvement in interregional equity. This was particularly evident in the case of Bolivia and seems also to have been the experience of Indonesia and South Africa. It seems likely that type B decentralizations (Brazil or India) will encounter less improvement with regard to interregional equity because of their inherent unevenness. This was highlighted in the evidence for the Indian state of West Bengal. Type C decentralizations are characterized by continuing control by the national government, so fiscal transfers could still be dominated by political discretion. The Chinese experience seems consistent with this interpretation: decentralization has not resulted in any noticeable improvement in interregional equity and has probably exacerbated previous inequalities. Nevertheless, confirmation of the hypothesis that type A decentralizations dominate the others with regard to their success in intercommunity targeting will have to await more detailed empirical evidence.

Type A decentralizations that devolve political and economic power evenly tend also to promote responsiveness with regard to local preferences over composition of local public spending. Here the only evidence available is from Bolivia, where there were striking compositional shifts in accordance with local needs.

Impacts on intracommunity targeting are more difficult to identify, owing to lack of suitable data at the micro household level. These are also subject to econometric problems of identification and have tended to be located in regions where the decentralization was more thoroughly implemented than others. So it is difficult to draw any general conclusions. In the few contexts where intracommunity targeting assessments have been carried out (such as West Bengal in chapter 6 in this volume), the results suggest that local governments are capable of achieving high levels of targeting the poor and responding to the needs of groups that were traditionally discriminated against (women and minorities).

Where detailed impact assessments were not feasible, the case studies attempted to appraise whether suitable preconditions for accountability improvements from local democracy existed. In this respect, there seems to be great heterogeneity. The studies for the more economically backward countries such as India, Pakistan, and Uganda were quite pessimistic, though the assessment of Bolivia and West Bengal were positive. There was also considerable heterogeneity across different regions within any given country, especially noticeable in the Brazil, Bolivia, and India studies. These highlight the importance of many ancillary institutions not directly included in the design of decentralization per se—traditions of political participation and voter awareness, citizen oversight groups, external media attention, literacy levels, and the extent of local social and economic equality. The importance of these was rendered especially salient in the comparative evaluation of two different municipalities within Bolivia in Faguet's study.

In light of this rich and varied experience, it is difficult to draw any simple conclusions concerning the general impact of decentralization on development or the way that decentralizations ought to be designed. Both theory and evidence suggest that outcomes are likely to be sensitive to context and design, in both respects of which there is great heterogeneity. The following general hypotheses nevertheless can be proposed.

Type A decentralizations tend to perform better than type B or C in the dimension of interregional targeting. This aspect is determined largely by the formal design of the decentralization.

Improvements in accountability (intracommunity targeting, specifically) or popular participation require a functioning democracy at the local level, which includes both a formal decentralization design (independent authority of local governments, direct elections, with political parties allowed to participate) as well as ancillary local institutions (a tradition of widespread political participation, lack of excessive social or economic inequality within the community, institutions such as citizen councils, NGOs, media or audit accounting mechanisms exercising oversight over actions of local governments). It is difficult to generalize beyond this. The effects on this dimension are therefore likely to vary greatly across communities or regions.

Most decentralizations have involved hard rather than soft budget constraints for local governments: expenditure responsibilities devolved have tended to outstrip revenues devolved, and independent revenue-raising powers have not risen much. Hence the decentralizations are unlikely to have much macroeconomic impact; underfunding of required expenditures on local infrastructure or social services has tended to continue. China is the only country where the local governments have played a leading role in increasing rates of growth.

The limited evidence available indicates that if properly designed and implemented, decentralization has significant potential for widening political representation and for targeting resources in favor of the poor. This is particularly evident for interregional allocations that moved in favor of backward regions in Bolivia and South Africa owing to formula-bound schemes of fiscal transfers. These programs replaced the political discretion of previous centralized administrations that disproportionately favored a few narrow, wealthy sets of constituencies.

In parts of Brazil and India where devolution was seriously implemented, poor and socially disadvantaged minorities interests were better represented.

Yet these are perhaps some extreme and unrepresentative cases. Overall, most country experts were more positive about the potential rather than actual achievements of decentralization in improving government performance or reducing poverty. They were most positive about the creation of new political space and the opportunities for innovation in public policy. This suggests that it may be too early to pass judgment. Short-run impacts may well differ from long-run impacts. Even limited forms of decentralization may unleash new political forces that affect the future dynamics of political innovation as communities learn from past experience and from each other and as patterns of political participation respond to devolution.

Acknowledgments

This introduction was prepared with the assistance of Patricia Meirelles and Catherine Rodriguez. We are grateful to the MacArthur Foundation Inequality Network and National Science Foundation Grant No. 0418434 for financial support. The views expressed here are our own and do not represent the views of the MacArthur Foundation or the National Science Foundation in any way.

Notes

1. For an account of this literature, see Oates (1972), Musgrave and Musgrave (1984, chap. 24), and Inman and Rubinfeld (1996, 1997).

2. Analysis, examples, and empirical evidence concerning such leakages and targeting failures are provided by Banerjee (1997), Bardhan (1996a, 1996b), Besley (1989), Besley and Kanbur (1993), Dreze and Saran (1995), Grosh (1991, 1995), Lipton and Ravallion (1995), van de Walle and Nead (1995), and the 1990, 1994, 1997, and 2004 *World Development Reports*.

3. An assumption implicit throughout that analysis was that each citizen is better informed than the government about the value of any good or service to her own welfare. This assumption, which may be violated in the context of health services or financial services, thus ought to be added to the list of preconditions for decentralization to perform effectively.

4. The important role of provincial elites in influencing the evolution of decentralization in Brazil is described in detail by Montero (2001) and Linz and Stepan (1996, ch. 11); the latter refer to these elites as the "barons of the federation."

References

Banerjee, A. (1997). "A Theory of Misgovernance." *Quarterly Journal of Economics* 62: 1289–1332.

Bardhan, P. (1996a). "Decentralized Development." *Indian Economic Review* 31(2): 139–156.

Bardhan, P. (1996b). "Efficiency, Equity, and Poverty Alleviation: Policy Issues in Less Developed Countries." *Economic Journal* 106: 1344–1356.

Bardhan, P. (2002). "Decentralization of Governance and Development." *Journal of Economic Perspectives* 16(4): 185–206.

Bardhan, P., and D. Mookherjee. (1998). "Expenditure Decentralization and Delivery of Public Services in Developing Countries." Working Paper, Institute for Economic Development, Boston University.

Bardhan, P., and D. Mookherjee. (2000). "Capture and Governance at Local and National Levels." *American Economic Review* 90(2): 135–139.

Bardhan, P., and D. Mookherjee. (2003). "Corruption and Decentralization of Infrastructure Delivery in Developing Countries." Working Paper, Institute for Economic Development, Boston University. Forthcoming, *Economic Journal.*

Bardhan, P., and D. Mookherjee. (2005). "Decentralizing Anti-Poverty Program Delivery in Developing Countries." *Journal of Public Economics* 89: 675–704.

Besley, T. (1989). "Targeting Taxes and Transfers: Administrative Costs and Policy Design in Developing Economies." Development Studies Working Paper 146, Princeton University, Woodrow Wilson School.

Besley, T., and R. Kanbur. (1993). "Principles of Targeting." In Michael Lipton and Jacques ven der Gaag (Eds.), *Including the Poor.* Washington, DC: World Bank.

Chattopadhyay, R., and E. Duflo. (2004). "Impact of Reservation in Panchayati Raj: Evidence from a Nationwide Randomised Experiment." *Economic and Political Weekly*, February 28, pp. 979–986.

Crook, R., and J. Manor. (1998). *Democracy and Decentralization in South Asia and West Africa.* Cambridge: Cambridge University Press.

Delli Carpini, M., and S. Keeter. (1996). *What Americans Know about Politics and Why It Matters.* New Haven: Yale University Press.

Dreze, J., and M. Saran. (1995). "Primary Education and Economic Development in China and India: Overview and Two Case Studies." In K. Basu et al. (Eds.), *Choice, Welfare, and Development: A Festschrift in Honor of Amartya K. Sen.* Oxford: Clarendon Press.

Galasso, E., and M. Ravallion. (2005). "Decentralized Targeting of Antipoverty Programs." *Journal of Development Economics* 89(4): 705–727.

Gaviria, A., U. Panizza, and J. Seddon. (2002). "Economic, Social, and Demographic Determinants of Political Participation in Latin America." Working Paper No. 472, Inter-American Development Bank, Washington, DC.

Grosh, M. E. (1991). "The Household Survey as a Tool for Policy Change: Lessons from the Jamaican Survey of Living Conditions." LSMS Working Paper 80, World Bank, Washington, DC.

Grosh, M. E. (1995). "Towards Quantifying the Tradeoff: Administrative Costs and Targeting Accuracy." In D. Van de Walle and K. Nead (Eds.), *Public Spending and the Poor: Theory and Evidence*. Baltimore: Johns Hopkins University Press.

Hamilton, A., J. Madison, and J. Jay. (1937). *The Federalist*. New York: Tudor. (Originally published in 1787).

Inman, R. P., and D. L. Rubinfeld. (1996). "Designing Tax Policies in Federalist Economies: An Overview." *Journal of Public Economics* 60(3): 307–334.

Inman, R. P., and D. L. Rubinfeld. (1997). "Rethinking Federalism." *Journal of Economic Perspectives* 11(4): 43–64.

Linz, J., and A. Stepan. (1996). *Problems of Democratic Transition and Consolidation: Southern Europe, South America and Post-Communist Europe*. Baltimore: Johns Hopkins University Press.

Lipton, M., and M. Ravallion. (1995). "Poverty and Policy." In J. Behrman and T. N. Srinivasan (Eds.), *Handbook of Development Economics* (Vol. 3, ch. 41). Amsterdam: North-Holland.

Litvack, J., J. Ahmed, and R. Bird. (1998). "Rethinking Decentralization at the World Bank." Discussion Paper, World Bank, Washington, DC.

Montero, A. P. (2001). "Decentralizing Democracy: Spain and Brazil in Comparative Perspective." *Comparative Politics* (January): 149–169.

Mookherjee, D. (2004). *The Crisis in Government Accountability: Governance Reforms and India's Economic Performance*. New Delhi: Oxford University Press.

Musgrave, R., and P. Musgrave. (1984). *Public Finance in Theory and Practice* (4th ed.). New York: McGraw Hill.

Oates, W. E. (1972). *Fiscal Federalism*. New York: Harcourt, Brace and Jovanovich.

Przeworski, A., S. C. Stokes, and B. Manin (Eds.). (1999). *Democracy, Accountability, and Representation*. New York: Cambridge University Press.

Putnam, R. (1993). *Making Democracy Work: Civic Traditions in Modern Italy*. Princeton: Princeton University Press.

Rodden, J., G. Eskeland, and J. Litvack (Eds.). (2003). *Fiscal Decentralization and the Challenge of Hard Budget Constraints*. Cambridge, MA: MIT Press.

Rosenstone, S., and J. Hansen. (1993). *Mobilization, Participation and Democracy in America*. New York: Macmillan.

Santos, B. (1998). "Participatory Budgeting in Porto Alegre: Towards a Redistributive Democracy." *Politics and Society* 26(4): 416–510.

Seabright, P. (1996). "Accountability and Decentralization in Government: An Incomplete Contracts Model." *European Economic Review* 40(1): 61–89.

Tendler, J. (1997). *Good Government in the Tropics*. Baltimore: Johns Hopkins University Press.

Tiebout, C. (1956). "A Pure Theory of Local Expenditures." *Journal of Political Economy* 64: 416–424.

Tommasi, M., and F. Weinschelbaum. (1999). "A Principal-Agent Building Block for the Study of Decentralisation and Integration." Working Paper, Universidad de San Andres, Buenos Aires.

United Nations. (Various years). *Human Development Report*. New York: Oxford University Press.

Van de Walle, D., and K. Nead (Eds.). (1995). *Public Spending and the Poor: Theory and Evidence*. Baltimore: Johns Hopkins University Press.

World Bank. (Various years). *World Development Reports*. New York: Oxford University Press.

2

Inequality and Innovation: Decentralization as an Opportunity Structure in Brazil

Gianpaolo Baiocchi

Introduction

Brazil's experiment with decentralization, codified in the 1988 postdictatorship constitution, has attracted a great deal of attention as one of the most far-reaching reforms conducted in Latin America and even in developing countries as a whole (Willis, Garmas, and Haggard, 1999). As the introduction to this volume makes clear, Brazil's decentralization was an extensive, big-bang set of reforms carried out in the context of marked regional heterogeneity. After more than a decade of continuing reforms, Brazil's decentralization has both its admirers and critics. Admirers point to subnational innovations in service provision and governance—such as the well-known examples of the municipalities of Curitiba and Porto Alegre and the state of Ceará—as "good governance in the tropics" made possible by decentralization (Tendler, 1997; Campbell, 1997; Peterson, 1997). Detractors note the ambiguities and incompleteness of Brazilian-style federalism, including the lack of central coordination on areas like fiscal and industrial policy. Other charges are that decentralization has provided a source of spoils for patrimonial elites and that the reforms have not ameliorated Brazil's longstanding regional inequalities. The unchecked and uncoordinated power of state governors, for example, has caused some to describe Brazil's system as the "most demos-constraining federation in the world" (Stepan, 2000, p. 143). Critics have also charged that the new arrangements do not enable municipalities, especially smaller ones, to provide the services for which they became responsible, a situation of an "unfunded mandate" (Pont, 2001, p. 1).

This chapter seeks to add to the debate on Brazilian decentralization and on the nature of decentralization of the state by reintroducing to the discussion the political dimension of the phenomenon. I argue that

Brazil's decentralization is partially guilty as charged: despite a complicated system of transfers and despite a decided overall improvement of
service delivery, it has not improved overall regional inequalities and
sometimes has exacerbated them. On the other hand, decentralization
has created the institutional opening for local actors to create a number
of local experiments in innovative governance, fulfilling the promise to
bring government closer to citizens that is implicit in decentralization.
I consider in the last section of the chapter participatory budgeting,
a local innovation that was made possible by the reforms and that
evidence suggests has generally increased democratic accountability
through citizen participation. The opportunity structure for these innovations is unevenly distributed, with poorer and smaller municipalities
less likely to have them.

The Context of Decentralization in Brazil

Brazil's decentralization was codified by its 1988 postdictatorship
constitution. To understand how the reforms were conceived and ultimately how they unfolded, it is important to understand the anteced-
ent conditions. First, democratization was happening concurrently
with decentralization, which was not inconsequential to the shape or
effect of the reforms. Reemerging regional elites that had negotiated
with the outgoing military dictatorship remained important through
the crafting of the constitution and ensured that it would protect their
interests. But the perceived opening of a political space during the
transition also meant that social movements pressured legislators to
include items in the constitution that would enhance local autonomy
and enshrine popular participation. New actors in civil society from
the prodemocracy movements would attempt to make use of these
openings. Second, the reforms were crafted after the debt crisis of the
1980s. International pressures to comply with fiscal austerity measures
as well as to modernize the state apparatus also contributed to the
pressures to transfer of government responsibilities since the late 1980s
in areas as education, social services, and health to municipal government (Alvarez, 1993; Nickson, 1995). The decentralization reforms
were thus conceived and implemented in ways that reflected these
contradictory pressures.

The Transition to Democracy
Since the late 1970s, social movements for democracy have become
increasingly visible in their demands, which have included political

reforms, accountability, and improved governance.[1] Throughout Brazil, participants in these movements sought ways to organize various local neighborhood associations and social movements into blocs that could make demands on city and state government and eventually coalesced into national movements like the Cost of Living Movement, the Housing Movement, and the Collective Transports Movement (Silva, 1990). Brazil's negotiated transition to democracy, beginning in 1985, took place at a time when poverty and exclusion had increased sharply throughout Brazilian cities, and the belts of poverty and exclusion around cities provided a further, powerful impetus for organizing.

In 1985, full municipal elections were held. A number of notable mayors were elected that year from Brazil's newly legal left-of-center parties with ties to these social movements. The Workers' Party (PT) emerged as one of the novelties of the period as a political party that had close ties to civil society, aspired to translate civil society demands into party platforms, and committed to the democratizing of state institutions (Branford and Kucinski, 1995; Keck, 1992a, 1992b; Lowy, 1987; Meneguello, 1989). With discussions about the new constitution beginning in 1986, urban social movements made demands for more accountable forms of city governance, calling for decentralization and citizen participation in the running of city affairs as a basic right of citizenship (Moura, 1989). Social movements mobilized around the legal proviso for popular amendments to the constitution. Caravans to Brasília accompanied the 122 popular amendments that were submitted to the congress, and social-movement representatives were eventually allowed to testify as consultants in the hearings (Alvarez, 1993).

Decentralization and the New Constitution

When the constitution was eventually ratified in 1988, it reflected the imprint of social movements and other sources of pressure as well, including from regional elites and from international bodies. Throughout the Americas in the 1980s, "decentralization of government" was also a catch phrase for policy makers who argued that a less centralized state would be a less bureaucratic, more responsive, and more efficient state.[2] Hardest hit by these austerity measures were urban services provided by central agencies. To adjust national fiscal spending to meet with International Monetary Fund conditionals, international lending agencies actively encouraged the transfer of responsibilities for social services to the local level. Most notably, the Inter-American Development Bank and the World Bank in the mid-1980s encouraged local institution building by offering loans and training programs directly to municipal governments (Nickson, 1995).

Regional elites also played an important role in the decentralization reforms. Brazil is a country with a long history of regional disparities and of region-based political and economic elites that have been able to influence national policy. Scholars have argued that Brazil's decentralization in the postdictatorship period should be understood as part of a continuum of "center-state-local power relationships" (Souza, 2002, p. 25). Since the founding of the Brazilian republic in 1889, municipalities and states have traditionally been the highly autonomous strongholds of a variety of regional elites with specific interests. The national state has sought to reign in states at various points, such as during the Vargas dictatorship (1930 to 1937) and again under the military regime (1964 to 1984), when government functions were recentralized, partially as a move to weaken the influence of regional elites. A variety of measures (including, for example, the abolishment of state constitutions and flags under the early years of the dictatorship) were sought as a way to strengthen the center.

Since the mid-1970s, however, there have been signs of decentralization, such as the incremental increase of transfers to states. Scholars have argued that this has been result of the national state's search for political legitimacy among regional elites represented by politicians in the two legal parties (Kugelmas and Sola, 1999). The first elections for governors in 1982 (ahead of the full transition to democracy) brought a number of opposition governors to power as well as a number of governors tied to regional elites. From then on, the dictatorship sought to appease these local power brokers, who were seen as the key to political legitimacy (Abrucio, 1998). Regional elites played a crucial role in ensuring a weakened center in the decentralization reforms, which has curtailed the ability of the national administration eventually to implement reforms evenly throughout the country.

The Design of the Reforms and the Constitution of 1988

In essence, the constitution reflected four broad transformations between national and local state power. First, local governments were given significantly more political autonomy from their district-level and national counterparts. In a rare constitutional arrangement, municipalities were to be thus considered state members of the national federation on equal footing as states. They were free to develop organic laws—municipal constitutions that were responsive to local needs. A number of cities in Brazil, including Recife and Porto Alegre, organized mass public debates on the new municipal constitutions. Cities were thus also allowed greater discretion with land legislation, particularly social-use and social-interest laws that guaranteed broad rights to municipal government to regulate the use of empty plots of land or to develop municipal policies to deal with squatters' settlements. Local autonomy in deciding land-rights questions would have important implications for the problem of urban poverty. On the other hand, the status of municipalities would also mean that there would be ambiguities in the coordination of the decentralizing efforts because it would not be legally possible for states or the federation to force municipalities to carry out services.

Second, local and state governments were given greater fiscal autonomy from the union, as the constitution codified a number of mechanisms of transfer of resources toward subnational government. Traditionally, the principal source of funding for local government came from federal revenue-sharing arrangements. The 1988 constitution shifted a significant number of resources toward states and municipalities, while increasing the number of taxes each could raise, such as vehicle, sales, and services taxes for municipalities. It also allowed for greater nondiscretionary transfers from the state and federal government to the local government. Five taxes, including ICMS (value-added tax), were transferred to states, which were free to set their own rates and were given discretion on its use, save for a provision that 25 percent would be transferred to municipalities in the state. The two funds of nondiscretionary transfers to states and cities, the participation funds (FPM and FPE), were augmented by increasing the proportion of the income tax (IR) and industrial products tax (IPI) transferred to it. These funds would be distributed according to states and municipalities on a formula based on per capita income and size.

Third, local governments were given the responsibility (or coresponsibility) for the some of the main aspects of social-service delivery that were municipalized. In 1987, the national health system was abolished in favor of a municipality-based service provision. The 1988 constitution formally recognized that cities would be responsible for health services, transportation, and primary education. As I discuss below, these devolutionary policies have led to mixed results because of ambiguities about which level of government would be responsible and accountable for provision.

Fourth, local governments became *free to institutionalize channels of direct popular participation into public affairs*. The 1988 constitution established legal provisos for participatory mechanisms calling for the input of popular councils in the development of social programs. At the same time, municipal governments were developing decentralization schemes. The well-known article 29 of the constitution calls for "the cooperation of representative associations in municipal planning" (Brazil, 1988).

Recentralizing Tendencies

The economic context under which these reforms were introduced was not an auspicious one. The late 1980s were a period of runaway inflation, difficulties with debt repayments, and constrained public investments. As a result of the economic changes of the 1980s and the dislocations of the population to urban peripheries, the tendency for city services and city hall offices to serve downtown areas instead of outlying areas was exacerbated. Newly elected local and state governments conflicted with the national government over service provision and acceptable levels of spending.

One of the conflicts involved the high levels of public expenditures of states by the early 1990s, particularly on personnel, which threatened fiscal stability. Newly elected governors in 1982 increased payrolls with 500,000 new employees at the state level (Samuels and Abrucio, 2000). Worries about the runaway spending of states (an increase in real terms of 33 percent between 1986 and 1995, a period when states' gross domestic product increased by only 16 percent), and several subsequent federal bailouts triggered a number of moves designed to foster fiscal recentralization (Kugelmas and Sola, 1999). The stabilization plan for the Brazilian real put forth by Fernando Henrique Cardoso in 1994 included several recentralizing measures as well as attempts to curb the spending of states. This included curbing the amounts of tax transfers to states and the creation of a new tax on transfers. A law on fiscal responsibility (the LRF) limited public-sector spending, and another law of 1996 (the Kandir law) then curbed the amount spent by subnational government on personnel (Souza, 2002).

Uneven Implementation

Observers have noted that the de facto implementation of decentralization has been extremely uneven. As mentioned earlier, a crucial factor in the crafting of the new constitution was the fact that parliamentarians involved in the Constitutional Assembly reflected disparate regional interests, and there was a general consensus that weakening the center as much as possible would lead to the most resources to regions (Montero, 1997, 2001; Samuels and Abrucio, 2000). This was reflected in some of the institutionally vague arrangement of the reforms. The constitution does not assign responsibility for provisions but instead assigns directives. Articles 198 and 204, for instance, assign directives for health and social assistance to municipalities without specifying the responsible entity. There are, in fact, thirty such areas of concurrent responsibilities in Brazil (Araujo, 1997; Medeiros, 1994).

A weakened center cannot implement reforms evenly or uniformly. One problem is the inability of local governments to assume responsibilities because of lack of capacity. According to Arretche (2000), the levels of "actual decentralization"—that is, the actual transfer of competencies to local units—is regionally varied. For instance, while the provision of school lunches has been turned over from the federal government to the municipal government and is essentially currently carried out locally, the story is different for social services and health, areas also deemed municipal competencies. Only 33 percent of municipalities by 1997 offered social services, and only 54 percent of medical consults in 1996 were offered in municipal clinics (Arretche, 2000). While Arretche finds clear variations by region and by size (and fiscal capacity) of municipality, it is not possible to assign a single causal explanatory variable to whether a municipality assumes services or not. Rather, a combination of political factors (such as whether local elected officials will take a risk), associative conditions, and resource constraints account for the outcome.

According to a study of the northern state of Bahia, a state with low municipal capacity and traditionally clientelistic politicians, that was carried out between 1987 and 1997, the decentralization of services was not met with any significant increase in local-level initiatives. In the case of housing, the dismantling of federal programs meant simply the virtual stoppage of housing assistance, and housing and infrastructure remained at roughly 1.5 percent of combined municipal budgets for the period. Health and education revealed similar features, and local-level social services were spent largely in clientelistic arrangements (Carvalho, 1997).

The Effects of Decentralization in Brazil

There is a wide-ranging discussion on the effects of decentralization in Brazil, and while there are disagreements, the literature as a whole describes "mixed but largely disappointing results in terms of service delivery, popular participation, strengthened local elites, and reform initiatives" (Weyland, 1999, p. 1006). Analysts of various stripes have consistently pointed to a number of persistent problems with Brazil's decentralization—the functional ambiguity of the reforms, regional inequalities, clientelism and elite capture, and runaway spending by governors—as reforms that have "tended to revitalize the power of traditional, patrimonial elites" (Montero, 1997, p. 32). Below, I review the evidence of the impact or reforms in terms of actual fiscal decentralization, provision of services, and regional and size disparities.

Fiscal Decentralization

By the year 2000, municipalities and states were spending over half of public expenditures and were becoming the dominant providers of health, education, and infrastructure. While the federal government was still spending the largest portion of public expenditures and was still the largest source of social spending, in 2000, 78 percent of federal spending went to debt amortization, and 65 percent of its social spending was in pensions, which highlights the importance of subnational units (Souza, 2002, p. 37). Table 2.1 shows the progression of social spending by source in Brazil from 1987 to 1996.

Table 2.2 shows the breakdown of spending by sector in Brazil by government level for 2000. It shows that municipalities and states have become the principal providers of a number of services, with municipalities accounting for 68.7 percent of housing, 30.9 percent of education and culture, and 30.3 percent of health expenditures. States account for 49.6 percent of education and culture, 47.3 percent of transportation, and 25.4 percent of health expenditures.

The resource base of municipalities and states, however, has increased in real terms over the period of the reforms, a growth in real

Table 2.1
Proportion of total social spending in Brazil by source, 1987 to 1996 (percentage)

Year	1987	1989	1992	1994	1996
Federal	63%	60%	56%	60%	57%
State	26	28	28	23	23
Municipal	11	12	16	17	19

Source: Souza (1997).

revenues of 161.5 percent between 1989 and 1995, causing some to declare Brazilian municipalities "the envy of the developing world" (Shah, 1991, p. 42). In fact, many scholars and practitioners have argued the opposite. While there has been an increase in resources, municipalities have been entrusted with an even greater responsibility for service provision as result of the dismantling of federal services, resulting in an overload of demands to local level institutions, particularly with smaller municipalities (Araujo, 1997; Arretche, 2000; Carvalho, 1997; Lebauspin, 2000; Pont, 2001; Souza, 1996, 1997). Table 2.3 shows the evolution of fiscal decentralization in Brazil and the distribution of total tax revenues available per level of government between 1987 and 2002. In addition to showing a tendency toward recentralization after 1991, the table shows (when compared to table 2.1) that social spending has fallen to municipalities in greater proportion than the increase in available budgets.

Among poorer municipalities, where per capita levels of municipal budgets are low, there is difficulty in raising independent revenues. According to Souza (2002, p. 36), three-quarters of municipalities and over 90 percent of towns with fewer than 10,000 inhabitants depend on transfers for over 90 percent of their revenue.

Table 2.2
Proportion of government expenditures in Brazil by level, 2000 (percentage)

Function	Union	States	Municipalities
Social insurance and social assistance	78.8%	16.2%	5.0%
Education, culture, sport, and leisure	19.5	49.6	30.9
Health and sanitation	44.2	25.4	30.3
Housing and urbanism	15.2	16.1	68.7
Labor	90.8	9.3	—
Environmental management	100.0	—	—
Energy and mineral resources	72.2	19.8	8.0
Transportation	23.8	47.3	28.9
Sectorial policies	58.9	33.0	8.1
Defense	100.0	—	—
Public security	15.2	82.2	2.5
Foreign affairs	100.0	0.0	—
Legislative branch	23.5	41.0	35.5
Judiciary branch	42.4	56.3	1.3
Total expenditures	45.5	37.9	16.5

Source: IBGE (2002).

Table 2.3
Fiscal decentralization in Brazil, distribution of tax revenues, 1987 to 2002 (percentage)

Year	Federal	States	Municipalities
1987	65.28%	23.98%	10.74%
1988	67.17	22.51	10.32
1989	62.93	25.72	11.35
1990	61.10	26.40	12.50
1991	58.55	28.40	13.05
1992	60.18	27.19	12.63
1993	62.55	25.26	12.19
1994	63.62	24.99	11.39
1995	61.73	26.00	12.28
1996	61.47	26.25	12.28
1997	62.48	25.43	12.09
1998	62.85	24.52	12.63
1999	63.18	24.00	12.82
2000	62.71	24.56	12.73
2001	62.44	24.54	13.02
2002	63.46	23.59	12.95

Source: BNDE, Termômetro da Descentralização.

Provision of Services

Assessing the impact of decentralization on the provision of services requires assessing changes in the provision by each level of government as well as overall changes. In addition to the difficulties in establishing baseline conditions or finding reliable data, as discussed in the introduction to this volume, the assessment is further complicated by the many redundancies in the institutional arrangements created by the new constitution. Because of overlapping responsibilities in most areas, de facto decentralization has been uneven, with lower levels of government often unwilling or unable to take over service provision. As Kugelmas and Sola ask, "How can decentralization be a success while states and municipalities lack the administrative, financial, and institutional conditions to implement programs?" (Kugelmas and Sola, 1999, p. 75)

Shortly after the constitution of 1988, the federal government undertook "Operação Desmonte," the dismantling operation that significantly removed funding for federal social programs. In this period, there was an aggregate decrease in per capita social expenditures for the nation as a whole—from U.S. $80 to U.S. $40 between 1988 and

1993 for health, for example, according to Workman (1997, p. 49). One of the downfalls of the devolution of government has been that smaller cities in cash-poor states have had to assume greater responsibilities for service delivery (Dowbor, 1998; Peterson, 1997; Willis, Garman, and Haggard, 1999).

The evidence about the performance of service provision under the regime of decentralization is mixed. Souza (1997), focusing on education, challenges the notion that decentralization has brought any improvements to performance and that it has exacerbated regional disparities. Other scholars examining education, health, and social service provision have also generally argued for modest overall improvements, pointing to local instances of innovation (Araujo, 1997; Arretche, 2000; Costa, 1996, 2002; Graham, 1997; Graham and Wilson, 1997; Jacobi, 1994; Sposati et al., 1990).

In terms of education, a principal problem with the decentralization reforms was the level of disparity in provision and the inability of municipalities to take over responsibilities. Some states, like Ceará, developed innovative ways of incetivizing municipalization in the early 1990s, but on whole the reforms had little success in altering the proportion of students in municipal schools throughout the 1990s. An effort in 1998 to equalize service provision was the creation of a federal fund (FUNDEF) to supplement local funds for education up to perstudent minimum, with an earmarking of 60 percent of funds to go to wages and salaries. As a result, there has been a significant increase in municipalization of education, supplementing the decision-making autonomy given by the constitution with an increase in the capacity to carry out those decisions. Between 1996 and 1999, the number of children in municipal schools nationally increased by over 6 million, bringing the proportion of all students in municipal schools to 40 percent from 31.8 percent (Afonso and Melo, 2000).

In terms of health-care provision, similar problems were faced by poorer municipalities, and efforts in the late 1990s to increase the equity in the resource base for health provision at the municipal level were somewhat successful in increasing access to health care. Transfers to meet per capita minimums for certain preventive-care programs were introduced, as was a mechanism to create intermunicipal consortia for health-care delivery since small municipalities do not have the means to meet the scale of invesment necessary for certain types of health-care services. The vast majority of such consortia are in the south and southeast regions of the country (Afonso and Melo, 2000;

Araujo, 1997; Costa, 1996). Table 2.4 offers some data on changes in terms of human-development indicators in Brazil between 1990 and 2000.

As the table suggests, education indicators have improved across the country, with the disparity between regions decreasing somewhat over the period. Adult literacy has increased from 68.84 to 78.23 percent over the period, and school attendance from 55.52 to 77.95 percent. The ratio of indicators for the southeastern region to the northeastern region gives a sense of the magnitude of the disparity between the country's richest and poorest regions. In terms of rates of school attendance, for example, the poorest regions have all but caught up with the richer ones, and the disparity in terms of adult literacy has also diminished. In terms of health between 1990 and 1998, there was a national increase in the life expectancy of four years, and infant mortality rates have decreased by over seven percentage points. In health, however, the disparities between regions have not been improved (such as for life expectancy) and actually increased in terms of infant mortality, with rates in 1998 almost three times as high in the northeast than in the southeast.

Regional and Size Disparities

While the constitution mandates a number of transfers that are, in principle, supposed to offset regional inequalities, scholars have pointed out that despite formal mechanisms to reduce regional inequalities, the economic supremacy of the industrialized Rio–São Paulo–Minas Gerais belt in the southeast worsened between 1988 and 2000. The available budgets for states and municipalities in different regions are also widely disparate, and despite attempts to equalize them, levels of social expenditure remain unequal.

Real disparities remain among municipalities of different sizes and in different regions. Table 2.5 offers some human-development indicators by municipality size according to 2000 data.

As the table shows, most indicators are significantly worse among smaller municipalities. Infant mortality in municipalities of up to 100,000 is almost 150 percent of the rate in the largest cities. Accordingly, rates of adult literacy, life expectancy, and school attendance are significantly higher in the larger cities. If we consider the fact that half of the country's population lives in municipalities of up to 100,000 inhabitants, this disparity becomes even more of a pressing issue.

Table 2.4
Selected human development indicators per region, 1990 to 2000

Region	Percentage of Adult Literacy			Percentage of School Literacy			Life Expectancy (years)			Percentage of Infant Mortality		
	1991	2000	Change 1991–2000	1991	2000	Change 1991–2000	1991	2000	Change 1991–2000	1990	1998	Change 1990–1998
North	63.76%	76.00%	12.24%	53.13%	74.53%	21.40%	61.30	65.72	4.43	48.41%	40.68%	-7.73%
Northeast	50.18	64.32	14.14	50.11	78.49	28.39	58.32	63.13	4.82	75.73	65.58	-10.14
Southeast	77.87	85.00	7.13	59.10	76.09	16.98	66.31	70.26	3.94	33.93	27.00	-6.93
South	84.14	88.89	4.75	58.49	80.30	21.81	67.81	71.54	3.73	27.83	22.62	-5.20
Central	75.19	83.22	8.03	58.58	80.13	21.55	64.13	68.94	4.82	37.54	30.06	-7.48
Ratio of south to northeast	1.68	1.38		1.17	1.02		1.16	1.13		0.37	0.34	
National average	68.84	78.23	9.39	55.52	77.95	22.43	63.45	67.74	4.29	47.68	39.96	-7.72

Sources: IBGE, 2001; SUS, 2001.

Table 2.5
Selected human development indicators per municipality size, 2000

Municipio Size	Number of Municipios	Population in Municipios (1994)	Percentage of Adult Literacy 2000	Percentage of School Attendance 2000	Life Expectancy (years, 2000)	Human Development Index (2000)	Percentage of Infant Mortality (1998)
Up to 20,000	4,066	30,737,394	77.48%	77.34%	67.60	0.69	39.31%
Up to 100,000	1,233	48,090,396	78.69	78.95	67.82	0.71	43.58
Up to 500,000	181	36,686,305	89.90	83.57	69.97	0.78	31.25
Up to 1 million	15	10,658,770	91.37	85.47	69.46	0.79	32.58
Greater than 1 millon	12	30,897,296	94.10	88.93	70.09	0.82	29.66
Total	5,507	157,070,161	78.23	77.95	67.74	0.70	39.96

Sources: IBGE, 2001; SUS, 2001.

Part of the problem lies in the disparate municipal budgets. The reforms gave municipalities additional powers to raise taxes, including a land-use tax (IPTU), a service tax (ISS), a real estate tax (ITBI), which altogether accounted for 15 percent of municipal income for 1997. The remaining municipal resources come from federal and state transfers; the federal transfer comes from a portion of federal income tax (IR) and the value-added tax (ICMS), which made up 60 percent of transfers into a municipal fund (FPM), which is then distributed according to a formula that favors smaller municipalities. State transfers come from a portion of state taxes over motor vehicles (IPVA) and valued-added tax (ICMS). Table 2.6 uses the example of health expenditures, where there are federal transfers, to illustrate the disparities between larger and smaller municipalities. Despite SUS transfers for health expenditures and the progressive transfers of the FPM, health expenditures remain disparate.

While smaller municipalities tend to be more dependent on transfers, the situation is also worse in the less economically developed areas of the country. Because the taxes that municipalities can raise privilege developed urban areas, the ability of municipalities to raise taxes is concentrated in the country's richer areas. In 1999, 71 percent of all municipal revenues were raised in the southeastern region, while the north, northeastern, and central west regions accounted for 15 percent of that (Afonso and Araújo, 2000; Neves, 1993; Nunes, 2001). Among northeastern municipalities, 60 percent were in a "high degree of dependency" for transfers; among smaller municipalities, own resources accounted to between 1.5 and 5 percent of total budgets for 1994, for example (Carvalho, 1997). In 2000, average per capita tax revenues raised by municipalities under 100,000 varied between 2 reais for Acre (in the north) and 77 reais for Rio de Janeiro (in the southeast). Even among state capitals, the disparity between per capita budgets in capitals in less developed regions and those in more developed regions is stark, with south and southeastern capitals having between two and three times the available per capita budgets than other capitals (Rosenblatt and Shildo, 1996). Among states, the picture is not much different. For 1999, states in the north, northeast, and central west depended on transfers for almost two-thirds of their state budgets, while the figure for south and southeast was closer to a third (Afonso and Melo, 2000).

In sum, the impact of decentralization has been mixed. The reforms' goals of improving service delivery at lower costs have been met,

Table 2.6
Health expenditures per capita per municipality size, 2000

Municipio Size	Own Health Expenditures per Capita (reals)	SUS Transfers per Capita (reals)	Average Population	FPM, ICMS Transfers per Capita (reals)	Own Income per Capita (reals)	Total Health Expenditures per Capita
Up to 20,000	59.97	31.20	8,324	402.39	18.57	**91.29**
Up to 100,000	34.20	35.97	40,896	212.72	33.51	**70.28**
Up to 500,000	45.44	54.47	223,435	199.07	81.96	**100.01**
Up to 1 million	54.52	73.15	760,461	204.84	107.17	**128.24**
Greater than 1 millon	41.45	88.31	2,739,665	157.56	176.95	**129.76**
Average	53.45	33.45	33,646	349.97	25.10	**87.02**

Source: SUS, 2001.

though their success must be qualified. Basic indicators show improvement across the decade but also show that size and regional disparities have not improved and, in some cases, such as the rates of child mortality, show an actual increase in levels of disparity. The reasons are not hard to fathom, as described above, and as noted by many scholars: the burden of the reforms has not been evenly shared. Despite federal transfers designed to ameliorate the situation, for many municipalities at the end of the decade the burden of meeting service provision was still difficult to meet. The reforms, however, also had another set of impacts having to do with opportunities for innovations.

Decentralization as Opportunity Structure: Democratic Innovation

The decentralization of government in Brazil has also opened up institutional spaces for local actors to carry out innovative reforms. The combination of increased political autonomy, greater discretion with regard to the allocation of resources, and a growing movement of local actors who have ties to social movements and are willing to contest elections has meant that conditions for democratic innovation have been made possible. Among the best-known examples of such innovation are instances of participatory governance, such as the ones noted in Belo Horizonte, Porto Alegre, Santos, or Diadema under the Workers' Party (PT). In Belo Horizonte, in the state of Minas Gerais, a *favela* urbanization program has helped several thousands of families of squatters to earn the title to their land. The city of Santos, also in São Paulo, under the PT developed innovative AIDS programs and community-based mental health programs that have become an international model (Branford and Kucinski, 1995, p. 85). Other innovations have been described in the literature, particularly in terms of municipal innovations, of "cities that work" or "islands of efficiency" (Figueiredo Júnior and Lamounier, 1997). These have been in the areas of environmental action, health provision, and computer resources at the municipal level (Figueiredo Júnior and Lamounier, 1997; Instituto Pólis, 2001; Jacobi, 2000; Lebauspin, 2000; Spink and Clemente, 1997). Given that these are islands and a minority of municipalities, I address the structures of opportunity afforded by the decentralizing reforms. While opportunity structures have often been considered in terms of understanding the way collective action is responsive to opportunities in the polity (Amenta and Zylan, 1991; Tarrow, 1996; Tilly, 1978), scholars of democratic innovations have pointed to the specific institutional and political contexts that made such innovations possible (Markoff, 2001).

The Range of Local-Level Reforms

Administrators from the first cohorts of opposition mayors of 1985 to 1988 experienced significant difficulties in carrying out effective governance and ensuring reelection. While these were often not radical programs that granted substantial decision-making powers to local groups, decentralization and participation were part of the municipal government plans of many cities in Brazil and Latin America at the time (Nickson, 1995). The capital cities of Curitiba, Rio de Janeiro, Recife, and Salvador developed some sort of participatory structures by 1989.[3] By the early 1990s, a number of notable experiments were being conducted throughout Brazil, varying widely in terms of district-level scope, composition, and decision-making power—including mutual-assistance programs, local management of specific municipal services, and sectoral councils, such as municipal health councils (Graham, 1997). Since 1993, dozens of municipalities in Brazil have been home to innovations, which have included participatory decision making about education, health, the municipal budget, municipal planning, and environmental regulation (Abers, 1996, 2000; Avritzer, 2000; Baiocchi, 2001; Branford and Kucinski, 1995; Campbell, 1997; Jacobi, 1991; Keck, 1992b; Kowarick and Singer, 1994; McCarney, 1996; Nylen, 1998; Reilly, 1995). While a number of early experiments ended in electoral failure and sometimes did not offer any improvement in service delivery, more recent versions of institutional designs have been more robust, though still vulnerable to losing electoral contests.

The reform that has attracted the most attention has been participatory budgeting (PB) reform, which aims to include ordinary citizens in binding discussions about the direction of municipal investments. Several municipalities, mostly under the PT, have carried out successful participatory reforms of this sort, often involving thousands of citizens or a significant proportion of the adult population in yearly meetings. The cities of Porto Alegre, Belém, Santos, Angra dos Reis, Belo Horizonte, and Campinas, among others, have achieved significant successes and have managed reelection. Participatory budgeting is currently the subject of much attention from within policy circles and academic circles, and while no comprehensive evidence exists yet about its various impacts across contexts, in a number of individual cases PB has been linked to redistributive outcomes (Calderón et al., 2002; Carvalho and Felgueiras, 2000; Lebauspin, 2000; Pont, 2001; Pontual, 1997; Pozzobon, 1998), increased governmental efficiency (Marquetti, 2002), increased civic activity, and a transformed political culture (Baiocchi, 2002). There are ongoing research efforts to establish the net impact of the range of PB reforms across Brazil.

One of the most successful examples of PB has been the city of Porto Alegre in the south of Brazil, which became a model administration as PB reforms became the model for many subsequent administrations. The PB has devolved decision making over new capital investments to citizen councils organized around the city's districts. Citizens participate as individuals and as representatives of various groups of civil society (neighborhood associations, cultural groups, special-interest groups) throughout a yearly cycle. They deliberate on projects for specific districts, and decide municipal investment priorities, and monitor the outcomes of these projects. Over the thirteen years of its existence, the citizen councils have decided on hundreds of projects accounting for almost 20 percent of the city's budget and have drawn in several thousand participants from poorer sectors.

The Porto Alegre experiment has become well known in and outside of Brazil, and research and indicators confirm that PB has indeed been successful in its innovations in governance and municipal decision making. Careful analysis has shown that PB investments have targeted poorer residents and needy areas (Marquetti, 2002). Although Porto Alegre had high indicators compared to previous administrations and to changes in Brazil as a whole, the PT administration in the city has brought significant improvements in service delivery, including achieving almost 100 percent coverage in basic sewage and water (up from 79 percent) in the ten years and has doubled the number of children in public primary schools (Abers, 1996; Baiocchi, 2001; Navarro, 1996; Santos, 1998; Utzig, 1996).

Participatory budgeting reforms were replicated (and transformed as they were copied) throughout Brazil. In addition to the twelve cities that carried it out between 1989 and 1992, thirty-six did so between 1993 and 1996, and at least 103 did so in the 1997 to 2000 tenure, according to surveys done by Brazilian nongovernmental organizations. A 2001 survey offers a snapshot of the practice in Brazil for the time period. The basic structure adopted by municipalities generally included an yearly cycle with district-level meetings, concurrent meetings of a main budget council, and somewhat less commonly,

municipal thematic meetings (Ribeiro and Grazia, 2002). According to
Teixeira (2002), many experiments begin as exact copies of the Porto
Alegre experiment, down to the names of the municipal departments
responsible for the process, and were modified after a year or two.
There is variation in how much decision making is afforded participants and how this decision making takes place. In Santo André, São
Paulo, at the Council of the Budget, municipal department heads have
the same number of votes as councilors (Carvalho and Felgueiras,
2000). In Belo Horizonte, only 50 percent of capital expedintures are
turned over to the PB, and in Recife district-level priorities are chosen
at the same time as delegates (Azevedo, 1997; Boschi, 1999; Somarriba
and Dulci, 1997). Preliminary results from a recent research project
has established that PB reforms across Brazil in 1997 to 2000 did have
some of the redistributive and development outcomes its proponents
have claimed. According to the research, they were associated with
increased municipal spending in health, the improved fiscal standing
of municipalities, some improved service provision (in areas like access
to drinking water), and some improved human development outcomes
(such as in poverty and enrollment rates) (Baiocchi, Chaudhuri, Heller,
and Silva, 2005).

The Uneven Diffusion of Innovation: Limits of Decentralization
Taking the set of cities with self-designated participatory budget experiments as a starting point, it is apparent that cities over 500,000
in the south and southeast of Brazil were overrepresented and that
smaller municipalities away from the more developed regions have
seldom had such reforms. Participatory budgeting has evolved geographically, moving away from its original home in the state of São
Paulo, where the majority of experiments took place in the 1989 to
1992 tenure, to the south, where a number of experiments were underway in the 1993 to 1996 period, to a move to the north and northeast,
where experiments took place in a significant way in the 1997 to 2000
period (table 2.7).

The case-study literature shows a number of difficulties faced by
administrators attempting to implement participatory reforms. Difficulties mentioned include the administration's fiscal standing, reprisal
from higher levels of government, pressures from local elites, electoral
pressures, and pressure from the party's own bases, among others.
Since most PT or left administrations have been elected by slim margins (often with protest votes that carry great expectations) and gener-

Table 2.7
Municipalities with participative budgeting by region and by size, 1997 to 2000

Region	North	North-east	South	South-east	Total PB Munici-palites	Total Munici-palites
Up to 20,000	2	1	23	4	30	4,066
20,000 to 100,000	1	2	8	21	32	1,233
100,000 to 500,000	0	6	7	19	32	181
500,000 to 1,000,000	0	3	0	1	4	15
1,000,000 and up	1	1	1	2	5	12
Total	4	13	39	47	103	5,507

Source: Ribeiro and Grazia (2002).

ally face the hostility of local elites and difficult governing conditions, the calculus for administrators often appears as the choices among a number of difficult options.

One constraint, related to the earlier discussion about the inequities among cities in Brazil during the period of decentralization, is the resource constraint. Among the cities that carried out PB in 1997 to 2001, "the municipalities, in relation to the total of Brazilian municipalities, presented, in the period in question, a more solid revenue base" (Ribeiro and Grazia, 2002, p. 87). It is crucial that the reforms actually deliver goods in a timely fashion to overcome cynicism and to convince persons who have a limited amount of time that participation is worthwhile. Participation may not make much sense for poor persons except for an assurance of timely returns. In highly fragmented social contexts or where persons are not accustomed to civic engagement, the equation may be even more stark. In addition, adequate administrative capacity to carry out the reforms is an important issue. With the decentralization reforms, cities gained new ways of raising revenue through vehicle, sales, and services taxes, but larger southern and southeastern capital cities were winners in this scheme. Porto Alegre, for example, with yearly revenues today well over U.S. $150 per person, has the capacity to offer many more returns to participation than the majority of other municipalities in Brazil.

A related constraint is the political constraint. While municipal elites have generally not posed the same problems that have all but blocked similar innovations at the state level, in the absence of an organized political force to pressure the administration to carry out reforms isolated reformers within administrations are unable to implement experiments like PB. The pattern of adoption of PB—first in São Paulo state, then in the south, and more recently in some places in the northeast—follows the evolution of the PT, which has gained a following away from its home state of São Paulo in the same period (Singer, 2001), as well as an evolution away from the PT as other political parties have begun to adopt the platform. While the vast majority of experiments were PT experiments for the first two periods, by 1997 to 2000 half the experiments were carried out by other political parties, though still mostly by left of center parties, with some notable exceptions.[4] But even the presence and electoral victory of a left of center party is not enough. The literature has established that internal ruling party fights and difficult relationships with municipal unions have sometimes been disabling to administrations attempting to implement PB. According to the 2001 survey, conflicts within the administrative apparatus were noted in almost half the cases, conflicts with the local legislative in a third of cases, and conflicts within the ruling political party in 20 percent of cases (Ribeiro and Grazia, 2002, p. 67). In the city of Betim, Minas Gerais, for example, where the administration carried out PB from 1997 to 2000, its inability to negotiate with its own bases of support cost it considerable legitimacy in an already inauspicious context and eventually rendered the administration unviable. The story the PT in São Paulo from 1989 to 1992 is another about how administrators' inability to negotiate sources of internal pressure within the PT immobilized it from even attempting some of the solutions that worked in other settings (Couto, 1995).

Lessons from Brazil's Decentralization

The ideal of bringing government closer to the people as defended by those who advocate decentralization on normative grounds may not find definite proof of its desirability when Brazil's reforms are considered as a whole. While the literature on the reforms is far from conclusive, there is agreement that, at least in its current incarnation, the reforms have had mixed results from the perspectives of service provisions, fiscal stability, regional disparities, and participation. Its positive results include the increase in social indicators in education and in health in the context of a decrease in net social spending and the opening up of local spaces for innovations in governance. Its principal negative results have been the regional and size disparities, which in some cases have increased as result of the reforms. In the case of health reforms, the portion of the country's population that lives in smaller and poorer municipalities and that is less likely to be able to afford private solutions faces worse health indicators as well as much less adequate and less well funded health services. Another negative impact, for which there is less systematic evidence, is the strengthening of the system of spoils for regional elites.

In this chapter, I have reviewed the context for and some of the principal features of Brazil's decentralization as codified in its 1988 constitution, devoting some effort to discussing the much-heralded experiments in participatory budgeting (PB) as a democratic innovation made possible by decentralization. Peculiarities of Brazil's history (such as the power of regional elites, high social deficit, and a history of high regional imbalances) help account for some of the undesirable results of the reforms, while features of the reforms themselves (such as the ambiguous concurrent responsibility provisions) are no doubt part of the story as well. I have briefly sought to explore the ways in which decentralization has made possible such innovation by addressing the structure of opportunity for it. I have argued that the decentralization of the state has opened up space for electoral competition at the municipal (and not necessarily the state) level and that new actors have translated civil society innovations into platforms for governance. In examining participatory budgeting, a reform that is thought to hold the potential for a number of positive outcomes, I have discussed the ways that it has been diffused as an innovation, first in the more developed regions in the country and later in northeastern regions. The structure of opportunity for this innovation is uneven, however, with local levels of revenue and presence of organized political actors interested in reforms as important preconditions. Brazil's decentralization has not done much to ameliorate the fiscal capacity of smaller and poorer municipalities, and thus these innovations cannot take place everywhere.

Notes

1. There is an extensive literature on the social movements of the 1970s and 1980s in Brazil, which is impossible to review here (Boschi, 1987; Cardoso, 1988; Evers, 1985; Telles, 1987; Viola and Mainwaring, 1987).

2. See, for instance, some representative positions in IDB (1997), IBAM (1988), Quercia (1984).

3. See Fischer, Colomer, and Teixeira (1989) for a more complete discussion of the details of these programs.

4. Of the 103, twenty-five were carried out by leftist parties traditionally tied to social movements (the PDT, the PPS, the PSB, the PV); twenty-two were carried out by left-of-center political parties originating in the country's prodemocracy movement of the 1980s, the PMDB and the PSDB; and four were carried out by right-wing parties (PTB and the PFL). The volatility of the Brazilian electorate, the lack of programmatic discipline, and the personalism of most political parties cautions against extrapolating much information from these data, however (Ames, 2001; Mainwaring, 1999).

References

Abers, Rebecca. (1996). "From Ideas to Practice: The Partido dos Trabalhadores and Participatory Governance in Brazil." *Latin American Perspectives* 23: 35–53.

Abers, Rebecca. (2000). *Inventing Local Democracy: Grassroots Politics in Brazil*. Boulder: Lynne Rienner.

Abrucio, Fernando. (1998). *Os Barões da Federação*. São Paulo: Hucitec/Edusp.

Afonso, José Roberto Rodrigues, and Erika Amorim Araújo. (2000). "A capacidade de gasto dos municípios brasileiros: Arrecadação Própria e Receita." *Cadernos Adenauer*: 35–53.

Afonso, José Roberto Rodrigues, and Luiz de Melo. (2000). "Brazil: An Evolving Federation." Paper presented at the IMF/FAD Seminar on Decentralization, Washington, DC.

Alvarez, Sonia. (1993). "Deepening Democracy: Popular Movement Networks, Constitutional Reform, and Radical Urban Regimes in Contemporary Brazil." In Joseph Kling (Ed.), *Mobilizing the Community*. Newbury Park, CA: Sage.

Amenta, Edwin, and Yvonne Zylan. (1991). "It Happened Here: Political Opportunity, the New Institutionalism, and the Townsend Movement." *American Sociological Review* 56: 250–265.

Ames, Barry. (2001). *The Deadlock of Democracy in Brazil*. Ann Arbor: University of Michigan Press.

Araujo, Jose. (1997). "Attempts to Decentralize in Recent Brazilian Health Policy." *International Journal of Health Services* 27: 109–124.

Arretche, Marta. (2000). *Estado Federativo E Politicas Sociais*. Rio de Janeiro: Editora Revan.

Avritzer, Leonardo. (2000). "Public Deliberation at the Local Level: Participatory Budgeting in Brazil." Paper presented at the Real Utopias Conference, Madison, WI.

Azevedo, Sérgio de. (1997). "Políticas Públicas e Governança em Belo Horizonte." *Cadernos IPPUR XI* 1: 63–74.

Baiocchi, Gianpaolo. (2001). "Activism, Participation, and Politics: The Porto Alegre Experiment and Deliberative Democratic Theory." *Politcs and Society* (March): 43–72.

Baiocchi, Gianpaolo. (2002). "Synergizing Civil Society; State-Civil Society Regimes and Democratic Decentralization in Porto Alegre, Brazil." *Political Power and Social Theory* 15: 3–86.

Baiocchi, Gianpaolo, Shubham Chaudhuri, and Patrick Heller. (2005). "Evaluating Empowerment: Participatory Budgeting in Brazil." Washington, DC: World Bank. Available at 〈http://siteresources.worldbank.org/intempowerment/Resources/Brazilpres .pdf〉.

BNDE. (2005). Banco Nacional de Desenvolvimento. "Termômetro da Descentralização 1988–2001" [database]. Available at 〈http://federativo.bndes.gov.br/destaques/ termometh2htm〉.

Boschi, Renato. (1987). *A arte da associacao; Politica de base e democracia no Brasil*. Sao Paulo: Vertice.

Boschi, Renato Raul. (1999). "Descentralização, clientelismo e capital social na governança urbana: Comparando belo horizonte e Salvador." *Dados* 42: 655–690.

Branford, Sue, and Bernardo Kucinski. (1995). *Brazil: Carnival of the Oppressed*. London: Latin American Bureau.

Brazil. (1988). Constituição da República Federative do Brasil: de 5 outubro de 1988 (3a edição) [Constitution of the Federal Republic of Brazil: 5 October 1988, 3d ed.]. São Paulo: Editora Atlas.

Calderón, Adolfo Ignacio, Vera Lúcia Michalany Chaia, Aldaíza de Oliveira Sposati, and Luiz Eduardo W. Wanderley. (2002). *Gestão municipal: Descentralização e participação popular*. São Paulo: Cortez Editora.

Campbell, Tim. (1997). "Innovations and Risk-Taking: The Engine of Reform in Latin American Countries." World Bank.

Cardoso, Ruth. (1988). "Os movimentos populares no contexto da consolidacao da democracia." in Guillermo O'Donnel (Ed.), *A democracia no Brasil*. Sao Paulo: Vertice.

Carvalho, A. A., and M. C. Felgueiras. (2000). *Orçamento participativo no ABC*. São Paulo: Pólis.

Carvalho, Inaia. (1997). "Decentralization and Social Policies in Bahia." *Caderno CRH* 26–27: 75–105.

Costa, Nilson. (1996). "Policy Innovation, Distributivism and Crisis: Health Care Policy in the 1980's and 1990's." *Dados* 39: 479–511.

Costa, Ricardo. (2002). "Decentralization, Financing and Regulation Reform of the Public Heath System in Brazil during the 1990's." *Revista de Sociologia e Politica* 18: 49–71.

Couto, Claudio Goncalves. (1995). *O desafio de ser governo: O PT na prefeitura de Sao Paulo*. Sao Paulo: Paz e Terra.

Dowbor, Ladislaw. (1998). "Decentralization and Governance." *Latin American Perspectives* 98: 28–44.

Evers, Tilman. (1985). "Identity: The Hidden Side of New Social Movements in Latin America." In David Slater (Ed.), *New Social Movements and the State in Latin America*. Amsterdam: CEDLA.

Figueiredo Júnior, José Rubens de Lima, and Bolivar Lamounier. (1997). *As cidades que dão certo: Experiências inovadoras na administração pública brasileira*. Brasília: MH Comunicação.

Graham, Lawrence. (1997). *Social Policy Dilemmas under Decentralization and Federalism*. Taeoe Kyongje Chongch'aek Yon'guwon Korea.

Graham, Lawrence, and Robert Wilson (Eds.). (1997). *Policymaking in a Redemocratized Brazil*. Austin: University of Texas Press.

IBGE. (2001). "Pesquisa de Informações Basicas Municipais" [database]. Available at ⟨http://www.ibge.gov.br/home/estatistica/economia/perfilmunic/default.shtm⟩.

IBGE. (2002). "Finanças Públicas do Brasil" [database]. Available at ⟨http://www.ibge.gov.br/home/estatistica/economia/despesaspublicas/financaspublicas_2001/default.shtm⟩.

Instituto Pólis. (2001). *125 dicas do Instituto Pólis*. São Paulo: Instituto Pólis.

Jacobi, Pedro. (1991). "Gestion municipal y conflicto: El municipio de Sao Paulo." In Alicia Ziccardi (Ed.), *Ciudades y gobiernos locales en la America Latina de los noventa*. Mexico City: Grupo Editorial M. A. Porrua.

Jacobi, Pedro. (1994). *Descentralização, política municipal de educação e participação no município de São Paulo*. Brasília: Ministério da Educação e do Desporto, Instituto Nacional de Estudos e Pesquisas Educacionais.

Jacobi, Pedro. (2000). *Politicas socias e ampliacao da cidadania*. Rio de Janeiro: FGV Editora.

Keck, Margaret. (1992a). "Brazil's PT: Socialism as Radical Democracy." *Report on the Americas* 25: 24–29.

Keck, Margaret. (1992b). *The Worker's Party and Democratization in Brazil*. New Haven: Yale University Press.

Kowarick, Lucio, and Andre Singer. (1994). "The Worker's Party in Sao Paulo." In Lucio Kowarick (Ed.), *Social Struggles and the City*. New York: Monthly Review Press.

Kugelmas, Eduardo, and Lourdes Sola. (1999). "Recentralization/Decentralization Dynamics of the Federative regime in 1990's Brazil." *Tempo Social* 11: 63–81.

Lebauspin, Ivo. (2000). *Poder local x exclusao social*. Petropolis: Vozes.

Lowy, Michael. (1987). "A New Type of Party: The Brazilian PT." *Latin American Perspectives* 14: 453–464.

Mainwaring, S. (1999). *Rethinking Party Systems in the Third Wave of Democratization*. Stanford: Stanford University Press.

Markoff, John. (1999). "From Center to Periphery and Back Again: The Geography of Democratic Innovation." In Michael Hanagan and Charles Tilly (Ed.), *Extending Citizenship, Reconfiguring State* (pp. 229–246). Lanham, MD: Rowman and Littlefield.

Marquetti, Adalmir. (2002). "Participação e redistribuição." In Zander Navarro (Ed.), *Inovação democrática no Brasil* (pp. 129–156). São Paulo: Cortez.

McCarney, Patricia. (1996). "New Considerations on the Notion of Governance." In Patricia McCarney (Ed.), *Cities and Governance: New Directions in Latin America, Asia, and Africa*.

Medeiros, Antonio Carlos. (1994). "The Politics of Decentralization in Brazil." *Review of Latin American and Carribean Studies* 57: 7–27.

Meneguello, Rachel. (1989). *PT: A formação de um partido 1979–1982*. Rio de Janeiro: Editora Paz e Terra.

Montero, Alfred. (1997). "Shifting States in Uneven Markets: Political Decentralization and Subnational Industrial Policy in Contemporary Brazil and Spain." Paper presented at the Inaugural Meeting of the International Working Group on Subnational Economic Governance in Latin America and Southern Europe, Columbia University, New York, September 12–14, 1997.

Montero, Alfred. (2001). "Decentralizing Democracy Spain and Brazil in Comparative Perspective." *Health Policy* 52: 113–127.

Moura, Maria Suzana de. (1989). "Limites a participacao popular na gestao da cidade." In *PROPUR*. Porto Alegre: UFRGS.

Navarro, Zander. (1996). "'Participatory Budgeting': The case of Porto Alegre (Brazil)." Paper presented at a Regional Workshop on Descentralization in Latin America: Innovations and Policy Implications. Caracas, Venezuela.

Neves, Gleisi. (1993). *Descentralizicao governmental municipio e democracia*. Rio de Janeiro: Instituto Brasileiro de Administracao Municipal.

Nickson, Andrew. (1995). *Local Governments in Latin America*. Boulder: Lynne Rienner.

Nunes, Ricardo. (2001). "Revenue Sharing a Problem of Federalism in Brasil." *Revista de Economia Politica* 20: 137–155.

Nylen, William. (1998). "Popular Participation in Brazil's Worker's Party: Democratizing Democracy in Municipal Politics." *Political Chronicle* 8: 1–9.

Peterson, George E. (1997). *Decentralization in Latin America*. Washington, DC: World Bank.

Pont, Raul. (2001). "Porto Alegre, e a luta pela democracia, igualdade e qualidade de vida." In Raul Pont (Ed.), *Porto Alegre: Uma cidade que conquista* (pp. 1–11). Porto Alegre: Artes e Oficios.

Pontual, Pedro. (1997). *Orcamento parcipativo em Sao Paulo na gestao luiza erundina*. Sao Paulo: FASE.

Pozzobon, Regina. (1998). *Porto Alegre: Os desafios da gestao democratica*. Sao Paulo: Instituto Polis.

Reilly, Charles (Ed.). (1995). *New Paths to Democratic Development in Latin America: The Rise of NGO-Municipal Collaboration*. Boulder: Lynne Reiner.

Ribeiro, Ana Clara de Torres, and Grazia de Grazia. (2002). *Experiências de orçamento participativo no Brasil*. São Paulo: Editora Vozes.

Rosenblatt, David, and Gil Shildo. (1996). "Quem tem recursos para governar?" *Revista de Economia Politica* 16: 101–106.

Samuels, David, and Fernando Abrucio. (2000). "Federalism and Democratic Transitions." *Publius* 30: 43–61.

Santos, Boaventura de Souza. (1998). "Participatory Budgeting in Porto Alegre: Toward a Redistributive Democracy." *Politics and Society* 4: 461–510.

Shah, Anwar. (1991). "The New Fiscal Federalism in Brazil." World Bank Discussion Paper No. 124, World Bank, Washington, DC.

Silva, Ana Amelia da. (1990). "A luta pelos direitos urbanos: Novas representacoes de cidade e cidadania." *Espaco e Debatte*: 28–40.

Singer, André. (2001). *O PT*. São Paulo: Publifolha.

Somarriba, Mescês, and Otavio Dulci. (1997). "A democratização do poder local e seus dilemas: A dinâmica atual da participação popular em Belo Horizonte." In E. Diniz and S. Azevedo (Ed.), *Reforma do estado e democracia no Brasil*. Brasília: Editora UnB.

Souza, Celina. (1996). "Redemocratization and Decentralization in Brazil the Strength of the Member States." *Development and Change* 27: 529.

Souza, Celina. (1997). *Constitutional Engineering in Brazil: The Politics of Federalism and Decentralization*. New York: St. Martin's.

Spink, Peter, and Roberta Clemente. (1997). *20 experiências de gestão pública e cidadania*. Rio de Janeiro: Fundação Getulio Vargas Editora.

Sposati, Aldaíza de Oliveira, Maria do Carmo Brant de Carvalho Falcão, Legião Brasileira de Assistência. Secretaria de Apoio Comunitário e Institucional. and Brazil. (1990). *A assistência social brasileira: Descentralização e municipalização*. São Paulo: Educ.

Stepan, Alfred. (2000). "Brazil's Decentralized Federalism." *Daedalus* 129: 145–163.

SUS. (2001). "Anuário Estatístico de Saúde do Brasil 2001" [database]. Available at ⟨http://portal.saude.gov.br/portal/aplicacoes/anuario2001/⟩.

Tarrow, Sidney. (1996). "Making Social Science Work across Space and Time: A Criticial Reflection on Robert Putnam's Making Democracy Work." *American Political Science Review* 90: 389–397.

Teixeira, Ana Claudia Chaves. (2002). "O OP em pequenos municípios rurais: Contextos, condições, e formatos de experiência." In Zander Navarro (Ed.), *A inovação democrática no Brasil*. São Paulo: Cortez.

Telles, Vera da Silva. (1987). "Movimentos sociais: Reflexoes sobre a experiencia dos anos 70." In Paulo Krische (Ed.), *Uma revolucao no cotidiano? Os novos movimentos sociais na America Latina*. Sao Paulo: Brasiliense.

Tendler, Judith. (1997). *Good Government in the Tropics*. Baltimore: Johns Hopkins University Press.

Tilly, Charles. (1978). *From Mobilization to Revolution*. Reading, MA: Addison-Wesley.

Utzig, José. (1996). "Notas sobre of Governo do PT em Porto Alegre." *Novos Estudos Cebrap*: 209–222.

Viola, Eduardo, and Scott Mainwaring. (1987). "Novos movimentos sociais: Cultura politica e democracia." In Paulo Krische (Ed.), *Uma revolucao no cotidiano? Os novos movimentos sociais na America Latina*. Sao Paulo: Brasiliense.

Weyland, Kurt. (1999). "Constitutional Engineering in Brazil." *American Political Science Review* 93: 1006.

Willis, Eiza, Christopher Garman, and Stephan Haggard. (1999). "The Politics of Decentralization in Latin America." *Latin American Research Review* 34: 7–56.

3

Decentralization, Democratic Transition, and Local Governance in Indonesia

Bert Hofman and Kai Kaiser

Introduction

Indonesia's big-bang decentralization occurred in the context of significant political and economic transition. The May 1998 collapse of President Suharto's centralist and authoritarian New Order regime in the wake of the East Asian economic crisis created the political space for a far-reaching decentralization in Indonesia's over four hundred local governments. The dynamics of decentralization were political—closely intertwined with the country's transition to democracy and marked by the first democratic elections in thirty years in 1999 and a second round of national and local elections five years later.

The 2001 decentralization provided local governments (kabupaten and kota) with significant additional fiscal resources, civil servants, responsibilities, and regulatory authorities (Hofman and Kaiser, 2002; World Bank, 2003). It is useful to distinguish between key elements of continuity versus change in the workings of state institutions. At the district level, Indonesia's decentralization built on relatively well developed sectorally deconcentrated as well as devolved local government structures. All core central ministries had well established bureaucratic outposts in each district that ultimately reported back to the capital, Jakarta. Local government structures were weak, beholden to the center, and not democratically accountable. The big-bang decentralization folded the deconcentrated agencies into the local government structures and sought to jettison the dominance of top-down accountabilities in favor of bottom-up or horizontal accountabilities (for example, between the local legislatures and executives). This form of devolution entailed a significant degree of continuity in the capacity of the local bureaucracy. At the same time, it has meant that the new accountability arrangements remain subject to consolidation.

Indonesia's decentralization was forged at a time where the archipelago's political economy was in a significant state of flux. Given a history of pent-up demand for more regional autonomy in Indonesia, it is questionable whether a more gradualist strategy of decentralization would have been feasible. Given the big-bang decentralization's short history, it remains an open question to what extent this new framework of governance will be consolidated and deepened or in parts reversed. The speed at which the two current cornerstones of decentralization—law 22 on governance and law 25 on fiscal relations (both 1999)—were drafted and implemented invariably has meant that the decentralization framework initially lacked broad-based participation and remains incomplete and contested in terms of clarifying roles and responsibilities across tiers of government and various executive and legislative actors (Turner and Podger, 2003). The recent revisions of the decentralization laws—laws 32 and 33 of 2004 supersede laws 22 and 25, implemented in 2001—suggests that the new prominence of local governance will not be overturned in the foreseeable future. While there have been efforts to limit local autonomy in a number of areas (for example, local governments have only limited authority to hire and fire civil servants), others (such as the direct rather than indirect popular regional elections) as of 2005 suggest that the system will be strengthened.

The apparent radical nature of the 2001 decentralization raised some fears that public services and national cohesion would have been direct victims rather than beneficiaries of this process. These initial fears were not realized. Yet the jury on big-bang decentralization's impact on national and local governance quality and public-service delivery levels and disparities remains out. This chapter describes the political context and institutions of Indonesia's decentralized governance, including special autonomy arrangements for Aceh and Papua. We discuss the associated fiscal and administrative arrangements, empirical evidence concerning the quality of decentralized governance, and the district characteristics associated with variations in local governance.

The Political Context of Big-Bang Decentralization

Indonesia is a sprawling archipelago of over thirteen thousand islands that stretches three thousand miles from east to west. It is characterized by significant regional, ethnic, religious, and linguistic diversity. Except for a brief federal constitution at the handover of sovereignty in 1949 (Schiller, 1955), it has remained a unitary state under the prevailing original constitution of 1945. Tensions between central-state control, territorial integrity, and regional autonomy demands have been a recurrent theme in Indonesian history. In fact, the republic's first law (law 1, 1945) was on regional autonomy, but this law, as many decentralization laws that followed, was never implemented. Following a brief spell of decentralized government in the mid-1950s (Legge, 1961), which ended in the secessionist Daruhl Islam (West Java and Sumatra) and PEMESTA (Sulawesi) movements, Indonesia experienced over forty years of centralization during the periods of Guided Democracy and the New Order (1966 to 1998).

A confluence of political and economic events led to a crisis for the authoritarian and centralist New Order regime and forced President Suharto to step down in May 1998. Popular pressures for reform (*reformasi*) were triggered by the perceived pervasive corruption up to the highest levels of government (KKN, *korupsi, kollusie, dan nepotism*), by economic crisis (*krismon*), and by loss of international confidence. For Suharto, this was compounded by the military's unwillingness to further prop up his rule. The failure of earlier attempts to decentralize combined with the extraordinary political circumstances in 1998 to become fertile ground for a big-bang approach to decentralization.

Long-suppressed regional separatist tendencies reappeared, and in regions with long-standing armed conflicts, such as Aceh and East Timor, the clamor for independence became louder. Added to this was the resentment felt by resource-rich regions against the central government that had "stolen their natural resources." Moreover, Suharto's successor, President Habibie (who had no intention of remaining an interim president or one presiding over a disintegrating Indonesia) was actively seeking the support of the regions. And regional autonomy seemed the right price for obtaining the support of regional representatives in the consultative assembly (MPR). Thus, the first instruction to develop new laws on regional autonomy came from the cabinet on May 24, and by July 10 the coordinating minister for state organization and supervision had tabled a first concept for regional autonomy.

The people who produced the early drafts of the decentralization plans were dedicated staff members who wanted to implement the presidential orders. They were later joined by strong political proponents for decentralization. Increasingly, regional autonomy was considered to be and presented as the natural complement to the emerging democracy at the central level. Yet the drafting of the law remained largely a bureaucratic process that received little feedback from politicians and even less from the regions (Turner and Podger, 2003). By the time the first drafts saw the light of day in late 1999, the basic structure for a radical decentralization was set.

President Habibie was not able to prevail in the 1999 legislative elections and the subsequent tumultuous multiparty legislative politics. He was initially succeeded by President Wahid, who was ultimately forced to resign in favor of Megawati Sukarno Putri, daughter of Indonesia's independence leader and head of its largest post-1999 election party (the PDI-P, which surpassed the previously ruling Golkar Party).[1] Whatever the changes in party representation in the post-1999 political landscape, the newly elected MPR reaffirmed the principles of regional autonomy. The second amendment of the 1945 constitution incorporated the basic principles of regional autonomy, decentralization, and devolution. Article 18 of the constitution embedded the principles of broad autonomy, the regions were given distinct status, and it was stipulated that that regional heads should be elected in a democratic manner, although direct elections were not specified.[2] The parliament initially also rebuked central government proposals, led by the ministry of home affairs, to revise law 22 of 1999, suggesting that decentralization is destined to remain a political reality for the foreseeable future.[3]

Tight deadlines and revenue assignment made Indonesia's decentralization even more radical. By law, within a year from approval, all implementing regulations were to be prepared, and by May 2001 (two years after parliamentary approval) the laws had to be implemented. Most likely, these deadlines were introduced in the law to prevent it from becoming just one more decentralization law that was never implemented. In a TAP (an instrument with higher status than a law), the MPR tightened the deadline to January 1, 2001. The aggressive assignment of revenues to the regions—without much analysis of what the regions actually needed—added to the pressure on government to decentralize responsibilities. Although the ministry of finance, on the advice of the International Monetary Fund (IMF) and the World Bank, had removed the specific assignment of revenues to the regions from the draft law,[4] Parliament quickly restored these revenue assignments. For the central government, the choice was now either to break the law or to devolve as many expenditures as possible to minimize the impact on the central government deficit. It chose the latter.

Provincial autonomy survived more or less by chance. The president's intention was to decentralize rapidly and radically to local governments, to eliminate the provinces as autonomous entities, and to keep them only as outposts of the central government. The provinces had been the center of regional unrest in the 1950s, and the military wanted to go along with regional autonomy only if there was no chance of a rerun. In their eyes, local government was easier to control than the larger, potentially more powerful provinces. However, by the time the decentralization laws saw their first draft, new election laws had been passed by Parliament. These laws specified in detail how the provincial parliament was to be elected. Since a provincial parliament could not exist without an autonomous provincial government, it was decided to restore the province as an autonomous region, while maintaining the role of the governor as the central government's representative in the region as well as the head of the autonomous region.

The founding moments and early implementation of Indonesia's big-bang decentralization have occurred in the context of notable changes to political landscape and its underlying institutions. According to its 1945 constitution, Indonesia is a unitary state. Authorities are granted to the regions by national laws passed by the national legislature (DPR) (see figure 3.1). Of the five hundred total members of the People's Assembly (DPR), 462 were elected and thirty-eight appointed by the military or police factions. The election of the president and modifications of the constitutions are the remit of the People's Consultative Assembly (MPR). The MRP consisted of a joint sitting of the DPR and regional and functional representatives (135 members selected by provincial regional legislatures (DPRDs) and sixty-five functional group members including military and police).

The president was elected by and accountable to the MPR. Through a so-called accountability speech, the president accounted annually for his policies. If rejected twice, the president is considered out of office.[5] Prior to 1999, the legislative was largely a rubber-stamp institution, but its powers expanded significantly in the wake of Suharto's resignation.

The 1999 electoral system was a hybrid of proportional and district elements based on closed party lists: voters could not vote for individuals at either the central or regional (provincial and local) elections. The district system allocated a disproportional amount of seats to the electoral districts off Java. While Java's population was 60 percent of the national total, it received only 50.6 percent of the parliamentary

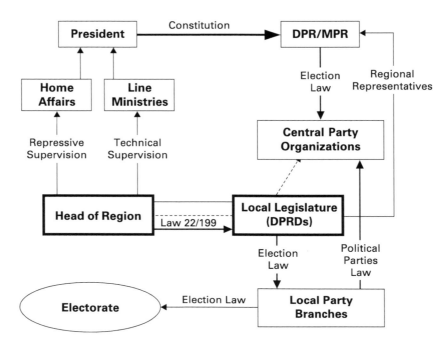

Figure 3.1
Indonesia's main political actors and accountability channels, 1999 to 2004
Source: World Bank (2003), with amendments.

seats. A parliamentary seat in East Java cost 287,000 votes versus 63,000 votes in Papua (Suryadinata, 2002). Thus the regions that had historic complaints about Javanese dominance and the extraction of natural resource rents were overrepresented in the national Parliament. At the same time, the closed party list system strengthened the position of central party boards, which also determined the lists for the regional elections.[6]

The 1999 electoral system and its outcome significantly altered the political landscape in Indonesia. In total, forty-eight parties contested the 1999 elections. Parties could participate, if they were recognized under law, had a committee in more than one-half of the number of provinces in Indonesia, and had a party committee in more than one-half of the number of districts or regencies in the same provinces (Suryadinata, 2002). This rule intended to prevent the emergence of regionally based parties. Only 23 percent of previous DPR members were reelected. After decades of dominance, Golkar's share of the vote crumbled from 74 percent in 1997 to 22 percent in 1999, but the party still emerged as the second largest after the PDI-P in terms of votes and seats. The relative advantage that the previous ruling party, Golkar, received from its stronger showing in the outer islands is reflected in its better national showing in terms of seats (26 versus 22 percent).[7]

The national accountability framework was significantly revised in advance of the 2004 elections. A new institution, the Regional Representative Council (DPD), with two directly representatives from the provinces, was also introduced, although unlike a full-fledged senate its roles appears to be largely advisory (Murray and Haysom, 2003). Reforms in advance of the 2004 elections retained rules to ensure national party presentation (although the military no longer retain its mandated representation). The system still sees national and regional legislative elections being held concurrently but now provides some scope for individual candidates to be selected direct and, provided enough votes, to supersede their ranking on the party lists. In 2004, the president was elected directly by popular majority for the first time. Following the April 2004 legislative elections, presidential candidates are now nominated by political parties and elected directly through majority (in up to two rounds of elections). After a second round of voting, President Susilo Bambang Yudhoyono (SBY) defeated President Megawati.

Local Political Accountability

Decentralization can be considered to be a rearrangement of accountability relationships among citizens, politicians, organizational providers, and service providers and the invariable ascendance of some actors relative to others (World Bank, 2004b). Law 22 of 1999 on regional governance shifted the balance from a largely top-down form of accountability in Indonesia (Panggabean, 1997) to local political accountability. At its core is the election of the head of the region and the annual accountability speech. The head is elected by and accountable to the local parliaments (DPRD). Law 22 of 1999, article 16(2), stipulates that the regional head of the executive (*bupati/walikota*) and legislative act in partnership (*kemitraan*). At the same time, the regional parliaments elect and can dismiss the head of the region through rejection of the annual accountability speech (LPJ, the *laporan pertanggung jawab*). Further powers of the DPRD include approval of the annual local budget (APBD) and approval of local laws and regulations

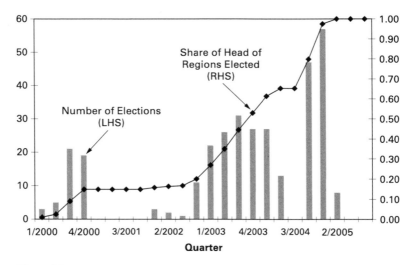

Figure 3.2
Elected head of regions and election schedule
Note: Number of regions refers to those existing in 2001.

(PERDAs), which in turn can regulate accountability relationships at lower tiers of village government.[8] Paralleling events at the national level for the presidential elections, the direct election of regional heads followed.

Not all regional heads were elected by local parliaments at the onset of decentralization. While regional legislatures were all elected in 1999, regional heads (which had effectively been appointed by the center in the past) were allowed to serve out their terms.[9] After the 1999 elections, new (*reformasi* regional head) regional heads were elected by the regional legislature (DPRDs) as the term of old (New Order) expired.[10] Unlike in the past, the central government has no formal authority to refuse the appointment of the regional heads.[11] Figure 3.2 presents data on the electoral cycle of local government heads based on their start of term. Few regional heads were appointed by the Suharto government in 1996 and 1997 in the run-up to the national elections, suggesting that a major wave of elections would be slated for 2003 and 2004. But the Ministry of Home Affairs again extended the tenures of regional heads during the 2004 elections (the April 2004 parliamentary elections followed by one or two rounds of presidential elections through October), believing that the absence of local elections and ongoing tenure of incumbent regional heads will enhance stability during the election season. At present, only a decision of the Ministry of Home Affairs was required to set the terms of the regional heads.

Another recent dynamic in the electoral cycle of regional heads has been the creation of new local jurisdictions. Between 1999 and 2003, the number of local governments in Indonesia increased from 292 to 410 (Fitrani, Hofman, and Kaiser, 2003). New regions received a new legislature and an interim regional head, with elections after about a year.[12]

Elections of new heads of region have not been without problems. Throughout the country, these elections are regularly surrounded by rumors of "money politics," at least as reported in the press.[13] Perhaps the most prominent case of this was the North Maluku governor, who was dismissed in September 2001 after allegations of corruption in the elections emerged ("North Maluku," 2001). Fueling suspicion of money politics in the elections is the surprisingly large number of newly elected heads of regions that are not affiliated with the majority or plurality party in the region. Election battles can end up worse than just corrupted, as was the case in Poso, where fierce competition for the mayor's office added to the violence that has marred this city in recent years (see Rohde, 2001).

Recent gubernatorial elections suggest that the central government under President Megawati took a special interest in the selection of governors. On a number of occasions, she has asserted her central control of the party against the choices of her own regional party fractions (in, for example, Jakarta, Lampung, and Surabaya).[14] At the same time, there are indications that the government wishes to strengthen the accountability of regional heads to the center by way of the governors.

The accountability speech of the head of the region is at the core of local governance. The law states that regional legislatures can dismiss the head of the region by rejecting the accountability speech twice: the original speech and the revised version presented by the regional head after the first rejection. In practice, the accountability report has created some confusion as to the exact powers of the legislative and the central government in the context of local executive accountability. Government regulation 108/2000 limits this wide-ranging power of the DPRDs: it states that an accountability speech can be rejected by two-thirds of the DPRD and requires that at least two-thirds of all members and all fractions be present (Podger, 2000). Once the DPRD has agreed to reject an accountability speech after a thirty-day period for resubmission, the case is sent to the governor (as the representative of the Minister of Home Affairs), who should set up a committee to evaluate the case. This committee seems to have the final word. Few regional heads have been ousted by the LPJ process, but frequent allegations of bribery in the accountability process have made it quite controversial and have been a key motive to the forthcoming change in the system to one of direct elections of regional heads.

In a recent survey conducted by the Ministry of Home Affairs of a sample of 128 regions, 6 percent of regional heads said that their LPJ had been rejected at some time during the first round. No formal records were available at the Ministry of Home Affairs of full-fledged dismissal procedures against regional heads. The four documented cases we found included three municipalities and one regency: the kota of Surabaya (2002), the kota Paya Kumbuh (estimates for 2001), the kota of Pontianak (estimates for 2001), and the kabupaten of Bankalan (2002). Only in the case of the kota of Paya Kumbuh had the central ministry team formally completed its work for dismissal, and the regional head been formally dismissed. Only in the kabupatens of Kepri (Riau) and Klaten were regional heads or public officials formally charged with corruption.

A third feature of political accountability is party control. As with the national elections, the participants of the regional parliamentary elections were parties. Participating parties had to meet the criteria for national parties (that is, the presence at least half the provinces and half the cities or districts within these provinces), and thus no local parties could emerge. For local parliamentary elections, the regency or city was the electoral territory. Candidate lists were registered in each kecamatan (subdistrict), and at least one seat was allocated to each of the subdistricts, but the overall result of the elections is determined by how well parties do districtwide. The size of the local DPRDs varies from twenty to forty-five per the criteria in law 3/1999. Candidates did not need to reside in the district in which they are candidates. As with the national Parliament, 10 percent of the seats in the DPRD was reserved for the military. In 1999, local elections were held at the same time as national elections, only two months after law 22 of 1999 passed.

While only twenty-one parties were able to enter the national Parliament (DPR), forty-six of the forty-eight parties that contested the 1999 elections were represented in at least one of the regional government legislatures. Thus, de facto localized parties emerged. The strength of the localized party showings may have been a mix of traditional regional allegiances or votes based on national leadership or issues. However, only a very small fraction of voters (0.05 percent) voted differently in the national and regional elections (Evans, 2003). This has left many regions with a high level of political fractionalization, coupled with the expectation that many representatives and smaller parties may not return to power with higher national entry barriers to the new elections meant to promote consolidation.

The central government can exercise repressive supervision of regional governments. The central government can annul regional bylaws and regulations (PERDAs) that conflict with national laws and regulations (including those on regional taxes and levies per law 34 of 2000). Line ministries are in charge of functional supervision—including a review of the regional regulations in their field of authority, while the Ministry of Home Affairs can cancel regulations, repressive supervision. Law 22 of 1999 gives the regions the right to appeal this cancellation at the Supreme Court. In contrast, the implementing regulation on supervision (government regulation 20/2001) allows for an appeal to the Minister of Home Affairs, the same that canceled the regulations in the first place. In the early days of decentralization, the cancellation process was far from smooth. As of September 2001, an interagency working group out of the Ministry of Home Affairs had reviewed and classified a total of 1,041 tax (116) and levy (933) PERDAs. Of these, 103 (94 levy, 9 tax) were submitted for cancellation. These were forwarded to the minister for signature, but at the end of 2001 he had still not signed. Despite the requirements in the law, many regional regulations also go unreported, and nuisance taxes based on such regulations have become a major issue.[15] In cases where the center did cancel local regulations, some regions did appeal. The central government has attempted to limit the regional budget (APBD) regional legislatures allocate themselves under government regulation 110 of 2000. On the basis of this regulation, it cancelled the West Sumatra budget that allocated generous remuneration to regional parliamentarians. West Sumatra appealed, and the Supreme Court annulled the cancellation and declared the regulation to contravene law 4 of 1999 (On the Position of Elected Bodies) and law 22 of 1999 ("Supreme Court Judge," 2003).

Audit and politicians asset declarations provide another possible accountability mechanism. Initial arrangements assigned responsibilities to multiple bodies, including the government's internal auditor

(BPKP), the supreme audit authority (BPK), the inspectorate general of the province, the inspectorate general of home affairs, and regional auditors (*bawasda*).[16] Public officials—including regional heads and legislatures—are also obliged to submit wealth declarations under law 28 of 1999 on Public Administration Free of KKN to the Commission to Audit the Wealth of State Officials (KPKPN). The law suggests that given indications that officials have acquired their wealth illicitly, they can be further investigation by KPKPN. At this stage, the law does not grant the KPKPN powers of sanction (Ekopuri, 2003). The effectiveness of both accountability mechanisms, however, relies on actual enforcement and sanctions in the case of infractions. In this regard, Indonesia is plagued by widespread concerns about the partiality and efficacy of the justice system ranging from the police to the attorney general's office (ADB, 2002).

Special Autonomy
De jure political institutions are largely uniform across Indonesia's decentralization landscape.[17] Exceptions are special autonomy for Aceh, Papua, Jakarta, and Yogyakarta. The special autonomy laws 18 and 21 of 2001 for Aceh and Papua attracted most attention. The two provinces account for about 3 percent of the national population and are located on the eastern- and westernmost flanks of the archipelago.[18] Both provinces are natural-resource rich and have history of secessionist movements, in part fueled by claims of unfair exploitation by the center. Special autonomy provided the provinces with additional natural-resource revenue shares, wider powers at the provincial level, and some concessions for local political and legal practices.[19] However, in both provinces the implementation of special autonomy has been stalled, with central and military authorities displaying an increasingly heavy hand in their dealings with these provinces. The imposition of martial law in Aceh under presidential decree 28 of May 2003 represents the continued frustration of the Jakarta government and especially fractions of the military with the independence aspirations of GAM.[20] Special autonomy for Papua is also pending because of a conflict between the Special Autonomy Law of 2001, and a previous law, law 45 of 1999, which calls for splitting the province into three. With presidential instruction 1 of 2003, the central government attempted to push the split but was met with resistance from the local population.[21]

Administrative and Fiscal Decentralization

Administratively Indonesia is divided into thirty provinces and more than four hundred local governments,[22] municipalities (kota), and regencies (kabupaten).[23] Local governments in turn encompass more than four thousand subdistricts (kecamatans) and 65,000 village and neighborhood communities (desa/kelurahan). The average local government has just over half a million inhabitants, but size and other characteristics differ vastly. Law 22 of 1999 on regional governance devolves all government functions to the regions, except those mentioned in the law. The exceptions are national defense, international relations, justice, police, monetary policy, development planning, religion, and finance. Local governments are obliged to perform a set of key functions, including the provision of health, education, environmental, and infrastructure services and may perform any function not explicitly reserved for the center or the provinces.

The province plays only a minor role, mainly in coordination and supervising rural regencies and urban municipalities that cannot yet perform their functions. The provincial governor also will continue to perform deconcentrated central government tasks, including supervision of local governments on behalf of the center. The fact that decentralization largely bypassed the provinces was influenced by government concerns that strong provinces might incite secessions, whereas smaller local governments would facilitate the center's divide-and-conquer approach.

The assignment of functions is far from clear. The lack of clarity is in part due to weaknesses in the decentralization laws themselves. Conflicting implementing regulations and sectoral laws that are out of line with law 22 of 1999 play their part as well. Some laws passed after law 22, such as the forestry law and the civil service law, largely ignore decentralization or indeed conflict with the very concept. Even some of the implementing regulations for law 22 itself seem to contradict the law. Furthermore, a presidential decree gave some agencies, including those for land and investment approval, temporary exemption from decentralization, thus further blurring the division of responsibility over levels of government. In addition, whereas implementing regulations for law 22 call for minimum standards to be formulated by provincial governments, this has thus far not yet been done. The upshot of this is that local governments have a large amount of discretion in implementing their responsibilities.

Law 25 of 1999 set out a revised intergovernmental fiscal framework (Hofman, Kadjadmiko, and Kaiser 2002b; World Bank, 2003). The law replaces the old system of earmarked grants (recurrent Subsidy for Autonomous Regions, SDO, and Presidential Instruction Grants, Inpres) and centralized control over local finances with one in which a general allocation grant (*dana alokasi umum*, DAU) and shared taxes provide the bulk of local revenues. Local tax authority remains limited. Regions can also special earmaked grants (*dana alokasi khusus*, DAK), although this channel remains limited. The center maintains control over the rate and base of the most buoyant taxes. Although local governments are allowed to raise their own taxes and levies per local regulation within the boundaries set by the center, these local revenues constitute on average less that 5 percent of the typical local budget (APBD).

Decentralization almost doubled the regional share in government spending. The expenditure share of regional—provincial and largely local—governments in overall public expenditures increased from about 17 percent in 2000 to over 30 percent of total government expenditures after 2001. This share is likely to grow over time to well over 40 percent, if central government would devolve the resources it currently spends on local tasks under the national development budget (APBD). Central spending in the regions amounted to 45.5 percent of total (central, provincial, local) development expenditures in 2002, up from 40.8 percent in 2001 (World Bank, 2004a).

The decentralization of significant shared revenues for natural resources and the income tax, coupled with incomplete fiscal equalization, in large part because the formula is still driven by historical allocations including wages, has meant that local governments are subject to significant disparities in per capita expenditures. Insufficient evidence exists on the geographic targeting of central development expenditures or on the extent to which these influence local allocative choices, especially give that the interjurisdictional allocation of these resources is largely up to the discretion of the central government and the various line ministries.

The 2001 decentralization reassigned some two-thirds of central civil servants to the regional governments. These civil servants worked in the deconcentrated central government offices that are now abolished or were seconded to local governments. Regional governments are now responsible for the employing three-quarters of civil servants, but their authority over civil-service management remains unclear. Law 22 of 1999 gives the regions the right to hire and fire its civil service, but conflicting laws and other forms of implementing regulations appear to circumscribe this autonomy. Articles 75 to 77 of law 22 give regions broad autonomy in civil-service management, and government regulation 97 of 2000 gives the head of the region authority to determine the number of civil servants in the region. In addition, presidential decree 159 of 2000 sets up regional civil-service agencies.

The local right to manage the civil service is limited in several ways. In contrast to law 22 of 1999, the civil-service law (law 43 of 1999) retains much control at the central level. The central government still determines to a large extent civil-service wages: base wage, position allowances, and family and rice allowances are still set by presidential instruction. In addition, the Ministry of Finance sets limits to honoraria to be received by civil servants for project management and the like. And BKN, the civil-service agency, is developing job classifications and accompanying qualification standards that it wants to see applied to the local civil service as well as the central civil service. Sector ministries such as education, health, and agriculture are developing similar standards for teachers, doctors, and agricultural extension workers. Moreover, the center recently hired almost 200,000 temporary teachers for placement with local governments (approaching 10 percent of the formal teacher workforce and about 1.4 percent of the DAU). Hiring procedures are further limited by government regulations. Among others, these require nationwide advertising for certain posts and local advertising for others.

Decentralized Governance and Service Delivery: Preliminary Evidence

The 2001 decentralization gave Indonesia's local governments more revenues and authorities. While the country did have a longstanding tradition of local governments, democratic institutions were weak, capacity limited, and governance in the bureaucracy poor. At the same time, responsibilities remain poorly defined in terms of expenditure assignments, and central-government oversight has been weakened. Moreover, central oversight and accountability functions such as the judiciary and the police underscore that poor governance and rent-seeking are not limited to local governments.

Despite its rapid implementation, decentralization in Indonesia did not appear to lead to a breakdown in service delivery. To a large extent, this can be attributed to bureaucratic continuity, as officials often remained performing their existing functions but under a new badge. Quantitative and qualitative evidence from the field, however, suggests significant concerns about the quality of governance at the local level.[24] Heightened attention to the behavior of politicians and bureaucrats at the local level could itself be viewed as a positive facet of the functioning of a new decentralized democracy. The effectiveness of the actual accountability mechanisms and the possibility that their absence will lead to transparency without accountability remain to be seen. Striking, however, is the degree of variation across local governments in terms of governance quality. Perceptions of service delivery were quite positive, probably because of the continuity in service delivery and the still evolving nature of standards and expectations.[25]

The Perception of Local Governance
A significant proportion of respondents perceives the local political process to be corrupt. In the average locality, over a third of households thought that the elections of the regional head were tainted by money politics, although 37 percent said they did not know (figure 3.3).[26] About one-fifth of households believed that money politics was involved in the accountability speech of the head of the region, although in general households seemed to have only limited information on or insight into this process.

Perception data on governance will invariably be subject to local norms (such as how outspoken citizens in a particular area are) or misperceptions. Based on fieldwork in Africa and South Asia, Crook and Manor (1998) suggest that popular perceptions of corruption may be on the rise with increasing transparency and political liberalization, even as insiders believe the situation in the bureaucracy is getting better. From the perspective of empirical work that retains broad coverage, this would imply drawing on the information from key respondents. Large disjunctures in popular and key respondent perception will in their own light be revealing. But household perceptions also potentially provide some indications about the legitimacy of political and bureaucratic leadership.

NGO and media respondents were consistently the most negative in their perception of corruption. Well over half found local regional heads and accountability speeches tainted by KKN. Public officials and legislative members were more sanguine, perhaps unwilling to admit abuses in their own ranks. Local-level bureaucrats were far more likely to attribute wrongdoings to those below them at the village level.

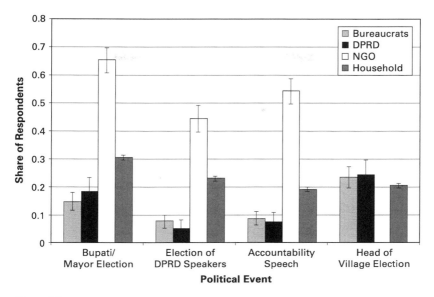

Figure 3.3
Money politics according to political events
Source: 2002 GDS (Bureaucrats = BGA4; DPRD = DGA5; NGO = LGA5; Household = RGA8).

While households saw the village level as the least afflicted by KKN in terms of shares (about 25 percent), bureaucrats and legislative members viewed them as the most corrupt on their own scale.

The Indonesian public lexicon for poor governance has adapted to decentralization. "Money politics" (*politik uang*) refers to concerns that local elections for regional heads and decision-making processes are bought. Local politicians in executive and legislature are accused of failing to heed the political aspirations of the wider public (*politik elit*). The new local heads are perceived to have started acting like little kings (*raja kecil*) who are not accountable to central authorities, local parliaments, or local constituencies. Meanwhile, rent-seeking is perceived to have proliferated in many regions because many new politicians are taking their turn at the trough ("many hands" or *campur tangan*). Cigarette money (*uang rokok*) continues to denote the pervasive petty corruption that most Indonesians face in daily life. Increased attention will therefore have to be devoted to understanding the dominant modes or patterns by which the quality of local governments appears to be undermined.

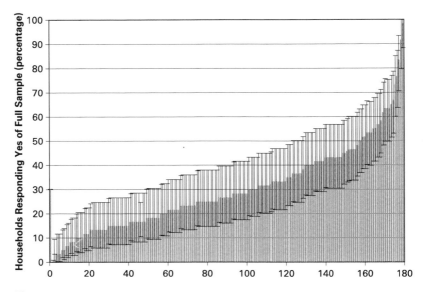

Figure 3.4
KKN in local head elections

Reported levels of KKN in local head elections varied significantly across localities (figure 3.4). In only a few localities (for example, several kabupaten in Bali) was the reported perception of corruption in the local elections negligible. Almost all respondents claimed money politics in others (the two worst-performing kabupaten were in Papua). In regions where elections are seen as tainted by corruption, the annual accountability mechanisms also are typically seen as corrupted as well, as denoted by the high correlation (0.9) of the two indicators.

The 2002 GDS inquired about the degree to which households followed political processes at various levels of government and their primary information source on these processes. The presidential elections attracted the most attention (86 percent in the average local government), bupati/walikota elections (55 percent), village head and representative body elections (55 and 49 percent), and the governor's elections (39 percent). At the time of the GDS, 82 percent of households said they have heard of regional autonomy, but this ranged from 48 to 100 percent across the jurisdictions sampled.

The media, both electronic and print, was the main source of information for most. The vast majority (88 percent) relied on television and radio for learning about decentralization, while 60 percent also drew on newspapers.[27] The print media were marginally the most important source of information for the case of governors and local government elections, compared to radio and television for the presidential elections. A range of other diverse sources influenced reported decisions. Community meetings (16 percent), local politicians (10 percent), and community leaders (10 percent) were also reported as information sources on elections for the heads of regions. On average, citizens said they relied on a variety of sources of information, led by community meetings (57 percent) and community leaders (30 percent) for local head elections. This diverse range of information sources reported by Indonesian households appears to underscore the increased level of transparency regarding local governance but again highlights diversity across districts. However, the penetration of local media varies significantly across the country, and anecdotal evidence suggests that journalists themselves can often be swayed by political interferences or payoffs, as "attendance money" is often considered an integral and accepted part many local government functions.

Households typically follow village and neighborhood institutions in detail but are likely to possess only general information about the functioning of local government.[28] Since households are typically best informed about community (village and neighborhood) dynamics, it is important to differentiate what changes are actually taking place at the local level (kabupaten and kota), which is the focal point of the main regulatory changes under decentralization. Figure 3.5 shows how NGOs rate the main local government institutions, with differences by urban-rural and on-Java versus off-Java. The legislative (DPRD) and local government executive office rate least favorably, whereas the village was considered to be least corrupt. Corruption was reported to be significantly higher in cities for the legislative, local government offices, and subdistrict offices. This result could be driven by a combination of greater access to information, transparency, and higher expectations among urban dwellers.

Charges of systematic corruption in the public sector preceded decentralization. Figure 3.6 shows that media and NGO respondents focused especially on poor governance in the area of recruitment and procurement.

The type of institutional subversion most prevalent in Indonesia appears to be the capturing of rents by old New Order executives, new legislatures, and the local contractor community from a largely

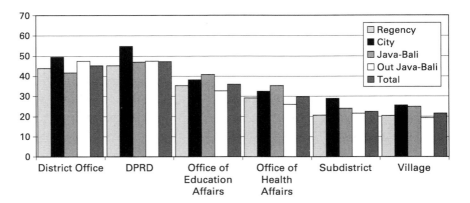

Figure 3.5
KKN in several government institutions based on NGO responses
Source: 2002 GDS (NGO = LGA1).

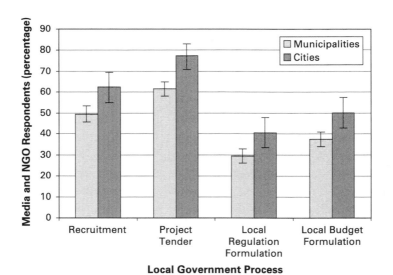

Figure 3.6
KKN in major local government process

revenue-led decentralization in the absence of effective accountability mechanisms in either the voice, compact, or client power dimensions. Capture of the formulation of local regulations or budgets is considered to be less prevalent than other types of abuse or at least has received less attention. Regional businesses have complained about the issuance of local taxes and levies under local regulations (PERDAs), based on a survey of 134 regions in 2002 (KPPOD 2003).[29] These figures appear to be consistent with anecdotal evidence that particular vested interests have not yet systematically tried to capture local policy making such as in Russian case, where collusion between business and government in the issuance of local regulations seems to have been more prevalent (Slinko, Yakovlev, and Zhravskaya, 2003). For example, the survey asked lawyers and prosecutors whether particular groups were now intervening more or less in legal processes. All respondents felt that the influence of civil society and NGOs had increased significantly. The relative influence of groups such as the military, the head of the region, and police were thought to have declined. Judges and prosecutors felt that the influence of entrepreneur groups had increased (four times as many respondents thought their influence had increased as thought it had declined), whereas lawyers were ambivalent about whether entrepreneurial influence had increased. Clearly, future work will have to assess emerging patterns of local capture and collusion, especially those that threaten to have the most detrimental effect on local service delivery and economic growth.

Figure 3.7 underscores the continued widespread presence of petty corruption (*pungli*, an abbreviation for "extra legal charges"). Households consistently reported paying more for basic services than the charges that were set out in local regulations. Official rates set by local regulations (PERDA) were consistently only about half of those that households actually reported paying. The entrenched nature of petty corruption at the village level is reflected by household responses to "cigarette money". While fewer than 20 percent of households had heard of corruption at the village level, over two-thirds were willing to answer a question about responses to cigarette money at the village level. Only 17 percent claimed to refuse paying cigarette money, whereas 63 percent paid while seeing this as an inevitable fact of life. The remaining 20 percent paid despite feeling angry. When asked about measures taken to combat corruption, 60 percent responded that no action was taken, 4 percent suggested the matter was solved with discrimination, 13 percent said the remedy was simply to ask for the

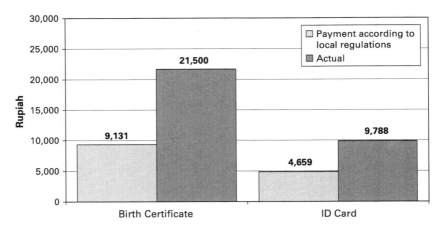

Figure 3.7
Comparison of the average actual payment for public-service delivery with the payment according to local regulations
Source: 2002 GDS (Household = RGE2) and local Perdas.

funds to be returned, 5 percent did not know, and only 18 percent felt that action was taken without discrimination. While pertaining to the village level, these responses raise some significant questions about the extent of accountability or popular constituency against KKN at the local level.

The GDS asked households if there were power abuses by village and neighborhood officials.[30] Only 21 percent perceived power abuses, although district averages ranged from 0 to 78 percent. Furthermore, the survey also asked what responses were made to infractions. Over three-quarters felt that nothing was done, that it was quietly settled, or that it was followed up and no sanction was ever imposed.

Budgets, Audits, and Wealth Declarations

Whereas perception-level data of local governance may not reflect the true underlying quality of local governance, systematic data on governance outcomes are often harder to come by and have their own limitations. Tables 3.1 and 3.2 summarize recent findings of the state auditor (BPK), broken down by central and regional government. These findings were presented to Parliament as part of the agency's annual accountability report. They are not audit findings per se but may provide some indications of the quality of financial management between the center and the regions and across regions.

Table 3.1
Major electoral processes by levels and local sources of information (percentage)

	Share of Households Following Electoral Processes (percentage)				Main Sources of Information for Those Responding Yes (percentage)				
	LG Aver-age	Mini-mum	Maxi-mum		Print Media	Elec-tronic Media (TV/ Radio)	Com-munity Meetings	Com-munity Leaders	Other
Presidential elections	86%	58%	100%	9%	5.7%	90.6%	1.0%	0.7%	1.9%
Governors elections	39	5	97	22	46	45.6	1.7	2.5	4.2
Local government heads	55	7	100	22	31.4	17.8	15.8	10.0	24.9
Village heads	55	2	100	27	1.1	0.5	56.3	27.1	14.9
Village repre-sentative body (BPD/LKMD)	49	3	97	24	0.4	0.2	57.3	28.9	13.2

Source: GDS 2002 (Household-RGP8 and RGP9).

Table 3.2
BPK audit findings (percentage)

	2001 (percentage of compliance deviations)	2002 (percentage of compliance deviations)
Central:	**13.6%**	**16.1%**[a]
Routine	20.5	9.8
Development	6.4	15.6
Province:	**3.7**	**27.9**
Routine	1.8	8.1
Development	5.1	30.7
District/cities:	**12.7**	**21.8**
Routine	13.8	21.6
Development	11.6	22.0

Source: Chairperson of BPK Welcome Speech at the Presentation of the Audit Results for Semester II of Fiscal Year 2002, Jakarta, February 2003.
a. Total includes military (TNI), which is excluded from the subtotals.

Table 3.3
Results of state official wealth audit committee

Institutions	Estimated Forms Required	Distributed Forms (actual)		Returned Forms	
		Number	Percentage	Number	Percentage
Executive	15,273	11,201	73.3%	4,902	43.76%
Legislature	14,000	12,368	88.3	1,811	14.64
Judicial	12,193	8,775	72.0	3,172	36.15
State-owned enterprise	10,000	9,056	90.6	3,788	41.83
Total	51,466	41,400	80.4%	13,673	33.03%

Source: KPKPN as of August 2, 2002.

These data suggest that administrative deviations have increased in all cases but central recurrent budgets. Deviations for local governments allegedly almost doubled and now exceed the national levels. These may reflect more rigorous investigations on the part of the auditor or just teething problems as regions are faced with increased financial-management responsibilities. Infractions are almost exclusively treated as administrative issues and are rarely sanctioned through the administrative or legal system. The full half yearly reports are contained in two volumes numbering thousands of pages and do not allow for easy sectoral or regional breakdowns. A closer investigation of these findings, however, suggested that these do not provide the basis for making an assessment about the general quality of central versus local governance or governance across regions.[31]

Table 3.3 provides data on the wealth and asset declarations actually submitted to State Official Wealth Audit Committee (KPKPN). Fewer than half of the regional heads returned forms, and only 14.6 percent of legislatures submitted their reports. In 2003, with over half their terms expired, only 21 percent of regional legislative members had submitted their reports. Regional reporting ranged from 0 to 100 percent by locality. The current efficacy of this type of information is further compounded by the fact that agencies in Indonesia either do not or cannot typically sanction illicit behavior or that such information is used only for political expediency, as is typically the case.[32]

Whereas budgets, audit reports, and wealth declarations could provide some more objective insights into local governance processes, they are at best inputs for relevant stakeholders. Evidence from the

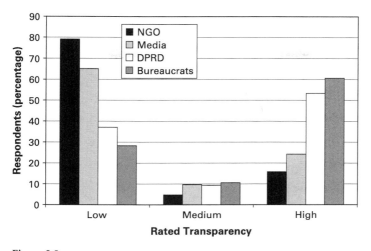

Figure 3.8
Transparency of local budget results (APBD)
Source: 2002 GDS (NGO = LGT11; Media = MGT9; DPRD = DGT14; Bureaucrats = BGT14).

GDS suggests that in this regard their accountability functions remain incomplete.

The regional budgets and internal auditors reports should serve as tools for citizens to monitor local governments. As figure 3.8 suggests, however, these documents also tend to be largely opaque. The perceived levels of transparency of the budgets differed across key stakeholders: 80 percent of NGOs thought they were of low transparency as opposed to just under 30 percent of bureaucrats. The majority of all key stakeholder felt local audit reports were of low transparency.

Local Public Services
The majority of GDS respondents appeared to be relatively optimistic about local service delivery. On average, between 50 and 60 percent of households rated services in their locality such as clinics and schools as good (4 or 5 on a five-point scale). Less than a third rated the police, a centralized agency, as good. Few respondents thought that services had gotten worse, and a large share actually felt that they had improved.

This is not to say that service delivery is not wanting or to invalidate the potentially corrosive impact of political KKN. The absence of minimum standards or comparative information on service provision in other regions (World Bank, 2003) means that local voters often do not know what they can expect from their representatives and therefore hold them accountable in terms of yardstick competition. In areas where transparency is low, voters may also implicitly assume that governance and service delivery is actually better that it is. Finally, citizens may have little information about how effectively public resources are being spent, especially if local governments were recently the beneficiaries of major transfer windfalls (as was the case in natural-resource-rich regions). Future work will clearly have to focus on whether local government budgets (APBD) are being reoriented to match local preferences. Given the rigidities in wage expenditures, these dynamics will initially be most evident in the for development expenditures. Equally important for intersectoral shifts will be the need to identify interjurisdictional (urban and rural or urban and community level) and interconstituency (by political, identity, and income group).

The overall relationship between the quality of local service delivery and indicators of poor governance is complex, if only because each encompasses a range of dimensions (both the level, mix, and quality of local services provided). The 2002 GDS found a significant negative relationship at the local level between the share of households that perceived that the individual services had improved since decentralization and the level of KKN. The strongest associations were for the village or neighborhood head (-0.46), the subdistrict or kecamatan office, schools, health clinics, and finally the regional heads office (-0.20). In terms of levels of good services, we found significant negative associations (at a 10 percent level) only with the village or neighborhood head (-0.48), the subdistrict office (-0.32), the police (-0.20), and public elementary schools (-0.15). Perhaps not surprisingly, there were high measures of association between village-level governance—such as, abuses of power by village heads (0.59) and perceived corruption in village or neighborhood (0.56)—and local-level KKN. These associations clearly raise some difficult questions about the relationship between village and neighborhood measures of governance and service delivery versus the quality of local governance, as well as the appreciation that citizens have of the importance of local-level government processes under decentralization.[33]

Local-Governance Outcomes

Theory and recent empirical evidence suggest various channels and conditions under which local political processes might be distorted.

We briefly investigate the relationship between perceived levels of distortions in the local politics process (KKN) with a range of local characteristics. We use variations in local-government jurisdiction (kabupaten or kota) (such as political, fiscal, bureaucratic, and accountability) to explain the variance in governance outcomes across these jurisdictions. To measure these characteristics, we use the following: political variables (political composition; term characteristics of regional heads; composition of the local electorate, including ethnic, religious, and electoral outcomes diversity), bureaucracy (size of the local civil service), fiscal variables (available resources and levels of tax yields), transparency (presence of media) that may make respondents more aware of corruption of KKN at the local (rather than just at the village, neighborhood, or subdistrict level), and finally indicators of possible accountability (legal and judicial) actually curb local KKN.

The international literature has attempted to examine the relationship between decentralization and quality of government. The often contradictory conclusions of these contributions may in large part be due to the fact that comparisons rely on different theoretical frameworks and actual types and contexts of decentralization (Treisman, 2000). Ethnic or religious diversity is often cited as an obstacle to good public policy. Evidence from the United States suggests that ethnic diversity can be associated with decreased expenditures on core services such as roads and education, but higher overall spending and deficits or debt per capita (Alesina, Baqir, and Easterly, 1999). The presence of multiple ethnic groups has often been associated with lower growth (Easterly and Levine, 1997) and a higher probability of conflict or even civil war. Miguel and Gugerty (2002) find that ethnic diversity in Kenya is associated with lower local voluntary school contributions, worse facilities, and poorer well maintenance. The main mechanisms suggested are that social sanctions against shirking become more difficult across ethnic groups, hence weakening cooperative outcomes. However, Collier (2001) suggests the impact of ethnicity on governance outcomes critically depends on the type of diversity—ethnic fragmentation across multiple groups versus dominance by one group—and the type of political regime. For example, international evidence suggests that ethnic diversity per se is not bad for governance but that it is largely bad under particular political regimes (such as dictatorships). International evidence suggests that a less fractionalized party system is associated with better outcomes in terms of economic growth, quality of government, and public-goods provision (Enikopolov and

Zhuravskaya, 2003). More politically fragmented governments may require more interests to be bought off (for example, through higher expenditures) to achieve a higher majority (Jones, Sanguinetti, and Tommasi, 2000) and hence higher levels of KKN. There is some presumption that higher female representation may have a positive impact on governance outcomes (World Bank, 2001). Although East Asia and the Pacific enjoy some of the highest rates of female parliamentary representation, Indonesia falls well below the regional average. Evidence from India, where heads of village councils (encompassing several villages) were randomly reserved for women, showed that women's leadership does affect the types of public goods provided. Generally, services were more in line with women's preferences (water, fuel, and roads versus education). However, there was no evidence that female leadership was associated with less corruption (Chattopadhyay and Duflo, 2001). In the Indonesian context, the presence of women on KKN may be more difficult to disentangle. The fact that women are more represented in a locality may be due to certain unobserved characteristics of that locality that are themselves responsible for better governance outcomes.

The analysis presented at this stage is exploratory, but our hope is that the stylized findings from this work will underscore the diversity across Indonesia's districts, lead us to better empirical proxies for studying local political elite capture, and open up the potential for a more rigorous modeling and testing of the issues. Unlike the significant body of empirical work in the United States linking regional political outcomes with institutional differences across states (for example, electoral rules and procedural rules) (Besley and Case, 2003), we can only exploit current cross-sectional differences. While we therefore do not offer tests of institutional reforms currently being proposed by the government of Indonesia (such as changes in electoral rules to consolidate party representation and allow for the direct election of regional heads, redistricting, and female participation quotas) but seek merely to raise some empirical findings for the policy debate.

Table 3.4 presents summary statistics for selected local-governance outcomes and determinant characteristics variables.[34] These also give some sense of the diversity across local governments in Indonesia. The dataset matches data from the Governance and Decentralization Survey with a wide range of fiscal and survey data—including the 2000 population census, the 2002 national household survey (SUSENAS),

Table 3.4
Summary statistics on local governance outcomes and characteristics

		Mean	Standard Deviation	Mini-mum	Maxi-mum
Perceptions of KKN in local head elections (% households)	KKNELE	30.5	18.0	0	98.3
Perceptions of KKN in local annual accountability speed (% households)	KKNACC	19.1	14.7	0	73.3
Population (000s)	POP	625.5	584.1	40.2	4,147
Area (km^2)	AREA	4,686	584.1	23	61,493
Density (pop/km^2)	DENSITY	1,030	8,245	2.5	12,172
Average years of schooling	YSCHOOL	5.12	1.38	1.28	8.55
Years of population with secondary schooling (% over)	SECSCHOOL	15.0	12.4	2.7	50.2
Poverty (%)	POOR	18.4	16.4	0	87.1
Inequality (Gini)	INEQU	0.28	0.04	0.20	0.42
Share of natural resource revenues (%)	PFSHSDA01	6.8	15.4	0	76.8
Share of development expenditures (%)	PFSHDEV01	29.9	13.1	3.3	80.4
Ethnic fractionalization	ELF	0.42	0.34	0.00	1.00
Major ethnic group (%)	ETHMAJ	70.4	27.7	12.1	99.8
Religious fractionalization	RELFRACI	0.19	0.20	0.00	0.77
Major religious group (%)	RELMAJ	87.7	15.8	31.9	99.9
Political fractionalization	POLFRAC	0.71	15.8	0.24	0.86
Major political party (%)	POLMAJ	43.6	39.0	20.9	86.8
Share of minor/ nonnational parities (%)	POLMINOR	11.0	5.6	0.5	32.8
Female representation (%)	POLFEM	4.7	3.7	0	16.7

Source: IDEA DataCore. Reported figures are for the randomly drawn GDS sample of 150 local governments. Figures in brackets refer to the overall sample of 348 local governments.

and local electoral data from the Elections Commission (KPU) from the
1999 elections.

Table 3.5 presents some regressions that help explain the relationship between perceived local governance and ethnic, political and religious diversity, fiscal revenue structure (including own revenues and
natural-resource revenue sharing), bureaucratic dynamics evidenced
by the fiscal expenditure structure, and finally variables denoting the
role of participation, transparency, and accountability.

We found support for the hypothesis that political and ethnic fragmentation makes better governance outcomes less likely. Given that
we are using perception data, however, special care much be taken to
interpret these results, as they may be driven largely by peer-group
effects. Greater diversity in political or group affiliation may mean that
the respondent is also less likely to share group or political affiliations
with the district leadership and hence be more likely to voice a negative judgment.[35]

Evidence of the impact of own revenue base on local governance
was weak, likely reflecting the fact that the local own tax base remains
very limited in Indonesia. Perhaps surprisingly, fiscal natural-resource
abundance (SDA) had a positive impact on governance quality. However, there were some indications that higher levels of services associated with greater public-resource abundance (lnPFPCREVTOT), since
decentralization may be contributing to this result (and reflecting the
large fiscal disparities suggested earlier in this chapter). We found
some evidence that kotas (municipalities) manifest higher levels of
reported KKN but remain uncertain whether this is due to better information and higher expectations by urban residents. Measures of regional per capita income (RGRP), inequality, education, or poverty did
not seem to influence KKN levels systematically. The variables on
democratically (post-1999) elected regional heads or military regional
heads (not reported) suggest that elections did not necessarily enhance
perceptions of governance. Neither did those for female participation.

Natural resources influence the structure of local revenues and also
their overall levels. The presence of natural-resource revenues (SDA)
typically means that regions have far more fiscal resources at their
disposal than the average local government in Indonesia. The share of
natural resources in the overall budget is positively correlated with
total per capita fiscal expenditures, per capita development expenditures, and the share of development expenditures (0.63, 0.74, and 0.66,
respectively).

Table 3.5
Effects on perception of KKN in local head election

Local Government Characteristics	(1) 2002	(2) 2002	(3) 2002	(4) 2002	(5) 2002	(6) 2002	(7) 2002
Ethnic fragmentation	0.124** [0.061]	0.119** [0.048]	0.130*** [0.047]	0.115** [0.058]	0.111** [0.049]	0.150*** [0.051]	0.144*** [0.051]
Political fragmentation index	0.342** [0.140]	0.327** [0.130]		0.305** [0.133]	0.372*** [0.136]	0.355*** [0.129]	0.329** [0.130]
Population density	0.005 [0.044]	0.016* [0.009]	0.017* [0.009]			0.012 [0.010]	0.013 [0.010]
Size (area)	0.003 [0.040]			−0.007 [0.017]			
Urban	0.030 [0.068]			0.029 [0.065]			
Public resource available	−0.053 [0.066]	−0.058** [0.026]	— −0.065*** [0.024]	— −0.073*** [0.027]	−0.062** [0.026]		−0.044 [0.031]
Share of PAD (% of total revenue)	0.175 [0.288]				0.323 [0.216]		
Share of natural resources on total revenue	−0.114 [0.180]					−0.230** [0.109]	−0.124 [0.132]
Local regulation rejected (political difficulty of incumbent)	−0.044 [0.035]					−0.047 [0.034]	−0.046 [0.034]
Constant	0.692 [1.318]	0.742** [0.370]	1.074*** [0.316]	1.096*** [0.410]	0.841** [0.366]	−0.006 [0.118]	0.581 [0.427]
Observations	141	141	148	141	141	141	141
R-squared	0.47	0.46	0.42	0.46	0.46	0.46	0.47

Note: Regional dummies were included. Standard errors are in brackets.
a. SIKD (2001).
*Significant at 10 percent.
**Significant at 5 percent.
***Significant at 1 percent.

One argument is that this makes the practice of arriving at rent shares (*bagi-bagi*) less contentious, at least in the immediate wake of the windfall, and that distribution occurs through a more formal padding of the budget, especially in the area of development. The availability of greater rents means that this can be done in the context of the formal budget and thereby manifests a less open process of money politics. While local capture is actually greater, households are not aware of this political KKN. With a negative interaction term, the effect of SDA will decrease with a higher level of rent pool (such as development budgets). However, we were not able to find significant results in this regard.

A dummy for Java tended to be significant, suggesting that political KKN was lower on the island. The kota variable consistently emerges as significant in the regressions. The urban result may be driven by higher levels of household awareness that has not been adequately controlled for in our regressions (such as by education levels and local media penetration variables). Similarly, urban areas may be characterized by higher demands on public resources, which put more pressure on local politicians to capture rents. An alternative interpretation is that the opportunities for rent-seeking outside the budget are greater in cities, therefore increasing the stakes and rewards to political KKN. Whereas the data are illustrative of some of the significant variations in local governance quality, future work will need to focus on devising better indicators and addressing issues of causality.

Conclusions

The 2001 big-bang decentralization has increased the fiscal, administrative, and political autonomy of Indonesia's local governments. These changes came at a time when the central government was significantly weakened in the midst of a period of political and economic upheaval. But decentralization must also be viewed as an integral part of the country's ongoing democratization process. At both the central and local government levels, it remains to be seen whether the new democratic institutions will enhance encompassing bureaucratic responsiveness, reduce corruption, and enhance service delivery at both the national and local levels.

A more definitive verdict on whether *reformasi* and regional autonomy (*otonomi daerah*) are leading to better local governance and service-delivery outcomes is premature. Democratization and devolution in Indonesia have had only a brief history. The underlying political, legal, fiscal, and administrative framework of decentralization continues to evolve. Moreover, Indonesia's regional heads (*bupatis* and *walikotas*) are undergoing a major transition from largely appointed to elected positions and will also be directly elected. Perhaps most important, the starting point of democratization and decentralization in Indonesia—and in many other international decentralizations—was *poor and declining levels* of political accountability and service delivery rather than the merely technocratic desire to *improve* governance and decentralization outcomes.[36] While this starting point for decentralization is not internationally unique, the magnitude of the concurrent democratic transition and decentralization suggests that we can expect import lags in outcomes.

Public services do not appear to have collapsed in the immediate wake of decentralization. Whereas there will most certainly be a great deal of inertia and lags in outcome measures, it is clearly too early to associate this with decentralization. Our expectation is that regions will increasingly perform differently over time, with some regions lagging behind and others forging ahead under decentralization. Capturing this process will require better indicators of levels and types of governance and public-service delivery. These will in turn require that the dynamics between service delivery and governance over time be better understood.[37] If ongoing assessments of decentralization are to be timely, it will be important to articulate potential leading indicators (for example, in governance), in the presence of lags or even U-curves (declines before improvements) in local service-delivery outcomes.[38]

As *transparency* has flourished in Indonesia, the question is whether this will serve as a bridge to enhanced *accountability*. Much of the applied work on local governance in Indonesia has rightly focused on enhanced transparency and participation as a means of reducing KKN and improving public-service delivery in Indonesia. While these are critical ingredients toward eroding political KKN, a range of accountability mechanisms (including elections, central oversight, and judicial sanction) will need to be strengthened given the initial conditions of governance and service delivery underlying Indonesia's decentralization.

We have argued that any forthcoming assessment of decentralization in Indonesia needs to evaluate the significant differences in performance already being observed across local governments over time. These dimensions might include a variety of dimensions (such as equity, quantity, or quality), which may actually rank on multiple dimensions (Hofman, Kaiser, and Schulze, 2003). While a number of recent theoretical contributions provide some useful guidance for analysis (Bardhan and Mookherjee, 2000), empirical work will have to draw on mixed quantitative and qualitative approaches in each given context. For example, one promising approach will be to focus on particular outliers (such as those with high or low KKN and different indicators of service delivery) identified by the survey approaches (such as the top and worst performers) to distill the major apparent dynamics in these regions.

Given the historical context of Indonesia's decentralization, the roles assumed by national and local governments have been the result of broader political dynamics and are often intertwined and overlapping in many arenas of service delivery. In many cases, the question of *whether* centralized or decentralized governments perform better or worse needs to provide a better understanding of *the conditions under which* particular local governments perform better than others. At the country level, this will depend on the starting point and particular characteristics of the decentralization. Locally, the presence or absence of various effective accountability mechanisms (and underlying capacity and local characteristics), especially how they are influenced by actors and relationships with higher tiers of government, needs to be carefully evaluated.

Some of the greatest challenges in more systematic evaluations of decentralization lie in our ability to measure local governance and service-delivery outcomes. We argue that the role of this type of information has two functions, which ideally should be complementary. Foremost, information on the performance of local governments in terms of quality of governance and service delivery should serve as an input to enhanced accountability at the level of citizens (such as particular facilities and their community and local governments), local governments, and higher levels of government. At the same time, these data could help untangle under which context particular accountability mechanisms in a given country or local context appear to function more effectively.[39]

The measurement of context-specific concepts such as local-governance and service-delivery dynamics will typically have to reach beyond household surveys, in part because of the high costs that these entail in terms of achieving significant subnational coverage. Perception measures of service delivery may or may not reflect actual underlying services or governance conditions for that matter and may be more influenced by group factors (Deichmann and Lall, 2003). While perception-based indicators are clearly less attractive from a research point of view, they do themselves provide intrinsically useful signals of how citizens perceive their local governments and what level of faith they place in the political processes that can hold them accountable (Paul, 2002). Empirical approaches will have to strike a balance between perception measures (such as the KNN variable used in this chapter) and more specific "harder" indicators (such as credible audit reports). At the same time, approaches that rely on key respondent approaches, such as village heads, may themselves also be subject to biases.

Many international donors and agencies are attempting to leverage decentralization for better development outcomes by promoting good governance at the local level. The apparent intractability of the governance reform agenda in Indonesia, most notably in such areas as legal and judicial reform, is leading many donors such as the World Bank to work with reform-minded local governments. As these projects seek to work with innovative local leaders, it will be important to be able to monitor the impact of these subnational governance interventions over time. However, this strategy does raise the question of how widespread or sustainable such governance reforms can prove in the absence of central inputs, such as a credible system of legal, administrative, or political party disciplines.

The significant changes in the roles and relationships of political actors in Indonesia's concurrent process of democratization and decentralization means that decentralization will remain contested for some time to come. Recent changes in the mode of election of the president and direct elections of regional heads underscore that the political system is still in a process of evolution. The anticipated formation of a new national government at the end of 2004, together with new political party constellations at both the local and national levels, will further define the contours of center and regional political, fiscal, administrative relations. Given the origins and rapid implementation of the 2001 decentralization, some pressure for recentralization have already emerged. With the increased diffusion of power and the broader process of democratization, however, the center is unlikely to reestablish the type of top-down control of the New Order. However, this contestation is likely to play itself out across a number of arenas (such as proposals to recentralized the civil-service wage bill), each with potential impacts for local governance and service-delivery outcomes at the local level.

Acknowledgments

The views in this chapter are attributable solely to the authors and not necessarily those of their organization. Special thanks goes to Fitria Fitrani, Bambang ("Koko") Suharnoko, and Silvia Irawan for assistance. We would like to thanks Pak Agus Dwiyanto and the team at CPPS-UGM for the ongoing partnership in the Governance and Decentralization Survey in the context of the Indonesian Decentralization Empirical Analysis (IDEA) project. Andrew Ellis was especially helpful in providing background on elections issues. Greatly appreciated were comments by Ella Jones and Paul Smoke. The authors would like to thank the Netherlands government for support in the context of the World Bank Dutch Trust Fund for Strengthening Indonesia's Decentralization. Funding for the 2002 GDS was provided by the Partnership for Governance Reform, the Partnership for Economic Growth (PEG-USAID), and the World Bank. An early version of this chapter was presented at the Decentralization Conference on the Rise of Local Governments, London School of Economics (LSE), May 23–25, 2003.

Notes

1. After 1971, the New Order regime greatly circumscribed political competition. Party representation was forced to amalgamate to the government's functional-groups vehicle (Golkar), a nationalist party (PDI, Indonesian Democratic Party), and an Islamist (PPP, United Development Party) party. The dominance of Golkar was underscored in the highly controversial 1997 elections, in which it gained 74 percent of the national vote. The regime had historically allowed some limited forms of opposition through two carefully managed Muslim (PPP) and nationalist opposition parties (PDI). The Muslim PPP Party achieved 23 percent. The support of the nationalist party PDI collapsed to 3 percent, following a government-orchestrated removal of its leadership led by now President Megawati (Suryadinata, 2002). The breakaway PDI Party (Party for Indonesian Democratic Struggle) subsequently became the single largest party.

2. Originals and English translations of Indonesia's major legal instruments related to decentralization are available at ⟨http://www.gtzsfdm.or.id⟩.

3. Garman, Haggard, and Willis (2001) suggest that the constellation and strength of central political parties can predict the degree of de- and recentralization. Notably, the proposed revisions were largely characterized by efforts to enhance the stature of the executive (Ellis and du Sautoy, 2001), especially compared with the newly empowered democratic institutions such as the local legislatures.

4. The World Bank and IMF commented on the draft laws in December 1999. The two main concerns that were raised were that expenditure assignments were extremely vague and that revenue assignments were very specific. Taken together, it was felt, the laws provided significant risk for macroeconomic stability and service delivery.

5. While Megawati Sukarno Putri of the PDI Party was the largest, the MPR voted in October 1999 to have Habibie succeeded by the moderate Muslim cleric Wahid after he emerged as a compromise candidate of the Islamic/Golkar axis. Despite some reformist instincts, Wahid proved an ineffective political negotiator. Under significant pressure by the legislature, Megawati, who was already in the role of vice president after being defeated by Wahid, was inaugurated on July 23, 2001. In the context of these political negotiations, Megawati received the implicit backing of the military.

6. Many of the political parties in Indonesia are new, thereby making it difficult to gauge their relative centralization. At the start of decentralization, many of the major parties were also closely linked to the strong personal identities (such as Megawati Sukarno Putri, the daughter of first President Sukarno, deposed by Suharto in the mid-1960s, for the PDI Party; Abdurachman Wahid, a moderate Muslim cleric chair of the NU, the largest Muslim organization in Indonesia, for PKB and initial successor to President Habibie; and Amien Rais, a *reformasi* leader for PPP.

7. Although the overall election was considered free and fair, there were some reports of systemic attempts at vote buying. Golkar was accused of vote buying in the outer islands (Suryadinata, 2002). Subsequently, the head of the Golkar Party in Indonesia, Akbar Tandjung, was convicted of diverting state funds from the state logistics agency (Bulog) to allegedly help finance the party's 1999 finance campaign (although he continues to lead the party).

8. The implementation of institutional arrangements for the lowest tier of government, the village (desa) and neighborhood (kelurahan), have now been delegated to the districts. However, especially in the case of villages, national laws prescribed accountability arrangements that include an elected council (BPD), which in turn can hold an elected village head accountable.

9. During the New Order, many military officials were demoted to civilian positions (*kekayaan*) (Kammen and Chandra, 1999). Just as the Suharto regime enforced regular rotations of regional military commanders to prevent them from establishing deep local roots and possibly developing into warlords of the 1950s variety, the New Order set limits on regional chief executives. The 1974 law on regional government set an explicit two-term limit on regional executives, and the government adhered to it consistently (Malley, 2000, p. 9). Evidence from the 1990s suggested that military officers held about half of all head of region positions (Malley, 2000). There were important regional variations, although the number of military officers being appointed as regional heads appears to have declined somewhat after the 1990s.

10. Article 41 of law 22 of 1999 defines the term of five years with up to one reelection.

11. The president refused to inaugurate Alzier Dianis Thabranie, who was elected as governor by the Lampung provincial legislature in November 2002, because the senior provincial official was accused of involvement in several corruption cases.

12. Typically, some legislators from the old local government move to the new legislative (DPRD), and then both legislatures are topped up to reestablish the old party balance. For newly created regions, the old region proposes a candidate for Bupati or Walikota to the provincial governor. After being processed in the provincial level, the candidate will then

be proposed to the Minister of Home Affairs. The minister will examine and issue a ministerial decree to the governor for appointing the head of the region. These are issues as decision letters (*surat keputusan*) stating the starting and end date of the appointment (MoHA, 2003). If there is no suitable candidate from the region, then the center can help appoint one from elsewhere. The practice appears to be that DPRD elections are then initiated a year later. The president then issues a letter of appointment for governors, whereas the Minister of Home Affairs issues letters for local government heads. The appointment of regional heads proceeds according to government regulation 151 of 2000. Following the election, the legislative sends notification (*Berita Acara Pemilihan*, BAP) to the central government and supporting documents (such as the qualifications of the candidate). Article 4 of government regulation 151 of 2000 requires that members of the armed forces and police receive a special permit from the Minister of Home Affairs in the name of the president.

13. Interview with Teten Masduki, Indonesia Corruption Watch, in *Van Zorge Report* 4(6) (April 2002).

14. The politics of these gubernatorial elections need to be seen in light of the upcoming 2004 elections. A full analysis of these dynamics is beyond the scope of this chapter but do suggest an area of future research.

15. There is some ambiguity, however, where the regions have legal recourse to a higher court if they are unhappy with these decisions.

16. Since then, presidential decree 74 of 2001 has been issued, changing the audit arrangement. The decree assigns three internal auditors the right to audit local governments' budgets: Badan Pengawas Daerah (Bawasda) Kabupaten, Badan Pengawas Daerah (Bawasda) Propinsi, and inspectors general of line ministries on the technical aspects. The inspector general of MOHA plays a role as coordinator of Bawasda assignment. In addition, BPK acts as the Parliament's audit body.

17. The decentralization laws provide local governments with increased leeway in organizing village governance. Subdistricts are led by a *camat*, who is typically an employee of the local government.

18. Yogjakarta also has some decree of special autonomy (Quinn, 2003), which link the governor's position to the royal house. Only in the case of Aceh and Papua do these special regulations appear to circumscribe the status of the local governments, as they do in the special metropolitan region of the capital, Jakarta. Tensions between local governments under law 22 of 1999 and the rights of the province under special autonomy have emerged in both Aceh and Papua.

19. The additional natural-resource shared revenues give Aceh about 1.5 Indonesian rupiahs trillion or Rps. 375,000 per capita for its population of 4 million. Special allocations for Papua (2 percent of the DAU amount) amount to Rps. 1.38 trillion, about Rps. 660,000 more for each of the 2.1 million Papuans, plus an initial additional Rps. 0.14 trillion, or Rps. 64,000 per capita from the more favorable oil and gas shares (Hofman, Kadjadmiko, and Kaiser, 2002a).

20. In Aceh, special autonomy allows for special governance arrangements (including direct elections of regional heads) and the implementation of Islamic sharia law. The implementation of special autonomy in Aceh requires the issuance of provincial regulations to implement the law called qanuns (or perdas in the rest of Indonesia). A particular sticking point has been the issuance of the direct elections of governor and vice governor, mayor and vice mayor, and regent and vice regent mandated by law 18 of 2001 (*pilsung*

or *pilihan langsung*). It is unclear whether regional heads have to be associated with national parties or can run as independent candidates (thereby presumably given space to a GAM associated political grouping). As about half of Aceh's twenty regional heads are up for election before the next general elections, local government legislators (and their provincial party compatriots) may also have a vested interest in maintaining the current system. The Political Party Law of 2002 does not allow regional parties, and at this stage it is difficult to imagine that a GAM as an organization seeking independence would join an existing national party.

21. The main political features of Papua's special autonomy include the establishment of a Papuan People's Assembly (MRP) with native representation and authority to regulate subprovincial jurisdictions (rather than by national law under decentralization). In contrast to the Aceh law, Papua's special autonomy (article 7) mandates indirect elections of the governor by the legislative (although it does not appear to specify regulations for local government heads). The MRP, however, is to be established by national government regulation (article 21), and its members must be approved by the Minister of Home Affairs. The law does accord for the formation of Papuan political parties (article 28) for participation in national elections. However, article 28b suggests that this be in done in accordance with prevailing laws, which would presumably mean the new political laws that do not allow for regional parties (a compromised apparently grudgingly accepted by Papuan negotiators at the time). Article 19 states that one-third be female, customary (*adat*), and religious representatives.

22. Kabupaten and kota are administrative and politically similar, but rural and urban government arrangements at the village and neighborhood level differ under law 22 of 1999. Local government is organized into subdistricts (kecamatans) and villages and neighborhoods (desa and kelurahan). The head of a subdistrict (camat) is typically a civil servant.

23. The term *region* (*daerah*) is used for provinces and local governments taken together. The special metropolitan area (DKI) of the national capital, Jakarta, also encompasses local governments. However, these are not vested with elected legislatures or regional heads. Originals and English translations of Indonesia's major legal instruments related to decentralization are available at ⟨http://www.gtzsfdm.or.id⟩.

24. This section presents initial evidence on this question, largely based on the 2002 Governance and Decentralization Survey (GDS). The GDS was conducted in 150 randomly drawn local governments out of a total 348 local governments. Further details and instruments are available at ⟨http://www.worldbank.or.id/decentralization⟩. The 150 local governments were selected randomly within provinces, and twenty-seven additional districts were samples as part of a World Bank project on reform-minded governments. The survey aimed to establish a baseline of evolving governance practices at the local level. Respondents to twelve structure questionnaires included households, officials, politicians, media, and other civil-society members. Questions focused on governance issues such as accountability, participation, rule of law, equity, responsiveness of politicians, corruption, collusion, and nepotism (KKN), and public-service delivery efficiency under decentralization. The GDS was conducted in Papua just prior to the implementation of special autonomy but not in Aceh. In each local government, sixty household respondents and thirty-six nonhousehold respondents were sampled. The surveyed households consist of fifteen randomly selected households from four randomly selected villages and neighborhoods in each kabupaten and kota, respectively. The nonhousehold respondents fall into three groups: government officials, representatives of the private business sector, and representatives of civil society. The first group includes officials from the local health

and education agencies, from local health centers (PUSKESMAS), members of the local parliament (DPRD), the head of a district (*bupati* or *walikota*) and his deputy, heads of the local finance and revenue office (DISPENDA) and monitoring offices (BAWASDA and BAPPEDA), senior judges and district attorneys, and school principals. The second and third groups comprise representatives of the local chamber of commerce and NGOs, lawyers, and print media journalists.

25. For example, when a respondent was asked to elaborate on what he meant when he said that service remained the same, he said that it was as bad as always.

26. It should be noted that in regions in which no elections for the head of the region had been held, some people indicated that there was corruption in the process.

27. Respondents could list up to three sources.

28. Households were asked about their views on transparency in key public processes of village and neighborhood life. These included village head elections, village representative body elections, village development finance, social safety net programs (JPS), and school assistance (BP3). While 55 percent of villagers claimed to have no information regarding the financing of development activities in their place of residence, 68 percent of those claimed that information was readily available. About a quarter of those, however, still claimed that the village rarely or never made an effort to publicize these.

29. This is a common problem in much of the empirical work on corruption. Mauro (1995) notes that the validity of international corruption indicators is underscored by the large amounts of money that companies pay for these indicators, presumably to make their business decisions.

30. A similar question was not asked about local-level officials because pilot tests showed that households were not sufficiently informed.

31. A more detailed assessment of these data suggests that they are a useful indication of the kinds of infractions found within government (such as abuse of the tender process) but are not substantial enough for actual rating purposes and reflected a number of inconsistencies. Although the report suggests that over seventy local governments were audited, the selection criteria were not clearly articulated. Actual data were presented for only fifty-six regions. The reports distinguished between three types of irregularities (noncompliance, inefficiency, and ineffectiveness), although the choice classification of actual instances was not always clear. Furthermore, the report classified instances as possible losses to the state, but it was not clear how these were acted on.

32. The State Official Wealth Audit Committee (KPKPN) recently announced that the governor of South Kalimantan had failed to declare all his assets at the time of his 2001 inauguration and wrote to the Minister of Home Affairs that he should therefore be dismissed. Members of the Muslim party (PPP) that nominated him, however, suggested that he should merely be allowed to update the declaration for the luxury cars and houses he had omitted as many other officials had not even submitted their reports *Jakarta Post*, (May 12, 2003). The accusation comes after an ongoing political tussle between the regional legislative and central government (see *GTZ Decentralization News*, issue 42). The DPRD insists it has dismissed him, while the Ministry of Home Affairs issued a decision in February 2003 stating that it had not followed government regulation 108 of 2000 in these proceedings (March 28, 2003).

33. The relationship between village and neighborhood and local governance perceptions clearly is an issue of concern, both in terms of the econometric specification and the

extent to which households differentiate between village and neighborhood level and local-level governance. While beyond the scope of this chapter, future work will seek to investigate intralocal jurisdiction differences in local governance and reported perceptions of the local government.

34. Households are expected to observe the local head elections at least every five years. As shown earlier, the timing of this event differs by region in Indonesia. The accountability speech occurs annually, typically in the first part of the year. The latter would therefore be the more theoretically correct measure.

35. Regrettably, we were not able to draw on perceptions of the national leadership or legislature, which might have served as a partial control for this effect.

36. While the New Order was especially successful at enhancing the quantity of public services in health, education, and infrastructure, it manifested growing concerns about the quality and sustainability of these services.

37. Our definition of *public-service delivery* is meant to encompass direct delivery of services (such as schools, clinics, hospitals, and identity cards) as well as regulatory services (such as the business environment).

38. For example, different types of political corruption may reduce the efficacy of public-service delivery to varying degrees with varying local welfare effects. The executive and legislative collude together to extract rents and engage in corruption through the local government. This could include creaming off projects, awarding jobs based on political considerations, and skewing overall expenditures to favor one group over another (such as, prorich or prourban expenditure rather than propoor or prorural expenditures).

39. Ratings and research do imply some tradeoffs. Ratings for yardstick competition would ideally include as many regions as possible, whereas research into local-level changes over time would deepen sampling in individual regions and not necessarily include all localities. Consequently, the depth of sampling ideally required to establish (1) causality between governance and service delivery and (2) the breath of coverage and the breath of local government coverage needed to promote widespread yardstick competition among comparable local jurisdictions in Indonesia presents clear tradeoffs. This sampling might require a two-stage approach of broad rankings and deepened samples that approach national representativity but cover fewer districts.

References

ADB. (2002). "Indonesia Governance Assessment." Manila: Asian Development Bank.

Alesina, Alberto, Reza Baqir, and William Easterly. (1999). "Public Goods and Ethnic Divisions." *Quarterly Journal of Economics* (November): 1243–1284.

Bardhan, Pranab, and Dilip Mookherjee. (2000). "Capture and Governance at Local and National Levels." *AER* 90(2): 135–139.

Besley, Timothy, and Anne Case. (2003). "Political Institutions and Policy Choices: Evidence from the United States." *Journal of Economic Literature* 41: 7–73.

Chattopadhyay, Raghaberndra, and Esther Duflo. (2001). "Woman's Leadership in Policy Decisions: Evidence from a Nationwide Randomized Experiment in India." Mimeo, Massachusetts Institute of Technology, Cambridge.

Collier, Paul. (2001). "Ethnic Diversity: An Economic Analysis." *Economic Policy*: 128–166.

Crook, Richard, and James Manor. (1998). *Decentralization and Democracy in South Asia and West Africa: Participation, Accountability and Performance.* Cambridge: Cambridge University Press.

Deichmann, Uwe, and Somik Lall. (2003). "Are You Satisfied? Citizen Feedback and Delivery of Urban Services." Washington, DC: World Bank.

Easterly, William, and Ross Levine. (1997). "Africa's Growth Tragedy: Policies and Ethnic Divisions." *QJE* (November): 1203–1250.

Ekopuri, Dyan Shinto. (2003). "Indonesia's New Institutions to Fight Corruption: Another Warriors with a Sword?" Mimeo, World Bank, Jakarta.

Ellis, Andrew, and Tony du Sautoy. (2001). "Proposals for Amendment of UU22/1999 on Regional Autonomy." Jakarta: National Democratic Institute for International Affairs.

Enikopolov, Ruben, and Ekaterina V. Zhuravskaya. (2003). "Decentralization and Political Institutions." Working Paper, CEFIR, Moscow.

Evans, Kevin Raymond. (2003). *The History of Political Parties and General Elections in Indonesia.* Jakarta: Arise Consultancies.

Fitrani, Fitria, Bert Hofman, and Kai Kaiser. (2003). "Unity in Diversity? The Creation of New Regions in a Decentralizing Indonesia." Mimeo, World Bank Office Jakarta, Jakarta.

Garman, Christopher, Stephen Haggard, and Eliza Willis. (2001). "Fiscal Recentralization: A Political Theory." *World Politics* 53(2): 205–236.

Hofman, Bert, Kadjadmiko, and Kai Kaiser. (2002a). "Evaluating Indonesia's Fiscal Equalization." Mimeo, World Bank, Jakarta.

Hofman, Bert, Kadjadmiko, and Kai Kaiser. (2002b). "Evaluation Fiscal Equalization in Indonesia." Mimeo, World Bank, Jakarta.

Hofman, Bert, and Kai Kaiser. (2002). "The Making of the Big Bang and Its Aftermath: A Political Economy Perspective." Paper prepared for a conference on Can Decentralization Help Rebuild Indonesia, Georgia State University, Atlanta, Georgia.

Hofman, Bert, Kai Kaiser, and Günther G. Schulze. (2003). "Decentralization, Governance, and Public Services: An Assessment of the Indonesian Experience." Reseach Concept Note, World Bank, University of Freiburg, Jakarta.

Jones, Mark P., Pablo Sanguinetti, and Mariano Tommasi. (2000). "Politics, Institutions, and Fiscal Performance in a Federal System: An Analysis of the Argentine Provinces." *Journal of Development Studies* 61: 305–333.

Kammen, Douglas Anton, and Siddharth Chandra. (1999). "A Tour of Duty: Changing Patterns of Military Politics in Indonesia in the 1990s." Cornell University Southeast Asia Project, Ithaca, New York.

Legge, J. D. (1961). *Central Authority and Regional Autonomy in Indonesia: A Study in Local Administration.* Ithaca, NY: Cornell University Press.

Malley, Michael. (2000). "Conflict, Reform, and Regional Political Leadership." Paper presented at the international seminar *Dinamika Politik Lokal di Indonesia: Perubahan, Tantangan dan Harapan*, Department of Political Science, Ohio University, Athens, OH.

Mauro, Paulo. (1995). "Corruption and Growth." *Quarterly Journal of Economics* 119(3): 681–712.

Miguel, Edward, and Mary Kay Gugerty. (2002). "Ethnic Diversity, Social Sanctions, and Public Goods in Kenya." University of California, Berkeley, and University of Washington, Seattle.

MoHA. (2003). "Daftar Nama Kepala Daerah dan Wakil Kepala Daerah Seluruh Indonesia (Names of Heads and Vice Heads of Regions for All of Indonesia) 2003." MoHA (Direktoral Pejabat Negara), Jakarta.

Murray, Christina, and Nicholas Haysom. (2003). "Political and Legal Obstacles to a Democratically Representative Council (DPD) in Indonesia." Policy Research Paper on Constitutional Reform, International Institute for Democracy and Electoral Assistance (IDEA), Jakarta.

"North Maluku Legislative Council Annuls Gafur's Election." (2001). *Jakarta Post*, October 11.

Panggabean, Adrian Toho Parada. (1997). "The Impact of the Intergovernmental Grant System on Interregional Growth and Equity: The Case of Indonesia." Department of Development Administration, University of Birmingham, Birmingham, Alabama.

Paul, Samuel. (2002). *Holding the State to Account: Citizen Monitoring in Action*. Bangalore, India: Books for Change.

Podger, Owen. (2000). "Comments on Government Regulation 108/2000 on the Form of Accountability of the Head of Region." Discussion Paper 32, ADB Capacity Building to Support Decentralized Adminsitrative Systems, Jakarta.

Quinn, George. (2003). "Coming Apart and Staying Together at the Centre: Debates over Provincial Status in Java and Madura." In Edward Aspinall and Greg Fealy (Eds.), *Who Are the Orang Riau? Negotiating Identity across Geographic and Ethnic Divides* (pp. 164–178). Singapore: Institute of Southeast Asian Studies.

Rohde, David. (2001). "Indonesia Unraveling?" *Foreign Affairs* (July/August).

Schiller, A. Arthur. (1955). *The Formation of Federal Indonesia, 1945–1949*. The Hague: W. van Hoeve.

Slinko, Irina, Evgeny Yakovlev, and Ekaterina Zhravskaya. (2003). "Institutional Subversion: Evidence from Russian Regions." Working Paper, Center for Economic and Financial Research (CEFIR), Moscow.

"Supreme Court Judge Confirms Revocation of pp 110/2000." *GTZ Decentralization News* 42, March 28.

Suryadinata, Leo. (2002). *Elections and Politics in Indonesia*. Singapore: Institute for Southeast Asian Studies.

Treisman, Daniel. (2000). "Decentralization and the Quality of Government." Mimeo, University of California, Los Angeles.

Turner, Mark, and Owen Podger. (2003). *Decentralisation in Indonesia: Redesigning the State*. Manila: Asian Development Bank.

World Bank. (2001). *Engendering Development: Through Gender Equality in Rights, Resources, and Voice*. New York: Oxford University Press.

World Bank. (2003). "Decentralizing Indonesia: A Regional Public Expenditure Overview Report." Report No. 26191-IND, World Bank East Asia Poverty Reduction and Economic Management Unit, Washington, DC.

World Bank. (2004a). "Development Spending in the Regions." World Bank Office Jakarta (Jasmin Chakeri and Blane Lewis), Jakarta.

World Bank. (2004b). "World Development Report 2004: Making Services Work for Poor People." World Bank, Washington, DC.

4 Decentralizing Bolivia: Local Government in the Jungle

Jean-Paul Faguet

Introduction

Does decentralization change policy outputs at the local level, and if it does, are the changes for better or worse? Do such changes reflect deep changes in the policy-making process itself, or are they related to technical parameters in the flow of funds? Why do some local governments respond well to decentralization while others respond badly? These are some of the most important questions surrounding the issue of decentralization, which—as Bardhan and Mookherjee point out in chapter 1—remain open despite a large related literature. This chapter seeks to answer some of these questions for the remarkable case of Bolivia, through a blend of econometric analysis at the national level and detailed qualitative research into local political and institutional processes. I argue that the "outputs" of decentralization are simply the aggregate of local-level political and institutional dynamics, and so to understand decentralization requires first understanding how local government works. This chapter examines what decentralization did at the national level and then digs into local government processes to understand how this was done. Employing a blended qualitative-quantitative approach allows us to benefit from econometric rigor and generality as well as from the deep insights of qualitative approaches, which in the best circumstances allow a researcher to choose among competing theories and pin down causality. Focusing on one country avoids problems of data comparability and controls for external shocks, political regime, institutions, and other exogenous factors. Bolivia is particularly deserving of study because reform there consisted of a large change in policy at a discrete point in time. The data available are of surprising scope and quality for a country of its socioeconomic characteristics, and they include information on the political, social and civic, economic, institutional, and administrative characteristics of all of Bolivia's municipalities. They beg to be exploited.

I define *decentralization* as the devolution by central (that is, national) government of specific functions—with all of the administrative, political, and economic attributes that these entail—to democratic local (that is, municipal) governments that are independent of the center within a legally delimited geographic and functional domain. The rest of the chapter is organized as follows. Bolivia's decentralization program is reviewed with a focus on its legal and budgetary aspects and a summarized analysis of the economic outcomes of decentralization. The second, qualitative half of the chapter examines local government in detail in Baures and Guayaramerín, two lowland municipalities in Bolivia's tropical northeast. The governance process in each is analyzed in terms of its local economy, local politics, and civil society. A conceptual model of local government is based on these fundamental concepts, and this analysis is connected to the broad trends in Bolivian public investment postdecentralization.

Decentralization in Bolivia

Historical Context

On the eve of revolution, Bolivia was a poor, backward country with a repressive state and extreme levels of inequality (Klein, 1993). The nationalist revolution of 1952 expropriated the "commanding heights" of the economy and launched a state-led strategy to create a modern, industrial, egalitarian society by breaking down provincial fiefdoms and transforming social relations (Dunkerley, 1984). To this end, revolutionaries built a monolithic state in which power and control cascaded downward from the presidential palace to the farthest corners of this large country.

Forty years of military coups, combined with the intellectual trends of the 1950s through the 1970s, contributed to this centralizing tendency (Klein, 1993). Such a regime had little need for municipalities. As a result, beyond the thirty or so largest cities local government existed at best in name as an honorary and ceremonial institution, devoid of administrative capability and starved for funds. And in most of Bolivia, it did not exist at all.

Although the 1994 reform was sprung on an unsuspecting nation, the concept of decentralization was by no means new. For more than thirty years, a decentralization debate focused on Bolivia's nine departments ebbed and flowed politically—at times taking on burning importance, at other times all but forgotten. The issue became caught up in the country's centrifugal tensions, as regional elites in Santa Cruz and Tarija manipulated the threat of secession to Brazil and Argentina, respectively—with which each is economically more integrated than with La Paz—to extract resources from the center. The Bolivian paradox of a highly centralized but weak state and a socially diverse population with weak national identity meant that such threats were taken seriously by the political class, which blocked all moves to devolve power and authority to Bolivia's regions.

So what spurred the change of tack, and why did it occur then? Two factors stand out. The less important one arises from Bolivia's failure to achieve sustained growth despite wrenching economic reform. Fifteen years of near-zero per capita growth sapped the credibility of the state and fomented social unrest. The new MNR administration of President Sánchez de Lozada saw the structure of government itself as an impediment to growth. Decentralization was an attempt to deepen structural reform to make the state more efficient and responsive to the population and so regain its legitimacy in the voters' eyes.

The more important factor is the rise of ethnic-based, populist politics in the 1980s, which undercut the MNR's traditional dominance of the rural vote and posed a serious challenge to its (self-declared) role as the "natural party of government." This rural dominance was itself born out of the MNR's agrarian reforms of the 1952 to 1953 revolution. A party with a tradition of radical reform, which found itself in secular decline, sought a second, redefining moment. In a typically bold move, it sought to reorganize government, recast the relationship between citizens and the state, and so win back the loyalty of Bolivians living outside major cities. To an important extent, decentralization was a gambit to capture rural voters for at least another generation.[1]

Reform Design: The Law of Popular Participation

Against this background, the Bolivian decentralization reform was announced in 1994. The Law of Popular Participation was developed almost in secret by a small number of technocrats in the president's office.[2] The law was announced to the nation to general surprise, followed first by ridicule and then by determined opposition by large parts of society.[3] First made public in January of that year, the law was promulgated by Congress in April and implemented in July. The scale of the change in resource flows and political power it brought about were enormous. The core of the law consists of four points (Secretaría Nacional de Participación Popular, 1994):

• *Resource allocation*   Funds devolved to municipalities doubled to 20 percent of all national tax revenue. More important, allocation among municipalities switched from unsystematic, highly political criteria to a strict per capita basis.

• *Responsibility for public services*   Ownership of local infrastructure in education, health, irrigation, roads, sports, and culture was given to municipalities, with the concomitant responsibility to maintain, equip, and administer these facilities and invest in new ones.

• *Oversight committees* (*comités de vigilancia*)   Established to provide an alternative channel for representing popular demand in the policy-making process. Composed of representatives from local, grassroots groups, these bodies propose projects and oversee municipal expenditures.

• *Municipalization*   Existing municipalities were expanded to include suburbs and surrounding rural areas, and 198 new municipalities (out of 311 in all) were created.

Before reform, local government was absent from most Bolivian territories, and the central state was present at most in the form of a military garrison, schoolhouse, or health post, each reporting to its respective ministry. After reform, elected local governments sprouted throughout the land.

The Economic Effects of Decentralization
The extent of the change is perhaps best appreciated by examining the changes in resource flows it catalyzed. Table 4.1 shows that before decentralization 308 Bolivian municipalities divided a mere 14 percent of all devolved funds, while the three main cities took 86 percent. After decentralization, their shares reversed to 73 and 27 percent, respectively. The per capita criterion resulted in a massive shift of resources in favor of smaller, poorer districts.

A more important and telling change was to the composition of investment. Figure 4.1 shows central and local government investment by sector for the periods 1991 to 1993 and 1994 to 1996. In the years leading up to reform, central government invested most in transport, hydrocarbons, multisectoral,[4] and energy, which together accounted for 73 percent of public investment during 1991 to 1993. After decen-

Table 4.1
The changing allocation of public funds

City	1993	1995	Percentage of Change 1993–1995	Percentage of Total 1993	1995
La Paz	Bs. 114,292	Bs. 61,976	−46%	51%	10%
Santa Cruz	51,278	63,076	23	23	10
Cochabamba	25,856	38,442	49	12	6
3 cities subtotal	**191,427**	**163,494**	**−15**	**86**	**27**
Rest of Bolivia	**32,099**	**444,786**	**1286**	**14**	**73**
Total	223,525	608,280	172%	100%	100%

Note: Average exchange rate is US$1 = 5 bolivianos.

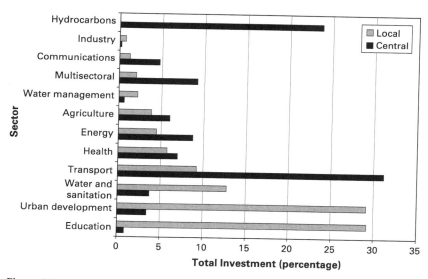

Figure 4.1
Local versus central government

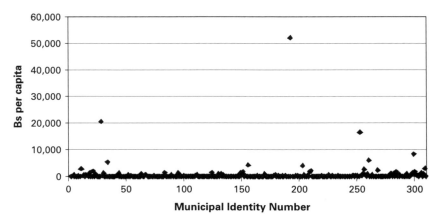

Figure 4.2
Investment per capita, 1991 to 1993

tralization, local governments invested most heavily in education, urban development, and water and sanitation, together accounting for 79 percent of municipal investment. Of the sectors accounting for roughly three-quarters of total investment in both cases, central and local government have not even one in common. The evidence implies that local and central governments have very different investment priorities.

It is also instructive to examine how investment was distributed geographically among Bolivia's municipalities before and after decentralization. Figures 4.2 to 4.4 give a rough sense of this by placing Bolivia's municipalities along the horizontal axis and measuring investment per capita as vertical displacement. A highly skewed allocation would appear as a few points strewn across the top of the graph, with most lying on the bottom; an equitable distribution would appear as a band of points at some intermediate level. What do the data show? Figure 4.2 shows that per capita investment before decentralization was indeed highly unequal, with large investments in three districts and the vast majority at or near zero. Figure 4.3 corrects for the skewing effect of the highest observations by excluding the upper twelve and showing only those below 2000 bolivianos per capita. Though the distribution now appears less unequal, there is still monotonically increasing density as we move downward, with fully one-half of all observations at zero. Investment under centralized government was thus hugely skewed in favor of a few municipalities that received enor-

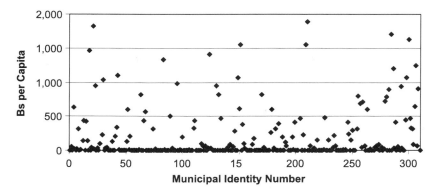

Figure 4.3
Investment per capita, 1991 to 1993 (highest 12 obs. dropped)

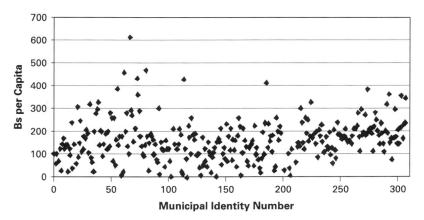

Figure 4.4
Local investment per capita, 1994 to 1996

mous sums, a second group where investment was significant, and the unfortunate half of districts that received nothing. Compare this with figure 4.4, which shows municipal investment after decentralization. This chart shows no district over Bs. 700 per capita, a broad band with greatest density between Bs. 100 to 200 per capita, and only a few points touching the axis.[5] These crude indicators imply that central government, with a much larger budget and free rein over all of Bolivia's municipalities, chose a very unequal distribution of investment across space, while decentralized government distributes public investment much more evenly throughout the country.

A third key fact comes from Faguet (2002b), who uses econometric models of public investment to show that decentralization increased government responsiveness to real local needs. After 1994, investment in education, water and sanitation, water management, and agriculture was a positive function of illiteracy rates, water and sewerage non-connection rates, and malnutrition rates, respectively. That is to say, although investment in these sectors increased throughout Bolivia after decentralization, the increase was disproportionate in those districts where the objective need for such services was greatest. I argue that these changes were driven by the actions of Bolivia's 250 smallest, poorest, mostly rural municipalities investing newly devolved public funds in their highest-priority projects.

The econometric models in (Faguet 2002b) yield a fourth notable fact: centralized investment was economically regressive, concentrating public investment in richer municipalities and ignoring poorer ones. Decentralization, by contrast, shifted resources toward poorer districts; after 1994, public investment rose in municipalities where indicators of wealth and income are lower. In short, the four key facts about decentralization in Bolivia are that it shifted public investment into social services and human capital formation, at the expense of economic production and infrastructure; distributed investment more equally across space; made investment more responsive to local needs; and shifted investment toward poorer districts.

Understanding Decentralization in Bolivia

Introduction
To say that decentralization drove these results is only to rephrase the fundamental question. How and why did decentralization achieve this? Why did central government behave so differently when all resources lay in its largely unfettered hands? To answer these questions, we must examine how local government works, as the effects of decentralization are inseparable from those of the local governments it empowers. The remainder of this chapter comprises a detailed examination of local government in two of the best and worst municipalities I was able to find in Bolivia—Baures and Guayaramerín. I focus on extremes of municipal performance to better highlight the systematic differences in decision making that characterize each, leading to their very different outcomes. The fact that both are located in the Beni department, in Bolivia's tropical northeast, strengthens the comparison.

I rely on qualitative information gathered during six months of field work in Bolivia, in a number of municipalities selected to control for size, region, economic base, rural versus urban setting, and cultural and ethnic characteristics. In each of these, I conducted extensive semi-structured and unstructured interviews of local government and community leaders, key informants, and citizens at the grassroots level. I spoke to over 300 people in more than 200 interviews, following a systematic program in which I put standard questionnaires to key local officials and central government representatives, local business and labor leaders, nongovernmental spokespeople, grassroots leaders, and ordinary citizens. Interviews were carried out in the main city or town and throughout the rural catchment area in each district. In each district, I was careful to visit a significant number of rural communities. The majority of the interviews by number (and duration) were with members and spokesmen of grassroots organizations. What follows is a highly summarized account of the findings of this research. A full account is given in Faguet (2002a).

Before commencing the analysis, it is useful to review quickly the institutional framework of local government in Bolivia. The Law of Popular Participation (LPP) stipulates that municipal councilors be elected from party lists in single-constituency elections. The council then elects the mayor indirectly from among those of them who garnered the most votes. Bolivia's fragmented political culture, grafted onto an American-style presidential system, ensures that most municipal (and national) governments are coalitions. Hereafter, this chapter uses *mayor* to refer to the mayor and executive branch of local government, including all appointed administrative and technical officials— by far the largest and most important of the three. The third institution of local government is the oversight committee (OC), which is composed of the representatives of grassroot organizations within each municipality. A municipality will typically be divided into four or more regions, each of which nominates one member to the OC from among its local grassroots leaders. OC members elect from among themselves a president, whose legal status is comparable to the mayor's. The OC's power lies in its natural moral authority, as well as the ability to suspend disbursements from central to local government if it judges that funds are being misused. Oversight committees thus comprise a parallel, corporatist form of social representation similar to an upper house of Parliament, enforcing accountability on the mayor and municipal council.

The Quality of Local Government in Baures

Top marks among civic leaders, grassroots respondents, business, union, and religious authorities, and other local notables clearly go to the youngest municipal government of the bunch, Baures. The quality of its investment projects and the public services it provides was judged good or very good by all of the respondents I spoke to, a standard that none of the others approached.[6] Its investment planning system was based on village-level assemblies that discussed and approved project requests, on which local government then based its annual operating plan (AOP). These meetings were reported to be extremely open and participatory ("even animals can attend," in the words of one respondent)[7] and won the broad approval of the local population. And the mayor and municipal council were deemed of high quality and eager to serve their jurisdiction. "Here they work well and the people are content with them," the leader of Jasiakiri said of the council. "They're with the people."[8] Several respondents from both town and countryside testified approvingly that town hall had so far favored rural farmers, "as they have the greatest needs and are in the majority here,"[9] and not cattle ranchers or miners, whose needs were less pressing. Baureños' contentment with their municipal government stood in stark contrast to their denunciation of the previous one, based in Magdalena, of which they were then a part. There was a broad consensus in Baures that Magdalena had ignored their needs and given them nothing and had run an untransparent administration that was possibly corrupt. Self-government, they testified, had solved these problems.

The Quality of Local Government in Guayaramerín

Guayaramerín presents a very different picture of governance. Most respondents testified that public investment and services in Guayaramerín were regular or bad. Planning procedures were dominated by municipal staff and closed to popular input. While some projects did originate in community ideas, others did not, and communities had little or no say in project planning or execution and no recourse for altering official plans. One technical officer in the municipality of Guayaramerín told me, "We reformulate the AOP as we see fit. We don't consult grassroots organizations because they bitch too much. We know we should, but we don't."[10]

Luckily for Guayaramerín's authorities, public opinion had not yet boiled over. In particular, in the city, in the wake of a previous mayor widely considered corrupt and ineffective, people suspended judgment as they waited to see what the current one might accomplish. Further out, however, rural community leaders attacked the mayor for grossly favoring the city at their expense. The municipal councils was widely held in very low esteem as a politicized, unresponsive institution, and councilors were generally considered corrupt. "The municipal council," observed the director of the Guayaramerín Hospital, "is worthless."[11]

Economics, Politics, and Society

Given a single reform program and the same institutional framework for local government nationwide, how can we explain such large differences in local government effectiveness? As I have said elsewhere (Faguet, 2005), an explanation of local government performance based on the quality of its institutions focuses only on proximate causes. More fundamental causes lie deep in the interactions of the local economy, political dynamics, and social structure of each municipality. Understanding these is the key to understanding *how* local government occurs and *why* it is good or bad in different places. We take each factor in turn.

The Local Economy

Baures is a farming community. The mainstay of its inhabitants is twofold—subsistence or near-subsistence agriculture on family plots and a cattle economy of 35,000 head. The few large farms in the district belong to ranchers based in La Paz, Santa Cruz, and Trinidad, and remaining ranchers are medium-sized to small.[12] Baures once had large landowners whose farm workers were virtual slaves.[13] But they entered decline in the 1970s and eventually died out. Partly as a result, land is not a source of social conflict. In a sparsely populated district, land is in abundance, is easily available, and has little competition for it.[14] The town primarily supports the farming economy through commerce and agricultural services and is essentially devoid of all other industry.

By contrast, Guayaramerín consists of a highly urbanized municipality with an extensive rural hinterland that, alone among our group, comprises a single agribusiness economy. It has the transport and trade-based economy of a frontier town but also benefits from large agricultural enterprises, including almond, Brazil nut, and heart-of-palm packagers and exporters, cattle ranchers, loggers and timber merchants, and a significant retail sector that exploits exchange-rate movements between the boliviano and the Brazilian real. This last spans the barrier of legality, running to drugs and contraband. The nature of these businesses implies that the urban and rural economies are intertwined: wealthy businessmen have large rural landholdings and employ many villagers, and the economic conditions that large and small actors face—given weather, disease, and infrastructure among others—are often the same. But this economy is dominated by a small group of powerful businessmen who collectively own much of the local economy and all of its large businesses. Some of the strongest among them are timber merchants and cattle ranchers, who also control the local political parties and through them local government, to which we return below. The most important two, Cacho and Gigi, were locked in a battle for influence that is typical of the dominance of the business elite to which they belong. Hernán "Cacho" Vargas Rivera is the most powerful businessman in Guayaramerín, with Brazil nut, heart-of-palm, and river and land transport companies, two television stations, and 140,000 hectares of land in Pando.[15] His rival, Adrián "Gigi" Rivera, is a hotel owner, president of the local electricity cooperative, and money lender at rates of 5 to 7 percent per month.[16] Their names came up often in my interviews throughout the district when respondents were asked "Quien manda?" ("Who runs the show?"). While Cacho attempted to gain control of municipal policy via the local Acción Democrática Nacionalista (ADN) party, which he leads, Gigi refused to lend the electricity cooperative $37,000 unless the municipality agreed to assume the debt, thus ensnaring it in his web. Though Cacho raged against this "scandal," he also admitted that, in his view, "the municipality has become an instrument" of powerful interests in Guayaramerín.[17]

Local Politics
Baures had a fully competitive party regime, where clearly delineated governing and opposition alliances existed that mirrored at least in form the national pattern of politics. Local government was in the hands of an ADN-MIR coalition, and the MNR was in opposition. Indeed, although politics in such a small population had an undeniably cozy air, and politicians knew each other and their families personally and well, politics was quite competitive in Baures, with rival blocs vying to unseat each other in local elections. "There's a lot of politics in this town," said one observer, referring to how party loyalties ran

deep in local society. "Yesterday the people [at the village festival] were absolutely divided by political party, each off to one side."[18] Not surprisingly, Baures had a low rate of electoral absenteeism: 24 percent. Perhaps as a result, politics was not dominated by powerful economic or other interests but was open to all and represented a broad range of views. Indeed, in the previous election the MNR had coopted the indigenous vote by naming a *Baureño* to its party list.[19] And unlike other municipalities, municipal councilors did not cover up each other's transgressions; thus two MNR councilors from the 1995 election had not yet been recognized, pending allegations against them from the previous government. But despite political competition that was often sharp, politicians managed to work relatively smoothly together, and it is telling that Baures's worst political conflict during this period came from the outside. This happened when the (MNR) prefect unilaterally donated a generator belonging to the town of Baures to nearby El Cairo when the latter's, used to pump water, broke down. The municipal council and oversight committee intervened at the scene of a public commotion and prevented him from doing so.[20] Their action was widely applauded throughout the district, even in the village of El Cairo.[21]

Guayaramerín, by contrast, suffered high rates of absenteeism and endemic interest-group capture. Money politics dominated. Prominent businesspeople—the spiritual descendants of the cattle barons of the past—were firmly in control of the major political parties and through them local government, using their resources to fight elections and expedite their political strategies. And once in power, officials and their businesses profited from the contracts, contacts, and policy-making powers that local government afforded to further their business interests. Thus when the MNR sought to prevent the reelection of Guayaramerín's long-time ADN mayor, who had won the popular vote,[22] it offered the MBL councilor $30,000 for his vote. This councilor, a former priest of modest means, used the money to buy a local television station and so became one of Guayaramerín's media magnates.[23] His vote elevated a prominent logging and timber merchant to the mayoralty of a district that contained large tropical forests. But it is notable that these political dealings occurred among individuals much more than among parties. Political alliances were much the same. Indeed, during my stay the mayor and senior ADN councilor inaugurated a new coalition between their respective parties with a karaoke duet in a local nightclub. This broke up the previous MNR-MBL pact. But the local ADN chief was unconvinced. "Ivan [the ADN councilor] and Tico [the mayor] don't seem to belong to any party anymore. They're just looking to accommodate themselves."[24] Political competition in Guayaramerín was the province of narrow interests—that is, individual businesspeople—vying for control over the machinery of government and its policy making. It was not a broader contest of ideas or ideologies, and in it broad collective interests were essentially unrepresented. Once elected, Guayaramerín's politicians were content to find an accommodation and did little to oversee or discipline each other's activity. The fact that they were friends and members of the same restricted social set greatly facilitated this process. The fate of the previous mayor, widely accused of embezzlement but never investigated by the municipal council on which he still sat, was illustrative.[25]

In a political system in which accountability did not obtain, voters not surprisingly reported a loss of faith in government and a loss of interest in politics. "The people here feel that their vote has no value," added an observer in Guayaramerín. "It's all cooked between them [politicians], so why vote?"[26] This worsened the problem of absenteeism, which in turn made it easier for elites to perpetuate themselves and decreased their accountability—a vicious cycle that was potentially difficult to break.

Civil Society
With five rural and three urban GROs, Baures comprised a compact society where whites lived largely in town, indigenous people in the countryside, and mestizos in both. The district had some 720 indigenous residents (self-identified), and people of mixed race made up the majority. But the social implications of this ethnic diversity were less than elsewhere in Bolivia due to the greater degree of assimilation by *Baureño* natives and mestizos. In linguistic terms, for example, 93 percent of Baures's people spoke only Spanish, 5 percent Spanish plus a native tongue, and 0.1 percent a native tongue only; this compares starkly with Bolivian averages of 32 percent, 19 percent, and 43 percent, respectively.[27] *Baureños'* dress was essentially Western dress, largely free of distinguishing features such as the multilayered skirts and bowler hats of the altiplano, and mixed *Baureño*-Spanish surnames abounded, indicating a high rate of intermarriage. Consistent with this, observers reported smooth social relations among these groups and described Baures as "pacific." "Here everyone gets along well," said

the nuns from CETHA. "All participate equally in each others' feast days."[28] Indeed, the controversy surrounding the generator and the prefect "was the first time since 1704 that there was a commotion in the town," the head of one GRO reported.[29]

Good social relations can be explained partly by the similar economic interests of its citizens, whether indigenous, mestizo, or white. As explained above, Baures comprised a single agricultural and cattle economy devoid of industry, lacking in trade, where small and medium-sized landowners prevailed. Town and countryside faced similar economic incentives, and when the countryside prospered, the town did too. There was thus an encompassing interest in Baures and one that expressed itself in a context of social harmony using a common language, Spanish. This bred a similarity of outlook that transcended politics and reached down into the social realm; as their goals were similar, the social organizations they employed to advance them were similar too. Rural and urban communities alike described their communities as "grassroots organizations" (*organizaciones territoriales de base*, or OTBs) using the language of the 1994 LPP reform, so eschewing the opposition between "indigenous/original communities" and urban "neighborhood councils" common in the rest of Bolivia. We might expect trust to flourish in such a context, and in Baures it did. "The distribution of money is much better now," said the head of Jasiakiri's GRO, explaining that his community was willing to forego investments in one year so that resources might flow to other communities. "Now communities take turns to receive investment. It's good this way."[30] This leader valued cooperation as such, illustrating an attitude that was common throughout the district.

With high levels of trust, a clear encompassing interest, and social relations that were close and smooth, Baures's civil society boasted a high level of institutional coherence and the ability to involve the people in their local government. Its geography may well help to explain these characteristics. Isolated by large plains that flooded half the year, its only reliable link to the rest of Bolivia was by air. With only 5,133 inhabitants and outside Bolivia's main west-east migratory flows, it comprised a microsociety with its own rules, traditions, and social patterns of interaction. It was a stable population that changed little from year to year, and its inhabitants knew that conflicts with their neighbors would not go unnoticed or become much diluted. With only the most limited of outside recourse, *Baureños* got along because they had to.

Guayaramerín was made up of eight rural and two urban GROs, and though 85 percent of its population claimed Spanish as their language, many also understood Portuguese. It had the typically mixed population of a thriving border town. But uncharacteristically, Guayaramerín was the product of a migratory boom that multiplied its population thirteen times during the previous half century.[31] As a result it was a relatively new town, the sum of many cultures and ethnic groups, with relatively little unity among its diverse population. "There is mutual tolerance here," said Sister Ana of Caritas, "but the people don't relate much among themselves. Each group celebrates its own feast day."[32] It was also a "very complex society" where enormous wealth rubbed shoulders with abject poverty[33] and drugs, prostitution, and alcoholism abounded.[34] New social organizations were slow to form in a context of high demographic flux, which provided local politicians with a valuable opportunity. When community groups finally did organize, it was at the instigation of local government. But rather than catalyze the sort of social self-organization that has been the rule throughout Bolivia, the government of Guayaramerín provided a channel for political parties to penetrate a weak and easily divisible civil society during GRO formation and so colonize civic institutions for political ends.[35] According to the secretary of the Chamber of Commerce,

The GROs are terrible here.... They're totally politicized. They make midnight deals in search of payoffs.... GROs don't consult their members before making decisions. Rather, the leaders meet with the parties, receive money, and then commit their misdeeds.[36]

By falling under the sway of the parties, GROs became complicit in the endemic corruption of Guayaramerín's local government. Such collusion was both a symptom of and contributing factor to the lack of social mobilization in Guayaramerín. Had organized civil society preceded politics, it might not have been coopted so easily nor so thoroughly, by the parties. Instead, GROs became political franchises that stifled civic participation in government. "The people are like children here," the Primero de Mayo community explained. "They receive misery [from local government] and are happy with that."[37] Lacking an autochthonous organization and excluded by their civic leaders, the people of Guayaramerín lay dormant before the government they had elected.

Guayaramerín, where urban and rural sectors were intertwined in a modern agribusiness economy, benefited from an encompassing interest. This gave city and countryside a common outlook and facilitated collective action for the progress of the municipality. "The development of this town has been through the money of its own citizens," reported the parish priest. "They pooled their efforts to form their own water, telephone, and other cooperatives" to provide basic services and improve the local standard of living.[38] These efforts were spearheaded by the city's well-organized business elite, which formed a powerful, all-party, pro-Guayaramerín lobby. They benefited from growth throughout the district and favored a comprehensive local development. If public services were better in richer than poorer areas, this was due as much to the financial constraints of cooperatives in a context of rapid population growth as to discrimination by the governing class.

Regarding trust, Guayaramerín's migrant peoples were simply too diverse and too unaccustomed to each other for trust to blossom among them. And the politicization of its civic institutions served to replace the logic of cooperation that operates at their core with a logic of (political) competition. Thus, on the few occasions when the practice of local government brought Guayaramerín's social groups into contact, it was not so much to organize collective action as to do battle on behalf of their political patrons. A process that might otherwise have promoted trust served instead to undermine it further. And a latent and potentially powerful encompassing interest was ultimately undone through the active subversion of society's organizational structure by political parties intent on partisan gain.

Theorizing Local Government[39]

Analytical Concepts

Now abstract away from the experiences of Baures and Guayaramerín to consider the processes by which local governance is produced. I take the three factors—economy, politics, and society—in turn. What is the role of the *local economy* in producing good or bad local governance? The striking contrast between Baures and Guayaramerín suggests a political version of economic orthodoxy in which open and competitive markets lead to the efficient allocation of resources. Parties— especially opposition parties—require resources to sustain themselves and to campaign. Where a municipality's economy is dominated by an economic hegemon, that hegemon will tend to reduce political competition by financing a favored party and may well abuse its position in other ways to hinder its political rivals. Thus, monopsony in the provision of political funds will tend to lead to monopoly in the party system. Such a reduction in political competition will reduce the level of oversight that local government institutions are subjected to as a by-product of political competition and may well leave sectors of the population unrepresented and effectively disenfranchised. An open and competitive local economy, by contrast, promotes competition in politics, leading to an increased diversity of ideas and policy proposals that compete for public favor as well as improved public accountability for government officials. Where an economic hegemon and a dominant political party actively collude, the effects can be multiplicative. Together they can distort the local party system, capture the institutions of government, and deform the governance process to their own ends.

With respect to the *local political system*, our comparison suggests that effective local governance requires a vigorous local politics in which competition spurs political entrepreneurship and policy innovation as parties vie to win new voters. The analysis above indicates two conditions necessary for such a local politics to obtain: an open and transparent electoral system that both promotes and is (indirectly) sustained by a competitive party regime. These combine naturally to produce a third, endogenous requirement of good local politics: a substantive focus on local issues and local people. Systemic electoral reforms that increase the transparency and ease of voting serve to increase participation by making voting both feasible and fair. Voters who are able to reach a polling center and cast a vote will be more likely to do so the less likely it is that results will be misrepresented or distorted by local interests. Reforms that promote all of these things encourage citizens to express their political preferences freely, both inside and outside the voting booth. This in turn raises the electoral return to parties that actively canvass local opinions and propose policies that respond to changing voter needs. Policy innovation of this sort can be termed *political entrepreneurship*.

But a competitive party system must be in place if the full beneficial effects of systemic opening are to occur. Political entrepreneurship that attempts to offer dissatisfied voters a political alternative will be thwarted by a party regime that is monopolized by one actor. In a way that is, again, closely analogous to the working of competitive markets, a competitive political environment will encourage policy entrepreneurs to innovate in the hopes of capturing electoral share from their rivals. Party systems that are characterized by multiple participants and free entry and that feature political agents who succeed or fail based on their ability to attract votes will tend to serve the welfare of their constituents better than those dominated by a single actor and hence by a narrower range of policy options. And a competitive local economy, as discussed above, will tend to promote a competitive political system.

The third key element in the local governance process is *civil society*. For civil society to provide useful oversight and a feedback mechanism for the governing process, it must be able to accomplish a limited but important set of tasks. First, it must be able to identify a specific failing of local policy at the community level. It must then formulate a coherent demand or complaint and transmit it upward through, typically, two or three of its own hierarchical levels. Finally, local civic leaders must be able to take up this complaint and communicate it convincingly to the mayor or municipal council. Such abilities are not culturally or organizationally specific, and thus a wide variety of societies are likely to have them. But they will all share four general traits that facilitate these tasks. The first is simply the ability to communicate, often across large areas and diverse ethnic groups. The second is norms of trust and responsibility, both within communities and across them (including leaders in the seat of government), as well as across time. Where community leaders do not comply with their duties of leadership and advocacy, government will not reap the information it needs to right policy mistakes. Communities must then trust leaders further up the hierarchy to accurately represent their interests before government, and leaders must trust that their information is correct. And civic leaders at the municipal level must then actively pursue communities' demands if government is to be held socially accountable for its policies at the community level.

The third trait is a minimum level of human capital among civic leaders such that those at the municipal level are able to interact productively with local government. This involves both cooperating with elected officials to advance policy goals and opposing their decisions in such a way as to modify their actions. The last trait, and often the most difficult to achieve in Bolivia, is a minimum level of resources required to carry out these activities. Even if civic officials are unpaid, there remain unavoidable and nontrivial transaction costs associated with their activities. Communities in Bolivia have for the most part longstanding traditions of reciprocal generosity that cover the transactions costs of community self-government. But the extension of these social institutions to the municipal level has in many places strained such finances beyond the breaking point.

A Model of Local Government

Local government is a hybrid. Its function is to produce local services and policies at the intersection of two market relationships and one organizational dynamic. Hence, local government occurs at the confluence of two distinct forms of social interaction. Political parties and politicians are at the center of both market relationships. The first of these occurs between parties and individual voters. This can be thought of as the primary, or retail, political market in which parties exchange ideas and declarations of principle for votes; parties compete with promises and ideas to attract voters, who vote for the party or candidate that inspires the most confidence. The second market connects parties to private firms, producer associations, and other economic and issue-oriented interest groups. This can be thought of as a secondary, or wholesale, political market in which specific policies or entire policy bundles, as well as broader influence over legislators and the policy-making process, are sold to interest groups in exchange for money. For simplicity, I assume from here onward that civic organizations do not engage in this market; the assumption is supported by evidence from all nine case studies. The first of these relationships is intrinsic to the process of representative democracy. The second is derivative but compelling, arising from political parties' need to fund election campaigns and sustain party operations.

It is important to emphasize the distinction between politicians or parties and government institutions: it is politicians and not governments who compete for votes in elections; likewise, it is not governments who sell influence in exchange for campaign and political funds but the parties and politicians who control them. I follow Downs in defining *party* as "a team seeking to control the governing apparatus by gaining office in a duly constituted election." This raises a wealth of complex ethical issues concerning the mechanics of political finance and the limits of official responsibility. For purposes of the analysis that follows, I sidestep these issues by assuming that elected politicians engage in this secondary market *as politicians* and not as governing officials, observing the organizational and behavioral constraints necessary to ensure this is so. The fact that such constraints are regularly violated in practice does not contradict the logic of the argument or its generality.

The second form of social interaction in local government involves civil society conceived as a collectivity or set of collectivities—as opposed to atomized individuals—and their relationship with the institutions of government. Where governance is concerned local civil society operates like a complex of organizations, aggregating preferences and representing communities' needs, mediating community participation in the production of certain services, facilitating social expression and the assertion of local identity, and enforcing political accountability on the institutions of government. It is not useful to conceive of it as a quasi-market, either internally or in its dealings with government, as its dynamics are not founded on buying and selling. It is rather a set of social organizations that develop their own norms of behavior and responsibility organically and over time may develop stores of trust and credibility that may or may not enhance capacity. Local government depends on the relationships that collectively comprise civil society to elicit information necessary to the policy-making process, judge the efficacy of previous interventions, and plan for the future. Politicians also depend on these relationships to gauge public satisfaction with their performance between elections. The organizational dynamic of civil society is thus intrinsic to the process of local governance. Figure 4.5 illustrates how civil society combines with the political markets described above to give rise to local government. In this diagram, the political parties that are most successful in competing for votes and resources win control of government institutions. These institutions then enter into a separate, more complex interaction with civic organizations that features varying degrees of feedback and social participation.

For local government to be effective, the market relationships and logic of social representation described above must counterbalance each other, and none must dominate the others. A stable tension between the three elements creates a self-limiting dynamic in which the impulses and imperatives of interest groups can be contained within the bounds of political competition and do not spill into the machinery of government or erupt as civil strife. This is equivalent to allowing the economic, political, and civic conditions outlined in the model above to obtain. Breaking this tension, on the other hand, can hobble government. Where the market for votes is weak or missing, government will tend to be undemocratic; where the economic market for political influence is weak, government may be insensitive to economic conditions; and where society's civic organizations are weak, government will be lacking in information, oversight, and accountability. In the interplay

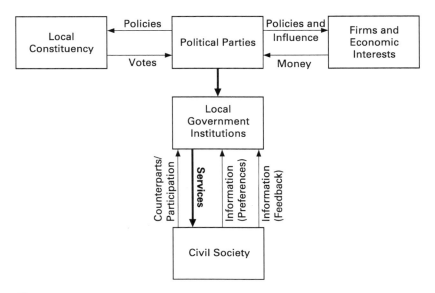

Figure 4.5
A model of local government

between these, the market for influence has the advantage of being a continuous process of exchange in which the priorities of economic interests are constantly brought to policy makers' attention. By contrast, the electoral dynamic is binding on local governors only intermittently at elections. This lower periodicity is balanced, however, by the severity of the potential consequences—the ejection of politicians from power. These imperatives are therefore roughly balanced.

Under usual circumstances, as discussed above, civil society is at a comparative disadvantage. Despite having the most pervasive network of the three, the instruments that civic leaders can deploy to influence policy define the extremes of costs and consequences. They carry in one hand the relatively inexpensive lever of public complaint and admonishment, including encouraging the grassroots to vote in a particular way. But experience indicates that this tool is weak against well-financed politicians with strong incentives to continue along a particular course. In its other hand, society carries the threat of demonstrations and civil disobedience, culminating in civil revolt. This instrument is powerful indeed but also very costly to deploy and is an effective threat only when levels of social discontent have passed a given, relatively high threshold. The genius of Bolivian decentralization was to include civil society directly in the local governance process via oversight committees, thus making accountability an explicit and continuous process. Bolivian society now has a third instrument at its disposal: the ability to freeze all central disbursements to municipalities—and thus effectively cripple the vast majority of the country's districts—if it is dissatisfied with local policy. This, along with the direct insertion of the OC into the policy-making process, gives it a permanent voice and continuous participation in how it is governed. It allows public problems to be identified at an incipient stage before discontent rises dangerously. It also levels the playing field between the competing logics of market and representation that are intrinsic to local government. But in doing so, it increases the premium on social trust and responsibility and the coherence of social organizations, which enable civil organizations to effectively represent their interests before government.

Conclusion

It is now time to stand back and consider what decentralization achieved in Bolivia. Detailed empirical evidence shows that decentralization made public investment more responsive to the real local needs of Bolivia's citizens and shifted resources toward poorer, mostly rural districts. As a result, public investment became much more equal across space, and investment shifted massively away from economic infrastructure in favor of social services and human capital. These results are impressive and do much to recommend reform to us. But *how* did decentralization achieve this?

Quantitative approaches are unsuited to a nuanced examination of such issues, and so in the second part of the chapter I turn to a qualitative analysis of one of the best and one of the worst municipalities I encountered during extended fieldwork in Bolivia. In little Baures, the institutions of government—mayor, municipal council, and oversight committee—operated transparently, boasting regular consultations with the populace and an easy openness to citizens and their concerns. In Guayaramerín, by contrast, power was openly bought and sold, and the institutions of local government were populated and dominated by a tiny clique of businesspeople who attended to themselves first, second, and third.

Based on this evidence, I develop a conceptual model of local government that construes local government as the nexus of two political quasi-markets and one organizational dynamic, where votes, money, influence, and information are freely exchanged. For local government to be effective, these three relationships must counterbalance each other, and none must dominate the other. Such a stable tension leads to a self-limiting dynamic where pressures from various interest groups are contained within the bounds of political competition.

Now, reconstruct Bolivia's decentralization story from the ground up. Decentralization created hundreds of local governments throughout the country. These proved more sensitive to local conditions and more accessible to lobbying and grassroots pressure than a central administration that simply abandoned large expanses of territory as convenience dictated. The superior responsiveness of local government is a product of the structure of local governance in which power and influence are nurtured and ultimately channeled by voting and information. Indeed, the effectiveness of decentralization as policy reform is largely the result of enabling such local government dynamics throughout the country, where previously no policy making took place. In so doing, decentralization engaged thousands of neighborhood councils, peasant communities, *ayllus*, and *mallkus*, as well as interest groups and business associations that previously had no voice in how their communities were run. By locating real resources and political power in municipal institutions, it reached out to rich and poor strata alike, offering them the means to improve their lives and a concrete incentive to participate.

And throughout Bolivia the people did participate. Their energies were channeled in positive ways that improved the quality of the nation's public investments. Of course, there were bad Guayaramerins alongside the good Baureses. But the Baureses were legion, and their effects were much greater.

This study has ultimately been about the possibility of change, and its message is hopeful. The reform of institutions and their associated incentives can bring about significant, nationwide changes in social and political behavior in the space of a few years. The Bolivian experiment argues against Putnamite assertions that policy performance is determined by thousand-year historical conditioning. When reform creates the opportunity to establish social organizations that improve group welfare, people can rise to the challenge and succeed. This includes the very poor and oppressed. The conditions necessary for reform to prosper are a complex of economic, political, and social characteristics and may well be lacking as often as they are present. But under the right circumstances, decentralizing resources and political authority can generate real accountability where none existed before and improve the quality of government a society achieves.

Acknowledgments

I am grateful for financial support from the World Bank Research Committee, the Economic and Social Research Council, the Crisis States Programme, and the London School of Economics' William Robson Memorial Prize. I am indebted to Tim Besley, Teddy Brett, and Paul Seabright for extensive criticisms and advice. I also wish to thank Pranab Bardhan, Shanta Devarajan, James Dunkerley, Armando Godínez, Dilip Mookherjee, François Ortalo-Magné, James Robinson, Fabio Sánchez, and seminar participants at the Development Studies Institute, the World Bank, and the Initiative for Policy Dialogue for their thoughtful comments and suggestions. All remaining errors are my own.

Notes

1. At the time, MNR strategists gleefully predicted such a result. They were proved wrong.

2. D. Tuchschneider, World Bank rural development officer, interview, La Paz, February 14, 1997.

3. "Injertos Tramposos en 'Participación Popular,'" *Hoy*, January 19, 1994; "La Declaratoria de Guerra del Primer Mandatario," *La Razon*, January 27, 1994; and "Arrogancia Insultante," *Presencia*, February 27, 1994, are only three of the many articles that appeared in the Bolivian press documenting popular reaction to the "Damned Law." These are documented in Unidad de Comunicación (1995).

4. This hodgepodge—including feasibility studies, technical assistance, and emergency relief—is difficult to categorize.

5. Investment sums here are much lower because they exclude central government funds.

6. All respondents were asked to rate public investment projects and the quality of local public services on the following scale: very bad, bad, regular, good, very good.

7. Oscar Durán, neighborhood council president, interview, Baures, May 2, 1997.

8. Juan Jahnsen, Jasiakiri community leader, interview, El Cairo, May 3, 1997.

9. Hugo Melgar Barbery and Erland Ayllón Parada, municipal council president (MIR) and member (independent, ex-MNR), interview, Baures, May 2, 1997.

10. Alberto Albert, municipal technical advisor and former municipal council president, interview, Guayaramerín, October 20, 1997.

11. Gabriel Sosa Salvatierra, hospital director, interview, Guayaramerín, October 22, 1997.

12. Hugo Ayllón Parada, Cattlemen's Association president, interview, Baures, May 2, 1997; Grover Martínez Franco, mayor, interview, Baures, May 2, 1997. I adhere to local definitions, where large is more than 1,000 head of cattle, medium is 300 to 600, and small is fewer than 300.

13. Jahnsen, note 8.

14. Ayllón Parada, note 12.

15. Hernán Vargas Rivera, agroindustrialist, television station owner, and ADN chief, interview, Guayaramerín, October 21, 1997.

16. Adrián Rivera, electricity cooperative president, money lender, and hotel owner, interview, Guayaramerín, October 21, 1997. The only bank in Guayaramerín is a branch of BIDESA, which dispenses local salaries but does not lend.

17. Vargas Rivera, note 15.

18. Sisters Pilar and Teresa and Oscar Velázquez, professor, CETHA, interview, Baures, May 4, 1997. CETHA is a church-supported institution specializing in adult education.

19. Juan Oni Antelo, municipal councilor (MNR), interview, Baures, May 2, 1997.

20. Melgar Barbery and Ayllón Parada, note 9.

21. Jahnsen, note 8.

22. Guido Roca.

23. Vargas Rivera, note 15. Cacho owned Guayaramerín's two other television stations.

24. Vargas Rivera, note 15.

25. Vargas Rivera, note 15. "Tilly" Rodríguez was widely denounced by people throughout Guayaramerín.

26. Sister Ana López, director of Caritas (NGO), interview, Guayaramerín, October 22, 1997.

27. 1992 census.

28. Pilar, Teresa, and Velázquez, note 18.

29. Oscar Durán, president of the Nicolás Carageorge neighborhood council, interview, Baures, May 2, 1997.

30. Jahnsen, note 8.

31. Sosa Salvatierra, note 11. According to him, the city's population rose from 3,000 to 38,000 over fifty-four years.

32. López, note 26.

33. López, note 26.

34. Fr. Julio Corredor, parish priest, interview, Guayaramerín, October 19, 1997.

35. Manlio Roca, port (customs) manager, former mayor and former member of Parliament, interview, Guayaramerín, October 21, 1997.

36. Elío Simoni Casangeli, Chamber of Industry and Commerce secretary, interview, Guayaramerín, October 21, 1997.

37. Dionisia Cuéllar Pérez, Emilse Choquere, and Santiago Méndez, community officers, interview, May 1 and October 23, 1997.

38. Corredor, note 33.

39. The arguments in this section are based on Faguet (2005).

References

Dunkerley, J. (1984). *Rebellion in the Veins: Political Struggle in Bolivia 1952–82.* London: Verso.

Faguet, J. P. (2002a). "Decentralizing the Provision of Public Services in Bolivia: Institutions, Political Competition and the Effectiveness of Local Government." Ph.D. dissertation, London School of Economics.

Faguet, J. P. (2002b). "The Determinants of Central vs. Local Government Investment: Institutions and Politics Matter." DESTIN Working Paper No. 02-38, London School of Economics. Available at ⟨http://www.lse.ac.uk/Depts/destin/workpapers/determinants-of-central.pdf⟩.

Faguet, J. P. (2005). "Governance from Below: A Theory of Local Government with Two Empirical Tests." STICERD Political Economy & Public Policy Discussion Paper No. 12.

Klein, H. (1993). *Historia de Bolivia.* La Paz: Libreria-Editorial Juventud.

Secretaría Nacional de Participación Popular, Ministerio de Desarrollo Sostenible y Medio Ambiente. (1994). *Ley de Participación Popular, Reglamento de las Organizaciones Territoriales de Base.* La Paz.

Unidad de Comunicación, Secretaría Nacional de Participación Popular. (1995). *Debate Nacional sobre la Ley de Participación Popular.* La Paz: Secretaría Nacional de Participación Popular.

5

What Difference Does a Constitutional Amendment Make? The 1994 Panchayati Raj Act and the Attempt to Revitalize Rural Local Government in India

Shubham Chaudhuri

If at the level of center-state relations the constitution gave us democracy, at the level of state-panchayat relations the constitution gave us bureaucracy.

—E. M. S. Namboodiripad,
Former chief minister, Government of Kerala

Introduction

The passage of the seventy-third and seventy-fourth constitutional amendments in 1994 has been hailed as a landmark in the evolution of local governments in India. The amendments provided rural and urban local governments with a constitutional status that they had previously lacked and reinforced this status by mandating regular elections to locally elected bodies. Further, the amendments mandated reservations of positions in these local bodies for women and for individuals from two traditionally disadvantaged (and constitutionally recognized) groups: Dalits (scheduled castes, which are castes at the bottom of or, more accurately, excluded from the traditional Hindu caste hierarchy) and Adivasis (scheduled tribes, which are the indigenous populations of the Indian subcontinent). Beyond this, the amendments called on (but did not explicitly require) individual states, the highest tier of subnational government within India's federal system, to enact legislation to devolve powers and resources to local bodies to enable the latter to function as institutions of self-government—to play a central role in the provision of public services, the creation and maintenance of local public goods, and the planning and implementation of developmental activities and programs to alleviate poverty and promote distributive equity.

At the national level, the ostensible aim of the constitutional amendments was clearly to revitalize local government. This was seen as a means of promoting greater community participation and involvement in developmental efforts, thereby improving the dismal record of the Indian developmental state in the sphere of human development and public-goods provision. In that the impetus for the amendments came from a widespread consensus regarding the failures of the bureaucratic and centralized apparatus of the Indian developmental state, supplemented, in certain circles, with a political agenda of democratic deepening, the attempt to revitalize local government in India mirrors attempts in other countries. But there are several key respects in which the Indian case stands out, and these need to be highlighted at the outset.

First, the Indian constitution assigns exclusive legislative domain over local governments to the states, unlike in many other countries where the impetus for decentralization originated at the national level and implementation responsibility also resided at the national level. In India, therefore, the final responsibility for the design and implementation of local government reforms lay with the states. Unsurprisingly, given the diversity in their historical trajectories and current sociopolitical and economic situations, across the states there has been tremendous variation in the design, scope, and extent of devolution to local governments.

Second, the Indian case also differs from some others in that there have been attempts in the past to empower local governments. Hence the latest effort to revitalize local government is by no means a "greenfield" initiative. In particular, this means that the novelty of the reforms—the extent to which they represent a significant departure from the pre-1993 scenario—varies across the states. For instance, the provision mandating regular elections to rural local bodies clearly has different implications in the state of Bihar (where elections to rural local bodies were last held in 1978) than it does in the state of West Bengal (where elections have been regularly held every five years since 1978).[1]

Lastly, it should also be noted that whereas in some countries the impetus for decentralization has come from external sources or has been triggered by an economic crisis, in India it was home-grown, and there was no single precipitating event that led to the reform. That is not to say, however, that the pressure for reforms came from the grassroots. Instead, the reforms reflected the emergence of a remarkable consensus among India's policy-making and intellectual elites.

In this chapter, I provide an overview of this large-scale and, in spirit, extremely ambitious initiative to revitalize local government in India. Because the specific design and implementation of the reforms were left to the discretion of individual states, the overview is naturally organized around and needs to consider the possibly divergent records of individual states. To keep the task manageable, I concentrate on the fourteen major Indian states, which together accounted for over 93 percent of India's population in 1991. The scope of the assessment is also inevitably limited by the information that is available. As a consequence, the assessment primarily focuses on the extent to which devolution has been attempted. On certain fronts, not enough time has passed, and in others, we simply do not know enough to say much about what the impacts of these reforms have been or are likely to be in the long run. Finally, as the title of the chapter indicates, the assessment is limited to the efforts to revitalize rural local governments and is concerned primarily with the state-level responses to the seventy-third amendment.

The overview provided in this chapter is very much a midterm assessment that is likely to become outdated within the near future. That is because the reform initiative is an ongoing process in two essential respects: first, though nine years have passed since the amendments went into effect, individual states continue to pass legislation in this area, and there continues to be a debate about the need for further formal institutional reform; and second, the dynamics and longer-term consequences of even the first set of reforms are still playing out.

The next sections detail the key provisions of the seventy-third amendment, lay out the historical context for these amendments, and pull together the available evidence on the design and scope of devolution at the level of individual states. I organize the discussion along the three main dimensions of devolution: political, administrative, and financial devolution. I then construct a crude index aggregating these different dimensions into a single measure of the overall extent of devolution in each of the fourteen states. I use this index and a review of the available case-study evidence to identify some of the patterns that appear to be emerging. Finally, I present some statistics on the progress various states have made in terms of human development in the last decade, which provide the basis for a rudimentary attempt to trace the impact of devolution at the state level. Some insights and thoughts on the future of the reforms are suggested by the Indian case, both from a policy perspective and from a more academic perspective.

The Constitutional Setting and the Seventy-third and Seventy-fourth Amendments

India is a federal parliamentary democracy made up of twenty-eight states and seven union territories.[2] At the national level, legislative authority rests with the two houses of the Parliament: the Lok Sabha (House of the People), which consists of 545 members, all but two of whom are directly elected from single-member parliamentary constituencies distributed proportionally on the basis of population among the states and union territories; and to a lesser extent, the Rajya Sabha (Council of States), which has no more than 250 members, most of whom are indirectly elected by the members of the state legislative assemblies of the various states.[3]

The titular head of state is the president. Executive authority, however, resides with the national government—in particular, the Council of Ministers—headed by the prime minister, who is the leader of the political party that is able to secure the support of the majority of the members of the Lok Sabha, either directly or through some form of coalitional agreement. Though the government enjoys broad powers and discretion in the design and implementation of programs and policies, it is ultimately answerable to the Parliament.

The parliamentary structure at the national level is, with some exceptions, replicated at the level of individual states. Each state has a legislative assembly, members of which are directly elected from single-member constituencies organized on the basis of population. The titular head of each state is the governor, who is appointed by the president. But as at the national level, executive authority rests effectively with the state government headed by the chief minister, the leader of the political party with majority support in the state legislature.

Until the passage of the seventy-third and seventy-fourth constitutional amendments, the states were the only subnational units officially recognized by the Indian constitution.[4] And the constitution grants individual states considerable legislative autonomy. Schedule 7 of the constitution explicitly demarcates the respective legislative domains of the state legislatures and the national Parliament. The functional areas over which the national Parliament has exclusive domain are specified in list I, also called the *Union List*. Items on this list include, among other things, defense, foreign affairs, currency, income taxes, interstate commerce, and key infrastructure. On the other hand, state legislatures have exclusive authority to enact legislation dealing with the items in list II, known as the *State List*. Included in this list are items such as law and order, public health, agriculture, wealth taxes, land tenure and land reforms, and most notably in the current context, functions of local governments. List III, the *Concurrent List*, includes items such as electricity, newspapers, education, and price controls, over which the national Parliament and the state legislatures share jurisdiction.

As mentioned earlier, the Indian constitution recognizes and makes special provisions for mandatory political representation (through reservation of seats in the legislative assemblies at both the state and the national levels) of two types of historically disadvantaged groups—Dalits and Adivasis.

The legislative origins of the seventy-third and seventy-fourth constitutional amendments date back to the Constitution (sixty-fourth amendment) Bill, which was introduced in the Parliament in July 1989 by the government of the then Prime Minister Rajiv Gandhi. The introduction of this bill represented the first attempt to confer constitutional status on rural local governments. Though the bill's broader aim of revitalizing rural local government was greeted favorably, some of the details were criticized, and the bill was ultimately defeated in the Rajya Sabha. It is worth noting that the main criticism leveled against the bill was that it offered the states little discretion in the design of local government reforms.

The seventy-third and seventy-fourth constitutional amendments were introduced in Parliament in September 1991 by the government of Prime Minister Narasimha Rao of the Congress(I) Party in the form of two separate bills: the Seventy-second Amendment Bill for rural local bodies (also known as panchayats) and the Seventy-third Amendment Bill for municipalities. They were referred to a Joint Select Committee of Parliament and were ultimately passed as the Seventy-third and Seventy-fourth Amendment Bills in December 1992.[5] After the bills were ratified by the state assemblies of more than half the states, the president gave his assent on April 20, 1993. The amendments were then officially enacted through the issuance of government notifications. The Constitution (Seventy-third Amendment) Act, 1992 (commonly referred to as the Panchayati Raj Act) went into effect on

April 24, 1993, and the Constitution (Seventy-fourth Amendment) Act, 1992 (the Nagarpalika Act), on June 1, 1993.

With local governments being a state subject in schedule 7 of the constitution, any legislation reforming the structure of local government has to be enacted at the state level. The first task of the states was therefore to pass conformity acts, which either introduced new legislation or amended existing legislation, to bring the state laws into line with the provisions of the amendment. Under the amendments, states had a year from the date the amendment went into effect to do so.

Because the amendments contain both mandatory and discretionary provisions, the degree of flexibility afforded the states in this task varied with the provision in question. The distinction between mandatory and discretionary provisions is embodied in the specific language adopted in the acts and carried over into the newly inserted articles of the constitution. The mandatory provisions were those that contain the word *shall* in referring to the steps that individual states needed to take. In the discretionary provisions, on the other hand, the word *may* figures prominently. And so while many of the discretionary provisions laid out a vision and created a space for individual states to legislatively innovate in reforming local government, ultimately, the design and scope of particular reforms was left to the discretion of individual state legislatures.

Of the mandatory provisions of the Panchayati Raj Act, the most critical are those that strengthen the structure of representative democracy and political representation at the local level. The following mandatory provisions are key:

• The establishment in every state (except those with populations below 2 million) of rural local bodies (panchayats) at the village, intermediate and district levels (article 243B).

• Direct elections to all seats in the panchayats at all levels (article 243C).

• Compulsory elections to panchayats every five years with the elections being held before the end of the term of the incumbent panchayat. In the event that a panchayat is dissolved prematurely, elections must be held within six months, with the newly elected members serving out the remainder of the five-year term (article 243E).

• Mandatory reservation of seats in all panchayats at all levels for Dalits and Adivasis in proportion to their share of the panchayat population (article 243D).

• Mandatory reservation of one-third of all seats in all panchayats at all levels for women, with the reservation for women applying to the seats reserved for Dalits and Adivasis as well (article 243D).

• Indirect elections to the position of panchayat chairperson at the intermediate and district levels (article 243C).

• Mandatory reservation of the position of panchayat chairperson at all levels for Dalits and Adivasis in proportion to their share in the state population (article 243D).

• Mandatory reservation of one-third of the positions of panchayat chairperson at all three levels for women (article 243D).

In addition, the act mandates the constitution of two state-level commissions—an independent election commission to supervise and manage elections to local bodies, much as the Election Commission of India manages state assembly and parliamentary elections (article 243K), and a state finance commission, established every five years, to review the financial position of local bodies and recommend the principles that should govern the allocation of funds and taxation authority to local bodies (article 243I).

Among the discretionary provisions, the two central ones, which in the opinion of many observers are the core of the amendment, call on the states to

• Endow the gram sabha—the electorate of a village panchayat—with powers and functions at the village level (article 243A) and

• Devolve powers and authority to panchayats to enable them to function as institutions of self-government. In particular, the provision calls for devolution of powers and responsibilities for the preparation of plans and implementation of schemes for development and social justice dealing with an impressively wide range of items, which are listed in a new schedule, schedule 11, of the constitution (article 243G).

A further discretionary provision (article 243H) authorizes states to pass legislation aimed at increasing the financial resources available to rural local bodies by increasing the latters' statutory taxation powers and by providing for grants-in-aid from the state government.

The newly introduced schedule 11 of the constitution contains a comprehensive list of functional items, ranging from agricultural extension, implementation of land reforms, poverty alleviation, and promotion of small-scale industries to health, primary and secondary education, and family welfare. In fact, there is considerable overlap between schedule 11 and the State List of schedule 7 of the constitution, with one of the notable omissions in schedule 11 being law and order.

Broad and impressive as the list of items in schedule 11 is, as De-Souza (2000) rightly points out, the language of the amendment itself indicates that the notion of local self-government is a fairly circumscribed one. While calling on states to empower panchayats to play a central role in planning and implementation of a variety of programs, the provision, despite the inclusion of the word *self-government*, makes no mention of transferring any legislative authority to rural local bodies. By omission, therefore, certain spheres of policy implicitly remain outside the realm of local governments.

Two other points need to be mentioned. The first is that while, for the most part, the seventy-fourth amendment act deals with urban local bodies, a key article contained in that amendment applies to rural local bodies as well. The article in question, article 243ZD, mandates the creation of district planning committees to consolidate the plans prepared by both rural and urban local bodies.

The second point is that the provisions of the seventy-third amendment did not apply to what are known as *scheduled areas*, constitutionally recognized areas of the country with large Adivasi populations. The amendment did, however, contain a provison reserving the right of Parliament to extend the amendments' provisions regarding local bodies to scheduled areas at a later date without the need for a further constitutional amendment. Parallel provisions regarding local governments in scheduled areas were ultimately enacted through the provisions of the Panchayats (Extension to the Scheduled Areas) Act of 1996.

Setting the Context

The public debate and discussion that preceded the adoption of the seventy-third and seventy-fourth constitutional amendments revolved almost entirely around the need to correct the multiple failures of the bureaucratic and centralized apparatus of the Indian developmental state—the failure to ensure the efficient and effective delivery of public services, to provide and maintain key infrastructure essential for economic growth, to promote equity, and to eliminate the multiple deprivations associated with poverty.

The basic claim made by proponents of the amendments was that by devolving powers to locally elected bodies the above-mentioned failures would be addressed. The fact that this claim was accepted, at least on the surface, by almost all participants in the public debate—differences of opinion concerned the details—is remarkable given the earlier more contested view of the virtues of localizing government in India's public discourse.

To better understand the roots of this consensus, the scope of the constitutional reforms at the national level, and the thinking behind the specific provisions of the amendment act, it helps to have a sense of the historical experience with local government, the political constraints imposed by India's federal structure, and the functioning of the Indian developmental state, particularly in rural areas.

As mentioned above, the passing of the seventy-third and seventy-fourth amendments marked a consensus concerning the desirability of governance structures that never existed in the public debate. Prior to that, the debate in the Constituent Assembly reflected contrasting positions of Gandhi and Ambedkar on the matter, and this contrast can be seen by the different phases in the history of panchayati raj in India and the associated committees: the Balwantrai Mehta Committee and the phase of ascendancy (1959 to 1964); the phase of stagnation (1965 to 1969); the phase of decline (1969 to 1977); and the Ashoka Mehta Committee and the revival of panchayats but as political institutions in a few states.[6]

Although some form local governments in India existed prior to the Independence, the Indian constitution did not provide constitutional status to local governments, and it assigned to the states the responsibility over local governments bodies. Consequently, the actual empowerment of local governments was in the hands of the states, which with few exceptions were unwilling to give away their power, creating a structure in which local governments were accountable to higher levels of government. An illustration of this lays in the fact that elections to local governments were frequently postponed at the discretion of the state governments or in many cases because of writ petitions to the courts. Also the great discretion given to the states made local government empowerments in India become extremely state variant.

Additionally, it was believed that revitalizing local governments would address the failures of the former Indian developmental state. Over the years, rural development in the Indian context came to be characterized by a proliferation of government schemes and programs staffed by civil servants who, at lower levels, were accountable only to their superiors in the administrative hierarchy of their respective agencies or line departments and, at upper levels, were motivated largely by career concerns in which the responsiveness to state-level elected representatives figured prominently. Moreover, under the planning approach, bureaucrats showed preoccupation with narrow sector-specific physical targets, and little attention was given to integrated outcomes.

Under this developmental model, the increasing flow of funds through panchayats in their role as implementing agencies for various schemes led to emergence of collusive networks connecting bureaucrats, local and higher-level elected representatives, and other members of dominant local elites. The result was that inefficiencies, leakages, and corruption associated with the plethora of government schemes undermined the legitimacy of the panchayats and wreaked havoc on the performance of various schemes.

Concomitantly with the ongoing debate concerning the empowerment of local government, in 1991 under the pressure of a severe balance-of-payments crisis and through a congruence of favorable political factors, the government then in power initiated a broad package of economic-policy reforms, which subsequent governments have, for the most part, maintained and supplemented. Under the new economic-policy regime, India's notorious industrial licensing regime has been largely dismantled, domestic industry has been deregulated, trade liberalization measures have been implemented, and the economy has been opened up to foreign direct investment. Financial-sector reforms have also been introduced at a slow but steady pace.

The timing of the 1991 trade and industrial-policy reforms happens to coincide roughly with the attempt to revitalize local government, but in terms of the initial impulse as well as the ultimate aim, these reforms are quite distinct. Trade and industrial policy reforms precipitated by balance-of-payments crisis and the poor performance in terms of economic growth. Their aim was to reduce the sphere of government influence and control. Consensus behind the need for local government reforms emerged more gradually and was borne out of the failures of the Indian state in terms of human development and poverty alleviation, particularly in rural areas. The aim was to reconfigure the structure of government.

The Panchayati Raj amendment has been hailed as a landmark in the evolution of rural local government in India. And it may well turn out to be so in the long run. But in many ways, the provisions of the amendment represent a marginal or incremental reform in that they are tailored to address some of the particular (perceived) problems with previous attempts to empower local government without radically reconstituting the balance of political power at the subnational level. The clearest indication of this is the seeming gap between the mandatory provisions requiring regular elections to local bodies and the weaker discretionary nature of the other parts of the amendment.

Assessing the Design and Scope of Devolution at the State Level

The task of assessing any reform initiative can be subdivided into two stages: documenting the extent and scope of the reforms and evaluating the effects of the reforms. Drawing causal inferences about the impact of particular changes in the policy environment is almost always difficult in the absence of policy experiments. With so-called stroke-of-the-pen reforms that are narrowly focused—for instance, a reduction in tariffs or the removal of industrial licensing requirements—the first stage is typically relatively straightforward. But with reforms that are broader in scope, in particular those that aim to bring about fundamental changes in the institutional context and practice of government, even the apparently simple task of documenting the scope and extent of the reforms becomes difficult.

There are two reasons why this is so. The first is the fact that these reforms are intrinsically multidimensional in nature. An attempt to revitalize local government and institutionalize more decentralized and participatory forms of local governance necessitates reforms along multiple dimensions. The structure and status of institutions of representative democracy need to be altered. Administrative reforms transferring control over civil servants from line departments to local governments have to be initiated. Administrative procedures, governing recruitment and promotion policies, reporting structures, and so on have to be reworked. Functional responsibilities for a wide range of items have to be reassigned. Various aspects of the devolution of financial resources have to be worked out—from changes in the assignment of taxes and the adoption of formulae for the transfer of funds to the relative shares of tied versus untied grants. Keeping track of the changes in all these dimensions is difficult.

A second and more prosaic reason is simply the practical difficulties of empirically distinguishing de jure or nominal reform measures from substantive de facto steps that actually alter day-to-day practices. There is a real danger that too much emphasis is placed on easily

recorded indicators of changes in legislative provisions and bureaucratic rules and processes and insufficient attention paid to whether
even clearly mandated changes are effected in practice. This is not to
say that changes in the formal legislative and institutional environment
are unimportant, only that in contexts where formal structures may
be imperfectly applied or enforced, the ground-level reality may differ
considerably. Changes in formal structures may well be important as
necessary conditions but are unlikely to prove sufficient.

A further important complication in the Indian context is one that
I have already alluded to above: although some provisions of the
seventy-third and seventy-fourth amendments were mandatory, the
design and degree of implementation of many of the key reforms
called for in these amendments were left to the discretion of individual
states. Not surprisingly, that has led to considerable variation in the
scope and extent of devolution across the Indian states.

With these difficulties in mind, I document the evidence of the scope
and extent of devolution along each of the three dimensions. The assessment is limited to the fourteen major states—states with populations exceeding 15 million that are not special category states. Where
relevant (and possible), I also provide some indication of the aggregate
India-wide picture as well.

The most striking feature of this selection is the variance between
states in several dimensions: size, population, per capita income, poverty, and human development indexes. Tables 5.1 and 5.2 provide an
evolution of some of these dimensions in the fourteen states for the
timespan of the analysis. In 1991, Punjab's per capita state domestic
product from agriculture of 2990 rupees (at constant 1980 to 1981
prices) was over six times that of Bihar, the poorest state. There was
tremendous variation in rural poverty as well, from a low of 6.2 percent in Punjab to a high of 48.6 percent in Bihar. Table 5.2 shows that
in terms of human development, the state of Kerala stood well apart
from the other states, a fact that has received much attention in international development circles. The so-called BIMARU states (Bihar,
Madhya Pradesh, Rajasthan, and Uttar Pradesh) lay at the opposite
extreme.

These observable differences in key economic, demographic, and human development indicators stem from and are supplemented by less
easily quantified differences in the states' colonial histories, political
culture, levels of social mobilization, and internal caste polarization.
To the extent that the prospects for participatory local governance

Table 5.1
Sampled states economic-development indicators

	Per Capita SDP from Agriculture			Rural per Capita Expenditure			Rural Headcount Index of Poverty			Percentage of Households with Electricity			Percentage of Households with Permanent Homes		
	1991–93	1995–97	Index of Progress	1993	1999	Index of Progress	1993	1999	Index of Progress	1991	2001	Index of Progress	1991	2001	Index of Progress
Andhra Pradesh	986	1,018	3.2	74	76	2.8	29.2	26.2	10.3	46.3	67.2	38.9	38.4	54.7	26.5
Bihar	430	424	−1.5	47	51	6.9	48.6	41.1	15.4	12.6	13.9	1.5	30.2	38.3	11.6
Gujarat	1,047	1,144	9.2	63	73	15.1	32.5	20.0	38.5	65.9	80.4	42.5	56.9	65.3	19.6
Haryana	2,257	2,292	1.6	74	97	31.0	17.0	5.7	66.5	70.4	82.9	42.3	50.1	65.8	31.4
Karnataka	1,276	1,320	3.5	63	68	9.5	37.9	30.7	19.0	52.5	78.5	54.9	42.5	54.9	21.5
Kerala	901	1,007	11.8	73	88	19.6	19.5	10.0	48.7	48.4	70.2	42.3	56.0	68.1	27.6
Madhya Pradesh	957	1,012	5.7	60	64	6.6	36.6	31.3	14.5	43.3	65.3	38.9	30.5	37.1	9.5
Maharashtra	1,227	1,344	9.5	61	69	14.1	42.9	31.9	25.6	69.4	77.5	26.4	52.2	57.8	11.7
Orissa	629	547	−13.1	61	62	1.4	43.5	43.0	1.1	23.5	26.9	4.4	18.7	27.6	10.9
Punjab	2,990	3,127	4.6	84	100	20.2	6.2	2.4	61.3	82.3	91.9	54.3	77.0	86.1	39.6
Rajasthan	1,063	1,273	19.7	58	62	7.0	23.0	17.3	24.8	35.0	54.7	30.3	56.1	64.9	20.1
Tamil Nadu	915	956	4.5	70	81	15.7	38.5	24.3	36.9	54.7	78.2	51.8	45.5	58.5	23.9
Uttar Pradesh	927	933	0.6	64	69	8.3	28.6	21.5	24.8	21.9	33.5	14.9	41.0	55.3	24.2
West Bengal	936	1,140	21.7	70	72	2.1	25.1	21.9	12.7	32.9	37.5	6.8	32.6	40.4	11.6
India							33.0	26.3	20.3	42.4	55.8	23.4	41.6	51.8	17.5

Table 5.2
Sampled states human-development indicators

	Rural Female Literacy Rate			School Attendance Rate			Percentage of Women Receiving Antenatal Checkup			Under-Five Mortality Rate			Percentage of Children Fully Vaccinated		
	1991	2001	Index of Progress	1992	1998	Index of Progress	1992	1998	Index of Progress	1992	1998	Index of Progress	1992	1998	Index of Progress
Andhra Pradesh	23.9	44.4	26.9	57.8	73.2	36.5	66	93	79.4	96	91	4.8	44.9	52.0	12.9
Bihar	17.9	30.1	14.9	47.3	61.8	27.5	27	36	12.3	137	110	19.3	10.7	10.6	-0.1
Gujarat	38.6	45.7	11.6	68.4	74.8	20.3	50	86	72.0	104	91	12.6	49.8	48.3	-3.0
Haryana	32.5	49.8	25.6	73.7	86.5	48.7	67	58	-27.3	108	79	26.5	53.5	60.3	14.6
Karnataka	34.8	48.5	21.0	64.7	77.0	34.8	65	86	60.0	102	83	18.3	52.1	56.0	8.1
Kerala	85.1	86.8	11.3	85.8	96.4	74.6	97	99	66.7	41	26	35.8	54.4	71.8	38.2
Madhya Pradesh	19.7	44.2	30.5	56.7	73.7	39.3	36	61	39.1	143	145	-1.1	29.2	20.6	-12.1
Maharashtra	41.0	59.1	30.7	75.1	86.7	46.6	70	90	66.7	76	70	8.1	64.2	72.7	23.7
Orissa	30.8	47.2	23.7	62.9	76.6	36.9	39	80	67.2	137	116	15.5	36.1	40.5	6.9
Punjab	43.9	57.9	25.0	73.3	89.3	59.9	86	74	-85.7	69	70	-1.0	61.9	71.4	24.9
Rajasthan	11.6	37.7	29.6	52.9	72.9	42.5	23	48	32.5	108	125	-16.2	21.1	16.0	-6.5
Tamil Nadu	41.8	55.8	24.1	74.1	86.7	48.6	78	99	95.5	95	65	32.2	64.9	88.0	65.8
Uttar Pradesh	19.0	38.6	24.2	56.2	74.0	40.6	30	35	7.1	162	132	18.3	19.8	20.1	0.4
West Bengal	38.1	53.8	25.4	61.6	75.8	37.0	69	90	67.7	107	71	33.8	34.3	43.6	14.2
India	30.6	46.6	23.0	61.6	76.4	38.5	49	65	31.4	119	101	14.6	35.4	39.4	6.2

depend in part on a variety of enabling features of the contexts in which it is attempted, as many have argued, this diversity in the initial conditions across the Indian states clearly needs to be borne in mind in considering the design, scope, and impact of state-level devolution efforts.

Political Devolution: Voice, Autonomy, and Accountability

Of the various institutional reforms, both nominal and substantive, that individual states have initiated since 1993, perhaps the most easily verifiable are the steps taken to meet the mandatory provisions of the constitutional amendment regarding the structure of political represen-tation below the state level. And so I begin by reviewing the progress on this front.

The constitutional amendment mandated the creation of a uniform three-tier structure of local government institutions at the substate level.[7] Immediately below the state are the district panchayats; below them, the block panchayats; and at the lowest level, the gram pan-chayats (village councils). Gram panchayats have existed in most states since at least the late 1950s (following the recommendations of the Balwantray Mehta Committee). However, in some states, there were no block panchayats (or their equivalent) or district panchayats, and in these states these higher tiers of substate local governments had to be created. The relevant states all enacted the necessary legislation to meet this requirement. Table 5.3 depicts the structure of representa-tive democracy that resulted. From a single national Parliament and twenty-five state legislative assemblies, India went to having 238, 682 additional constitutionally recognized representative bodies, 499 at the district level, 5,905 at the block level, and 232,278 at the village level. And for the first time, there exists a uniform three-tier structure of rural local governments in India. But as table 5.3 indicates, there remains considerable variation across states in the makeup of the three-tier structure, the details of which were left to the discretion of the states and were in part determined by varied historical legacies. In particular, village panchayats in Kerala and West Bengal stand out in being con-siderably larger in terms of population than village panchayats in other states.

Much of the rhetoric that accompanies initiatives to empower local governments highlights the need to downscale government to "bring government closer to the people." At least on one dimension—the "closeness" of the electorate to their elected representatives (as measured by the number of individuals represented by each elected

Table 5.3
Structure representative democracy

| State | Number of Rural Local Bodies (RLBs) | | | Population per Elected Body (000s) | | | | Area per Village LB | Number of Urban Local Bodies | Population per Urban Local Body (000s) |
| | District | Block | Village | State Assembly | Rural Local Bodies | | | | | |
					District	Block	Village			
Andhra Pradesh	22	1,093	21,784	66,508	2,210.0	44.5	2.2	12	116	154.2
Bihar	55	726	12,181	86,374	1,364.0	103.3	6.2	14	170	66.8
Gujarat	19	184	13,547	41,310	1,424.4	147.1	2.0	14	149	95.6
Haryana	16	111	5,958	16,464	775.6	111.8	2.1	7	82	49.4
Karnataka	27	175	5,673	44,977	1,150.7	177.5	5.5	33	215	64.7
Kerala	14	152	990	29,099	1,529.9	140.9	21.6	36	58	132.4
Madhya Pradesh	45	459	31,126	66,181	1,129.8	110.8	1.6	14	404	38.0
Maharashtra	29	319	27,611	78,937	1,668.8	151.7	1.8	11	244	125.2
Orissa	30	314	5,255	31,660	914.2	87.3	5.2	29	102	41.5
Punjab	17	138	11,591	20,282	840.5	103.5	1.2	4	137	43.7
Rajasthan	32	237	9,184	44,006	1,060.6	143.2	3.7	37	183	55.0
Tamil Nadu	28	385	12,593	55,859	1,313.6	95.5	2.9	10	744	25.6
Uttar Pradesh	83	904	58,620	139,112	1,343.5	123.3	1.9	5	684	40.4
West Bengal	17	340	3,314	68,078	2,904.1	145.2	14.9	26	122	153.3
India	499	5,905	232,278		1,259.9	106.5	2.7	13	3,682	59.1

representative)—that is literally what the mandated creation of these locally elected bodies did. Before 1994, the elected representatives effectively closest to the voters were the state legislative assembly members (MLAs). As table 5.4 indicates, on average, this meant a population of nearly 200,000 or more per MLA. After 1994, this number has, in principle, come down to a few hundred in most states, with the village panchayat representative being closest to the population. These numbers overstate the contrast, since village panchayats did exist even prior to the amendment. But given the irregularity of local body elections in most states, it is not clear that panchayat members could reasonably be considered "elected" representatives. The larger point though is that by increasing the pool of constitutionally protected elected representatives some five hundredfold, the amendment brought about a dramatic broadening of the representative democratic base of India.

For this new structure to meaningfully increase the closeness of elected representative, elections have to be held regularly. Prior to 1994, with the exception of West Bengal since 1978, local body elections had not been held on a regular schedule in most states. In many cases, elections were delayed as a result of writ petitions submitted to the courts by groups other than the state government. In others, state governments themselves unilaterally postponed elections, putting forward a variety of reasons for the postponement, from natural disasters to civil unrest to school holidays. By mandating regular elections to local government institutions, the constitutional amendment sought to restrict the discretionary authority of the state governments. The amendment even contains a provision (article 243O) barring interference by the courts in electoral matters.

Have these provisions made a difference? The second column of table 5.5 provides a partial answer. Shown there are the dates of elections to village panchayats in the last ten years. Since the constitutional amendment calls for a uniform and unalterable term of five years, each state should have had two elections, and the period between elections should not have exceeded five years. Table 5.5 indicates that the first standard has mostly been met. But fewer than half the states have met the second constitutionally mandated standard. And in the case of Orissa and Uttar Pradesh, which did hold elections within five years, elections were held only as a result of court interventions overturning the state governments' decision to postpone elections (Matthew, 2001).

Table 5.4
Structure representative democracy

| | Number of Elected Representatives to: | | | | | Population per Elected Representative to: | | | | |
| | Parlia-ment | State Assembly | Rural Local Bodies | | | Parliament | State Assembly | Rural Local Bodies | | |
			District	Block	Village			District	Block	Village
Andhra Pradesh	42	294	1,093	14,644	230,529	1,583,524	226,218	44,484	3,320	211
Bihar	54	324	1,585	15,344	165,452	1,599,527	266,588	47,332	4,889	453
Gujarat	26	182	761	3,814	123,470	1,588,830	226,976	35,563	7,096	219
Haryana	10	90	303	2,418	54,159	1,646,365	182,929	40,953	5,132	229
Karnataka	28	224	919	3,340	80,627	1,606,329	200,791	33,808	9,302	385
Kerala	20	140	300	1,547	10,270	1,454,926	207,847	71,394	13,845	2,086
Madhya Pradesh	40	320	946	9,097	474,351	1,654,529	206,816	53,745	5,589	107
Maharashtra	48	288	1,762	3,524	303,545	1,644,525	274,087	27,466	13,733	159
Orissa	21	147	854	5,260	81,077	1,507,606	215,372	32,113	5,214	338
Punjab	13	117	274	2,441	87,842	1,560,151	173,350	52,149	5,854	163
Rajasthan	25	200	997	5,257	119,419	1,760,240	220,030	34,041	6,456	284
Tamil Nadu	39	234	648	6,499	97,398	1,432,281	238,713	56,761	5,660	378
Uttar Pradesh	85	473	2,551	58,165	682,670	1,636,615	294,106	43,711	1,917	163
West Bengal	42	294	723	8,579	50,345	1,620,904	231,558	68,285	5,755	981
India	543	4,120	13,484	128,581	2,580,261	1,558,568				

Table 5.5
Structure representative democracy

| State | Elections to Village Local Bodies, 1993–2002 | Percentage of Elected Representatives Women | | | Relative Representation Ratio | | | | Reservations for Backward Castes |
| | | District | Block | Village | Dalits (SCs) | | Adivasis (STs) | | |
					District	Village	District	Village	
Andhra Pradesh	1995, 2001	33.2	37.0	33.8	0.7	0.9	0.8	0.8	Fixed share
Bihar	2001	.	.	.	.	.	.	.	Proportional
Gujarat	1995, 2002	33.4	33.4	33.4	1.1	0.5	0.7	0.4	Fixed share
Haryana	1994, 2000	33.3	33.4	33.1	1.0	0.2	N.A.	N.A.	Conditional
Karnataka	1993, 2000	36.5	40.2	43.8	1.0	1.2	1.0	1.8	Fixed share
Kerala	1995, 2000	34.7	36.4	32.9	0.9	1.1	1.0	0.9	None
Madhya Pradesh	1994, 2000	33.7	34.2	32.9	1.0	0.9	1.0	1.0	Conditional
Maharashtra	1997, 2002	33.3	33.3	33.0	1.0	1.2	1.0	1.0	Fixed share
Orissa	1997, 2002	34.4	35.6	35.3	0.6	0.5	0.6	0.9	None
Punjab	1998	32.5	13.4	35.4	1.0	1.0	N.A.	N.A.	Conditional
Rajasthan	1995, 2000	33.2	33.1	32.5	1.0	0.8	1.0	0.8	Proportional
Tamil Nadu	1996, 2001	34.7	35.3	33.7	0.9	0.9	0.3	0.5	None
Uttar Pradesh	1995, 2000	25.4	24.1	25.5	0.7	0.6	1.4	0.6	Proportional
West Bengal	1993, 1998	34.0	35.1	35.6	1.4	1.0	1.3	1.0	None

Even when elections have been held, some states have failed to meet the provisions regarding mandatory representation for women, Dalits, and Adivasis. Drawing on the most recent local body elections for which data are available, the second through eighth columns of table 5.5 provide an indication of the extent to which this particular mandate was met. The constitutional provision mandated that a third of all seats at all levels be reserved for women. In most states, this mandate was met, and some (such as Karnataka, Tamil Nadu, and West Bengal) even exceeded it. However, in Punjab and Uttar Pradesh the mandate was not met. The fifth through eighth columns display the relative representation ratios of Dalits and Adivasis at the lowest and highest tiers of local government. The relative representation ratio of a group is defined as the ratio of the fraction of elected representatives from that group to that group's share in the state's population. By consitutional mandate, this ratio ought to be 1. That clearly is not the case in a number of states. The fact that the problem appears to be worse at the level of village panchayats is suggestive of the social and exclusionary dynamics operating in the villages of the states in question. At the district level, with fewer seats to fill in absolute terms, this appears to have been less of an issue, presumably because almost all the major political parties have, for purely instrumental electoral reasons, recruited some members from traditionally disadvantaged groups into their ranks.

Regular elections may ensure, albeit crudely, some degree of accountability and provide some legitimacy to locally elected representatives, but they represent only one step in the process of political devolution. Equally important is the degree of political autonomy afforded locally elected bodies. On this front, there is little variation across the states. Reviews of the various state conformity acts indicate that even at the statutory level—let alone in terms of actual practice— state governments have, against the spirit of the amendment, retained considerable powers over the rural local bodies. As table 5.6 indicates, in all states, the state-level legislation vests various functionaries of the state government—for instance, the district collector (the chief civil servant at the district level)—with the authority to intervene in the functioning of rural local bodies. These provisions have been criticized by many proponents of local government—not because they do not recognize the need to have some accountability and oversight mechanisms in place but because the provisions violate the separation of powers and such authority is better retained by the courts.

Table 5.6
Structure representative democracy

State	Head of VP Directly Elected?	MPs/MLAs Members of Local Bodies?	State Government Has Power to:					
			Suspend or Remove Head of Local Body		Suspend or Dissolve Local Body		Countermand Orders of Local Body	
			Village	District	Village	District	Village	District
Andhra Pradesh	Yes	Both	Yes	Yes	Yes	Yes	Yes	Yes
Bihar	Yes	Both	Yes	Yes	Yes	Yes	Yes	Yes
Gujarat	Yes	MLAs	Yes	Yes	Yes	Yes	Yes	Yes
Haryana	Yes	Both	Yes	Yes	Yes	Yes	Yes	Yes
Karnataka	No	Both	Yes	Yes	Yes	Yes	Yes	Yes
Kerala	No	Both	Yes	Yes	Yes	Yes	Yes	Yes
Madhya Pradesh	Yes	MLAs	Yes	Yes	Yes	Yes	Yes	Yes
Maharashtra	No	Both	Yes	Yes	Yes	Yes	Yes	Yes
Orissa	Yes	MLAs	Yes	Yes	Yes	Yes	Yes	Yes
Punjab	Yes	MLAs	Yes	Yes	Yes	Yes	Yes	Yes
Rajasthan	Yes	MLAs	Yes	Yes	Yes	Yes	Yes	Yes
Tamil Nadu	Yes	Both	Yes	Yes	Yes	Yes	Yes	Yes
Uttar Pradesh	Yes	Both	Yes	Yes	Yes	Yes	Yes	Yes
West Bengal	No	Both	Yes	Yes	Yes	Yes	Yes	Yes

As indicated in the second column of table 5.6, all the states also acknowledge a role for elected representatives to higher levels of government—namely, members of parliament (MP) and members of the legislative assembly (MLA)—in the two higher tiers of rural local government. Again, this has been criticized because of concerns about the disproportionate influence that MPs and MLAs are likely to enjoy.

The first column of table 5.6 reveals the state-level variation in one aspect of the design of political devolution that is of particular concern in the Indian context. And that has to do with whether the village panchayat chairperson is selected through direct elections. Apart from Karnataka, Kerala, Maharashtra, and West Bengal, all the states require direct elections. The inclusion of this feature of a presidential system of government has been decried by many who see in it the potential for perpetuating the status of panchayat chairperson as a "first among equals." The concern regarding this provision stems from the experience of the last five decades.

Lastly, by explicitly recognizing the gram sabha—the electorate of a village panchayat—the constitutional amendment envisioned a more direct channel through which citizens could exercise "voice" and participate in local governance. The hope was that the gram sabha, through regular meetings over the course of the year, could become the fulcrum of the community development process, playing a key role in both the planning and subsequent monitoring of development activities. The particular roles and functions entrusted to the gram sabha were however left to the discretion of state legislatures. The state-level legislation, in most states, does little more than mechanically list a variety of nominal functions and duties to be performed by gram sabhas. Only in Kerala, has there been an effort to seriously engage the gram sabha. I detail the Kerala experience in a later section.

Functional and Financial Devolution

Article 243G of the constitutional amendment—which calls on state governments to devolve power, authority, and responsibilities to rural local bodies so as to enable them to "functions as institutions of self-government"—captures the core ostensible aim of the constitutional reform. And that was to empower and enable rural local bodies to play the central role in the provision of public services, the creation and maintenance of local public goods, and the planning and implementation of developmental activities and programs to alleviate poverty and promote distributive equity.

At the time the constitutional amendments were introduced, the situation in most states was almost farcically far from this ideal. The functional domain of rural local bodies was limited largely to the provision of some core services such as street lighting, water supply, sanitation, and local roads. To the extent that panchayats were involved in developmental activities, they played the role of implementing agencies at the local level for various schemes sponsored by either central government or state government departments. In this capacity, panchayats helped identify beneficiaries for a number of transfer schemes and oversaw the management and implementation of various local infrastructure schemes funded through various state government departments.

The picture presented above is an aggregated one. There have been attempts at various points in time and in various states to enhance the role of local governments. At the national level, the initiative for community development following the Balwantray Mehta Committee has already been mentioned. The experience of a few selected states also bears mentioning. The western states of Gujarat and Maharashtra were early reformers, passing legislation in the 1960s transferring many activities (including primary health care and education) to district panchayats. In both states, funds were devolved as well and a separate administrative service—the Panchayat Service in Gujarat and the Maharashtra Development Service in Maharashtra—was set up to facilitate the transfer (or deputation) of state-level civil servants to work with the district panchayats.

More recently, in the mid-1980s, the southern state of Karnataka undertook a significant and, in many respects, far-reaching devolution of functional responsibilities to the district panchayats. The Karnataka experience is described in some detail in Crook and Manor (1998). But as in the cases of Gujarat and Maharashtra, the original vision behind the decentralization effort has not been sustained.

Significant attempts to broaden the functional domain of village panchayats have been rarer. West Bengal, since 1978, has involved more directly village panchayats in the implementation of various programs (an issue discussed in more detail in chapter 6 by Bardhan and Mookherjee in this volume).

To what extent has the passage of the constitutional amendments changed the situation? While a definitive response to this question is not possible without a detailed empirical study, which has yet to be done, of the institutional arrangements under which local governments operate on a day-to-day basis, anecdotal reports, media accounts, and a myriad of case-studies suggest that, with perhaps a couple of exceptions, the progress by the states in genuine functional and financial devolution has been extremely limited.

At the statutory level, almost all the states have enacted new or amended previous legislation to broaden the functional domain of panchayats. But as Vijayanand (2001) points out, statutory provisions, unless they are extremely detailed, provide "only the skeletal framework and form" for the day-to-day workings of government and for the design and implementation of public programs. The "flesh and blood of administration," in practice, comes from the myriad of administrative rules and procedures—procurement rules, reporting structures, compensation schemes, accounting systems, and so on—that are put in place by the executive branch of government.

A number of reports that review the state-level legislation indicate that, in most instances, the statutes merely provide a "shopping list" of various activities and sectors for which panchayats would be newly responsible (Government of India, 2001a, 2001b). Little detail is provided in the legislation in terms of the specific roles and responsibilities of the different tiers of panchayats relative to the other tiers and to the existing line departments of the state governments.

Whether the lack of specificity and clarity in the state conformity legislation was strategic, as some have argued, can be debated. State legislatures were under some pressure to enact the conformity legislation within a prescribed time frame. Articulating a detailed road map for administrative devolution may not have been feasible within this time frame. However, if that were the sole reason for the omission of details regarding the framework for functional devolution, one would expect to see, subsequent to the initial legislation, significant administrative steps being taken.

In ascertaining the extent of administrative devolution, it is therefore necessary to go beyond the legislative statutes and review whether the administrative steps—issuance of government orders and circulars, notification of changes in administrative rules and procedures—needed to fully operationalize the intent of any new legislation have in fact been taken. A thorough and direct review of the gamut of statutory and administrative measures that the major Indian states have undertaken is beyond the scope of this chapter. I rely instead on a number of detailed studies to piece together an overall picture.

One such study is the Report of the Working Group on Decentralized Planning and Panchayati Raj Institutions (Government of India,
2001a, 2001b), a high-level task force of the central government. Table
5.7 displays the report's findings, based on information compiled by
the Ministry of Rural Development, on the extent to which functions,
funds, and functionaries have been transferred to rural local bodies.
The second column displays the count of activities—of the twenty-
nine listed in schedule 11 of the constitution—that individual states
have transferred to local governments. In several states, all the functions appear to have been transferred (though what exactly this means
is unclear). But from the third and fourth columns, it is clear that even
when functions have been statutorily or even administratively transferred to panchayats, in most states the funds and personnel necessary
for meaningfully carrying out these functions remain under the administrative control of the state-level bureaucracy (departments of the state
governments). Karnataka, Kerala, Maharashtra, and West Bengal are
the exceptions to this norm.

Yet another indicator of the failure of the states to make any serious
efforts to implement the spirit of the amendment comes from looking
at the status of the district planning committees, the constitution of
which was mandated by article 243ZD. As can be seen from the last
two columns of table 5.7, many states have yet to establish the district
planning committee. The significance of this is that it indicates that
funds for a variety of central and state-sponsored schemes are still being routed through the district rural development agencies and line
departments. It is also an indication that the rural local bodies are yet
to be genuinely involved in the planning process. Even when the district planning committee has been constituted, in some states, contrary
to the spirit of the amendment, it is headed by a state minister rather
than the chairperson of the district panchayat.

A central theme in the economic literature on decentralization is that
the functional and fiscal domain—taxation and spending authority—
of local governments should, to the extent possible, overlap. In a perverse sense, the preamendment situation in most Indian states satisfied
this basic tenet in that the severely circumscribed functional domain
of panchayats described above was mirrored by an equally limited fiscal domain. In principle, panchayats (and in particular, village panchayats) did have powers to impose local taxes and assess a variety of
fees. In practice, given the limited capacity and effective authority of

Table 5.7
Extent of devolution to rural bodies

State	Number of Schedule 11 Items for Which Legislation Enacted And/or Government Orders Issued Transferring:			Status (as of 2001) of District Planning Committee	
	Functions	Functionaries	Funds	Constituted?	Chairperson
Andhra Pradesh	13	2	5	No	—
Bihar	—	—	—	No	—
Gujarat	—	—	—	No	—
Haryana	16	—	—	Partially	—
Karnataka	29	29	29	Partially	—
Kerala	29	15	15	Yes	District panchayat head
Madhya Pradesh	23	9	10	Yes	State minister
Maharashtra	18	18	18	No	—
Orissa	25	3	5	Yes	District panchayat head
Punjab	7	—	—	No	—
Rajasthan	29	—	—	Yes	District panchayat head
Tamil Nadu	29	—	—	Yes	District panchayat head
Uttar Pradesh	13	9	12	Yes	State minister
West Bengal	29	12	12	Yes	District panchayat head

village panchayats to enforce tax collection and the even more limited incentives they had to do so under the prevailing system of transfers from the state and central governments, local revenue collection was negligible, and revenue dependency—the share of panchayat total income that came from external sources—was in most states very high.

Panchayat revenues fall into two main categories: own revenues and transfers from higher levels of government.[8] Own revenues (revenues that are collected locally) come from two sources: nontax sources (such as user fees for local public goods and commons and income from panchayat-owned properties) and own tax revenues. Own taxes are those that are statutorily assigned to local bodies and collected by the local bodies. Typically, own taxes have included items such as entertainment taxes, dwelling taxes, taxes on professions, and levies on pumps, tractors, and so on.

The other main category of revenues, intergovernmental transfers, can be subdivided into tax and nontax components as well. The tax component consists of revenues from both assigned taxes (taxes statutorily assigned to local bodies but collected by the state government and transferred to the local body) and shared taxes (taxes assigned to the state and entirely collected by the state government but subsequently shared with local bodies). The nontax component of intergovernmental transfers takes the form of grants from the central and state governments, tied in most cases to a variety of state-sponsored and centrally sponsored development schemes.

On the expenditure side, because their effective functional domain was so limited, panchayats had few areas over which they have enjoyed discretionary decision-making authority and budgeting autonomy. The bulk of the expenditures that were incurred by (that is, were nominally routed through) the panchayats were financed by the tied grants linked to specific state- and centrally sponsored schemes. That panchayats lacked genuine spending authority for much of their expenditures is indicated by the restrictions that most states placed on the power of village panchayats to sanction expenditures above a prespecified cap (table 5.8).

The second, fifth, and eighth columns of tables 5.9 to 5.12 give some sense of the state of panchayat finances in the years, from 1990 to 1995, immediately preceding and subsequent to the passage of the constitutional amendments and before, presumably, any reforms had taken effect. A couple of disclaimers need to be made about the information presented in these tables. First, data on local government finances

Table 5.8
Extent of devolution to rural bodies

State	Restrictions on Powers of Village Panchayats to Sanction Expenditures (as of 1999)
Andhra Pradesh	Capped at 10,000 rupees
Bihar	.
Gujarat	Uncapped for own resources
Haryana	Capped at Rs 25,000
Karnataka	Capped at Rs 10,000
Kerala	Uncapped regardless of source
Madhya Pradesh	Rs 300,000 for own resources
Maharashtra	Uncapped for own resources
Orissa	Capped at Rs 1,000
Punjab	Capped at Rs 10,000
Rajasthan	Capped at Rs 100,000
Tamil Nadu	Uncapped for own resources
Uttar Pradesh	Capped at Rs 20,000
West Bengal	Uncapped regardless of source

in India (and it must be said, in most poor developing economies) are extremely hard to come by and can be quite unreliable when they are available, which in itself is an indication of the status of local governments. The scale of the problem is reflected in the fact that the Eleventh Finance Commission, a statutory body at the national level that prescribes the rules for transfers between the national government and the state governments, specifically set aside funds to assist panchayats in the maintenance of accounts and to set up a database on local government finances (Government of India, 2000). The second caveat is simply that data on the flow of funds through panchayats, no matter how accurate, do not indicate which tier of government has ultimate decision-making authority.

Table 5.9 clearly indicates the dismal record of rural local bodies in collecting revenues locally. On a per capita basis, own revenues were laughably low. What revenues were derived locally were generally collected by the village panchayats with whom the statutory powers of taxation resided in most states. Village panchayats in ten of the fourteen states reported own revenues of less than 10 rupees per year on a per capita basis. Given the relatively small populations of most village panchayats, these figures translate into aggregate own revenues—for instance, Rs. 760 for Uttar Pradesh, or Rs. 11,310 for Tamil Nadu—that

Table 5.9
Local finances

State	Annual per Capita Own Revenues (rupees)						Ratio of Own Revenue to Total Revenue: All RLBs		
	Village Local Bodies			All RLBs					
	1990–1995	1995–1998	Percent-age Change	1990–1995	1995–1998	Percent-age Change	1990–1995	1995–1998	Differ-ence
Andhra Pradesh	13.5	20.2	49.7	16.2	23.9	48.2	6.1	6.1	0.0
Bihar	0.0	0.0	.	0.0	0.0	.	0.0	0.0	0.0
Gujarat	8.4	10.1	21.0	11.2	13.1	17.3	2.6	1.9	−0.7
Haryana	28.5	32.2	12.9	28.5	32.3	13.2	68.4	61.8	−6.7
Karnataka	6.3	8.6	37.5	6.3	8.6	37.5	1.1	0.9	−0.2
Kerala	19.3	39.5	104.1	19.3	39.5	104.1	31.3	17.7	−13.6
Madhya Pradesh	3.1	4.7	53.8	3.3	5.6	69.9	6.0	4.1	−1.9
Maharashtra	8.8	16.8	90.6	9.7	18.2	88.2	3.1	3.3	0.1
Orissa	2.6	2.4	−6.2	2.6	2.4	−6.2	3.0	1.2	−1.8
Punjab	18.7	28.5	52.0	22.1	33.2	50.6	24.3	34.0	9.7
Rajasthan	4.0	3.4	−13.6	6.7	7.7	14.1	3.0	2.1	−0.9
Tamil Nadu	3.9	6.8	72.2	5.4	8.9	62.8	5.7	8.2	2.4
Uttar Pradesh	0.4	0.3	−24.6	2.7	3.3	23.2	6.3	5.9	−0.4
West Bengal	1.7	1.9	13.5	2.9	3.1	7.8	7.6	3.2	−4.4
India	5.1	7.4	44.4	6.2	8.9	42.5	4.5	3.7	−0.7

are insufficient to cover even minimal establishment costs. The only exceptions to this generally bleak picture were Haryana, Punjab, and Kerala.

Not surprisingly given the low absolute levels of own revenues, revenue dependency levels were high in most states, with Haryana, Kerala, and Punjab again being the exceptions. The level of revenue dependency is a normalized measure that obscures differences in scale. From table 5.10, it is clear that there were significant differences in the volume of revenues flowing through local governments in different states. Per capita total revenues of all rural local bodies combined were highest—an order of magnitude higher than in some of the other states—in the states of Gujarat, Karnataka, and Maharastra, reflecting their respective legacies of devolution to the district level.

Since own revenues were likely to be the sole source of funding for the discretionary expenditures by village panchayats, the low levels

Table 5.10
Local finances

State	Annual per Capita Total Revenue (rupees)						Ratio of RLB Revenues to State Revenues: All RLB		
	Village Local Bodies			All RLBs					
	1990–1995	1995–1998	Percentage Change	1990–1995	1995–1998	Percentage Change	1990–1995	1995–1998	Difference
Andhra Pradesh	55	58	5.5	268	397	48.2	25.0	24.2	−0.8
Bihar	31	38	22.8	39	47	21.5	3.7	5.8	2.0
Gujarat	27	35	31.3	439	709	61.5	36.5	33.3	−3.2
Haryana	38	47	24.6	42	52	25.8	2.7	1.7	−0.9
Karnataka	46	69	52.0	592	992	67.4	49.3	50.4	1.1
Kerala	63	199	217.0	63	274	335.5	5.3	12.9	7.7
Madhya Pradesh	51	91	77.9	54	176	223.0	6.1	12.5	6.4
Maharashtra	38	81	114.7	310	555	78.9	20.4	26.0	5.7
Orissa	38	47	26.1	94	202	114.1	10.2	16.2	5.9
Punjab	76	78	1.8	89	100	11.3	5.9	3.9	−2.0
Rajasthan	93	192	105.7	231	367	58.7	22.5	23.5	1.0
Tamil Nadu	40	72	80.5	97	110	13.6	.	5.5	.
Uttar Pradesh	41	51	24.7	42	56	33.0	5.9	5.4	−0.5
West Bengal	41	54	34.0	58	97	66.4	6.1	8.8	2.7
India	43	69	59.3	142	239	68.0	13.2	14.5	1.4

of own revenues are mirrored, as one would expect, by low levels of expenditures on core services by village panchayats. This is apparent from table 5.11. Somewhat surprising in light of the fact that the core services in question are truly local in nature is the fact that in a few states—Andhra Pradesh, Karnataka, Maharashtra, and Uttar Pradesh—there is a jump in reported expenditures on core services in going from the village panchayat to the higher tiers of local government.

To address the weak financial position of panchayats, in article 243H the constitutional amendment authorizes states to pass legislation aimed at increasing the financial resources available to rural local bodies by increasing the latter's statutory taxation powers and by providing for grants-in-aid from the state government. To assist the state governments in this process, the amendment mandates the constitu-

Table 5.11
Local finances

State	Annual per Capita Total Expenditure (rupees)						Ratio of Core Services to Total Expenditures: All RLBs		
	Village Local Bodies			All RLBs					
	1990–1995	1995–1998	Percentage Change	1990–1995	1995–1998	Percentage Change	1990–1995	1995–1998	Difference
Andhra Pradesh	9.0	16.3	81.4	26.4	55.9	111.5	9.8	13.8	4.0
Bihar	.	.	.	0.0	0.0	.	.	.	.
Gujarat	4.0	5.0	25.2	4.0	5.0	25.2	0.8	0.7	−0.1
Haryana	.	.	.	0.0	0.0	.	.	.	.
Karnataka	8.4	15.9	89.1	53.8	96.2	78.9	9.9	10.0	0.1
Kerala	18.0	24.2	34.5	18.0	27.8	54.6	28.4	12.0	−16.5
Madhya Pradesh	1.9	4.1	115.5	2.4	8.7	261.5	4.4	6.1	1.7
Maharashtra	8.1	14.2	76.6	30.6	59.9	95.9	6.9	8.1	1.2
Orissa	1.6	1.5	−1.3	4.8	2.9	−39.6	5.8	1.5	−4.3
Punjab	37.9	38.0	0.2	37.9	38.0	0.2	41.6	33.5	−8.1
Rajasthan	0.0	0.0	.	0.9	2.8	218.7	0.4	0.8	0.4
Tamil Nadu	16.3	26.4	61.8	19.4	33.4	72.0	30.5	30.7	0.1
Uttar Pradesh	0.4	1.7	296.6	45.0	59.6	32.4	0.9	2.6	1.6
West Bengal	0.1	0.1	−3.6	0.4	0.4	−4.9	0.7	0.4	−0.4
India	4.6	7.2	57.4	10.3	18.7	80.8	6.6	7.3	0.6

tion of a State Finance Commission every five years. Under this provision, the State Finance Commissions are charged with advising the state governments on the principles to be adopted in determining the allocation of funds to local bodies and the range of taxes to be devolved to local bodies.

The fourteen major states all constituted State Finance Commissions by the prescribed deadline (within a year of the amendment coming into effect). Thereafter, however, the record of individual states has varied significantly. It is worth spelling out the sources of this variation, not so much because the work of the State Finance Commissions represents a key element of the constitutional reforms but rather because it provides yet another example of how, within India's federal structure, even a mandatory constitutional provision can be ignored or deliberately misimplemented. In four of the states—Bihar, Gujarat,

Madhya Pradesh, and Orissa—the commission had to be reconstituted because the original commission was not, for a variety of reasons, able to submit its report. In most states, there were delays of two to three years before the commission was able to submit its report, often because the information on local government finances and needs was not readily available. There were further delays still, often over a year after the submission of the commission's report, before the state government submitted an action-taken report to the state legislative assembly. And even then, only in some states (for instance, Kerala) did the government accept and pledge to implement all of the recommendations made by the finance commission.

A number of studies have examined the reports of the state finance commissions in some detail. These suggest that for the most part the finance commissions have attempted to balance the natural limits, both economic and political, to the tax base of local governments, the need for interjurisdictional equity given the heterogeneity in local economies, and the need to preserve the incentives of local governments to raise revenue locally.

From an economic perspective, the natural tax base of local governments consists of taxes on immovable property and user fees for local public goods and commons. In rural India, the predominant form of property is agricultural land. There is a levy on agricultural land in most states—based not on the value of the land but on the potential income from it as determined by its productivity—but it is not seriously enforced.[9] The "settlement rates" (the assessed productivity of the land used to calculate the levy) have been so rarely revised and updated that revenues from this particular source have become insignificant (Rajaraman, 2000). Perhaps anticipating the political constraints on doing so, none of the state finance commissions appear to have seriously considered proposals, such as that put forward by Rajaraman and Bhende (1998), to revive the land levy as a source of income for rural local bodies. Instead, the recommendations have largely been limited to reassignment of some minor taxes, such as imposition of surcharges and the like.

If indeed, as many claim, there are few elastic sources of local revenue for rural local bodies, the only real avenues that remain for enhancing the financial resources of rural local bodies while ensuring some degree of budgeting autonomy are, on the one hand, to identify mechanisms for improving the tax effort (better collection and enforcement of existing taxes and fees) of local bodies and, on the other, to increase the transfer of untied block grants from the state governments. Concerns have been expressed about the incentive effects of a move toward untied block grants on the tax effort or, more broadly, own resource mobilization efforts of rural local bodies. These concerns are in principle legitimate, but given the empirical evidence on the limited tax effort of rural local bodies even in the absence of untied grants, they seem misplaced. It is hard to see how tax efforts could get any worse.

The way forward would therefore appear to be to consider increasing the use of untied block grants while exploring ways of improving the tax effort of local bodies. The use of matching grants as incentive devices risks worsening cross-jurisdictional inequality. Matching grants, though ideally based on tax effort relative to the tax base, in practice tend to be based on observed tax revenues because tax effort is difficult to directly ascertain. In settings where the tax bases of local bodies vary greatly because of inherited disparities in infrastructure and levels of economic activity, the use of these matching grants is clearly likely to exacerbate rather than mitigate these existing disparities. The alternate route considered by some of the state finance commissions was therefore to make "obligatory" the collection of certain taxes and fees and moreover to specify a floor on the minimum tax rates that local bodies could impose.

The state finance commission reports, even when they have been accepted in principle, do not reveal the extent to which financial devolution has actually taken place. Again, without further detailed empirical research, it is impossible to say definitively what the situation is in individual states. But a sense of the overall trend can be obtained by returning to the data on panchayat finances presented in tables 5.9 to 5.12.

The third, sixth, and ninth columns of these tables present summary statistics on local government finances at the state level for the most recent three years, 1995 to 1998, for which they are available. Table 5.10 indicates that in a few states, whether or not there was genuine financial devolution, there was at least a dramatic rise in the flow of funds to rural local bodies. Nationwide, per capita total revenues of village panchayats rose by nearly 60 percent in the relatively short span of five years or so. In Kerala, Madhya Pradesh, Maharashtra, Rajasthan, and Tamil Nadu the growth in village panchayat revenues exceeded the national rate, in the case of Kerala (217 percent), Maharashtra (114 percent), and Rajasthan (106 percent), by a considerable margin. In Kerala and Madhya Pradesh, the total revenues of all rural local bodies

Table 5.12
Local finances

State	Annual per Capita Total Expenditure (rupees)						Ratio of RLB Expenditure to State Development Expenditures: All RLBs		
	Village Local Bodies			All RLBs			All RLBs		
	1990– 1995	1995– 1998	Percent-age Change	1990– 1995	1995– 1998	Percent-age Change	1990– 1995	1995– 1998	Differ-ence
Andhra Pradesh	50	55	9.8	268	398	48.3	30.5	27.8	−2.7
Bihar	35	43	23.6	65	74	13.7	12.4	13.6	1.2
Gujarat	13	17	33.2	477	687	44.1	39.5	36.7	2.8
Haryana	61	82	34.5	66	89	35.4	5.5	4.8	−0.7
Karnataka	43	68	60.3	538	968	79.7	54.4	61.1	6.7
Kerala	64	156	143.6	64	235	268.0	6.9	14.6	7.7
Madhya Pradesh	52	94	83.2	54	178	227.1	6.9	15.3	8.4
Maharashtra	51	77	49.2	449	749	67.0	39.0	40.1	1.1
Orissa	38	47	26.1	94	202	114.1	11.5	17.8	4.3
Punjab	75	90	19.8	90	111	23.6	6.6	6.5	−0.1
Rajasthan	94	196	109.5	230	369	60.2	22.8	26.0	3.2
Tamil Nadu	34	57	67.0	63	109	71.2	.	6.3	.
Uttar Pradesh	41	52	25.1	45	60	33.1	8.7	8.0	−0.7
West Bengal	51	62	20.9	69	103	49.9	12.1	11.0	−1.1
India	45	69	52.5	154	256	66.2	17.7	19.6	1.9

combined also grew at a rate far exceeding the national average. The numbers for Madhya Pradesh suggest a bias in favor of district panchayats relative to village panchayats. In contrast, in the case of Maharashtra there appears to have been some movement toward redressing the previous focus on district panchayats. Rajasthan and Tamil Nadu are the only two other states where the recorded per capita revenues of village panchayats grew at a faster rate than did the revenues of block and district panchayats.

In terms of the impact of increased grants-in-aid to local bodies on the own revenues of local bodies, some of the worst fears seem to have been unfounded. Though measured levels of revenue dependency did increase in some of the states (such as Kerala and Madhya Pradesh) that had the highest rates of overall revenue growth, in absolute terms own revenues increased appreciably in the same states.

Overall, the available information suggests that in most states there has been very limited progress in terms of administrative and financial devolution. What is one to make of this? It suggests a lack of political will and significant bureaucratic resistance. But to attribute it entirely to efforts to preserve rents would be to risk oversimplifying the nature of the problem.

A more nuanced perspective would also recognize that the process of transferring funds and functionaries can be quite complicated. In terms of transferring personnel, two sets of issues arise. The first is a practical one—the need to address bureaucratic career concerns to retain and attract suitably qualified individuals to these positions. The smaller scale of the bureaucracies supporting local governments potentially limits the upward promotion possibilities for civil servants, and practical ways have to be devised to get around these limits.

A second issue that arises is the tension between the need to make bureaucrats accountable to elected representatives and also ensure some degree of insulation for the bureaucracy from political pressures. The basic tension between bureaucratic accountability and autonomy does not exist only at the local level, but it does complicate the process of reconfiguring bureaucratic structures.

An Aggregate Index of Devolution

Having provided a more disaggregated account of the scope and extent of devolution attempted (or not) by individual states along the various relevant dimensions of devolution, and at the risk of considerable oversimplification, in this section I make an admittedly crude and speculative attempt to partition the fourteen major states into categories based on the overall extent of devolution. I do this for two reasons. First, such a categorization provides an initial reference point, a sort of benchmark, through which the more detailed case-study investigations of the specifics of each state can be filtered in a way that facilitates cross-state comparisons. Second, without some degree of aggregation, the task of empirically assessing the impacts of devolution, even in a very exploratory fashion, becomes unmanageable.

Needless to say, others reviewing the same information may have arrived at a different way of organizing and categorizing it. And so, in the interests of transparency, table 5.13 displays all the values that I assigned based on a review of the evidence. Table 5.13 also reports the comparative rankings that emerge from a couple of other multistate studies. The first is a study by the Eleventh Finance Commission,

Shubham Chaudhuri

Table 5.13
Aggregated index of devolution

Dimensions of devolution	AP	BI	GU	HA	KA	KE	MP	MA	OR	PU	RA	TN	UP	WB
Political devolution														
Regular elections	0	−1	−1	0	−1	1	0	1	0	−1	1	1	1	1
Women's representation	1	−1	1	1	1	1	1	1	1	−1	1	1	−1	1
Dalit/Adivasi representation	−1	−1	−1	−1	1	1	1	1	−1	1	−1	−1	−1	1
Political autonomy	−1	−1	−1	−1	−1	−1	−1	−1	−1	−1	−1	−1	−1	−1
Functional devolution														
Transfer of functions	0	−1	0	0	1	1	1	1	1	−1	1	1	0	1
Transfer of functionaries	−1	−1	−1	−1	1	1	1	1	−1	−1	−1	−1	1	1
District Planning Committee	−1	−1	−1	−1	−1	1	0	−1	1	−1	1	1	0	1
Expenditure autonomy	−1	−1	0	−1	−1	1	0	0	−1	−1	0	0	−1	1

Financial devolution

Transfer of funds	0	−1	−1	0	1	1	1	1	0	0	−1	−1	1	1
Flow of funds	−1	−1	0	0	1	1	1	0	0	−1	1	1	0	0
Share of funds	1	−1	−1	1	1	0	0	1	0	−1	1	−1	−1	0
Crude overall index	−4	−10	−6	−3	6	8	5	5	−1	−9	2	0	−2	7
Rank	11	14	12	10	6	1	4	4	8	13	6	7	9	2
Category	Minimal	Minimal	Minimal	Minimal	Modest	Significant	Modest	Modest	Minimal	Minimal	Modest	Minimal	Minimal	Significant
Index of decentralization	Above average	Below average	Average	Average	Above average	Above average	Above average	Above average	Average	Average	Above average	Above average	Average	Above average
11th Finance Commission	Minimal					Significant	Minimal						Minimal	
World Bank study	Minimal						Modest				Minimal			

which put together a state-level index of decentralization.[10] This index was used by the Eleventh Finance Commission in its formula for allocating funds to the states. The second is a study sponsored by the World Bank looking intensively at the experiences in seven major states.

The outcome of this crude exercise yields the following categorization of states. Kerala and West Bengal emerge as the only two states to have undertaken significant devolution. Maharashtra, Madhya Pradesh, Karnataka, and Rajasthan come next as states with modest records of devolution. I aggregate the remaining states into a single third category of states that displayed minimal progress toward devolution.

A State-Level Initiative in Kerala: The People's Campaign for Decentralized Planning

Before I turn to a consideration of some of the broader patterns that appear to be emerging at the national level, I briefly describe a state-level initiative that has received attention: Kerala. Chapter 6 of this book provides a detailed description of the experience of West Bengal. As I argued in the previous section, Kerala and West Bengal are the two only states that experienced a significant level of devolution, and therefore a more detailed account of these two experiences become relevant.

In 1996, the Left Democratic Front (LDF) coalition returned to power in Kerala, and the government (led by the Communist Party of India–Marxist, CPM) immediately fulfilled one of its most important campaign pledges by launching the People's Campaign for Decentralized Planning. All 1,214 local governments in Kerala—municipalities and the three rural tiers of district, block, and village panchayats—were given new functions and powers of decision making and were granted discretionary budgeting authority over 40 percent of the state's developmental expenditures. The campaign went well beyond the devolution of governance functions. As structured by the implementing agency—the Kerala State Planning Board—the campaign was designed to create an active role for local citizens in shaping local development policy making and budgeting. Thus, not only were local governments charged with designing and implementing their own development plans (which included designing and financing projects across the full range of development sectors), but they were mandated to do so through an elaborate series of participatory exercises. The building block of this process was the holding of two annual gram sabhas (ward-level assemblies), one at the beginning of the planning cycle and one at the end of the budgeting process.

The first gram sabha serves as an open forum in which residents identify local development problems, generate priorities, and form subsector development seminars in which specific proposals first take shape. The gram sabhas are open meetings, are presided over by local elected officials, and are facilitated by "key resource persons" trained by the State Planning Board. They are always held on weekdays and in public buildings (usually schools). Preparations for the assemblies include extensive publicity and the distribution of various planning documents. Minutes are kept, and each subsector group presents a report of its deliberations and produces a list of "felt needs." These are in turn translated into specific projects by task forces and submitted to the elected panchayat council for final budgetary approval.[11]

Beyond its institutional design, there are two critical features of the campaign that need to be highlighted. The first is that in addition to providing the fiscal resources, the procedural templates, the enabling regulations and laws, key oversight functions, and administrative capacity, the Kerala state government—and specifically the SPB—also orchestrated a massive training exercise, described by one observer as "the largest nonformal education program ever undertaken in India." In the first year, in seven rounds of training at state, district, and local levels, some 15,000 elected representatives, 25,000 officials, and 75,000 volunteers were given training. About 600 state-level trainees—called key resource persons (KRPs)—received nearly twenty days of training. Some 12,000 district-level trainees—district resource persons (DRPs)—received ten days of training, and at the local level more than 100,000 persons received at least five days of training. In subsequent years, these training programs were extended and were more specifically targeted at women and Dalits and Adivasis.[12] The second point is that at every stage of this process, a range of civil society organizations have played an active role. Most notable has been the role of the Kerala Sastra Sahitya Parishad (KSSP)—the Kerala People's Science Movement. With its 50,000 members recruited predominantly from the white-collar professions of civil servants and school teachers, the KSSP has an organized presence in almost every village in Kerala and is by far the most active and influential nonparty affiliated, secular organization in the state. In addition to playing an active role in the campaign itself (supplying for example many of the local key resource persons), it is important to emphasize that in designing the campaign the SPB relied heavily on a stock of practical knowledge, ideas, and experiences drawn from twenty-five years of local-level experiments in sustainable development conducted by the KSSP.

Interstate Patterns in the Scale and Scope of Devolution

Combining the picture of the interstate variation that table 5.13 suggests with the various case studies that have been done looking at individual states, the following preliminary observations may be made.

Economic prosperity, far from being a facilitating contextual factor, may actually provide a disincentive for devolution. Of the high- and middle-income states, only Maharashtra, West Bengal, Kerala, and to a lesser extent Karnataka appear to have attempted any meaningful measure of devolution. On the other hand, Madhya Pradesh and Rajasthan, usually lumped together with Bihar and Uttar Pradesh in the BIMARU group of underperforming states, have taken measurable steps toward devolution.

Second, the imperatives of electoral politics appear to figure prominently. In particular, the combination of a change of government within a bipolar party system is a common feature of all instances but Maharashtra: CPI(M) in West Bengal in 1978 with Congress in opposition, Janata Party in Karnataka in 1983 with Congress in opposition, CPI(M) in Kerala in 1995 with Congress in opposition, Congress in Madhya Pradesh in 1994 with BJP in opposition, and BJP in Rajasthan in 1994 with Congress in opposition. Andhra Pradesh, Tamil Nadu, and Gujarat are all exceptions to this particular combination.

If we limit our focus to the states where there have been meaningful (if not entirely successful) attempts at devolution, three separate approaches to devolution are evident: a phased or stepping-stone approach as in West Bengal, a big-bang approach as in Kerala, and a thematically oriented demand-driven approach as in Madhya Pradesh.

Finally, an increasing emphasis on participatory approaches is often accompanied by greater involvement of nongovernmental actors.

Tracing the Impact of the Reforms

A growing literature in economics has used policy variation across political jurisdictions to econometrically estimate the effects of key policy innovations on various outcomes of interest.[13] The typical approach involves the use of longitudinal data on outcomes for a panel of jurisdictions (such as states in India) coupled with data (often categorical) capturing the timing and magnitude of reforms. The basic intuition behind this approach—often labeled *difference-in-differences*—is that the difference between the changes (*difference*) over time in the outcome of interest in a jurisdiction that experienced a policy change and the changes in outcomes in a jurisdiction that did not, ought to (subject to some caveats and complications) provide a rough estimate of the impact of the policy change. In the Indian context, a number of papers have adopted this approach. These include, among others, Banerjee, Gertler, and Ghatak (2002), who look at the efficiency effects of tenancy reform in the state of West Bengal; Besley and Burgess (2000), who consider the poverty-reducing and growth impacts of land reform legislation more broadly; and Pande (2003), who examines the effects of mandated political representation in state legislative assemblies for traditionally disadvantaged groups, on patterns of public expenditure.

For a number of reasons, all of which have been previously mentioned in other contexts, a formal implementation of this approach is not feasible in tracing the impact of the constitutional amendments at the state level. To begin with, given the paucity of information regarding the substantive reform measures adopted by individual states, even a crude assessment of the true extent of the devolution in individual states is difficult. In principle, this problem can be circumvented by reframing the problem as one of estimating the reduced-form effect of what is acknowledged to be possibly only a nominal reform effort— that is, an estimate of the impact of the promulgation of a new policy that incorporates and reflects the possibility that the policy may have been imperfectly implemented.[14] And in fact, a case can be made that this reduced-form effect should be the object of inference since the impact of institutional reforms is inevitably mediated through the political and societal context within which they are attempted (Besley and Case, 2002).

However, even if a reduced-form approach is adopted, other hurdles remain. One is the multidimensional nature of the reforms. In particular, given the heterogeneity across the states in the scope of devolution along different dimensions, a complete overall ordering is simply not possible. Another is the relatively short time since the introduction of the reforms.

The task is complicated further by the fact that the Panchayati Raj initiative roughly coincided with a major program of economic liberalization at the national level. The liberalization program initiated in 1991 reduced the span of central-government control and thereby opened up the space for a variety of state-level initiatives to promote industrial development and economic growth—for instance, by offering tax incentives to attract private investment (Ahluwalia, 2000). This makes it yet more difficult to disentangle the impact of local government reforms from that of these other initiatives.

In light of these difficulties, what appears below can be described as a highly exploratory analysis, loosely motivated by the differences-in-differences intuition underlying more formal investigations. Basically, I focus on cross-state variation in the changes in a number of state-level indicators of development outcomes over a period spanning the passage of the constitutional amendment and the subsequent state-level reforms. I restrict the analysis to a subset of outcomes that are plausibly less directly influenced by changes in the trade and industrial policy regimes. The state-level outcomes I consider, along with the relevant dates at which they are observed, are listed below:

• Per capita state domestic product from agriculture (1991 to 1993 average, 1995 to 1997 average),

• Mean rural per capita expenditure (1993, 1999),

• The rural headcount index of poverty (1993, 1999),

• The fraction of households with electricity connections (1991, 2001),

• The fraction of households living in permanent structures (1991, 2001),

• The rural female literacy rate (1991, 2001),

• The school attendance rate of school-age children (1992 to 1993, 1998 to 1999),

• The fraction of pregnant women who receive antenatal care (1992 to 1993, 1998 to 1999),

• The under-five mortality rate (1992 to 1993, 1998 to 1999), and

• The percentage of children between one and two years old who are fully vaccinated (who have received vaccines for BCG, measles, and three doses of DPT and polio) (1992 to 1993, 1998 to 1999).

The first three measures, particularly the rural poverty rate, though certainly affected by the quality of governance in rural areas, are also influenced by the overall economic conditions in the state and in the country. The remaining indicators, on the other hand, are likely to more directly reflect the quality of public-service delivery.

Tables 5.1 and 5.2 display the basic data on the performance of the Indian states during the 1990s. For each of the variables, the first column displays the level of the variable in the early 1990s, prior to the passage of the constitutional amendment. The second column displays the level in the late 1990s (or in some cases, 2001), five years or more after the state conformity acts were enacted. The third column displays an index of the progress made by each state between the two dates.

For the two straight economic variables, per capita state domestic product from agriculture and rural per capita expenditures, the index of progress is simply the percentage change between the two dates.

All the remaining variables admit of a natural target level (a maximum or minimum attainable level), and for these variables the index of progress (between two dates) is defined as the proportionate reduction in the distance to the target. For instance, a reduction in the head-count index of poverty (for which the natural target level is 0) of five percentage points from 25 percent to 15 percent would translate into an index of progress of 40 percent (100 multiplied by 10/25). Similarly, an increase in the school attendance rate from 50 percent to 60 percent translates into an index of progress of 20 percent. For aggregate welfare indicators that have a natural upper bound (or lower bound), defining the index of progress in this way avoids some of the conceptual difficulties that arise in measuring progress simply in terms of changes. For instance, in assessing progress in poverty reduction, if we adopt as our index the percentage-point difference in poverty rates at two dates, we would end up attributing greater progress in poverty reduction to a state where the poverty rate decreased by ten percentage points from 30 percent to 20 percent than we would a state where poverty was eradicated starting from an initial rate of 5 percent and further reductions were simply not possible.

Tables 5.1 and 5.2 indicate that there was great variation in the progress made during the 1990s, both across states for a given indicator and across indicators for a given state. The question then is whether some of the variation across states can be traced back to differences in the scope and extent of devolution. A crude way of getting at this question is to overlay the pattern of deviations at the state level from the mean index of progress across the fourteen states with the crude categorization of states in terms of devolution in table 5.13. The mean across the fourteen states controls for any common factors, such as increases or decreases in allocations for centrally sponsored schemes, that might influence the index of progress for a particular indicator. The deviation from this mean then captures the influence of any factors specific to the state, among them the degree of devolution. This is a crude proxy for the actual extent of devolution. In particular, it is likely to be confounded by other state-specific factors that are unrelated to the process of devolution (for instance, a variety of economic shocks), and so I also construct a set of adjusted deviations that account for growth in per capita expenditures in the state. It should be noted that by examining deviations in the index of progress for an indicator, which is constructed from changes in the indicator across two points in time, I am implicitly controlling for any time-invariant state-specific effects. Lastly, I compared these deviations state by state, and perhaps not surprisingly, these deviations, adjusted and unadjusted, do not indicate any clear and consistent patterns across the range of indicators.

Viewing the Reforms through an Analytic Lens

The relative merits of the two approaches to reform—big-bang and stepping-stone, shock therapy and gradualism—can and have been debated, if not in the Indian context, certainly in the case of the reform programs in Eastern Europe and the former Soviet Union. The usual line is that, whatever the domain of the reforms, the choice between the two depends on the institutional and political context in which the reforms are being contemplated. At some level, this claim obviously is right. But the Kerala approach suggests the intriguing possibility that what may be a more critical element in the long-term success of a reform process than the choice that is made at the outset is the conscious recognition of the power of agency and the adoption of a learning-by-doing mentality. As Thomas Isaac, the principal architect of the People's Campaign describes it: "in short, the preconditions for successful decentralization are to be created in the very process of decentralization" (Isaac, 2000). Essentially, this approach treats as central the dynamic and contingent nature of directed institutional change. Similar themes are stressed in the literature on participatory democracy— participation inculcates the capacity for participation—and in a more recent literature on the constructability of collective capacities for change.

This point about the need to incorporate or at least recognize the dynamic and contingent elements of the processes of institutional change carries over to the economic literature on decentralization. There are three separate strands of the literature, distinguished by the implicit or explicit view that is taken of the nature of state-society interactions. The literature on fiscal federalism, dating back to Tiebout and Oates, implicitly views government (and governmental actors, whether bureaucrats or politicians) as benevolent if not omniscient decision makers who are motivated only by the disinterested pursuit of economic efficiency and limited only by informational constraints in the population at large. As Bardhan (2002) points out, the realities of governance in most developing economies make this framework largely irrelevant in that context. In a subsequent work, Seabright (1996) recognizes potential agency problems between the electorate and bureaucrats and politicians—for instance, by viewing government as a set of elected representatives motivated by electoral imperatives. But this literature is of limited relevance in the Indian context because it implicitly assumes reasonably well-functioning representative democracies in that the channels of political influence are limited to the act of voting and hence influence is equitably distributed. A third strand, Bardhan and Mookherjee (2000), explicitly incorporates the possibility of uneven influence and capture by elites at both the local and higher levels, and hence provides a much more useful framework for thinking about decentralization in developing countries. But even this strand of the literature ignores the possibility of dynamic agency.

However, even if, as I suggest above, preexisting conditions at the local level are less immutable than much of the current thinking presumes—which is to say, the possibility of local capture may itself be diminished and the prospects for participation enhanced through the process of decentralization—there are clearly contextual prerequisites at higher levels, of which the most important is the political will and capacity at the level of government contemplating decentralization. Put another way, while local context may be less important to the normative questions of how and whether to decentralize, the primacy of politics and the broader context manifests itself in the positive questions of where, when, and if meaningful decentralization is attempted in the first place.

Looking Ahead: Is the Glass a Quarter Full or Three-Quarters Empty?

With the slow progress that is evident in most Indian states on genuine functional devolution and the many instances where preexisting inequities and patterns of social exclusion and domination have thwarted even genuine attempts at devolution, some observers have worried that this latest initiative to revitalize local government will also fail. Clearly, institutional reforms initiated through state-level legislation are not irreversible. The decline of panchayats in the 1970s and 1980s in most states or the failure to sustain the Karnataka reforms all attest to that.

The question then is whether the one element that thus far has distinguished this latest attempt to foster Panchayati Raj—the fact that it has constitutional backing—will make a difference in the long run. There is undoubtedly considerable uncertainly about how exactly events will unfold this time around. But constitutional reforms lie at the top of the reform hierarchy in terms of their purported impact and degree of irreversibility. And while it is true that, in practice, the Indian experience has revealed that the implementation of constitutional mandates remains vulnerable to various forms of filibustering because constitutional contracts are inevitably incomplete, it is also the case that they can be made more complete by more clearly outlining the consequences of noncompliance. And that increasingly is happening in the Indian context.

The courts have begun to play a more assertive role as witnessed by the intervention of the Supreme Court and the Andhra Pradesh High Court, respectively, in ensuring that panchayat elections went ahead as scheduled in Orissa and Andhra Pradesh. The Indian government too has begun considering introducing progress in devolution as a key element in the formulas determining intergovernmental transfers.

Ultimately, though, the main reasons for optimism are the scattered but numerous accounts of developments at the community level, where the space created for participation is being occupied and contested by those previously excluded. If participatory democratization involves learning by doing, there is increasing evidence that the learning is taking place in disparate communities all over India. The learning may be slow and sporadic, and much of rural India is still on the flat portion of the learning curve, but it does appear to be taking place. And just as the extension of the franchise and mandatory representation manifested itself, albeit with considerable lags, in the growing political participation of subordinate groups (other backward classes), there is the distinct possibility that just the sheer numbers of individuals, the more than 2 million locally elected representatives who now have a stake in the system will make a difference. In effect, a new interest group has been created that potentially cuts across preexisting lines of division providing a new axis along which interests may align. The gathering of panchayat representatives in New Delhi in April 2002 is one early sign of the potential emergence of a new coalition.

Notes

1. This does not mean that this particular provision has no implications in the case of West Bengal because it does. By reducing the discretionary powers that state governments effectively enjoyed in the holding of elections to local bodies, the amendment takes away an option that the state government previously had though chose not to exercise. And in politics, as in finance, options have value even if not ultimately exercised.

2. The number of states has increased over time, with various state reorganization initiatives. The latest occurred in 2000, when three new states were created: Chhattisgarh, by partitioning the state of Madhya Pradesh; Jharkand, from the state of Bihar; and Uttaranchal, from the state of Uttar Pradesh.

3. Two members of the Lok Sabha and twelve members of the Rajya Sabha are directly appointed by the president to represent, respectively, the small Anglo-Indian community and various fields of human endeavor such as literature, sciences, arts, and social service.

4. The constitution of India came into effect on January 26, 1950, just over two years after India attained its independence on August 15, 1947.

5. In the fifteen months between the time the bills were introduced and the time they were finally passed, the numbering changed.

6. See chapter 6 on West Bengal for a more detailed discussion of the recommendations of these committees and subsequent responses by different state governments.

7. Smaller states with populations below 2 million are exempt from this requirement.

8. Other potential sources of funds are loans from financial institutions, public and private, and voluntary contributions from panchayat residents. Historically, these have been uniformly negligible, though this may change with proposals to set up a Panchayat Finance Institution.

9. In rural India (as in many poor agrarian economies), the distinction between a tax on the value of land and a tax on the potential income from the land would be irrelevant with well-functioning land markets since the potential income stream from the land would be capitalized into the value of the land.

10. The index aggregates ten different design elements and implementation steps that states incorporated or undertook: enactment or amendment of state panchayat and municipal legislation; intervention or restriction in the functioning of the local bodies; assignment of functions to the local bodies by state legislation; actual transfer of functions to these bodies by way of rules, notifications, and orders; assignment of powers of taxation to the local bodies and the extent of exercise of such powers; constitution of the SFCs and the extent of action taken on their reports; elections to the local bodies; and constitution of district planning committees per the letter and spirit of article 243ZD.

11. The design and politics of the campaign created a wide range of mechanisms that make elected panchayat councilors de facto—if not de jure—accountable to the gram sabha mandates. Needless to say, the degree of accountability varied widely and calls

for further research. However, previous fieldwork, other research, and some simple but significant aggregate shifts in expenditures leave little doubt that popular mandates significantly impacted budgetary outcomes.

12. As of the 1991 census, Dalits and Adivasis represented 11.9 percent of Kerala's rural population.

13. A parallel and much more established (though still very active) literature uses microeconometric techniques to evaluate the effects of particular programs on a range of outcomes at the individual and household levels. The literature on policy impacts at the aggregate level, using aggregate jurisdiction-level data, has increasingly drawn on this literature in framing the analysis in terms of estimating "treatment" effects and in taking seriously the possibility that "treatments" may be endogenous.

14. The analog in the program-evaluation literature is the distinction between the intention-to-treat effect and the effect of treatment on the treated. The former incorporates the possibility of selective compliance with the treatment and therefore provides, in some senses, a more robust estimate.

References

Ahluwalia, M. (2000). "Economic Performance of the States in Post-reforms Period." *Economic and Political Weekly*, May 6, pp. 1673–1648.

Banerjee, A., P. Gertler, and M. Ghatak. (2002). "Empowerment and Efficiency: Tenancy Reform in West Bengal." *Journal of Political Economy* 110(2): 239–280.

Bardhan, P. (2002). "Decentralization of Governance and Development." *Journal of Economic Perspectives* 16(4): 185–206.

Bardhan, P., and D. Mookherjee. (2000). "Capture and Governance at Local and National Levels." *American Economic Review* 90(2): 135–139.

Besley, T., and R. Burgess. (2000). "Land Reform, Poverty Reduction and Growth: Evidence from India." *Quarterly Journal of Economics* 105(2): 389–430.

Besley, T., and A. Case. (2002). "Political Institutions and Policy Choices: Evidence from the United States." Mimeo, London School of Economics.

Crook, R., and J. Manor. (1998). *Democracy and Decentralization in South Asia and West Africa*. Cambridge: Cambridge University Press.

Deaton, A., and J. Dreze. (2002). "Poverty and Inequality in India: A Reexamination." *Economic and Political Weekly*, September 7, pp. 3729–3748.

DeSouza, Peter. (2000). "Multi-State Study of Panchayati RajLegislation and Administrative Reform." In *Rural Decentralization in India* (vol. 3). Washington, DC: World Bank.

Ghatak, M., and M. Ghatak. (2002). "Recent Reforms in the Panchayat System in West Bengal: Toward Greater Participatory Governance?" *Economic and Political Weekly*, January 5, pp. 45–58.

Government of India. (1985). "Administrative Arrangements for Rural Development: A Perspective—Proceedings of the National Workshop Held at NIRD." Hyderabad: National Institute for Rural Development.

Government of India. (2000). *Report of the Eleventh Finance Commission*. New Delhi: Ministry of Finance.

Government of India. (2001a). *Report of the Task Force on Panchayati Raj Institutions*. New Delhi: Planning Commission.

Government of India. (2001b). *Report of the Working Group on Decentralized Planning and Panchayati Raj Institutions*. New Delhi: Ministry of Rural Development.

Government of India. (2002). *National Human Development Report*. New Delhi: Planning Commission.

Grindle, M. (2001). "In Quest of the Political: The Political Economy of Development Policymaking." In G. Meier and J. Stiglitz (Eds.), *Frontiers of Development Economics: The Future in Perspective*. New York: Oxford University Press.

Isaac, T. M. Thomas. (2000). "Decentralization, Democracy and Development: A Case Study of the People's Campaign for Decentralised Planning in Kerala." Mimeo.

Kohli, A. (1987). *The State and Poverty in India*. Cambridge: Cambridge University Press.

Manor, J. (1999). *The Political Economy of Democratic Decentralization*. Washington, DC: World Bank.

Matthew, G. (2001). "Panchayat Elections: Dismal Record." *Economic and Political Weekly*, January 20, pp. 183–184.

Mookherjee, D. (2001). "Combating the Crisis in Government Accountability: A Review of Recent International Experience." Boston University Institute for Economic Development Discussion Paper No. 117.

Oates, W. E. (1972). *Fiscal Federalism*. New York: Harcourt, Brace and Jovanovich.

Pande, R. (2003). "Can Mandated Political Representation Provide Disadvantaged Minorities Policy Influence? Theory and Evidence from India." *American Economic Review* 93(4): 1132–1151.

PRIA. (2001). *The State of Panchayats: A Participatory Perspective*. New Delhi: Samskriti.

Rajaraman, I. (2000). "Fiscal Features of Local Government in India." In Jean-Jacques Dethier (Eds.), *Governance, Decentralization and Reform in China, India and Russia*. Boston: Kluwer Academic.

Rajaraman, I., and M. J. Bhende. (1998). "A Land-Based Agricultural Presumptive Tax Designed for Levy by Panchayats." *Economic and Political Weekly*, April 4, pp. 4–10.

Seabright, P. (1996). "Accountability and Decentralization in Government: An Incomplete Contracts Model." *European Economic Review* 40: 61–89.

Tiebout, C. (1956). "A Pure Theory of Local Expenditures." *Journal of Political Economy* 64: 416–424.

Vijayanand, S. M. (2001). "Issues Related to Administrative Decentralization and Administering Decentralization: Lessons from the Kerala Experience." Paper presented at the Workshop on Decentralization, Institute for Social and Economic Change, Bangalore, May 31–June 1.

6   Decentralization in West Bengal: Origins, Functioning, and Impact

Pranab Bardhan and
Dilip Mookherjee

Introduction

The eastern state of West Bengal in India has been characterized by devolution to local governments (panchayats) for over a quarter century now, in striking contrast to much of the rest of India. This is primarily the result of a conscious strategy of agrarian transformation pursued by a coalition of left parties (known as the Left Front) that has held power at the state government continuously since 1977. While a handful of other Indian states periodically experimented with decentralization prior to the 1990s, it is only since the passage of the seventy-third and seventy-fourth constitutional amendments in 1993 that the rest of India has systematically begun to implement such a system. The West Bengal decentralization experiment thus predated the all-India experiment and is frequently hailed as an instance of successful implementation of decentralization that other Indian states would do well to emulate.

In this chapter, we provide an account of the origins of the panchayat system in West Bengal, followed by a description of the range of responsibilities devolved and their functioning. We subsequently summarize results of recent research concerning patterns of local participation of local residents and their success in targeting resources to intended beneficiaries of various developmental programs. We conclude with an assessment of the system on normative grounds (the extent to which they have promoted accountability and responsiveness in the delivery of public services) as well as the political economy of the reforms (how well they have secured the political objectives of the Left Front government).

Historical Origins

The origins of the system can be traced to the efforts of the British colonial state to create a system of self-government in the late nineteenth century, starting with the 1882 Ripon Resolutions, the 1885 Bengal Local Self-Government Act, and the 1919 Bengal Village Self-Government Act. These acts culminated in a system of union boards, with each board covering eight to ten villages with a total population of 10,000. The jurisdiction of these union boards coincides with the current-day gram panchayat (GP). The union boards brought village administration into the formal administrative and revenue structure of the colonial state. Not surprisingly, these boards made no efforts to encourage popular participation of local residents. Their main purpose was to coopt local elites into the power structure of the colonial state, partly in response to the threat of rising nationalism among these elites. The range of powers or finances devolved were negligible. If anything, the boards served to reinforce traditional patterns of agrarian inequality between a narrow landowning elite and large masses of poor tenants and agricultural workers.

Following independence, the Constitution of the new Indian republic encouraged decentralization to village governments but left the responsibility for implementing such a system to state governments. To assist this process, the central government set up the Balwantrai Mehta Committee in 1957, which provided a detailed set of suggestions for a three-tier system of local government.

The recommendations of this committee led to the formation of a model that has substantially affected the actual process followed in India in the subsequent half century. The lowest tier was proposed to be the village panchayat, whose members would be elected directly with special provision for representation of scheduled castes (SCs), scheduled tribes (STs), and women. Their duties would include managing local roads, water, sanitation, land management, and the welfare of underprivileged classes. Above these would be the panchayat samiti (PS) at the block level, with members indirectly elected from representatives of the village panchayats and also with special provision for representation of women, SC, and ST residents. The PS was to be assigned responsibility for development of agriculture, livestock, public health, welfare, administration of primary schools, and the implementation of special development schemes entrusted to it by the central government. They were to be primarily financed by grants and aid from the state and central governments. The top tier of the system was to be composed of the zilla parishad (ZP), regarding which the Mehta Committee provided three alternative structures varying with regard to range of powers and mode of election.

The structure proposed thus allowed very limited financial autonomy to local governments, which would have to rely on aid and grants from state and central governments. The range of responsibilities devolved excluded administration of public education (above primary schools) and was insufficiently detailed in its definition of public-health responsibilities to be assigned to local bodies. In other words, the system was to be part of a top-down centralized state, where the role of local governments would be to provide municipal services and implement development programs mandated by state and central governments. No mention was made of the processes by which local populations could express their need for different public services to higher levels of government. The administration of the three key areas of irrigation, schools, and health facilities could be retained by the bureaucracy appointed at the state or central government levels, without seriously contravening the recommendations of the committee. The seeds of the current system of limited decentralization prevailing throughout India were thus sown at this early stage in the life of the new republic. It reflected the consensus in the middle of the twentieth century that the centralized state would be the principal agent of economic development.

The Balwantrai Mehta Committee also left room for state governments to experiment with the system as they saw fit, consistent with the constitutional assignment of responsibility, and was endorsed in this respect by the National Development Council in January 1958. The central government created a Ministry of Community Development, Panchayati Raj, and Cooperation in 1958 and issued a publication in 1962 entitled *A Digest on Panchayati Raj* reiterating its encouragement to state governments to implement a three tier system of local government. In the absence of any concrete political pressure from the center, state governments (with few exceptions such as Maharashtra and Gujarat in the late 1960s) were unwilling to embark on any serious effort to devolve powers to local governments at their own expense (Government of West Bengal, 1980).

West Bengal's own experience during this period was similar (Government of West Bengal, 1980). It passed a Panchayat Act in 1957, followed by the Zilla Parishad Act of 1963, which established a four-tier

system comprising village panchayats, anchal parishads with a jurisdiction of eight to ten villages, anchalik parishads at the block level,
and zilla parishads at the district level. These were supposed to have
four-year terms of office, with indirect elections at all levels above the
village panchayats from representatives at lower levels and with representation of women, underprivileged communities, ranking bureaucrats at the block level and above, and elected politicians from local
constituencies. Approximately 19,000 village panchayats, 3,000 anchal
panchayats, 300 anchalik parishads, and 15 zilla parishads were formally constituted by the mid-1960s. Yet these institutions were not
delegated much effective responsibility or provided much financial
support. Elections were rarely held, meetings of local gram sabhas (village assemblies) were poorly attended, and local political leadership
was yet to emerge. In the words of Uday Bhaduri, the assistant director
of panchayats in 1980:

This was undoubtedly an important step towards democratic decentralization;
its socio-economic significance is indisputable. But in the economic base
on which the gradual evolution lay, there was very little place for the poor.
The rural and panchayat leadership was one that emerged out of the green revolution in the farms of the big landholders. The zilla parishads and anchalik
parishads met their inglorious death as soon as they were born. The reason behind this fact was that the unorganized landholder [jotedar] class could not be a
match for the neobourgeoisie, a product of the industrial cities. Beginning right
from the national movement up to the second decade after independence the
national leadership was mainly in the urban areas. Therefore, though the rural
institutions got the theoretical recognition, in practice it was beyond the notice
of national leadership.

Webster (1992) identifies the two key problems that rendered these
governments ineffective. First, responsibility for delivery of most important public services and developmental programs were retained
by departments and ministries of the state government. Bureaucrats
appointed by the state government and accountable only to their
hierarchical superiors in the district and state capitals were the principal agents in the delivery system. There was no scope for the voice
of the local governments to be heard by the bureaucrats. Second,
there was no scope for representation of the interests of the vast
majority of tenants and agricultural workers, while the existing
structure of land relations continued to remain highly unequal owing
to the failure of the state government to implement any serious land
reform.

Reorganization of Panchayats under the Left Front

All this changed with the ascendance of a Left Front government to power at the state-government level in 1977. A decade earlier, they had shared a coalition United Front government with a breakaway faction from the Congress Party for two brief years (1967 to 1969). This period was marked by growing unrest and anarchy, originating in a peasant rebellion led by the ultraleft Naxalite movement. This ended with the imposition of president's rule by the central government then dominated by the Congress Party headed by Indira Gandhi. The elections of 1972 saw the Congress back in power for a full five-year term at the state. The next state assembly elections in 1977 saw the Left Front coalition attain an absolute majority.

The newly elected government set about implementing two key initiatives in the agrarian sector: land reforms and reconstitution of local governments. The former was intended to decisively alter patterns of agrarian relations, with recording and protection of sharecropping tenants from eviction (Operation Barga), vesting of land owned by large landowners above the legal ceiling and distribution of vested lands in the form of land titles to the landless. At the same time, it set about creating a three-tier system of local government analogous to the formula suggested by the Balwantrai Mehta Committee. With the continuation of the Left Front at the state government through six successive elections, this structure is essentially the system prevailing today, though modified and amended in a variety of ways in the interim.

The lowest tier is the gram panchayat (GP), with a jurisdiction comparable to the British union boards or the postindependence anchal parishads; they cover eight to ten villages, with approximately ten to eighteen elected members (each representing 500 voters in nonhill areas and 125 voters in hill areas). A bold departure from the Mehta Committee required the representatives at two tiers above comprising panchayat samities (PS) and zilla parishads (ZP) to also be elected directly by voters. These elections are held every five years on a mandatory basis, starting with 1978. In other respects, the structure is quite similar to that recommended by the Mehta Committee.

Of particular note is the political will of the state government to devolve significant responsibilities to the panchayats, reducing the near monopoly power of bureaucratic departments in the previous regime. Relevant bureaucrats such as the block development officer at the PS level and the district magistrate at the ZP level have positions in the corresponding PSs and ZPs but need to work with politically elected representatives who retain the chairperson authority in these bodies. Elections to these positions in local government are characterized by high voter turnout and are increasingly subject to greater contestation between the Left Front and its principal rival the Congress (and its breakaway faction the Trinamool Congress since 1998).

Range of Responsibilities and Finances Devolved

The principal responsibilities of the panchayats have included the following:

• Implementation of land reforms, chiefly identification of sharecroppers and of those entitled to receive land titles;

• Selection and monitoring beneficiaries of various agricultural development (such as distribution of agricultural minikits and extension services) and antipoverty programs, including the Integrated Rural Development Program (IRDP), employment-generation programs creating rural infrastructure (including the National Rural Employment Program, NREP, and the Rural Labour Employment Guarantee Program, NRLEGP, during the 1980s, subsequently consolidated into the Jawahar Rozgar Yojana, JRY, from 1989), and various welfare schemes (such as housing, old age assistance, pensions, and disaster relief);

• Construction and management of local roads, school buildings, and irrigation facilities (such as tanks, ponds, riverlift schemes, and wells);

• Community and cooperative projects, including management of common property resources such as wasteland, and forests;

• Collection of local taxes, levies and fees; and

• Since the early 1990s, administration of Shishu Shiksha Kendras (SSKs), alternatives to the primary schools run by the state government.

Conspicuous by their absence are the management of primary and secondary schools and management of principal health facilities, which remain under the jurisdiction of relevant departments of the state government.

   The extent of financial autonomy is also limited, with the panchayats relying principally on grants from state and central governments under various schemes. In the sample of panchayats that we have surveyed (described below in greater detail), employment grants comprised approximately 50 to 60 percent of the resources available to gram panchayats in any given year. A number of other fiscal grants tied to specific projects collectively accounted for another 25 percent of panchayat revenues. The rest was raised by the gram panchayats from local sources, mostly in the form of schemes involving sale of assets and collectively produced goods (such as fish produced in community ponds). Taxes and fees accounted for a minuscule fraction of panchayat revenues—less than 4 percent on average.

The panchayat system was amended significantly in 1985 and then again in 1992 and 1993 and in 1998. The 1985 amendment sought to create a system of decentralized planning or budgeting whereby panchayats would communicate their priorities and needs to higher-level tiers, which would subsequently incorporate them into allocations across districts, blocks, and GPs. The extent to which this has been effectively operationalized is difficult to assess, with some accounts suggesting that allocations depend insignificantly on upward flows of information from bottom levels. The 1992 and 1993 amendment created mandatory reservation of one-third of panchayat seats to women and a share equal to their population share for SCs and STs; this was supplemented by the 1998 amendment to include reservation of positions of pradhan (chair of the GP) for women, SCs, and STs. Apart from reservation for minorities, the 1992 Amendment also mandated twice yearly meetings of the gram sabha (village assembly) where accounts for the preceding period would have to be presented by GP officers, past developmental projects could be publicly discussed, and complaints or critical questions could be raised by local citizens.

The role of the GPs is partly to allocate resources within its jurisdiction—allocation of funds under various employment programs to different forms of rural infrastructure such as roads, water, sanitation, irrigation, or public buildings; the execution of such projects (selection of location, procurement of materials, selection of those employed from within the village); selection of beneficiaries of various programs, taking the form of creating a below-the-poverty-line (BPL) list of local residents; and selection of (or recommendation to the concerned block office about) recipients for specific programs from this list. It will also include subsequent monitoring of these recipients, such as for those receiving an IRDP loan, the use of the proceeds of the loan, or assisting in the recovery of the loan. The intra-GP allocation is highly visible within the village, as a result of requirements to have a system of accounts publicly available to local residents, which can be discussed at gram sabha meetings. These accounts and minutes of GP meetings are legally required to be maintained by the GP secretary and to be submitted and audited by the PS directly above the GP in question.

The other role of the GP is to participate with higher-level bodies in determining how many resources it is to receive under various program heads. The inter-GP and sometimes also the inter-PS or interdistrict (ZP) allocations are rarely defined by transparent formulas, with the exception of the centrally sponsored employment programs. With respect to the IRDP program or the distribution of agricultural minikits, for instance, discretion plays a big role in the deliberations at the PS level, involving a large number of elected representatives from the panchayats, bureaucrats of the concerned state departments, and other implementing agencies (such as loan officers in the corresponding lead banks administering the IRDP loans). Some formulas appear to exist for vertical allocation of funds across different tiers of the system (across ZP, PS, or GP levels), but there are comparatively few for their horizontal allocation at any given vertical tier.

The interjurisdictional resource allocations are complex in other ways as well. There is a bewilderingly large array of developmental schemes flowing down from various ministries or various upper-level governments. Our review of the budgets of GPs indicated at least one thousand different schemes in operation at different times, contributing to the revenues and expenditure responsibilities of the GPs. These may flow from the central government, the state government, or a combination of the two (such as the majority of funds flow from centrally sponsored schemes where the bulk of funding comes from the central government, with matching contributions from the state government). They may flow from various employment programs or other welfare programs. Apart from the programs showing up in GP budgets, there are others in which they have significant responsibility, such as land reforms, selection of beneficiaries of agricultural services, or the IRDP program.

Participation Patterns

We now turn to available empirical evidence concerning various aspects of the functioning of the panchayats. Many case studies are available, but these are usually conducted in one or two locations, and there is heavy reliance on the subjective impressions of the investigators (see, for example, Lieten, 1992; Pramanick and Datta, 1994; Webster, 1992). So the representativeness of their conclusions can be questioned. For this reason, we report the results of recent studies based on larger and more representative samples, relying on empirical data generated by these studies that are far more reliable than subjective impressions reported by surveyed individuals or of investigators.

One such study involves a sample of over eighty villages throughout the state from which have collected data concerning the operation of panchayats between 1978 and 1998, covering five successive panchayat elections. Details of this sample have been described in Bardhan and Mookherjee (2003, 2004, 2005). This study collected data on panchayat composition, GP meetings, GP budgets, distribution of IRDP loans and agricultural minikits, employment programs, and details of expenditures on road construction and maintenance. In addition, it included land reforms implemented, a listing of all households in the village in 1978 and 1998 including landownership, irrigation status of land owned, occupation, SC or ST status, literacy, and gender of head of household. A survey of eight randomly selected farms across different size classes carried out by the Socio-Economic Evaluation Branch of the Department of Agriculture of the state government for a period of between three and fifteen years generates data on production in these farms and details of relevant prices and wage rates. This study focuses mainly on patterns in the activities of the panchayats with respect to implementation of land reforms and other developmental programs and how they changed in response to variations in landownership, demographic composition, occupational patterns, and literacy within the villages over the twenty-year period.

Another study has been carried out by Chattopadhyay and Duflo (2004) of all GPs (166 in number) in the district of Birbhum, focused specifically on the effect of reservation of GP and Pradhan positions for women, SC, and ST candidates on participation patterns in GPs and village meetings and on the allocation of public-service delivery between 1998 and 2000. It relies on cross-sectional comparisons between villages with and without reserved seats.

These two studies allow us to infer patterns of representation of different landowning classes and of minority groups in GPs. Table 6.1 presents the proportion of GP seats secured by landless, marginal (0 to 2.5 acres), and small (2.5 to 5 acres) landowners in different GP elections. It shows that these three groups collectively comprised approximately two-thirds of all GP seats throughout the period. From this

Table 6.1
Representation of poor households in GP seats (percentage)

	1978–1983	1983–1988	1988–1993	1993–1998	1998–2003
GP seats					
Landless	9.6%	11.2%	10.9%	20.8%	19.9%
Marginal	38.5	39.6	37.6	37.8	35.2
Small	18.3	16.9	21.7	12.1	15.7
Total	66.4	67.7	70.2	70.7	70.8
Households (landless, marginal, and small)	96.1				99.2

Source: Author survey.

point of view, they tended to retain majority control of GPs. On the other hand, these three groups were underrepresented relative to their demographic share, which rose from 96 percent of the village population to over 99 percent. This implies that households owning more than five acres of land were vastly overrepresented in the GPs: a group of less than 4 percent households in the village held approximately one-third of GP seats throughout the period. The underrepresentation was greatest for the landless, whose demographic weight was 44 percent in 1978 and 49 percent in 1998. While the proportion of seats secured by them approximately doubled from 10 to 20 percent over the period, their representation rate was less than half their demographic weight. In 1998, one out of every two households was landless, but only one out of every five seats in the GP was secured by a landless candidate. While the representation of the landless poor improved markedly (compared to the pre-1978 period or also during the period 1978 to 1998), clearly there is some way to go before they are to be effectively represented. If there is an issue that divides the interests between suppliers and employers of hired labor (such as an agitation for higher wages, distribution of surplus land to the landless, or allocation of panchayat funds between less employment-intensive and more employment-intensive infrastructure projects, such as irrigation versus roads), it would not be surprising if the majority of GP members would vote in favor of the interests of the employers.

Table 6.2 provides data on representation of women, SC, and ST categories in the population. Prior to 1993, when the mandatory seat-reservation policy was introduced, women were heavily underrepresented. This changed drastically from 1993 onward, when they secured approximately one-third of all GP seats. SC and ST candidates also

Table 6.2
Representation of minorities in GP seats (percentage)

	1978–1983	1983–1988	1988–1993	1993–1998	1998–2003
GP seats					
Women	2.4%	1.7%	1.3%	31.1%	34.1%
SC/ST	23.1	20.3	22.1	33.9	33.4
SC/ST households	32.8				34.4

Source: Author survey.

Table 6.3
Minority participation in Birbhum GPs with and without reservations (percentage)

	GPs with Reserved Pradhan Positions	GPs without Reservations
GP with female pradhans	100.0%	6.5%
GP with SC/ST pradhans	100.0	7.5
Women attending gram sabha meetings	9.8	6.9
GPs where women file complaints six months prior to survey	20.0	11.0

Source: Chattopadhyay and Duflo (2004, tables 1 and 3).

tended to be underrepresented before 1993 but to a substantially less degree. They secured approximately one out of every four or five GP seats, while representing one out of every three households. The reservation policy ensured that they were evenly represented from 1993 onward.

The effect of reservations policy on representation is also borne out by the Chattopadhyay-Duflo study, as indicated in table 6.3. Seat reservations for women, SC, and ST candidates for the position of GP pradhan were properly implemented, and increased the frequency of minority Pradhans dramatically. The seat reservation for the women increased the participation of women in gram sabha meetings and in their filing of complaints or requests to the GP; these differences were statistically significant.

A detailed study of attendance at gram sansad meetings in a sample of twenty panchayat constituencies has been carried out by Ghatak and Ghatak (2002). This study covers constituencies located in fourteen GPs in three different districts—twenty-four Parganas (N), twenty-four Parganas (S), and South Dinajpur—in May 1999. It is based on a survey of villagers by the authors following recent gram sansad

Table 6.4
Gram sansad attendance rates (percentage)

	Men	Women	SC	ST	Mus-lims	Land-less	Marginal and Small Land-owners	Left Front Political Affilia-tion
Attending	91%	9%	55%	13%	3%	43%	41%	67%
Voters	54	46	58	15	4			65[a]

Source: Ghatak and Ghatak (2002, tables 4, 5, 6).
Note: a. Constituencies secured by Left Front candidates.

meetings and concerning their participation in these meetings. The sample is smaller and less representative than the other two studies reported above but covers a larger range of situations than most other case studies (which typically focus on two or three villages). It provides valuable insights into the extent and nature of popular participation in meetings discussing the activities of the GPs.

Table 6.4 presents some of the participation rates in the gram sansad meetings reported by Ghatak and Ghatak. The overall participation rate in these meetings was 12 percent of all voters, somewhat below the 16 percent rate they report for West Bengal as a whole. This suggests one out of every seven or eight voters attended the gram sansad meetings, where the minimum required for a quorum is one out of ten. Of those attending, 43 percent on average were landless, 41 percent were marginal or small landowners, and the remaining 16 percent were medium or large landowners. Similar to the GP representation rates, a majority of attendees were therefore small landowners or poorer, but medium and large landowners were vastly overrepresented. However, the landless were more evenly represented in the meetings than in GP positions.

Minority groups such as SC or ST voters or Muslims were evenly represented. However, the most pronounced asymmetries arose with respect to gender and political affiliation. Women were vastly underrepresented, with a 9 percent attendance rate (roughly consistent with gram sabha attendance rates reported by Chattopadhyay and Duflo in their study). Moreover, there was a marked tendency for attendees to be associated with one of the main political parties, with a heavy bias in favor of the dominant party in the constituency. On average, two-thirds of the constituencies were secured by the Left Front, and a similar proportion of attendees reported a political affiliation with a left party. In constituencies where a non-Left Front candidate had secured the seat, the attendance rate of Left Front–affiliated voters was conversely less than one-third uniformly. Hence those voters who were affiliated with the opposition tended to stay away from these meetings disproportionately.

The Ghatak and Ghatak study also provides details of the nature of discussions in these gram sansad meetings. The main issues concerned review and monitoring of past and current GP projects (including location of projects, quality complaints, and corruption or mismanagement complaints); agenda for future projects (demands for new programs and priorities for GP spending); and selection of beneficiaries (distribution of water or housing benefits). Their account suggests a forum that enables genuine participation by diverse groups within these villages in public discussions, inducing a measure of accountability of elected members to their constituency (Ghatak and Ghatak, 2002, p. 53):

The participants actively voice demand for new projects, suggest how allocated funds should be spent and debate how projects should be designed. The pradhan and the local representatives are questioned on the progress of implementation of projects, and often face allegations about misuse of funds and selection of beneficiaries. The response of elected officials to these criticisms showed that they could not take the voters present at the meeting for granted. In some cases where there was overwhelming evidence in favour of the criticisms raised by the people, the village council officials admitted their error.... Sometimes the elected representatives and other village council functionaries gave a detailed account of the financial situation in respect of various schemes and tried to explain their poor performance in terms of delay of arrival of funds from the state government.

This represents a marked improvement over the previous situation where the power of the village council [gram panchayat] was totally concentrated in the hands of the pradhan.... The pradhan's power could be maintained mainly by the fact that the common villagers were not privy to information about the allocation of resources and there was no forum to voice their opinions and criticisms. The village constituency meetings seem to be an important institutional innovation to contribute to the ideal of participatory governance, although from our study we cannot judge how much of an effect it will have in making the allocation of resources responsive to public demand, or improving the implementation of projects.

Impact on Resource Allocation

In this section, we report on the principal findings of our own study (Bardhan and Mookherjee, 2005) and that of Chattopadhyay and

Duflo (2004) concerning resource allocation decisions made by the panchayats.

Chattopadhyay and Duflo find that reservation of Pradhan positions for women caused a statistically significant shift in allocation of public spending of GPs. Since the reservations were randomized, the cross-sectional differences between GPs with and without reserved positions represent the causal impact of reservations. Spending on drinking water facilities were higher by 7 percent, on road maintenance by 39 percent, and on informal education centers was down by about 20 percent. These accord with relative priorities expressed by women and men in their complaints or suggestions to the GP. The two highest items of women's complaints consisted of drinking water and road improvement (31 percent each), while irrigation and education centers were among their lowest priorities (4 and 6 percent, respectively). In contrast, the composition of complaints filed by men consisted of road improvement (25 percent), irrigation (20 percent), drinking water (17 percent), and education center (12 percent).

Our study focused on patterns of how resources are targeted within and across villages and how these varied with changes in demographic composition, land inequality, and literacy over time. The performance of panchayats with respect to selection of beneficiaries of IRDP loans and agricultural minikits across different landowning classes provides an indication of their responsiveness to the needs of the poor. An additional measure is the extent of employment generated per rupee of employment funds received by the panchayat, as this indicates incomes generated for the working poor.

Table 6.5 shows shares of IRDP loan subsidies, agricultural minikits, and employment days generated per rupee of employment grants received by GPs.[1] Shares of the landless, "upto small" category that aggregates landless, marginal, and small landowners in the IRDP program subsidies are depicted. The IRDP program is exclusively earmarked for households owning less than five acres, with preferential allotments for SC and ST categories and women. Table 6.5 shows that the leakage rate of this program to medium or large landowners was quite small, below 4 percent on average. Shares of the landless and "upto small" category exceeded their corresponding demographic weights. A similar pattern obtains for allocation of agricultural minikits, 98 percent of which were allocated to the "upto small" category, exceeding their share of cultivable land in the village. This indicates

Table 6.5
Intravillage targeting patterns

	IRDP Landless Share	IRDP "Upto Small" Share	Minikits "Upto Small" Share	Days Employment Generated per Rupee of Employment Grant
Average (s.d.)	45	97	98	.024
	(39)	(14)	(8)	(.095)
Effect of:				
2.5% more households landless rather than medium landowners	*i*	*i*	*i*	−0.010**
10% cultivable land shifts to small landowners from big landowners	*i*	*i*	*i*	*i*
5% more poor households are SC or ST	*i*	−*i*	*i*	*i*

Source: Bardhan-Mookherjee (2005).
Notes: *i* denotes statistically insignificant effect.
**Significant at 5 percent.

that GPs were quite effective on average in channeling developmental resources to the poor.

Table 6.5 provides estimates of the effect of changing some key distributional parameters within the village on intravillage targeting: landlessness, distribution of cultivable land between small and big landowners, and proportion of SC and ST households among the poor (defined as landless or marginal landowners). The magnitudes of these hypothetical changes were chosen to be approximately the same as the average change between between 1978 and 1998 (with the exception of the SC and ST proportion, which changed by fewer than five percentage points). The effects of these shifts on intravillage targeting turn out not to be significant, either statistically or quantitatively. In other words, there is little evidence of elite capture within villages.

Table 6.6 indicates the allocation of resources *across* GPs. We noted previously that the inter-GP allocation is complex and substantially less transparent to local citizens. Here there is scope for substantial political biases, which show up in the results for inter-GP allocation

Table 6.6
Intervillage targeting of resources

	IRDP Credit Subsidy (Rs)	Minikits Distributed	Employ-ment Grants Received by GP (Rs)	Total Fiscal Grants Received by GP (Rs)
Per household	24	.085	195	464
average (s.d.)	(66)	(.114)	(366)	(1247)
Effect of:				
2.5% more households landless rather than medium landowners	−*i*	−*i*	−*i*	−84*
10% cultivable land shifts to small landowners from big landowners	−*i*	*i*	55**	146*
5% more households are SC/ST	*i*	−.078***	−*i*	−125***

Source: Bardhan-Mookherjee (2005).
Notes: All rupee figures expressed in 1980 prices.
i denotes statistically insignificant effect.
*Significant at 10 percent.
**Significant at 5 percent.
***Significant at 1 percent.

of employment grants, and fiscal grants received from upper-level governments. These presumably reflect the discretion of upper-level politicians and bureaucrats combined with the political skill of local panchayat officials and awareness of local residents (related to socio-economic status) in directing resources toward their jurisdictions.[2] A shift of 10 percent cultivable land from small to big landowners or rise in the proportion of SC and ST households among the poor by 5 percent was associated with a decline in the per capita allotment of employment grants and all fiscal grants by approximately 25 percent. Rising landlessness by 2.5 percent was associated with an 18 percent decline in fiscal grants.

Assessment

To what extent have the West Bengal panchayats promoted account-ability to local citizens concerning delivery of public services? The answer to this question depends primarily on the relevant criterion of accountability. In the context of rural India and West Bengal in particular, one of the primary criteria involve their responsiveness to the poor compared with more affluent citizens, owing to the high degree of poverty and inequality. Both the extent of deprivation of the poor and their numerical majority implies that a key criterion of accountability is the extent to which the system is responsive to the needs of the poor, relative to the nonpoor. With regard to this aspect of distributive justice, the West Bengal panchayats certainly appear to be quite successful. This is both in terms of providing an opportunity for the poor to be heard and represented in the formal system of government and for resources in developmental programs to flow toward the poor. In this respect, the panchayats have reversed century-old traditions of hierarchy of power within the Bengal countryside based on high inequality in land relations. Landless agricultural workers, women, and SC and ST members can now stand up in public meetings and openly pose critical questions regarding public services to village leaders. The fraction of resources in credit, agricultural minikit delivery, or other welfare schemes reaching the poor has equaled or exceeded their demographic shares. Leakages in the IRDP program earmarked for the poor amounted to less than 4 percent on average throughout two decades of operation of the program.

In other respects, the provision of benefits of the system has been uneven. Women, SC and ST members, and those not politically affiliated with the party in power in the local area still participate at low levels, though seat reservations for minorities have helped alleviate this imbalance. The intervillage allocation of resources was subject to high levels of discretion, reflecting both political priorities of upper-level governments and the political bargaining strength of local governments and local citizens. Villages with greater landlessness, land inequality, or low-caste status among the poor received substantially fewer resources as a whole. Anecdotes and case studies indicate that the allocation of benefits follow political party lines. Those that do not belong to the party locally in power get severely discriminated against.

The extent of autonomy of the panchayats is also quite limited in comparison with local governments in many other countries. They rely principally on grants from state and central governments, the allocation of which is based on either political or bureaucratic discretion. The system responds perversely to variation in local needs, reducing allocations to more needy villages. The scale of resources channeled through the panchayats remains pitifully low. They do not have access to elastic revenue bases, nor do they have skill or experience with raising revenues locally. Hence their capacity to make a serious dent on local poverty is limited. They also lack authority over the administration of vital education and health services, which remain in the hands of the state bureaucracy.

Both the strengths and weaknesses of the West Bengal panchayats can be explained by political economy considerations—the political compulsions of the Left Front. Their sustained political will to create a functioning panchayat system even in the absence of any constitutional mandates—in contrast to all other Indian states—has been a joint outcome of both their political ideology and more pragmatic compulsions of consolidating their political power. Ideologically, the left parties have been committed to empowering poorer sections of the peasantry at the expense of landed elites, which required the creation of an institutional mechanism that would be the source of political power of the poor. Implementing the land reforms required the state government to seek the active collaboration of local citizens, who were better informed than urban-based political leaders or bureaucrats temporarily assigned to district or block headquarters concerning how much land was owned by any given household in the village or who was whose tenant. Given the traditional nexus of collusion between local landed elites and the state bureaucrats, it was necessary to transfer authority over the delivery of key public benefits from the bureaucracy to politically elected local leaders.

The pragmatic need to consolidate power also necessitated the creation of a system of local government. Having shared power briefly in a coalition United Front government in the late 1960s that was subsequently dismissed by the central government (dominated by the opposition Congress Party) on grounds of growing anarchy in the state, the Left Front was anxious to consolidate its political power in the state in 1977, when it won a majority in the state assembly for the first time. Creating a system of village panchayats throughout the state where it might expect to also secure a majority, would ensure that the political power of the Left Front in the state would no longer be at the mercy of the central government. A second source of political compulsion arose from the need to neutralize the threat from the ultraleft Naxalite Party that had fomented the peasant rebellion in the late 1960s. It needed to implement land reforms and extend political power to the poor peasantry to prevent a recurrence of such rebellions in the future. In addition, it was important to convince hardliners within the left parties growing increasingly disenchanted with the compromises made by the party relative to its traditional ideology of encouraging confrontation and class conflict. As vividly described by Lieten (1992) and Bhattacharya (1999), the policy of the party veered increasingly toward the pragmatic objective of consolidating political power through a democratic system, what Bhattacharya labels as the "politics of middleness." This required the creation of local democratic institutions forming part of the overall system of government, which would seek to represent the poorer sections of the peasantry and minority groups. As the case study of two villages in Bardhaman district by Ruud (1999) indicates, pragmatic compulsions often led to the coopting of some backward castes but not others.

The panchayat system has served the political purposes of the Left Front reasonably well. They have formed the base of political support of the party, as weaknesses in industrial performance have caused their support in urban areas to wane. Our study (Bardhan and Mookherjee, 2003) of the success of the left in successive GP elections indicate a strong proincumbent effect, after controlling for various community characteristics (such as distribution of land, literacy, occupations, and population across different socioeconomic groups) and measures of past performance (with respect to implementation of land reforms) that might affect loyalties of local voters. In other words, community characteristics and past performance remaining the same, a village GP in which the Left Front secured a higher proportion of seats in any given election was more likely to win a majority in the next election. This may either reflect genuine proincumbency sentiment among voters or the ability of incumbents to use their command over local law and order or electoral machines to gain an advantage over their political rivals. Whatever the source, this proincumbency effect implies that the panchayats enabled the left to consolidate their power over time, though the last two elections (1998 and 2003) have been marred by increasing violence and contestation with rival parties.

Some of the weaknesses of the panchayats also derive from the political compulsions of the Left Front. The party has a tradition of strong centralized party discipline. Accordingly, there is a tendency to use local panchayats by the central committees at the state level as an instrument of political mobilization and cultivation of political clientelism at the local level. This explains the partisan character of distribution of resources at the local level by the GPs, combined with centralized party control of interregional allocation of development funds.

Notes

1. The IRDP subsidy includes the subsidy portion of the loan that is not meant to be repaid, in addition to an imputed subsidy rate applied to the remainder based on assumption of an annual informal interest rate of 80 percent per annum and normalized to a per year equivalent.

2. The IRDP and minikit data pertain to specific villages rather than GPs, whereas the data on grants pertain to GPs.

References

Bardhan, P., and D. Mookherjee. (2003). "Political Economy of Land Reform in West Bengal 1978–98." Mimeo, Institute for Economic Development, Boston University.

Bardhan, P., and D. Mookherjee. (2004). "Poverty Alleviation Efforts of Pacnhayats in West Bengal." *Economic and Political Weekly*, February 28, pp. 965–974.

Bardhan, P., and D. Mookherjee. (2005). "Pro-Poor Targeting and Accountability of West Bengal Panchayats 1978–98." Mimeo, Institute for Economic Development, Boston University. Forthcoming, *Journal of Development Economics*.

Bhattacharya, D. (1999). "Politics of Middleness: The Changing Character of the Communist Party of India (Marxist) in Rural Bengal (1977–90)." In B. Rogaly, B. Harriss-White, and S. Bose (Eds.), *Sonar Bangla? Agricultural Growth and Agrarian Change in West Bengal and Bangladesh*. New Delhi: Sage.

Chattopadhyay, R., and E. Duflo. (2004). "Impact of Reservation in Panchayati Raj: Evidence from a Nationwide Randomised Experiment." *Economic and Political Weekly*, February 28, pp. 979–986.

Ghatak, M., and M. Ghatak. (2002). "Recent Reforms in the Panchayat System in West Bengal: Towards Greater Participatory Governance?" *Economic and Political Weekly*, January 5, pp. 45–58.

Government of West Bengal. (1980). *Panchayati Review*. Calcutta: Government of West Bengal.

Lieten, G. K. (1992). *Continuity and Change in Rural West Bengal*. New Delhi: Sage.

Pramanick, S. K., and P. Datta. (1994). *Panchayats and People: The West Bengal Experience*. Calcutta: Bagchi.

Ruud, A. E. (1999). "From Untouchable to Communist: Wealth, Power and Status among Supporters of the Communist Party (Marxist) in Rural West Bengal." In B. Rogaly, B. Harriss-White, and S. Bose (Eds.), *Sonar Bangla? Agricultural Growth and Agrarian Change in West Bengal and Bangladesh*. New Delhi: Sage.

Webster, N. (1992). *Panchayati Raj and the Decentralisation of Development Planning in West Bengal*. Calcutta: Bagchi.

7 Decentralization in Uganda

Omar Azfar, Jeffrey
Livingston, and Patrick
Meagher

Introduction

Uganda experienced a tumultuous postindependence period, with power passing to Milton Obote, to Idi Amin, back to Obote, and eventually to Yoweri Museveni and his National Resistance Movement (NRM). Idi Amin's regime, among its other excesses, savaged the social sector by forcing the migration of many Asian doctors, pharmacists, and teachers. Since Museveni's takeover in 1986, Uganda has been something of a regional success in terms of stability and economic growth, but social indicators have shown lackluster performance.[1] There is hope that the latter might improve with the devolution of health and education provision to the local level. It is argued that local governments produce the same goods at lower costs than the central government and that local governments are likely to be better able to provide the public goods that are demanded by citizens.[2]

In this chapter, we examine whether Uganda's decentralization reforms are having these benefits—specifically, in the health and education sectors. The literature on fiscal federalism and related perspectives suggests several reasons, or "federalist disciplines," to expect Uganda's devolution of authority to lead to significant improvements in service delivery. Devolution will theoretically be successful only if local democracies work better than national democracies, if local officials are well informed about the preferences of their constituents, and if local governments are both able and willing to fund projects that are needed or demanded in their jurisdictions. Further, there must be diverse preferences across localities, and there must be de facto devolution of power to the local level (Tiebout, 1956; Oates, 1972; Oates and Schwab, 1988; Inman and Rubinfeld, 1996; Bardhan and Mookherjee, 1998). We evaluate the evidence on each of these points concerning

Uganda—first analyzing the structure and process of decentralization and then presenting empirical data.

The Structure of Ugandan Decentralization[3]

President Museveni came to power as the head of a victorious guerilla movement that followed the common revolutionary formula of establishing popular local councils (resistance councils) to administer territory under the NRM's control. Having consolidated their hold on national authority, Museveni and the NRM set about formalizing the council structure, linking individual councils in a hierarchy leading up to the districts and from there to the center. The councils, which originally served the security and mobilization needs of a guerilla movement, evolved into organs of state administrative control and forums for local political participation in Uganda's "no-party democracy."

Museveni's top priority was to amalgamate as many significant political forces as possible—regardless of past political affiliation—into the NRM structure (Khadiagala, 1995). Bringing the population into this framework of local participation and representation seemed to offer the NRM a way to sideline the old political parties, the traditional chiefs, and the major ethnic groups such as the Baganda that wanted autonomous status. Consolidating NRM control at the center and extending it out through the NRM structure and the councils were necessary parts of this strategy. Thus, the NRM could exert influence from the top down and expand its reach through mobilization and patronage—while offering limited recognition to political parties and to traditional leaders such as the Kabaka (Kasfir, 2000; Makara, 1998; Mukyala-Makiika, 1998). From a position of strength, Museveni could head off the challenges of multipartyism and federalism and move decisively on economic liberalization (Oetemoeller, 1996).

The Gradual Devolution of Responsibilities

Here and in the next section, we assess the extent of decentralization in Uganda, including the evidence on the de facto authority of local-governance units (LGUs). Later, we test this empirically, looking at officials' ability to respond to local demands.

In the Ugandan context, decentralization meant conferring formal political authority on the councils, converting them from appointed to elected bodies, and devolving the resources necessary for public services and administration. Uganda has devolved state power in stages over the years. The resistance councils were formalized in 1987 and strengthened by the 1993 Decentralization Act, which also made primary health and education the responsibility of the districts. The decentralization of recurrent budgets was phased in from 1993 to 1997.

The 1995 constitution sets forth a general framework for decentralization, which is further elaborated in the 1997 Local Governments Act. There are five levels of local government—village, parish, subcounty, county, and district. Of these, only the district and subcounty levels have both political authority and significant resources. Hence, the forty-five districts and the eight hundred subcounties are the focus of this research. Local governments have legislative and executive authority within their listed areas of jurisdiction. The district council list includes primary and secondary education, a range of primary health services, and basic services in the areas of water provision, roads, planning, and licensing. Several listed areas—including primary education, community-based health services, and hygiene—are to be devolved by the district to lower-level councils.

Two (potentially) important checks are provided between levels in the governmental hierarchy: lower-level enactments must be forwarded for constitutional review to higher levels, and lower-level governments are charged with monitoring the performance of higher-level public officials working in their areas, as well as the provision of services and implementation of projects by higher-level governments. The law also defines exacting standards and procedural requirements for the convening of ministerial commissions of inquiry and for the takeover of local administrations by the president.

The division of powers under the Local Governments Act is not always clear. The district and subcounty levels have popularly elected chairs, designated as the political head of the relevant jurisdiction. Districts and subcounties also have administrative chiefs who monitor local-government department activities and delivery of services, reporting to the local council. Additionally, the president appoints resident district commissioners (RDCs) to represent central government interests, monitor governmental activities, and provide advice to each district. The balance of power between the district chair and the RDC is nebulous and seems to create conflict.

Local Resources and Administration
Uganda has moved significant resources and responsibilities to local governments. In the past, central ministries essentially decided on

funding allocations for district-level services, and the Ministry of Finance, Planning, and Economic Development (MFPED) routed funds through the relevant line ministries. Now, the districts are given budget ceilings within which to operate, and the MFPED directly transmits grant funds to district administrators, thus removing one link in the chain (Lubanga, 1998). However, most funds are allocated to the district in the form of conditional grants.

Local government revenue sources include the graduated (head) tax, property tax, and some licenses and fees. The two most important sources of revenue are the graduated tax and grants from the central government. Local governance units have some discretion in setting tax rates. They may adopt additional taxes, but only at the discretion of the Ministry of Local Government (or Parliament). The subcounty level acts as the primary local tax collector, remitting 35 percent of collections to the district level (50 percent in urban areas) and passing on smaller shares to lower-level governments. District governments are supposed to distribute 30 percent of own revenues to lower levels of government following a formula taking account of child mortality and school-age population.

Central grants include equalization transfers directed to localities lagging behind in public-service provision. These policies raise the concerns of Persson and Tabellini (1996) about risk-sharing versus incentives facing local governments. Indeed, some authors have raised concerns about the perverse incentives created by equalization grants in Uganda (Hutchinson, 1999). To address this, some districts have apparently designed schemes to reward subordinate units for good performance.

The local budget planning process requires districts to prioritize funding needs within a ceiling imposed by the center. As between the district and subcounty levels, planning and budgeting decisions are, in theory, to be driven by the subcounty as the relevant political and fiscal unit supporting local public services. In practice, these processes vary with local capacity and with local tolerance for the time-consuming procedures. In many cases, data are simply sent up from the subcounties, and the districts make decisions unilaterally on that basis.

Nongovernmental organizations (NGOs) are substantially involved in service delivery. They receive conditional grants directly from the center (via the district) and sometimes participate in planning with the districts. NGO contributions to public services are now expected to be included in local government budgets. However, the districts have a strong countervailing incentive not to disclose information on NGO contributions or donor funds, fearing that this will lead to cuts in block grants.

It is frequently observed that local governments, from the district level downward, have little overall flexibility in the use of funds. Conditional grant terms contain not only affirmative duties but also lists of things that the grants cannot be used for, and conditional grant-reporting requirements are said to be onerous. These rigidities appear to encourage undesirable outcomes such as overinvestment in facilities and informal accommodation of needs identified by district officials. Other standards tie the hands of local governments but are not as well monitored—including the Local Governments Act cap on local council allowances, at 15 percent of the previous year's revenue. The 15 percent rule is said to be routinely flouted, with the bulk of local revenues being used for council salaries and allowances (Francis and James, 2003).

Another public-finance problem is delay in local governments' receipt of grant funds. Opinions differ on whether the banking system or the administration is at fault here. Under Uganda's system of cash budgeting, if a district does not receive a grant by the end of its fiscal year, the funds are lost (Barnes, 1999). Since development budgets have begun to be devolved, affected districts (such as Mukono) say that public funding is becoming more stable and reliable. But as of early 2000, the center still handled over 70 percent of the development budget for local (district and below) activities (Kiyaga-Nsubuga, 2000).

Local expenditure in Uganda is essentially a matter of personnel: payrolls claim the lion's share of public finance. Civil-service reform reduced public sector staff overall from 320,000 in 1992 to below 140,000 by the end of 1994 (Kisubi, 1998). This number rebounded to 170,000 in 1999 (Kiyaga-Nsubuga, 2000). Thus the perception has become widespread in Uganda that decentralization raises the overall public sector wage bill due to inevitable overlap at different levels of government. At the same time, the districts are hemmed in by central budget programming decisions and civil service protections. Many districts manage to alleviate their situation, passing on some personnel costs to the subcounties.

When a local government does bear the full cost of a public employee, it tends to use this for political advantage. Local politicians have two sources of cover for favoritism in recruitment: first, the constitution requires that local government staff should live in the districts where they serve; and second, the district service commissions (DSCs), which should monitor civil service practices independently of the local councils, seem rarely to do so in practice. This has fostered perceptions that public sector jobs go to "sons of the soil."

Devolution of the Social Sectors

Education services and a range of health-care functions have been devolved to local governments. The latter include primary care, certain hospitals, and communicable disease control. Health specialists often express alarm at the likely impact of decentralization on health services. They point out that successful decentralization of health services can be expected to take five to ten years and requires reorganization of the Ministry of Health (MOH).

Two main problems arise in decentralization of health services in Uganda. First, health units have little incentive to manage costs effectively or to respond to local demands. Salaries and staffing decisions come from the district, drugs are sent mainly from the center, and conditional grants for health contain recommended staffing patterns and other restrictions—creating an "inefficient centralized system within each district" (Hutchinson, 1999, p. 75). Moreover, politicians seek to build new health units to increase their influence locally but without considering recurrent costs.

Second, the expansion of local power into areas of health care that have spillover effects is bound to create anomalies. Decentralization by definition potentially endangers vertical programs. It requires new systems at the district level that did not exist before, and it inevitably confronts contrary preferences and incentives of local governments. Immunization programs are a responsibility of the center in Uganda, but the districts control supplies and maintain the cold chain. In the case of malaria control, the Ministry of Health contributes by setting standards and guidelines, providing technical support and supervision, supporting epidemic control, and conducting monitoring and training. At the same time, however, local fiscal contributions and to a lesser extent conditional grants for primary health care are subject to being diverted toward competing local health-care priorities.

This finding receives further support in recent health-sector research in Uganda. Akin, Hutchinson, and Strumpf (2001) suggest that small (subnational) governments tend to provide the goods for which citizens reveal preferences—and as a result focus expenditure more on goods with private characteristics, such as curative-care clinics, than would central government. Thus, decentralization of health care may direct spending away from public goods such as communicable disease control and thus reduce societal welfare. Data from Uganda on the allocation of local budgets to health care during the mid- to late 1990s supports this view. Budgets tended to favor construction of offices and clinics to the detriment of primary health care and other public goods.

Uganda's decentralization has prompted a number of steps aimed at combating corruption and inefficiency in the health sector. Whereas vaccines and essential drug kits were formerly distributed to the districts based on local returns, now the Ministry of Health collects data and projects these needs, allocating supplies accordingly. Also, Uganda's Health Management Information System collects and manages data on health-system inputs, needs, and outcomes. These approaches help to dilute previously strong incentives to overreport both input needs and outputs such as immunization coverage. To increase transparency, health-unit fees (but not budgets) are required to be posted, and overcharging has often led clients to complain to the local health committees. Some local health committees have taken the further step of opening the drug kits sent to the districts and comparing quantities to official records.

In the case of primary education, the curriculum and most funding flow from the center. New transparency mechanisms have accompanied the increased flow of funds to primary schools. Under Uganda's universal primary education (UPE) program, begun in 1997, school fees were abolished and funding augmented by central grants financed through a combination of debt-relief funds, national revenues, and donor funding. These grants include capitation grants (per student, up to four per family), classroom construction funds (based on enrollment levels), teacher salary grants based on a periodically fixed pupil-teacher ratio, and (initially) in-kind grants of materials. Families were also allowed to choose among public schools. As a result, primary enrollment jumped from about 3 million in 1996 to nearly 7 million in 2001, and spending on education as a share of government expenditure rose from approximately 20 to 26 percent (Suzuki, 2002; Stasavage, 2003). To cope with the increased flow of funding, UPE required school grants to be advertised and posted at the schools. The grants are now routinely announced in the newspapers and on radio. The evidence presented in World Bank tracking studies strongly suggests that these steps, along with the political visibility of universal primary education, helped drastically increase the proportion of primary education funding reported to be reaching the schools from 13 percent in the early 1990s to 90 percent or more recently (Ablo and Reinikka, 1998; Stasavage, 2003).

It is much less clear that the reforms offer a way to address school quality or to make the schools accountable in practice to the parents (Suzuki, 2002). Divergent spending priorities in education usually involve conflicts between the needs of teacher payrolls and those of school buildings. Teacher pay is a problem. The districts recruit teachers and pay them with conditional grant funds according to uniform pay scales approved by the Ministry of Education and Sports (MOES). Teacher pay has been increased since the universal primary education policy was adopted (to cope with the loss of phased-out parent-teacher association contributions, which in large part went to teachers). Yet some districts report that teacher salaries cover only a fraction of living costs and that payroll problems require some teachers to work as long as two years without pay.

Administrative and Political Disciplines

In this section, we turn to the vertical structures of government in Uganda that correspond to the federalist disciplines anticipated by the theoretical literature. Here, we examine two categories of disciplines—those exercised by central government and those imposed by the populace through the political system and local committees. The effectiveness of these disciplines is tested in the later empirical parts of the chapter.

Central Government Oversight

We begin with constraints imposed on local governments by intergovernmental relations—regarding central government oversight, fiscal authority, and planning and budgeting arrangements. Uganda is decentralizing while its government retains a unitary structure. Thus, local initiatives occur within an institutional structure defined and monitored by the center. This discipline has two primary formal channels: the resident district commissioner and the national oversight agencies. The Local Governments Act allows the center to deal directly only with districts but shields lower-level jurisdictions, bringing them under direct oversight by the districts. However, these formal relations are unlikely to be the whole story. The more important source of hierarchical pressure is probably political, and this is most likely to take place informally within the NRM structure.

Most changes brought about by decentralization are aimed at disciplining the local rather than central government. The Local Governments Act defines an array of procedures and standards for district government budgeting, audit, accountability, and financial allocations to lower levels. The resident district commissioner handles the formal monitoring, coordination, and advisory needs of local governance units. This may take on the aspect of directing and overruling (as well as political indoctrination and control) in those areas of Uganda with the lowest levels of political mobilization and media exposure. The Local Governments Act spells out dispute-resolution processes to be used in cases of conflict of authority, but these apparently have been little used (Kiyaga-Nsubuga, 2000).

In addition, the principal oversight bodies at the national level—the Inspector General of Government (IGG), the Treasury Inspectorate, the Auditor General, the Attorney General, and the Public Accounts Committee of Parliament—have direct jurisdiction over local government units. The main development program financed with budgetary savings from international debt relief, the Poverty Action Fund (PAF), has since 1998 provided monitoring funds to support some of these agencies in the oversight of local projects and services funded by the PAF. Fund releases are also to be advertised in the press.

This vertical arrangement may help to control corruption. Still, accounts of corruption affecting local health and education services are numerous, and there are significant weaknesses in the oversight process. The front-line internal auditors, at the district level, appear to lack the necessary skills and resources. The district chief administrative officers (CAOs), appointed by the district service commissions, have often proven to be inexperienced. Constraints on the DSCs' factual independence, reported by some observers, likely affect the CAOs as well.

In practice, hierarchical discipline in the system appears to be ad hoc. When a local government underperforms in a key sector (such as health), overspends its budget, or makes an invalid funding reallocation, the disciplinary responses available are numerous. They range from suspension or dismissal of the responsible bureaucrat to investigation by national authorities. Yet the perception is widespread that the center does not back up its policies with sanctions. The biggest "stick" held by the central government, the president's power to dissolve district governments, appears politically impossible to use.[4]

The center also appears to avoid any attempt to restrict district funding as a disciplinary measure—for political reasons. In fact, the usual response in the case of bad sectoral indicators appears to be *increasing* the central grant to the district to help it deal with the problem. However, the districts themselves have been less shy. The initial pilot districts that were given authority over their development budgets have instituted semiannual evaluations of subcounties and parishes. Those that perform well receive a 20 percent budget increase, while those faring badly suffer a 20 percent cut.

Political Accountability and Competition in Uganda

Political mobilization is high in Uganda by most accounts, and democratic practice has improved—but the "no-party" system, which increasingly affects local politics, raises questions. The nonpartisanship requirement for national political campaigns was extended to local elections under the Local Governments Act (article 126). This is bound to have an impact on political expression and competition. No-partyism has been criticized as antidemocratic: a 1999 report by Human Rights Watch interpreted the National Resistance Movement as essentially a state party. The NRM hierarchy in Kampala has a decisive voice in most policy matters. Thus, local council accountability runs at least as much to the NRM bosses as to the local population, and the NRM's expressed preferences place firm limits on political freedom and contestability.

The NRM has a representative structure that parallels the decentralized government councils at every level, with the National Movement Conference and its permanent secretariat at the pinnacle. Human Rights Watch suggests that this duplication—completely funded by the state—has no other evident function than as a partisan political apparatus of the type used in one-party states. This aim gains further support from the constitutional prohibition on conventions by other parties, the use of sedition laws against selected criticisms, intimidation by police and security forces of some parties and independent journals, mandatory political education for state functionaries, and state control of newspapers and radio stations reaching rural audiences (U.S. State Department, 2000; Human Rights Watch, 1999; Freedom House, 1999). Analysis by Ugandan scholars seems to confirm this view (Oloka-Onyango, 2000; Kasfir, 2000).

Yet there appears to be some space for contestability of elections and of public debate on political issues. According to the U.S. State Department's *1999 Country Reports on Human Rights Practices* (p. 17), "Individual parliamentarians who claim non-Movement party affiliation fully participate in the legislature." The report also suggests that the national legislature took a relatively "independent and assertive" posture during 1999 (p. 16). Most of the directly elected seats in Parliament were in fact contested during the 1996 national elections. In addition, parties were allowed to campaign in the 2000 referendum on the no-party system, and Paul Ssemogerere, leader of the Democratic Party, ran a competitive (but unsuccessful) presidential campaign against Museveni in 2001. There is also consensus that the government generally respects freedom of expression, despite its use of some restrictions, and indeed hard-hitting stories of scandal and corruption appear in both print and electronic media (U.S. State Department, 2000; Freedom House, 1999). The no-party system won decisive reaffirmation in the 2000 referendum, although the victory was tarnished by criticisms and relatively low turnout (Bratton and Lambright, 2001).

The extent of open political space at the district and local levels is more difficult to assess. No reliable information was available to us on the extent of competition in local elections. Experts agree that a divide exists between local and national-level politics but differ as to which is more democratic and accountable. Field studies suggest that people have usually viewed the resistance councils, now local councils, as legitimate forums of local consultative democracy (Tidemand, 1994; Oettemoeller, 1996). The problem, in this view, is that local transparency may be real, but it does not extend to higher levels (Human Rights Watch, 1999). Also, local government units have been held accountable legally—for example, by being sued on employment issues (Lubanga, 1998). Subcounties benefit from traditions of local consultative governance and from relatively high trust—although migration, especially in the south, is changing this.

In many respects, politics and institutions are more democratic at the national level than the local level. First, media and party activities appear most intensive in the national arena and in Kampala (we present evidence comparing the use of media for news on local and national politics in the empirical section of this chapter). Second, since the early days of the resistance councils, local government has become more integrated into the public sector. As a result, recent observations suggest that the state and the local councils have greater authority in the provinces than in the capital and other large cities (within the limits of geographic spread and security). Human Rights Watch cites evidence that both the local councils and the resident district commissioners do much of the NRM's work in the interior, providing platforms for candidates, spreading the NRM's ideology, administering political training, and performing other functions (Human Rights Watch, 1999). This suggests that political competition is probably much more limited in rural areas than major urban centers, that heavy-handed tactics are less likely to be opposed or publicized, and that political information is more controlled and less available in those areas.

Last, the committee structures set up under the Local Governments Act appear to have created at least as many governance problems as they have resolved. School management committees are empowered to sign checks for the headmaster, oversee the schools, and investigate problems. The committees also oversee school construction and improvements under regulations that exempt primary school-building from local tender board requirements. Communities are not always aware of the committees' operations and are not encouraged to participate (Uganda Debt Network, 1999). The committees, it seems, provide a sense of participation to families without providing them actual influence. They have often been run by members of the local councils, which are seen by many as tools of top-down political management rather than local accountability (Tukahebwa, 1998; Suzuki, 2002; Francis and James, 2003). The committees are said to divert funds and materials to alternative uses, including personal benefit.

Similarly, health-unit management committees are believed to be major culprits in the drug leakage problem. In a recent study, surveyed communities did not know the appointment methods used in filling these committees. They also viewed the committees as ineffective and said that they gave themselves large sitting allowances and engaged in patronage (Asiimwe, Mwesigye, McPake, and Streefland, 1997). Committees at the subcounty and village levels frequently do not exist or do not function well (Hutchinson, 1999).

Surveys and Data

To examine the extent of Uganda's devolution, the sources of political disciplines on local government, and the consequences of these political disciplines, surveys of eight different groups were undertaken:

households, district health officials, district education officials, subcounty health officials, subcounty education officials, subcounty education chiefs, health facilities, and primary school principals. A test of
primary school pupils was also administered. The surveys were conducted in spring 2000.

Data were collected from seventy-five subcounties chosen randomly
from ten quasi-randomly selected districts.[5] In each subcounty, fifteen
households were chosen from four randomly selected villages. Either a
primary school principal or a health facility worker was interviewed
in each of these villages, thereby allowing facilities and schools to be
matched to households. In each subcounty, the survey team tried to
survey the subcounty chief and the education officer with the education instrument and to survey the health inspector and subcounty
health chief with the health instrument. If any of these officers was
not available, the survey team tried to interview another person at the
relevant office. Two health and two education officers were also interviewed in each district. The topics covered in the surveys and the number of observations are shown in table 7.1. There were some missing
observations in most of these surveys.

The household survey covers basic demographic information, information on health knowledge and usage (with a focus on immunization
and malaria control), primary education, preferences, voting patterns,
political action, media exposure, and mobility. The public official surveys also asked questions about their knowledge of citizen's preferences and numerous questions about public sector management that
are presented in Azfar, Kahkonen, and Meagher (2001).

Sources of Information on Politics and Government

In this section and the sections that follow, we turn to an analysis of
our survey data and its bearing on the questions of federalist disciplines that have been raised. We first address the issue of citizen information sources concerning local governance.

Decentralization will improve efficiency only if local democracies
work well. Local governments will act more efficiently than national
governments only if political disciplines can be better exerted on local
government officials. For this to be the case, it is argued that citizens
should get information about the conduct of local government officials
from independent media sources because they will be better informed
in this case than if information comes from alternative sources such as

Table 7.1
Surveys

Household	Public Official Education	Public Official Health	School Principal	Health-Facility Worker
Basic demographics on respondent and family	Basic demographic on respondent	Basic demographic on respondent	Basic demographic on respondent	Basic demographic on respondent
Health-care use	Demand responsiveness of service delivery	Demand responsiveness of service delivery	Demand responsiveness of service delivery	Demand responsiveness of service delivery
Knowledge of immunizations	Government-run primary schools	Government-run health units	General primary-school information	General health-unit information
Closest government and private unit	Role of local government in education delivery	Planning of service delivery, supplies of vaccines and medicines	School supplies, facilities, and equipment	Supplies of vaccines and medicines
Immunizations of infants		Performance standards and monitoring of service delivery	Performance standards and monitoring of service delivery	Availability of equipment
Malaria	Performance of service delivery	Performance of service delivery	Performance of service delivery	Performance of service delivery
Village health committee	Funding of overall service delivery	Funding of service delivery	Funding of service delivery	Funding of service delivery
Primary school	Personnel, recruitment, salaries, and allowances	Personnel, recruitment, salaries, and allowances	Personnel, recruitment, salaries, and allowances	Personnel, recruitment, salaries, and allowances
Parent-teacher association	Disciplining and firing of staff	Disciplining and firing of staff	Disciplining and firing of staff	Disciplining and firing of staff
Mobility	Individual performance evaluation	Individual performance evaluation	Individual performance evaluation	Individual performance evaluation
Access to media	Corruption	Corruption	Corruption	Corruption

Table 7.1
(continued)

Household	Public Official Education	Public Official Health	School Principal	Health-Facility Worker
Knowledge and awareness of government actions	Education committee	Health committee	Parent-teacher association	Health-unit management committee
Voting and political action			Immunization in schools	
Social cohesion				
	Data sheet: Overall revenues and expenditures	Data sheet: Overall revenues and expenditures Immunization and malaria	Data sheet: Performance of service delivery Funding of service delivery	Data sheet: Performance of service delivery Funding of service delivery Supplies and vaccines
$n = 1{,}126$	$n = 137$ subcounties $n = 18$ districts	$n = 125$ subcounties $n = 20$ districts	$n = 145$	$n = 140$

word of mouth. To consider this question, we look at how Ugandans get news about both local and national politics. In our survey, households were first asked whether they followed politics. Almost all said yes to both local (95 percent) and national (94 percent) politics.[6] They were then asked the following questions:

• What is your family's main source of information about events and politics in this area?
• What is your main source of information about national events and politics? (Surveyor: Do not read out answers.)

The survey results show that Ugandans use the media as the main source of information for national politics (64 percent) more often than they use the media for local news (20 percent), as presented in table 7.2. These patterns are clear for *all* sources of media, local newspapers, national newspapers, local radio, national radio, and television, and the difference is significant in each case. By far the most important source of information on national politics is the radio, with 65 percent of Ugandans citing national (40 percent) or local (25 percent) radio as

Table 7.2
Sources of information about politics: Percentage of people using each source

	Local Politics ($n = 1{,}067$)	National Politics ($n = 1{,}052$)	t-Statistic[a]
Local newspaper	0.47% (0.002)	1.14% (0.015)	−1.53
National newspaper	0.28% (0.002)	1.90% (0.003)	−3.61
Local radio	15.37% (0.011)	25.76% (0.004)	−5.97
National radio	4.69% (0.006)	39.73% (0.013)	−21.42
TV	0.09% (0.001)	0.57% (0.015)	−1.91
Friends and family	8.43% (0.009)	3.52% (0.002)	4.79
Community leaders	70.48% (0.014)	27.66% (0.006)	21.68
Other	0.66% (0.002)	0.10% (0.014)	2.11
Total media	19.8% (0.011)	64.5% (0.014)	24.11

Notes: n is the number of people who follow the news or who heard reports of corruption. Standard error is in parentheses. Means, standard errors, and t-statistics shown are calculated treating those who do not follow politics (or did not hear reports of corruption) as a missing value. There are no significant differences in the results if such people are treated as nonusers of the information source.
a. t-statistic of test of hypothesis that the percentage of people using a source of information is different for local issues and national issues.

their main source of information on national politics. By contrast, radio is the main source of news for local politics for only 20 percent of Ugandans.

The most worrisome finding might be the extent of reliance on community leaders as a source of news on local politics. In an almost diametrical reversal of the results on radio usage, 70 percent of Ugandans use community leaders as their main source of information on local politics, while only 28 percent use community leaders as their main source of information on national politics.[7] Worse yet, people who used community leaders as their main source of information on local politics were significantly less likely to have heard reports of corruption. Using regression analysis, we find that people who rely on community leaders for news are eleven percentage points less likely to have heard reports of corruption than people who rely on the media as their main source of information.[8] A comparison of sources of information on politics and sources of information on corruption also suggest that reliance on community leaders for news on local politics affects knowledge of forms of misgovernance such as corruption. While 70 percent rely on community leaders for news on local politics, only 28 percent get news on local corruption from community leaders (the main source of information about local corruption is "friends and family"). One plausible explanation for this is that community leaders underreport corruption in their communications with their communities. This evidence might be a sign of elite capture, a notion analyzed notably by Bardhan and Mookherjee (1998), who comment that elite individuals or groups may find means of dominating local politics and will act in ways that serve their own interests rather than the interests of their constituents. If this is a correct interpretation of these results, the results would seem to cast doubt on the effectiveness of local politics as a disciplining device for local government, despite the high turnouts in elections.

In terms of comparison across sectors, public officials were asked whether there was media coverage of their sector and many more education officials reported coverage than health officials. This could be a reason that education might be a more appropriate sector to decentralize than health. It could also show the influence of the transparency procedures used under UPE.

Voting and Political Action

For local democracy to work, citizens must not only be well informed about their government but also must use this information to penalize officials who do not respond to citizen concerns—by voting against them or participating in other political action. Local demand for public goods emerges in policy discourse, political action, and elections— collectively known as *voice*.

This section reports results on the sources of direct political discipline on local and national governments. More specifically, these results shed light on the following:

• Whether voter turnout is greater in local or national elections,

• Whether people vote for different reasons in local or national elections,

• What the determinants are of membership on health and education committees, and

• What levels of success are met by political action.

Households were asked the following questions:

• Did you vote in the last Parliamentary elections?

• (If yes, ask) What factors influenced who you voted for? (Surveyor: Do not read out answers.)

• Did you vote in the last district (LC5) or subcounty (LC3) elections?

• (If yes, ask) What factors influenced who you voted for? (Surveyor: Do not read out answers.)

Reported turnouts are very high in both local (80 percent) and national elections (83 percent).[9] In addition to turnout, the reasons for voting may also affect the quality of local government. If citizens vote on the basis of the candidate's experience or agenda, this might provide incentives for better overall public services. However, if citizens vote on the basis of race, religion, or language, this may induce officials to adopt policies not aimed at improving general welfare (like diverting public resources to particular sections of the population). The reported reasons for voting appear to be "good" in both local and national elections: the vast majority (74 percent) cited the candidate's agenda as a reason in both local and national elections, and almost all (91 percent) reported the agenda, prior experience or political affiliation as a reason, with very few (4.6 percent) citing at least one "poor" reason, such as being paid by a candidate (2 percent), religion (0.7 percent), race (1.8 percent), or language (1.6 percent). Voting patterns, which have been shown to affect service delivery elsewhere,[10] are thus uniformly encouraging for Ugandan politics but give no indication that they are more encouraging for local than for national politics. In fact, it is unclear to what extent either national or local elections are genuinely contested. As previously mentioned, the NRM dominates both levels, and it would be difficult to interpret the importance of differences in voting behavior even if there were significant differences.

Next, the determinants of membership in village health committees and school management committees were estimated. Unsurprisingly, education and income predicted committee membership. While these results might suggest there is elite capture of health and education committees, it can reasonably be countered that membership of committees by well-educated people would improve performance.[11] (Detailed results are omitted here for reasons of brevity.)

Finally, with regard to the extent of political action, respondents were asked the following:

• In the past year, have people in your village or town met to request that officials address a specific issue (for example, improvement of health provision, local roads, or water delivery)?

• (If yes, ask) Were these actions successful?

Most people (56 percent) said they had participated in political action and 63 percent of these people said they had participated with at least partial success. We have no evidence that these high rates of participation are due to decentralization. However, if one is willing to accept a priori that political action is a more important discipline on local than on national government, then these results could be interpreted as suggesting one reason for improved public-service delivery following decentralization.

Local Demand for Public Goods and Services

One of the classic arguments for fiscal federalism as narrated by Tiebout (1956) and Oates (1972) is that local governments can better match goods to preferences. It is important therefore to investigate whether demand really varies in important ways across jurisdictions—and in the case of Uganda, whether these variations are across districts or across subcounties within districts (or both). It is equally important to investigate whether differences in household demand are reflected in the perceptions and actions of public officials. If there are significant differences across jurisdictions and local public officials display knowledge of these differences, then this can provide an argument for decentralization.[12] Data on demand were collected from households and public officials to examine these issues. In this section, we look at local demand for public goods and the extent to which officials are informed of local demand. We later examine local governments' flexibility in responding to this demand.

What Do Households Demand, and Do Demands Vary across Jurisdictions?

In our surveys, households were asked the following question (U.S. $1 = 1,000 Ugandan shillings):

• If the subcounty government received 10 million Ugandan shillings, on which activity would you want most of the money spent? (Surveyor: Do not read out answers.)

The question is asked in this way to facilitate the respondents' understanding the question and being able to answer it. In principle, better data could be collected if respondents were asked to rank several different publicly provided goods, but this is liable to confuse respondents as has been discovered in previous attempts to do so. The answer, which measures deficient demand, also conflates demand and supply. Adequate public provision of a public good, which saturates demand, might lead respondents to pick some other good as their first choice. We try to deal with this concern in the discussion below.

Two items are of particular interest: primary education and immunization. Twenty-two percent of respondents stated they would prefer the money to be spent on primary education (only water at 31 percent was ranked higher). This interest of citizens in primary education suggests they would exert political pressure to improve primary-education delivery in their localities. There are also large differences in demand for primary education across districts, which varies from a low of 7 percent in Tororo to a high of 39 percent in Apac. A more sophisticated analysis, the details of which can be found in Azfar and Livingston (2001), suggests that there were indeed statistically significant and economically meaningful deviations in the demand for education across districts (the standard deviation being around 35 percent of the mean). A similar test for the deviation in demand across subcounties within districts found less evidence of the dispersion of preferences across subcounties within districts.

Remarkably, however, only 1 percent of households responded to this survey question with "immunization." For other goods, this might have been an argument for not supplying goods that are not demanded, but in the case of immunization this contradicts accepted scientific knowledge on the cost effectiveness of preventative and curative medicine.[13] Even when asked to pick among different forms of health provision, households did not show any evidence of demand for immunizations. For a question that asked which health service citizens would want money spent on, only 0.45 percent of respondents wanted money spent on immunization as compared to 52 percent on medicines.[14]

This apparently wide divergence between accepted scientific knowledge and citizen demand raises concerns about the decentralization of public-health responsibilities in Uganda.[15] It is not meaningful to talk about differences in demand from such a low base, and indeed there are no perceptible differences in demand for immunization in Uganda across districts or subcounties.

Do Local Public Officials Know What Households Demand?

For local government to match service provision to citizen preferences, local officials need to know and act on citizen demands for public goods. To determine whether differences in household demands are reflected in the perceptions and actions of public officials, the latter were asked two questions:

• If this subcounty government received 10 million Ugandan shillings, on which activity would local people want most of the money spent? (Surveyor: Do not read out answers.)

• In the last year, on which activity did this subcounty government spend most of its local tax revenues? (Surveyor: Do not read out answers.)

To examine whether local officials actually had knowledge of local preferences, we regressed the responses of public officials in each district on the difference between households' demands in that district from the national average (the interested reader can consult Azfar et al., 2001, for the statistical results). No evidence was found of any correlation between household demands and either public officials' knowledge of these demands or resource allocation decisions at the district level.

This exercise was then repeated at the subcounty level, where we found evidence of some congruence between household and public-official preferences. A literal interpretation of our regression results is that "subcounty officials reflect 20 percent of the population's preferences." Subcounty officials, unlike district officials, do seem to reflect the demand of the citizenry to some extent.

Similar but weaker results were found for actual resource allocation: there is a positive but statistically insignificant relationship between household demand and subcounty-level resource allocation. One possible explanation for the weakness of this relationship may be that if resources were actually allocated to a public good in the previous year, the marginal demand for the good this year would fall.

In general, this analysis of household demand for public services in Uganda gives only weak support to the decentralization of primary education and malaria control to subnational levels and gives no support to the decentralization of immunization provision. Among immunization, malaria control, and primary education, the only good with sizeable household demand was primary education. Differences in demand were really significant only across districts for primary education and malaria and not significant across subcounties within districts. However, only differences in demand across subcounties were reflected in public officials' perceptions.

Mobility

A second key method of demand revelation, apart from politics, is "exit"—that is, migration. Following Tiebout's classic (1956) analysis, mobility is often cited as a reason that decentralization will improve productive and allocative efficiency. The movement of people to jurisdictions that supply the mix of public goods they prefer creates a first-order improvement in allocative efficiency. Additionally, if local governments are reluctant to lose their citizens or desire to attract citizens from elsewhere, then mobility may create pressures for more productively efficient local government. To assess whether mobility might be an important source of improvements in the delivery of health and education, Ugandan households were asked two sets of questions:

• Why do you live in this village/town? (Surveyor: Do not read out answers.)

• Do you have plans to move to another village or town in the next year?

• (If yes, ask) Why are you planning to move? (Surveyor: Do not read out answers.)

The majority (82 percent) cited spouse or parents as the reason that they lived where they did: only 1.3 percent cited health care, and only 1.2 percent cited education as reasons. There was significant overlap (around 60 percent) between citing health and education as a reason for residence, and even among this small number most of these households also cited other reasons for their choice of location.

A total of thirty-six (3.3 percent) households said they were planning to migrate in the next year. This is not a small number and is comparable to the United States—a relatively mobile society. Thus, the reason for questioning the relevance of mobility as a motivating factor for improvements in the delivery of health or education is not that illiquid land or labor markets have rendered the population immobile but rather that mobility is not driven by the provision of health and education delivery. The most significant reason for migration seems to be employment. Employment is prominently cited both as a reason for people living where they do (14.7 percent) and as a reason for planning to move (1.8 percent).

By contrast, there is little evidence of mobility driven by the quality of health or education provision. Only one household cited schooling as the only reason for planning to move, and one other household cited all three of education, health, and employment as reasons for moving. Thus, one cannot be confident that migrations based on health or education delivery are either a direct or indirect source of better allocative or productive efficiency in Uganda.[16]

Can Local Officials Adjust Services to Reflect Demand?

Our analysis continues with an empirical examination of the de facto discretion and flexibility that local governments enjoy in delivering public services. In all four surveys of public officials, they were asked the following question:

• In general, how easily can you adjust in this district (subcounty) the provision of health (education) services to respond to the suggestions of local people?

Respondents could answer "cannot adjust," "can adjust with great difficulty," "can adjust with some difficulty," or "can adjust easily." Table 7.3 shows the distribution of answers to these questions by the various public officials. The modal response was clearly "can adjust with some difficulty." On the basis of these results, an adjustability index was created:

$$\text{Adjustability index} = (\text{Can adjust with great difficulty} \\ + 2 * \text{Can adjust with some difficulty} \\ + 3 * \text{Can adjust easily})/3$$

The index is thus equal to 0 if the official responded "cannot adjust," equal to $1/3$ if the official responded "with great difficulty," equal to $2/3$ if the official responded "with some difficulty," and equal to 1 if the official responded "easily." There is an element of arbitrariness in

Table 7.3
Discretion: How easily can you adjust services provision to respond to the suggestions of local people? (percentages)

	Subcounty Health Office	Subcounty Education Office	District Health Office	District Education Office
Cannot adjust	12%	5%	0%	0%
Can adjust with great difficulty	24	26	10	22
Can adjust with some difficulty	47	52	75	67
Can adjust easily	17	16	15	11
Adjustability index[a]	0.56	0.59	0.68	0.63
n	124	134	20	18

Note: a. Adjustability index = (Can adjust with great difficulty + 2 ∗ Can adjust with some difficulty + 3 ∗ Can adjust easily)/3.

constructing any such index from ordinal answers, but this seemed like the least controversial way to do so. This index, whose mean can take values between 0 and 1, showed adjustability at 0.56 for the subcounty health office, at 0.59 for the subcounty education or chief's office, at 0.68 for the district health office, and 0.63 for the district education office (table 7.3).

Next, similar adjustability indexes were created for several specific functions: hiring, salaries, purchases, raising revenues, and resource allocation. For most of these functions, local governments reported some flexibility, and the averages for the four levels of local government were between 0.3 and 0.5 (see Azfar et al., 2001, for a tabulation).

For health, there were several comparable questions on hiring officials, hiring workers, and deciding what type of health service to provide, how to combat malaria, and how much money to allocate to immunization. District officials report often significantly more discretion for each of these categories. The average discretion reported by district health officials (0.50) is 66 percent higher than the average discretion reported by subcounty health officials (0.30). There are also significant differences in the responses of subcounty and district health officials about whether their suggestions were incorporated into subcounty or district development plans, respectively, and local government budget framework papers. All this suggests that district health officials enjoy more discretion and flexibility than subcounty officials, which corresponds to the de jure allocation of authority by the Local Governments Act.

It was difficult to compare the levels of discretion enjoyed by district and subcounty governments in education as not enough similar questions were asked and the education questionnaire at the subcounty level was, by design, often administered to the subcounty chief. The questionnaire focused on general administrative questions rather than exclusively on education. The only question (on funds) for which answers are presented for both district and subcounty governments was consequently phrased differently in the two questionnaires. The differences in the responses of subcounty and district education officials about whether their suggestions were incorporated into local government plans are only marginally significant for subcounty or district development plans and are insignificant for local government budget framework papers.

In summary, the survey results indicate that local governments at both the district and subcounty levels do in fact have some autonomy in the delivery of public services. The findings discussed previously suggest that there is reason, based on officials' awareness of local demands at the subcounty level, to expect this autonomy to increase the demand responsiveness of resource allocations for local public services.

Political Disciplines and Socioeconomic Outcomes

The most challenging aspect of our empirical research was to test whether the political disciplines documented in the previous sections of this chapter in fact affect public service delivery. This is difficult because comparisons can be made only across jurisdictions; consequently, there are only seventy-five observations, of middling quality, based on the assessments of fifteen households each. Measurement error could easily prevent discovery of a relationship even if one exists. We tried to minimize measurement error by using composite indexes for the variables of interest, but this is an inevitably imperfect exercise.

Before analyzing the impact of political disciplines at the subcounty level, one must ask whether a subcounty-level analysis is a valid exercise if most resource allocation decisions are made at the district or national level. We believe it is for three reasons. First, subcounty officials do appear to have some authority over resource allocation and the management of public services, as reported in the previous section. Second, our regression technique holds constant any effects that occur at the district level, so if we find that political disciplines have any effect on public-service delivery, we can reasonably assert that this is occurring at the subcounty level. Third, even if decisions are being made at the district level, media use and voting propensities at the subcounty level could affect resource allocation decisions at the district level. District-level officials might find it more politically expedient to concentrate on service delivery in subcounties that have a better informed and more politically active citizenry—as Betancourt and Gleason (2000) found in India. The interpretation of the result would in that case be different, but it is nonetheless interesting.

Our surveys contained two measures of education quality, making it possible to see whether the political disciplines we have studied—such as having "good" sources of information about local politics and whether people vote in local elections and vote for "good" reasons—result in better education delivery and outcomes. The first is "test score," which is the average score of primary-school students on tests administered in the primary schools surveyed. The test consisted of fourteen simple mathematics questions and nine simple language and general-knowledge questions. These questions were preceded by a short demographic questionnaire, which asked if the child's parents were alive and could read. The test was administered to 6,035 students. The variable "test score" depends on the number of correct answers to the twenty-three mathematics, language, and general-knowledge questions. "Test score" may be an imperfect measure for two reasons: it is based on only two villages per subcounty, and test scores may not capture everything about the quality of education. The second measure of education quality is an average of the normalized value of "test score" and a subjective assessment of education quality from the household questionnaire. This has the advantage of being a broader question and having information from four rather than two villages but has the disadvantage of being less precise. It is reassuring that the correlation between "test score" and the answer to the subjective question is positive and statistically significant (the correlation coefficient between the two variables is 0.44, and a statistical test suggests that there is a less than 0.01 percent chance that there is actually no relationship between our two measures). This suggests that each of these variables is a reasonable measure for some underlying quality of education and that the average of these two measures might be a better measure than either.

A regression analysis was used to see how these measures are related to two indexes, "voting" and "media access and use." Results are presented in table 7.4. The variable "voting" is the average of the nor-

Table 7.4
Federalist disciplines and the quality of education

Independent Variable	Score, GLS Random Effects (5)	Index, GLS Random Effects (6)
Intercept	−29.273***	−6.879***
	(11.403)	(2.074)
Media index[a]	2.807***	0.522***
	(0.943)	(0.171)
Voting index[b]	0.292	−0.002
	(1.918)	(0.349)
log(income)	2.963**	0.510**
	(1.158)	(0.211)
Inequality[c]	−0.242	0.003
	(0.870)	(0.158)
Mother's education	1.950***	0.343**
	(0.962)	(0.175)
Father's education	−1.347**	−0.187*
	(0.618)	(0.112)
Rural dummy	2.581*	0.470*
	(1.535)	(0.279)
Ethnic dispersion[d]	2.679	0.259
	(1.934)	(0.352)
R^2	0.359	0.339
n	75	75

Notes: Standard errors in parentheses. Overall R^2 is reported. The dependent variable is the residuals from the subcounty dummies from the regression described in Azfar and Livingston (2001, table 15). The education index takes the average of household reports of education quality and the residuals from the subcounty dummies in Azfar and Livingston (2001, table 15), standardized as mean 0 and standard deviation 1 variables, if both are available. If one is not available, the index is just the variable that is not missing.
a. The media index is the sum of the coefficients of subcounty dummy variables from three regressions: whether the media is a household's primary source of information on local politics, how often the household listens to the radio, and how often the household reads the local newspaper.
b. The voting index is the sum of the coefficients of subcounty dummy variables from three regressions: whether a household voted, whether a household voted for a good reason, and whether the household participated in political action.
c. The inequality measure is the subcounty average of the interquartile range of log(income).
d. Ethnic dispersion is measured by calculating the probability that two randomly selected individuals within a subcounty will speak a different language.
*Significant at the 10 percent level.
**Significant at the 5 percent level.
***Significant at the 1 percent level.

malized value of voting in local elections and voting for a good reason (the candidates' experience, agenda, or political affiliation rather than bribery or the candidates' race or religion). The variable "media access and use" is the average of the normalized values of whether the media are the primary source of local news, how often the household listens to the radio, and how often the household reads the local newspaper. The particular regression technique used is sophisticated and holds many other possible effects constant, such as the impacts of income, whether the child's parents are alive, the education level of the child's parents, and the child's gender and age.

The results indicate that test scores in subcounties where everyone reads newspapers, listens to the radio often, and uses the media as their main sources of local news are 2.8 points higher than subcounties with no media use. This is nearly twice as high as the most significant individual-level determinant of scores—whether the mother was alive. There is no perceptible effect of "voting and political action." Media use also has a positive impact on the broader "education index," but the impact of "voting and political action" appears to be negative; however, our statistical test cannot conclusively say that voting really does have an impact on the index.

We tried to repeat this exercise for vaccinations but were frustrated by the poor quality of the data. One problem was that the surveyors could see only vaccination cards about half the time and a response "yes, but card not seen" could not reasonably be coded as either a yes or a no.

Overall, the evidence suggests that media access and use have a positive effect on the quality of education delivery. However, there is no perceptible effect of voting on education quality. Combined with the evidence presented earlier suggesting that communities that instead rely on community leaders as sources for news are less likely to have heard reports of corruption, the results reported in this section—that the use of media as the source of news on local politics (the opposite of using community leaders as the source of news) is related to better performance—suggest that elite capture might be undermining education provision in Uganda.

Conclusion

In this chapter, we presented evidence from Uganda on the presumed federalist disciplines at work in a decentralized system. The results provide little reason to expect better provision of public services by local governments.

Our findings on demand for public goods show worryingly little demand for immunizations—an important publicly provided good that is well known to be cost effective. This may be the cause of the reported diversion of public resources away from immunization following decentralization, though there was no way of showing a formal link between the weak demand and the reported diversion of resources. For primary education, there was both evidence of significant demand and of significant differences in demand across districts; however, there was no evidence of public officials' having better knowledge of demand for public goods in their district. There was, however, some evidence of differences in demand for education across subcounties and for public officials' having better knowledge of demands within their subcounties.

On voting, there were reports of both high rates of voting and generally good reasons for voting in both local and national elections. Committee membership seemed skewed toward more educated and wealthier people. While this might indicate elite capture, it may in fact improve performance. Also, there is little evidence of mobility or potential mobility being driven by the quality of publicly provided health or education services.

The results on sources of information on politics are perhaps the most interesting and worrisome. While the vast majority of Ugandan households use the media as their source of information on national politics, the vast majority also rely on community leaders as their source of information on local politics. The reliance on community leaders appears to undermine citizens' knowledge of some aspects of local politics like corruption. Subcounties where people rely on the media for news of local politics seem to have better service delivery as measured by test scores and satisfaction ratings with education. Taken together, these findings may indicate that elites control information flows on local politics and thus dominate local politics more than national politics.

These empirical findings, along with our analysis of the decentralization program in Uganda, suggest that this experiment in governance reform is having difficulty in delivering the expected benefits. Imperfections in design (such as devolution of certain public-health responsibilities), constraints to political competition, and deficits in local information flows and accountability mechanisms all play a role.

Uganda's experience sheds light more generally on the preconditions and disciplines needed for successful decentralization.

Acknowledgments

The research underlying this chapter was supported by a grant from the World Bank financed by the Netherlands Trust Fund. We are grateful to Tony Lanyi for his management of this project, to Satu Kahkonen for survey design and implementation (assisted by the Makerere Institute of Social Research), and to Diana Rutherford for excellent research assistance and project support. We thank Shanta Devarajan, Malika Krishnamurty, Jennie Litvack, and Ritva Reinikka at the World Bank for their support. We are also grateful for comments on the chapter from those already mentioned, as well as from Roger Betancourt, Peter Murrell, Malgosia Madejewicz, Wally Oates, and participants in the 2003 London School of Economics conference. All errors are our own.

Notes

1. An exception may be HIV/AIDS control, where Uganda is a rare African success story.

2. See, e.g., Oates's classic work *Fiscal Federalism* (1972).

3. Most of this section and the next was written soon after the data were collected in summer 2000. The data reflect the situation that obtained in the second half of 2000, which has not changed dramatically since then. For a fuller treatment, see Meagher (2000).

4. As of late 2000, it had never been used, and we are unaware of any cases since then.

5. Some districts were taken out of the data pool before the sample was randomly selected because they could not be surveyed for safety reasons. Thus, our sample might be biased toward better-run districts with more exacting political disciplines.

6. We tried to assess people's knowledge of local and national politics by asking them the names of the president and their subcounty chair. The test is unfair as Museveni is a charismatic figure who's been in power more than fifteen years. The results showed essentially everybody (98 percent) could name the president but only 70 percent could name the subcounty chair, giving little reason to hope for better knowledge of local rather than national politics.

7. Seventy percent of those who follow local politics report using community leaders as their primary source, which corresponds to 67 percent of the entire sample, similarly 27 percent use community leaders as their main source for national politics.

8. The interested reader may consult Azfar and Livingston (2001) for a full description of this analysis and a tabulation of the results. The results may be biased because we have omitted some explanatory variables.

9. The interested reader can read Azfar and Livingston (2001) for tabulations of these results.

10. For example, Betancourt and Gleason (2000) find that voter turnout affects the allocation of doctors and nurses to Indian districts.

11. We thank Wally Oates for this point.

12. The argument also requires that central-government officials have a poorer understanding of the demand for different public goods than local officials. The data did not allow an examination of this question. In principle, data could be collected from central government officials to answer this question.

13. It is theoretically possible that many people rank immunization as their second preference, and there is significant demand for immunization that cannot be observed because the question was asked only about the most preferred good. This would not be unlikely if everyone expressed the same top preference. However, since there is considerable variation in the top preference, this seems less likely. It is also theoretically possible that there is little demand for immunizations because they have already been adequately provided. However, it is more likely that children in fact are not adequately immunized. If citizens believe that they are, however, then the lack of observed demand remains worrisome. In fact, immunization rates for diphtheria, polio, measles, and tetanus are below 50 percent according to UNICEF. These rates actually appear to be lower than the rates reported for 1994 and 1995 by Hutchinson (1999).

14. A detailed table of results for this answer is available from the authors on request.

15. Immunization programs are provided by the central government, and local-government decisions do not countermand them but determine whether necessary local support is provided. It is conceivable that local survey respondents understood this and reflected this in their answers—but this is essentially the same as saturation of demand, an unlikely possibility, as we have suggested.

16. One reading of the evidence, suggested by some readers, is that even marginal choices of where to locate once the employment decision had been taken may motivate local officials to improve service delivery.

References

Ablo, Emmanuel, and Ritva Reinikka. (1998). "Do Budgets Really Matter? Evidence from Public Spending on Education and Health in Uganda." Policy Research Working Paper 1926, Africa Region, Macroeconomics 2, World Bank.

Akin, John, Paul Hutchinson, and Koleman Strumpf. (2001). "Decentralization and Provision of Public Goods: The Public Health Sector in Uganda." Draft Paper, MEASURE Evaluation Project/USAID, Carolina Population Center, University of North Carolina, Chapel Hill.

Asiimwe, Delius, F. Mwesigye, B. McPake, and P. Streefland. (1997). "Informal Health Markets and Formal Health Financing Policy in Uganda." Mimeo, Makerere Institute of Social Research.

Azfar, Omar, Satu Kahkonen, and Patrick Meagher. (2001). "Conditions for Effective Decentralized Governance: A Synthesis of Research Findings." Mimeo, Center for Institutional Reform and Informal Sector, University of Maryland, College Park.

Azfar, Omar, and Jeffrey Livingston. (2001). "Federalist Disciplines or Local Capture: An Empirical Analysis of Decentralization in Uganda." Mimeo, Center for Institutional Reform and Informal Sector, University of Maryland, College Park.

Bardhan, Pranab, and Dilip Mookherjee. (1998). "Expenditure Decentralization and the Delivery of Public Services in Developing Countries." Institute for Economic Development Discussion Paper, Boston University.

Barnes, Nicole. (1999). "How Local Can Government Go? Lessons from Fiscal Decentralization in Uganda." Master's thesis, Massachusetts Institute of Technology, Cambridge, MA.

Betancourt, Roger, and Suzanne Gleason. (2000). "The Allocation of Publicly Provided Goods to Rural Households in India: On Some Consequences of Caste, Religion and Democracy." World Development 28(2): 2169–2182.

Bratton, Michael, and Gina Lambright. (2001). "Uganda's Referendum 2000: The Silent Boycott." African Affairs 100(400): 429–452.

Francis, Paul, and Robert James. (2003). "Balancing Rural Poverty Reduction and Citizen Participation: The Contradictions of Uganda's Decentralization Program." World Development 31(2): 325–337.

Freedom House. (1999). Survey 1999: Uganda. Available at ⟨http://www.freedomhouse .org⟩.

Human Rights Watch. (1999). Hostile to Democracy: The Movement System and Political Repression in Uganda. New York: Human Rights Watch.

Hutchinson, Paul, with Demissie Habte and Mary Mulusa. (1999). "Health Care Issues in Uganda," World Bank Discussion Paper No. 404, Washington, D.C.

Inman, Robert, and Daniel Rubinfeld. (1996). "Designing Tax Policies in Federalist Economies: An Overview." Journal of Public Economics 60(3): 307–334.

Kasfir, Nelson. (2000). "'Movement' Democracy, Legitimacy and Power in Uganda." In Justus Mugaju and J. Oloka-Onyango (Eds.), No-Party Democracy in Uganda: Myths and Realities (pp. 60–78). Kampala: Fountain.

Khadiagala, Gilbert. (1995). "State Collapse and Reconstruction in Uganda." In Zartman, William (Ed.), Collapsed States: The Disintegration and Restoration of Legitimate Authority. Boulder: Lynne Rienner.

Kisubi, Mohammed. (1998). "Capacity Building with Results-Orientation and Integrity in Mind: The Experience of Uganda." In A. Ruzindana, P. Langseth, and A. Gakwandi (Eds.), Fighting Corruption in Uganda: The Process of Building a National Integrity System (pp. 97–108). Kampala: Fountain.

Kiyaga-Nsubuga, John. (2000). "Issues in Uganda's Decentralisation Approach to Governance." Conference Paper, U.N. Centre for Regional Development, Nagoya.

Lubanga, F. X. (1998). "On-Going Reforms Relevant to Curbing Corruption: The Contribution of Decentralization." In A. Ruzindana, P. Langseth, and A. Gakwandi (Eds.), Fighting Corruption in Uganda: The Process of Building a National Integrity System (pp. 91–96). Kampala: Fountain.

Makara, Sabiti. (1998). "Political and Administrative Relations in Decentralisation." In Apolo Nsibambi (Ed.), Decentralisation and Civil Society in Uganda: The Quest for Good Governance (pp. 31–46). Kampala: Fountain.

Meagher, Patrick. (2000). "Overview of Decentralization and Governance of Public Services in Uganda: Institutions, Processes, Practices." Mimeo, Center for Institutional Reform and Informal Sector, University of Maryland.

Mukyala-Makiika, Rebecca. (1998). "Traditional Leaders and Decentralisation." In Apolo Nsibambi (Ed.), *Decentralisation and Civil Society in Uganda: The Quest for Good Governance* (pp. 96–109). Kampala: Fountain.

Oates, Wallace. (1972). *Fiscal Federalism.* New York: Harcourt Brace Jovanovich.

Oates, Wallace, and Robert Schwab. (1988). "Economic Competition among Jurisdictions: Efficiency Enhancing or Distortion Inducing?" *Journal of Public Economics* 35: 333–354.

Oetemoeller, Daniel. (1996). "Institutionalization and Democratization: The Case of the Uganda Resistance Councils." Dissertation, University of Florida.

Oloka-Onyango, J. (2000). "New Wine or New Bottles? Movement Politics and One-partyism in Uganda." In Justus Mugaju and J. Oloka-Onyango, *No-Party Democracy in Uganda: Myths and Realities* (pp. 40–59). Kampala: Fountain.

Persson, Torsten, and Guido Tabellini. (1996). "Federal Fiscal Constitutions: Risk Sharing and Moral Hazard." *Econometrica* 64(3): 623–646.

Stasavage, David. (2003). "On the Role of Democracy in Uganda's Move to Universal Primary Education." Mimeo, London School of Economics.

Suzuki, Ikuko. (2002). "Parental Participation and Accountability in Primary Schools in Uganda." *Compare* 32(2): 243–259.

Tidemand, Per. (1994). "The Resistance Councils in Uganda: A Study of Rural Politics and Popular Democracy in Africa." Dissertation, Roskilde University, Denmark.

Tiebout, C. (1956). "A Pure Theory of Local Expenditures." *Journal of Political Economy* 64: 416–424.

Tukahebwa, Geoffrey. (1998). "The Role of District Councils in Decentralisation." In Apolo Nsibambi (Ed.), *Decentralisation and Civil Society in Uganda: The Quest for Good Governance* (pp. 12–30). Kampala: Fountain.

Uganda Debt Network. (1999). "Implementation of the Poverty Action Fund in Uganda." Draft report.

U.S. State Department. (2000). *1999 Country Report on Human Rights Practices: Uganda.* Available at ⟨http://www.state.gov⟩.

8

Local Government Reforms in Pakistan: Context, Content, and Causes

Ali Cheema, Asim Ijaz Khwaja, and Adnan Qadir

Introduction

This chapter examines the recent decentralization reforms in Pakistan under General Pervez Musharraf. We highlight major aspects of this reform and analyze its evolution in a historical context to explore the potential causes behind this current decentralization. Analyzing the evolution of local government reforms in Pakistan is interesting because each of the three major reform experiments has been instituted at the behest of a nonrepresentative center using a top-down approach. Each of these reform experiments is a complementary change to a wider constitutional reengineering strategy devised to further centralization of political power in the hands of the nonrepresentative center. We argue that the design of the local government reforms in these contexts becomes endogenous to the centralization objectives of the nonrepresentative center. It is hoped that analyzing the Pakistani experience will help shed light on the positive political economy question of why nonrepresentative regimes have been willing proponents of decentralization to the local level.

We provide a historical overview of decentralization reforms, starting with the preindependence period up to the revival of local governments under General Musharraf, describe salient features of the current decentralization reform, and interpret the current reform in light of its historical context. The potential impact of the current decentralization reforms in Pakistan is addressed in chapter 9.

The History of Decentralization in Pakistan

While providing a detailed history of local governments in Pakistan is beyond the scope of this chapter, aspects of this history can shed light on the current decentralization. After briefly examining the pre- and postindependence period, we look at the two most significant decentralization reforms prior to the current one, begun under the nonrepresentative military regimes of General Muhammad Zia-ul-Haq and General Ayub Khan, respectively.

The Preindependence Period

Local Governments under the British   The British introduced local governments in India[1] not by building on the traditional structures of local governance, such as the village panchayats, but instead from scratch, following the annexation of Sindh in 1843 and of Punjab in 1849 (Nath, 1929; Tinker, 1968; Venkatarangaiya and Pattabhiram, 1969). The main objective of the system was to coopt the native elites by establishing representative local governments. However, local governments were never substantively empowered as they were formed in a top-down manner in urban and rural areas, with extremely circumscribed functions and members who were not locally elected but nominated by the British bureaucracy (Tinker, 1968). Instead, the deputy commissioner (DC), a district[2]-level agent of the nonrepresentative central bureaucracy, emerged as principle actor at the local level (Ahmed, 1964).

Democratic Processes at the Provincial Level   Given the structure of the nonrepresentative state, it is not surprising that the initial focus of political demands made by nationalist parties was for greater representation in provincial and central governments where substantive power lay. This shifted focus away from local governments, and the strength of the nationalist movement in the early twentieth century prompted the British government to make political concessions to Indian political parties by granting more autonomy at the provincial level.[3] These changes contributed to the evolution of local governments since they sharpened the contrast between these nascent representative governments at the center or province and the existing local governments, as the latter became less relevant as means of representation and the public debate shifted to the more regional and central arena of the nationalist movement. This shift in political emphasis was a major factor behind the dormancy of local governments in the areas that were to constitute Pakistan (Rizvi, 1976).

Patronage and Rural Biases under the British Another important feature of the British system of administration and local government was the creation of a rural-urban divide. Urban local councils were established by the British to provide essential municipal services in urban areas. In contrast, rural councils were explicitly used to coopt the local elites by giving them limited representation, and as a result their capacity to provide essential municipal services became even more circumscribed than the capacity found in urban areas (Siddiqui, 1992).

The British center used the deconcentrated agents of the central-district bureaucracy to coopt and entrench local elites through a selective but extensive system of patronage (van den Dungen, 1972). This was particularly true of the Punjab, where the colonial bureaucracy had ample opportunities for providing patronage through land-settlement policy, grant of colony lands in the canal colony districts of Punjab, and the use of protective legislation like the Punjab Land Alienation Act of 1900 and the Punjab Pre-Emption Act of 1913, which prohibited transfer of land from agricultural to nonagricultural classes (Ali, 1988; Pasha, 1998; Metcalfe, 1962).

The Punjab tradition of establishing patron-client relationships between the central bureaucracy and the local elite resulted in a rural-urban division, which restricted politics away from the urban middle classes. Safeguarding the loyal landowning classes from economic and political domination by the urban elites became colonial policy (Talbot, 1996). The dominance of the Unionist Party (representing large landowners of all religions) in Punjab's politics during the early decades of this century was a direct manifestation of this phenomenon.

Thus what emerges from this brief history of colonial local governments is that the system was not introduced in response to popular demand or local pressure but primarily as a result of the central government's initiative and functioned under the imperial bureaucracy's control. Moreover, from the beginning, there was a contradiction between the development of autonomous local self-governing institutions and imperialist local-level bureaucratic control with the imperative of creating a loyal native class, and it is the latter that dominated. The rise of the nationalist movement during the early twentieth century demanded more political space at the central and provincial levels. As a result, these higher tiers emerged as the hub of political activity, which not only shifted political focus away from local governments but also resulted in a lack of political ownership to build local governments by nationalist politicians. However, even the provincial autonomy that was granted was heavily circumscribed and extensively loaded in favor of the nonrepresentative bureaucracy at the imperial center.

Postindependence to Ayub
Given that the independence movement was driven by political party mobilizations at the provincial and higher levels, postindependence there was understandably little emphasis on local governments. The limited local governments that existed were controlled and superseded by the central bureaucracy by not holding elections and, where elections were held, by limited franchise and massive malpractice (Waseem, 1994). During the decade of the 1950s, weakening local governments coincided with increasing centralization and a center increasingly dominated by the civil and armed bureaucracy (Jalal, 1995; Callard, 1957; Talbot, 1998).

The Ayub Period: Decentralization and the Politics of Legitimacy
Pakistan's first bold experiment with local governments occurred under the 1958 martial law, which set back representative politics at the central and provincial levels by disbanding national and provincial assemblies. Following the dissolution of the higher-tier elected governments, General Ayub, as the British colonialists before him, revived local governments as the only representative tier of government. The new local governments, established under the Basic Democracies Ordinance of 1959 and the Municipal Administration Ordinance of 1960, comprised a hierarchical system of four linked tiers.[4] At the lowest tier, which was the union councils, members were elected on the basis of adult franchise, and they, in turn, elected a chairperson from among themselves. The higher tiers of local government had some members elected indirectly by these directly elected members, some official members nominated by the government, and these officials as chairpersons (Rizvi, 1976; Siddiqui, 1992).

Similar to the British period, Ayub's local-government system was controlled by the bureaucracy through controlling authority vested in the deputy commissioner, commissioner, and the government for different tiers. The controlling authority had the power to quash the proceedings, suspend resolutions passed or orders made by any local body, prohibit the doing of any proposal, and require the local body to take action. Although the system assigned several regulatory and development functions to the local governments, especially at the lowest tiers and at the district level, few functions could be performed due to a severely curtailed fiscal capacity (Siddiqui, 1992).

The most controversial aspect of the local government system was that it came to be used by Ayub to legitimize his essentially unitary Presidential Constitution (1962), which gave effective state power to the armed forces through the office of the president. The 1962 constitution (articles 155, 158, and 229) explicitly linked the office of the president to the newly created local bodies by declaring the 80,000 Basic Democrats as the electoral college for the election of the president and national and provincial assemblies. The electoral function of the Basic Democrats system, based on Ayub's concept of controlled democracy, was a carryover from the paternalistic colonial view of guardianship whereby the colonial bureaucracy was supposed to guide the politicians while resisting their corrosive influences. This partly bureaucratic and partly political system was explicitly used for distributing resources and patronage "to secure a mandate for Ayub" (Gauhar, 1996, p. 84) and to build a constituency for the military regime (Burki, 1980).

There were continuities between British management of urban and rural political and economic competition and that of Ayub. At the level of local governments, a legislative divide was maintained between urban areas, which were governed through the Municipal Administration Ordinance (MAO) (1960), and the rural areas governed by the Basic Democracies Ordinance (BDO) (1959). However, Ayub, like the British, increased the share of targeted provincial and federal development resources in favor of the rural areas because his main source of support lay in these areas[5] and these allocations reversed the significant urban bias in federal and provincial development spending that had emerged during the 1950s (Ahmed and Amjad, 1984). Rural local representatives, who formed a majority in the local-government system (Rizvi, 1976), were associated with development plans and projects at the local level both on account of program design[6] and because of their electoral importance in the wider state system (Rizvi 1976; Ahmed and Amjad, 1984).

The Zia and Post-Zia Period

Local Government Reforms 1979 to 1985   After a nascent period under Prime Minister Zulfiqar Ali Bhutto (1971 to 1977), local governments were revived under General Zia-ul-Haq's military regime. Like

Ayub, Zia-ul-Haq combined political centralization at the federal and provincial levels with a legitimization strategy that instituted electoral representation only at the local level. Political centralization was achieved during the early years (1977 to 1985) of the regime through the imposition of martial law, which held the 1973 constitution in abeyance, and was followed in 1985 by the eighth constitutional amendment that established indirect military rule through a quasi-presidential form of government (Noman, 1988). Local governments were revived through the promulgation of Local government ordinances (LGOs) and local bodies were elected in all four provinces during 1979 and 1980. In essence, the army sought to use its old strategy of divide and rule by creating a new and competing class of collaborative local-level politicians (Jalal, 1995).

However, the increased political importance of local bodies was not complemented by any further decentralization of federal or provincial administrative functions or financial powers to the local level. Cheema and Mohmand's (2003) comparison of the Local Government Ordinance (1979), the Basic Democracies Ordinance (1959), and the Municipal Administration Ordinance (MAO) (1960) shows that there was little change in the functions and financial powers assigned to local governments during the Zia and Ayub periods. Therefore, the increased importance of local governments as a means of political legitimacy did not translate into their substantive empowerment during either the Ayub or Zia periods. In fact, local governments continued to lack constitutional protection and their creation and maintenance remained at the whim of the provinces, which retained suspension powers.[7]

In spite of these differences Zia's LGO (1979) differed from Ayub's BDO (1959) in important respects. Zia consciously adopted populist measures introduced by Bhutto's unimplemented local-government legislations (1972 and 1975), which abolished the direct representation of the bureaucracy in local governments as members and chairpersons and instead stipulated that all members (including chairpersons) of all tiers of local government were to be directly elected through adult franchise (sections 12 and 13 of LGO 1979).[8] This was a significant change from BDO (1959) and MAO (1960). Although, the provincial administration retained suspension powers and the powers to quash resolutions and proceedings during the Zia period; nonetheless, their control over local government functioning through direct representation was loosened. This was perhaps a circumscribed response to the emergence of mass-based politics during the 1960s and 1970s.

However, the unequivocal adoption of the representative principle was significantly weakened as Zia retained the historical principle of holding local elections on a nonparty basis. Although, nonparty local-level elections had been the general principle in areas that comprise Pakistan since the colonial period, the adoption of this principle by Zia-ul-Haq represented an important reversal because mass-based political parties had emerged as important players in the electoral arena since the 1970 federal and provincial elections. Zia retained this principle to neutralize the influence of political parties at the local level. Evidence suggests that these measures resulted in the localization and personalization of politics at the local level (Wilder, 1999).

Another continuity between Zia's legislation and the British and Ayub legislations is the rural-urban divide at the level of rural or district councils and town and municipal committees and corporations.[9] In addition, Zia-ul-Haq abolished the district (rural) councils' function of rural-urban coordination, which made the district council responsible only for governance in rural areas. However, increased urbanization, the growing size of urban markets, the heightened flow of rural goods into urban areas, and the selected adoption of tax farming (AERC, 1990) resulted in a significant increase in the per capita income of urban local councils[10] as octroi[11] and UIPT revenues started to increase in response to these sociodemographic changes, and this trend continued well into the 1990s (table 8.1). However, the Zia regime consciously persisted with the rural-urban divide, which meant that the urban councils did not need to share the benefits from this increase in their per capita incomes with their rural hinterland.[12] Historical evidence suggests that during the early part of his regime, Zia sought to accommodate the interests of the urban middle classes,[13] who had formed the core of the anti-Bhutto movement.[14] It appears that the decision to retain the urban-rural divide, at a time when urban local council incomes were increasing, allowed the state to accommodate strong anti-Bhutto urban middle-class political mobilizations by giving them control, albeit circumscribed, over funds that could be used for the entrenchment of localized clientelist networks. The absence of buoyant sources of revenue in the hands of rural local councils, however, meant that their capacity to deliver on even their meager compulsory functions remained limited.[15] The precarious revenue situation of rural local councils combined with a legislative rule that denied rural areas access to urban revenues resulted in these areas becoming increasingly dependent on the provincial tier for service delivery.

Table 8.1
Income per capita by type of council

	Income per Capita			
	Urban Councils			Rural Council
	Municipal Corp.	Municipal Committee	Town Committee	District Council
1985				
Punjab	131.7	147.9	126.0	16.5
Sindh	239.0	150.4	147.3	21.8
NWFP	109.1	140.1	113.5	14.5
Balochistan	187.4	146.2	249.1	0.3
1990				
Punjab	327.9	187.3	135.0	21.4
1995				
Punjab	282.3	290.4	176.5	45.7

Source: AERC (1990), World Bank (2000), Population Census (1981, 1998).

The Evolution of the Local Government Structure from 1985 to 1999   The revival of elected provincial and federal governments in 1985 reinforced the localization of politics that had begun with the 1979 local bodies' elections. The dominance of these revived assemblies by local bodies' politicians[16] helped transplant the culture of local body politics to the provincial and national levels (Wilder, 1999). This tendency was reinforced by the nonparty nature of the 1985 assemblies and governments ("personalized patronage")[17] as elected government ministers began to use development funds to increase their individual chances of reelection.[18] Moreover, this personalization of politics did not reverse despite the revival of party-based federal and provincial assemblies and governments in 1988. The persistence of this tendency is partly an outcome of weakening party organizations, which is due to adverse de jure and de facto measures instituted by the Bhutto and Zia regimes (Wilder, 1999).

Furthermore, the absence of political linkages between different tiers of government, which was an outcome of the nonparty basis for politics, created tensions between provincial and local politicians with the local tier being viewed as a competing structure of patronage (Wilder, 1999). The tension between the province and local governments was exacerbated because of the federal government's encroachment on provincial functions, which was seen as a way to weaken the purview of the provinces (World Bank, 2000). This created a lack of political ownership with regard to the local tier that resulted in a number of serious consequences. Discretionary special development programs became widespread at the higher tiers and became an effective means for federal and provincial politicians to obtain unaudited control over local-level development allocations (AERC, 1990; Nasim, 1999; World Bank, 2000). Moreover, the concentration of buoyant revenues in the hands of the federal and provincial governments[19] constrained the financial capacity of local governments, prompting the provinces to play an ever-increasing role in service provision, especially post-1990.[20] Finally, this tension between provincial and local tiers resulted in the suspension of local bodies between 1993 and 1998, and as in the period immediately following independence, somewhat paradoxically it was democratic forces at the provincial and higher levels that pushed for a retrenchment of local governments and further centralized expenditures functions in the higher tiers of the state.

The New Devolution of Power Plan

This section gives an overview of the current decentralization reforms introduced as the Devolution-of-Power Plan by General Musharraf in January 2000 and implemented after a series of local-government elections that ended by August 2001.[21]

Several aspects of the reform are worth highlighting. First, in addition to devolving administrative and expenditure responsibilities to local governments, the decentralization involved, to differing degrees, changes in the administrative level of decision making, the accountability of the decision-making authority (political or bureaucratic), and the nature and amount of fiscal resources available.[22] Second, the decentralization process was not uniform across all functions, with significant heterogeneity in its extent not only across administrative departments but also across services within a department. Finally, the reform took place fairly rapidly and under military rule and hence at the time when no provincial and federal elected governments were in power. As a result, its implementation is still in a process of flux and is undergoing changes. While one can foresee some of these changes, a note of caution needs to be raised in taking any description of the current decentralization as final.

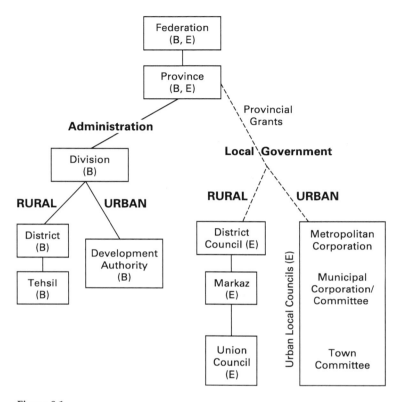

Figure 8.1
Predevolution structure (Zia)
Note: B represents a bureaucrat and E an elected official.

Overview

With this caveat in mind, we start with a stylized description of the devolution plan. In a nutshell, the devolution process substantially restructured the subprovincial (district and below) government structure (figures 8.1 and 8.2). We highlight the major changes brought about by the current devolution plan:

• *Engendering electoral accountability*   Under the recent reforms, a new elected government has been created at the district level headed by an elected nazim (mayor), and the district administration head, the district coordination officer (DCO), reports directly to the elected head of the government. This is a significant departure from the previous sys-

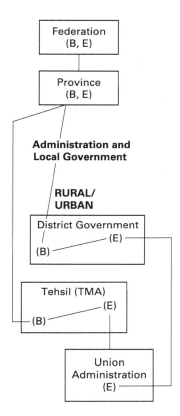

Figure 8.2
Postdevolution structure (Musharraf)
Notes: The police department is an exception to the above structure since it has not been devolved to the local level under the new structure. B represents a bureaucrat and E an elected official.

tem, where the de facto head of the district administration, the deputy commissioner (DC), reported to the nonelected provincial secretariat.

• *Reducing bureaucratic power*   The recent reforms are an attempt to curb bureaucratic power by abolishing the office of the DC. In addition, the new head of district administration, the DCO, no longer retains the executive magistracy and revenue-collection powers of the old DC.

• *Greater presence and scope of elected government at the local level*   While local governments did exist in periods prior to devolution, they did not have any significant role because these local governments, especially in rural areas, were practically inactive[23] and because most of the state functions were carried out by the provincial bureaucracy. Postdevolution, most public services that were previously under the purview of the deconcentrated district administration have been transferred to elected local governments. As a result, the scope of local governments in terms of the services they are responsible for and how they allocate district-level expenditures across services increased substantially post-devolution (Cheema, Khwaja, and Qadir, 2005).

• *Changed local electoral processes*   Prior to devolution, members of urban local councils and district councils were directly elected, and then they elected the heads of their respective councils. Under devolution, both the members and heads of the lowest level of government, the union council, are elected through public vote as before. However, the new legislation has created intergovernmental political linkages by ensuring that the majority (two-thirds) of the members of the Tehsil and district councils are these elected heads. The remaining one-third members of district and tehsil councils and the heads of district and tehsil governments are elected indirectly by the directly elected union-council members. Thus in particular, the head of the district government, the district nazim, need not command a majority of the public vote in a district but rather a majority of the union councilors and union nazims elected in the district (Cheema, Khwaja; Qadir, 2005). Another important electoral change has been a significant increase in reservation for peasants and women with a total of one-third seats reserved for both as compared to 5 and 10 percent in the district councils previously.

• *Limited constitutional support*   Despite the new local government structure, Pakistan is constitutionally still a two-level federal state (the local governments are not recognized as the third tier of government by the 1973 constitution). The seventeenth constitutional amendment provides limited protection to the local governments for a period of only six years, during which provinces can make changes to the local government legislation with the concurrence of the president.

• *Provincial to local decentralization with no federal decentralization*   Equally important, devolution involved a transfer of provincial powers and responsibilities to the district and lower levels of governments but no decentralization of any federal powers to either the provincial or local level.[24]

• *Uneasy integration between provincial/federal- and district-level elected governments*   Whereas prior to devolution, there was no significant link between the elected provincial/federal and the local governments, it did not matter since most of the state services were provided through the deconcentrated provincial administration, which was indirectly responsible to the provincial elected representatives. However, post-devolution, the elected local government was transferred a large proportion of these services. Given that the devolution process took place at a time when there was no provincial/federal elected government and the local government elections were held on a nonparty basis, no effort was made to integrate the newly elected local government with the soon to be elected provincial/federal governments. This has resulted in an interesting but not so surprising conflict between the local and provincial/federal elected representatives, which we address more explicitly in the next section (see also Cheema and Mohmand, 2003).

Characterizing Devolution

While the previous overview provides an illustration of the changes brought about through the current decentralization process, it misses some of the interesting details. In this section, we elaborate on some of these aspects.

Since the primary goal of a state is to provide public goods and services to its constituents, a useful way to categorize the devolution process is in terms of the changes in administrative level, accountability, and fiscal resources available to these services. To this end, we carried out a detailed exercise of mapping out the extent of devolution, at least as envisaged on paper, under the local-government ordinances. Moreover, for select departments this mapping was tallied with actual practice by conducting detailed interviews with members of these departments. While presenting the details of this mapping is beyond the scope of the current chapter, we use examples from this exercise to illustrate the type of changes brought about by devolution and the heterogeneity in these changes both across and within different departments.[25]

Level Changes

Level changes occur where a particular service is still decided by a similar agent (bureaucrat or politician) but at a different level in the government hierarchy as compared to before. While theoretically all types of changes are possible, devolution has primarily involved the following.

Province to Province   For the sake of completeness, we start with instances where there has been no change in the administrative level. This can happen for one of the following reasons:

• An entire department is not devolved. Examples include departments like irrigation, which has not been devolved because of significant interjurisdictional spillovers.

• Certain activities in a department have been retained at the provincial level. For example, university education has remained a provincial subject despite most of the remaining educational services having been devolved to the district level.

• Certain budgetary heads of expenditures have effectively been retained at the provincial level. The most important example is salary and allowance expenditures of all department employees. Since most employees in the administrative departments remain provincial employees, the district cannot create or reduce posts or adjust their salary structure, and therefore, a large fraction of the district budget is fixed.[26] Thus for departments where a large fraction of the current expenditure incurred is on salaries, such as the education department, which spends around 90 percent of its nondevelopment budget on salaries, this is a significant factor limiting the extent of decentralization.

Province to District   The most common and significant change involved shifting the budgeting, planning, and development functions related to services from the provincial level to the district level. Since a large part of these activities were decided at the provincial level before, this has entailed devolution of administrative level (these decisions formerly were based primarily on the Provincial Secretariat and the Provincial Cabinet. Now the analogous decision makers are at the district level—the district nazim, the executive district officer for finance and planning, and the executive district officer of the relevant line department.

Urban/Rural Local Council to Tehsil   Spatial and functional integration occurred as several of the services that were previously the domain of urban or rural local councils were integrated at the tehsil level. Among others, these include key municipal services such as water supply, sewerage, sanitation, drainage schemes, and street lights.

Accountability Changes

Accountability changes involve a particular service that is now decided by an agent who differs in his accountability to the public. In particular, devolution brought such an accountability change primarily at the district level. Whereas prior to devolution, the deconcentrated provincial bureaucracy at the district level was accountable to their nonelected provincial secretariat, under the present system they are accountable to the elected heads of district and tehsil governments. Rather than going through illustrations of which services underwent such a change, it is sufficient to note that any service that was under the purview of the district officer of a provincial line department and is now placed under the district government has effectively undergone such an accountability change. That is, the ultimate decision maker changed from a provincial government district officer who reported to the provincial bureaucracy to an elected nazim who ultimately is answerable to his district's constituents.

The most significant accountability change is that the de facto head of district administration under the previous system, the deputy commissioner (DC), used to report to the nonelected provincial bureaucracy, whereas in the present system the head of the district administration, the district coordination officer (DCO) reports to the elected district nazim. Although it needs to be pointed out that the authority of the nazim over the DCO and executive district officers (EDOs) is circumscribed in matters of transfers and promotions, which continue to remain under the purview of the provincial secretariat, and as a result this accountability change remains circumscribed in both a de jure sense and a de facto sense (Manning, Porter, Charlton, Cyan, and Hasnain, 2003).

Financial Changes

Some fiscal changes that have accompanied the devolution process that, while not necessarily directly affecting the allocation of funds to a particular service, are likely to have an indirect effect on such allocations insofar as they change the total amount of funds available to each local government.

Changes in Budgetary Transfers: Nondiscretionary and Nonlapsable   A significant financial change accompanying decentralization has been the establishment of a rule-based fiscal transfer system between

the provinces and the local governments. Previous local government reforms failed to establish an adequate fiscal transfer system with the result that local councils were unable to perform even the limited expenditure functions assigned to them (AERC, 1990; Nasim, 1999). The nondiscretionary intergovernmental fiscal transfer process is determined by the Provincial Finance Commission awards.[27] In addition to this nondiscretionary aspect, these budgetary transfers have also changed in that they are no longer lapsable and continue to be retained by the relevant local governments. It should be noted though that while the interim Provincial Finance Commission (PFC) awards have established a rule-based transfer mechanism for the distribution of the provincial allocable amount between local governments, the PFCs are yet to establish well defined rules for the division of the Provincial Consolidated Fund between the province and the local governments, even though this is required by the legislation (Cheema and Ali, 2005).

The extent of financial decentralization, however, remains limited, despite these reforms. Districts governments continue to have the same restricted revenue collection mandates and are excessively reliant on provincial and ultimately federal funds, through the provincial finance commission awards.[28] Furthermore, a significant proportion of district expenditures are "establishment charges,"[29] which, while incurred by the district, cannot be altered by the district. These expenditures include salaries of administrative personnel who continue to be provincial employees, and as such the district cannot fire them or adjust their wages.

Urban-Rural Reunification The integration of urban and rural administrative areas (at the tehsil level) also has significant implications on the flow of funds between urban and rural areas. In particular, until 1999 a major source of revenue for the urban areas was octroi levied in urban areas for all goods, regardless of whether they were eventually consumed in a rural area.[30] This resulted in a disproportionate access of resources for urban areas. After devolution, however, there is no longer any rural-urban distinction as both such areas within a tehsil fall under the jurisdiction of the same tehsil government. In such a case, the resources for both areas for a given tehsil are pooled, and in the likely situation that the rural area has greater voting importance, one may expect to see a correction of the urban bias in funding and perhaps even a bias toward the rural areas. This issue is addressed in detail in the next section.

The Political Economy of Decentralization

The first section of this chapter presented a history and context of decentralization in Pakistan and helped shed light on the political economy of decentralization, particularly for the most recent reforms under General Musharraf. In this section, we recap some of the salient trends identified in the previous sections to explain why centralized regimes are seemingly willing to shed their own powers. Our contention is that the recent devolution, while more ambitious and broader in scope than previous attempts, is in several important ways a natural continuation of previous decentralization attempts and is best understood in light of this context.

Nonrepresentative Centers and Local-Government Reforms

The central tendency revealed by our historical analysis is that local governments have been enacted by nonrepresentative regimes to legitimize their control over the state.[31] Legitimacy has been sought by creating a localized patronage structure that produces a class of collaborative politicians who act as a conduit between local-level constituencies and the nonrepresentative center. This is as true of the British period as it is of the postindependence period. The difference between these periods lies in the nature of the nonrepresentative institution that established its authority over the state. In the preindependence period, it was the British imperial state that introduced modern local self-government. In the postindependence period, it has been the Pakistani military.

Musharraf's local-government reforms represent a continuity of this central historical tendency. Unlike attempts at decentralization in some other countries, which appear to have been motivated more by changes in state ideology or multilateral pressure, in Pakistan the military's need for legitimization of state control appears to be a prime reason behind the recurring attempts at local-government reform. Multilateral pressure for decentralization in Pakistan has existed since the mid-1990s (World Bank, 1996, 1998). However, no major attempts at decentralization were initiated by the Pakistani state until General Musharraf's takeover in 1999.

A corollary to this central tendency is that local-government empowerment has always been combined with centralization of political power in the hands of the nonrepresentative center. The centralization of political power has undermined representative institutions at the levels of the center and the provinces. Each attempt at centralization of political power by the military during the postindependence period has initially involved the dissolution of elected provincial and federal assemblies and has invariably been followed by the enactment of a presidential or a quasi-presidential constitution, which preserves the nonrepresentative institution's role at the center even after the revival of representative governments. Centralization of political power has also involved selective disqualification of political party representatives and at times outright bans on all or certain political parties. As a result, these attempts at centralization of political power have considerably weakened the organizational structure of political parties and have distorted electoral competition at the local, provincial, and central levels.

The Musharraf regime represents another attempt at combining the empowerment of local governments with the centralization of political power through the establishment of a quasi-presidential constitution. General Musharraf's Legal Framework Order (2002) as enshrined in the seventeenth constitutional amendment institutionalizes the role of the military in the center by strengthening the powers of the president compared with the elected prime minister.[32] The current attempt at centralization of political power by the military has again been accompanied by a number of interventions against politicians and political parties. These interventions include selective accountability and disqualification of politicians, the enactment of an educational criterion for electoral candidacy, and the creation of a promilitary political party, the Pakistan Muslim League (Q), which currently retains political power in the center and in the Punjab.

Limited Local Governments
While all nonrepresentative governments have been the protagonists of local-government reforms, they have not given complete autonomy to these governments by design. This is perhaps another manifestation of the desire of the nonrepresentative center to retain political control over local governments. Political control was directly exercised by the center through the bureaucracy during the British and Ayub periods. Neither the British nor the Zia regimes gave constitutional cover to the local tier, which reflects the center's lack of commitment to entrench an autonomous and self-sustaining local tier. In addition, during the Zia period local government reforms were designed to give suspension power to provincial military governors, which established a credible

threat of removal over local politicians.[33] Equally important and as we have argued above, local governments were never financially empowered, which weakened their ability to meet even their own restricted expenditure mandates. This was perhaps a safeguard exercised by the nonrepresentative center against the emergence of a politically independent local tier.

Moreover, the current regime has provided only a limited six-year constitutional protection to the reform through the seventeenth constitutional amendment. As discussed above, the financial autonomy of the new local governments also remains circumscribed on both the revenue and expenditure sides. It is therefore unclear whether the long-term sustainability of the reform is ensured in light of both the limited financial autonomy and constitutional protection, especially given the lack of political ownership of these reforms (see the next section).

Distortions and Conflicts in Politics: Local Governments versus the Province?

Not surprisingly, given the central tendency identified above, non-representative designers of local-government electoral processes have invariably placed a series of limitations on organized political representation, which has distorted electoral competition at the local level. The most extreme limitation was placed during the early British period when local-government members were nominated by the center, a rule designed to undermine local electoral competition. All military governments, including the current regime, have required local-government elections to be held on a nonparty basis. A likely objective of this measure has been to weaken the presence of opposition political parties at the local level. Under the Zia regime, successful candidates with a Pakistan People's Party (PPP) affiliation were disqualified on different pretexts in the 1979 local bodies' elections (Wilder, 1999). Similarly, recent press reports indicate that candidates with opposition-party affiliations, who were successful in southern Punjab and rural Sindh, were pressurized to withdraw their party affiliations. Opposition politicians have interpreted these interventions as a means to create a competing class of collaborative politicians and to weaken the base of political parties at the provincial level.

The nonparty basis of local-government elections has invariably ended up weakening political linkages between elected provincial governments, which have tended to be party based, and local governments. Political parties, when in government at the provincial and federal levels, have tended to view local governments as a competing tier of patronage (Wilder, 1999), and as a result they have not made any attempt at empowering the local-government system. If anything, *they have tended to suspend or abolish established local governments when in power.* Thus each elected federal government that has followed the military regimes that introduced local governments has at the very least ignored these local governments and often suspended them altogether. This antagonistic relationship between local and provincial governments also arises because local government reforms are perceived as a way to weaken the authority and the delivery functions assigned to provincial politicians without a commensurate compensation in the form of devolution of powers and resources from the federal to the provincial level.

These provincial-local government tensions have heightened during the current reform period.[34] Among other reasons, this is because no attempt was made to build political ownership of these reforms among elected provincial governments. This is in part because local government reforms, which represented a major reassignment of provincial functions and resources to the local tier, were enacted prior to the establishment of elected provincial governments. Local governments were again legally empowered in the absence of elected provincial governments, despite the fact that local government is a provincial subject under the 1973 constitution. Given this history and the fact that the powers, authorities, and resources of elected members of the provincial assemblies (MPAs) have been significantly curtailed by the current system, it is not surprising that there is poor ownership of the local government system among provinces and some of the major political parties. In fact, in Sindh and NWFP there have been open conflicts between the two tiers (Manning et al., 2003), which have been managed through the intervention of the federal government. Even in the Punjab, where the PML (Q) is in power, it is unclear whether MPAs have tendered widespread acceptance of the present system.

The Role of the Bureaucracy

The historical analysis shows that there has been a change in the tendency of nonrepresentative centers to use the bureaucracy to control local governments. Bureaucratic control over local governments was most explicit during the British and Ayub periods. The Zia regime circumscribed direct bureaucratic representation in local governments, which resulted in greater autonomy for the elected tier at the local level. The Musharraf regime has furthered this trend through two means: First, it has considerably weakened the provincial bureaucracy by reassigning a large proportion of their functions to elected local governments and by abolishing the office of the deputy commissioner. Second, and more important, are the accountability changes brought about by the present system whereby the provincial bureaucracy at the local level has been made accountable to the elected heads of district and tehsil municipal administration. It needs to be pointed out that the weakening of the provincial bureaucracy is circumscribed as the provincial secretariats still retain considerable administrative authority over district bureaucrats (Manning et al., 2003), which at times has been used to trump the authority of the nazim, even though the relative de jure bargaining power between the district bureaucracy and the nazim has been tilted in favor of the latter.

The historical evidence thus suggests a trend toward loosening bureaucratic control of local governments, and Musharaf's reforms have been the most radical in this regard.[35] However, it is unclear that the de jure shift in emphasis toward elected representatives and away from the bureaucracy has been matched by their substantive de facto empowerment. In fact, even during the current reforms the relationship between the bureaucracy and elected heads of local governments remains uncharted and at times highly conflictual. Manning et al. (2003, p. 51) argue that local governments continue to have little de facto control over the appointment, transfer, and firing authorities of local-government bureaucrats and in particular the new heads of local administration and the line departments (the DCOs and EDOs, respectively).

Rural-Urban Dynamics

Our analysis shows the existence of a strong rural bias in central and provincial government policies during the British period in an effort to maintain social order among the majority rural population. We have also argued that Ayub in part reflected a similar rural bias by increasing the share of targeted provincial and federal development resources in favor of rural areas, which reversed the urban bias in the provision of these resources that had arisen during the 1950s. This preference is not surprising given that the rural areas formed a majority in Ayub's electoral college. However, while Zia-ul-Haq continued the rural-urban divide at the local level, in his period this meant a relative tilt in favor of urban local governments as increasing urbanization during this time resulted in significant relative increases in per capita tax income of urban local councils as compared to rural councils. In Zia's case, this appears to be an attempt to accommodate the interests of the urban middle classes that had formed the core of the anti-PPP movement. Thus in general, these changes appear to reflect the political judgment of the nonrepresentative center at particular historical junctures regarding the relevant political population that needed to be accommodated to deliver sustained political support at the local level. This judgment is apparently based on the numerical importance of a population and by the ability of mobilized groups to impose heavy electoral, political, and disruption costs on the state.

What is important is that the judgment of different regimes regarding the political importance of rural and urban areas appears to have differentially benefited these areas in terms of public spending at different levels of the state. We have shown that the current plan has reversed the trend set under the previous regimes as it has legislatively eliminated the rural-urban divide in local governments by integrating urban and rural local councils at the tehsil level and by ensuring that a rural-urban distinction is not present within district governments. While the reasons behind the reversal of the rural-urban divide under the current reforms are not obvious, given that the previous rural-urban proclivities all reflected the changing importance of urban/rural constituents in harnessing local support and legitimacy, it is likely that the same reasons are at play.

Thus it is plausible that the current decision to eliminate the rural-urban divide is partly explained by sociodemographic changes that have taken place in Pakistan since the 1980s. Recent demographic work (Ali, 2003) indicates that Pakistan's primary cities have emerged as major urban systems, with their rural suburbs or "peri-urban" settlements integrated into the city economies. This phenomenon is most apparent in central Punjab's heartland, where contiguous districts (comprising major cities, medium-sized towns, and peri-urban settlements) have formed into a significant population agglomeration that has increased its political and economic importance (Ali, 2003). More important, approximately half of this population resides in peri-urban settlements that had not been recognized as urban under the previous local government system, a legislative rule that denied them access to the administrative benefits associated with urban local councils such as octroi revenue and better delivery of municipal services. The integration of urban and rural councils into tehsil administrations will certainly benefit this population by creating tehsils where the peri-urban vote is in a majority.

In general, however, the effects of eliminating this urban-rural administrative distinction are not as simply classified. While we have argued above that in central Punjab this was likely to favor peri-urban areas, in the more agrarian regions, such as Sindh and southern and western Punjab (Gazdar, 1999), this change is likely to benefit rural areas due to their majority rural vote as the relatively economically prosperous urban areas will now have to share the benefits of their incomes with their rural and peri-urban hinterlands.[36] In this sense, the Musharraf system is more flexible in that it allocates relative power to whatever demographic group is in majority in the local area.

Concluding Thoughts

This chapter has argued that to understand the current decentralization in Pakistan it is imperative to view the reform in the historical context of previous reforms. In particular, a continuing theme that emerges in this context is that these reforms have somewhat paradoxically been brought about by nonrepresentative regimes such as the British during the preindependence period and the military during the postindependence period. In fact, each of the three military regimes in Pakistan has implemented local-government reforms, and each political government that has followed has undermined these reforms or at best simply ignored the local governments. These reforms have all involved decentralizing from the province level to the local level but often a recentralization at the federal level. Our interpretation is that these reforms have been used as a means for a nonrepresentative center to gain legitimacy by bypassing the political agents at the provincial and national levels.

Moreover, the conflict between the provincial representatives and local governments we have highlighted does not bode well for the future of the current decentralization program. Already, with elected provincial and national governments in place, we have begun to see conflicts arising between the province and local governments. However, what is different about the current decentralization reforms is that they have gone much further in terms of their extent and scope. While the local governments still have little revenue-raising abilities and have effectively limited ability to decide their expenditures given that the majority expenditure is in the forms of fixed establishment costs, the delivery of most public services has now come under their purview. While these local governments' future is still uncertain given their time-bound constitutional protection, their limited financial support, and conflict with the provincial governments, if they remain, we are likely to see an impact on the delivery of these public services. Whether this will be for the better (as local governments may become more accountable to the general public) or for the worse (if local governments fall into patronage and biraderi politics) remains to be seen.

Acknowledgments

The authors would like to acknowledge invaluable research assistance provided by Usman Talat, Mariam Mufti, and Ali Fareed Khwaja. We would like to thank Daron Acemoglu, Mahmood Hasan Khan, Reza Ali, Haris Gazdar, Shandana Mohmand, and Anjum Nasim for their comments. This work would not have been possible without support from the CIDA-funded LUMS-McGill Social Enterprise Development Programme.

Notes

1. We are referring to areas of India that came to constitute Pakistan.

2. The district was the principle unit of government in colonial India.

3. For details of this transition, see Cheema, Khwaja, and Qadir (2005).

4. For details of the system, see Cheema, Khwaja, and Qadir (2005).

5. In the 1965 presidential election, Ayub secured most of his votes from rural areas, while urban areas mostly went against him because Ayub's local government system placed rural representatives in a majority (Rizvi, 1976).

6. "The Rural Works Programme had been evolved in 1961 to utilize the concealed unemployment in the agricultural sector through the institutions of Basic Democracies" (Ahmed and Amjad, 1984, pp. 187–188).

7. See Cheema, Khwaja, and Qadir (2005) for details.

8. We would like to thank Reza Ali for bringing this point to our notice.

9. For details of Zia's local-government structure, see Cheema, Khwaja, and Qadir (2005).

10. During the Zia regime, an area was classified as urban (as given in the 1981 census) if it had the *administrative status* of municipal corporation, municipal or town committee, or cantonment board, regardless of its population size. This was a departure from the previous system, which combined the administrative criterion with a population criterion and gave census commissioners discretion to declare an area urban if they felt it had "ur-

ban characteristics" (Ali, 2003). Therefore, our use of the term *urban* implies administered urban areas.

11. Octroi was a tax on goods imported into municipal limits for production or consumption. Before it was abolished by the federal government in 1999 and 2000, octroi had been the biggest source of revenue for urban councils, contributing on average 50 to 60 percent of these councils' income. In Punjab and Sindh, the octroi was biased in favor of larger urban councils (Nasim, 1999; World Bank, 2000).

12. For example, in the Punjab the average per capita octroi receipts for urban local councils were 74.5 rupees in 1985. In the absence of the urban-rural divide, the per capita octroi revenue for rural and urban areas would have fallen to a meager 19 rupees (AERC, 1990).

13. For example, Wilder (1999). Hasan (2002) argues that the increasing importance of urban middle classes in Punjabi politics, during the 1970s and 1980s, is underpinned by socioeconomic changes that made agriculturalists dependent on mandi (market) arhtis (middlemen) and their transporters, who controlled credit as well as access to mandis with the connivance of the bureaucracy.

14. The anti-Bhutto coalition in 1977 included middlemen, traders and shopkeepers from Punjab's mandi (market) towns, small and large industrialists, and urban professionals (Noman, 1988; Wilder, 1999). For details, see Cheema and Mohmand (2003).

15. This situation was somewhat rectified post-1990 because more items were placed on the district (export) tax list during the 1980s and because of the adoption of tax farming for collection purposes (AERC, 1990). This is shown by table 8.1, which shows a narrowing of the gap between rural council and urban council per capita incomes in the Punjab during the 1990 to 1995 period.

16. For example, nearly 50 percent of the elected members of the Punjab Provincial Assembly were sitting local councilors (Zaidi, 1999, p. 439).

17. The term *personalized politics* describes the tendency among powerful ministers to use state resources to capture influential local factions based on party, *biradari* (community), *quam* (tribe or nation), or *zat* (caste). Keefer, Narayan, and Vishwanath in chapter 9 (this volume) analyze the effect that personalized politics has on service provision outcomes.

18. As one minister put it during the 1985 National Assembly's first budget session, "We don't have one party, or ten parties...; we have two hundred parties. Each member of the assembly considers himself responsible only to himself" (Haq, 1985, p. 5).

19. Over 96 percent of Pakistan's revenue was controlled by the federal and provincial governments in the last two decades (World Bank, 2000).

20. Data show that the ratio of municipal corporation per capita income (the richest tier of local governments) to provincial per capita income decreased from 0.78 in 1990 to 0.32 in 1995.

21. This section draws upon both the Local Government Plan (2000) and the local Government Ordinance (2001).

22. These reforms were brought about through a new local-government ordinance, a new Police Order (2002), and abolition of executive magistracy through amendments in relevant laws.

23. Even these limited local governments were mostly suspended during the 1990s, so prior to the current devolution there were no elected representatives at the local

level, and their powers were exercised by provincial bureaucrats as local-government administrators.

24. The National Reconstruction Bureau established the Higher Government Restructuring Committee in 2001 to suggest devolution of powers from the federal level to the provincial level. However, no concrete steps have been taken on this front as of today.

25. For a detailed rendering, see Cheema, Khwaja, and Qadir (2005).

26. In the Punjab, district governments are empowered to create contractual posts, provided they fund them from own source revenues and are able to obtain the "concurrence" of the provincial finance department.

27. For details, see Manning et al. (2003) and Cheema, Khwaja, and Qadir (2005).

28. Manning et al. (2003) show that the legislatively mandated transfers of the provincial consolidated fund to local governments amounts to less than 25 percent. They also show that provincially controlled programs still account for 30 to 60 percent of local governments' development expenditure. Also see chapter 9 in this volume.

29. Manning et al.'s (2003) six-district study shows that the salary component in total district expenditure in their sample districts ranged from 82 to 94 percent. Also see chapter 9 in this volume.

30. The octroi and zila taxes were abolished in 1999.

31. An alternative explanation would be that the military needs to create a local-level preference aggregation mechanism that effectively reveals the demands of civil society in the absence of elected higher tiers of government. We would like to thank Daron Acemoglu for suggesting this point. However, the legitimacy and demand-aggregation explanations need not be mutually exclusive.

32. Substantive powers include the revival of article 58-2(b), which empowers the president to dissolve the elected assemblies.

33. For example, see section 29 of Punjab LGO (1979).

34. It is therefore not surprising that the Punjab province's most important recent initiative, the Punjab Education Sector Reform Program, mandates members of the provincial assemblies to select primary- and secondary-school schemes, even though these services have been devolved to the district.

35. Cheema, Khwaja, and Qadir (2005) provide a political-economy explanation for the historical trend toward loosening bureaucratic control.

36. Despite the NRB Local Government Plan's (2000) explicit recognition that there was a case for declaring the city areas in at least eleven districts of Pakistan as city districts, the Musharraf regime chose to declare only the four provincial capitals as city districts. This effectively gave the rural areas and rural politicians of the remaining seven districts a claim over the resources of the larger and richer urban areas.

References

Ahmed, M. (1964). *The Civil Servant in Pakistan*. Karachi: Oxford University Press.

Ahmed, V., and R. Amjad. (1984). *The Management of Pakistan's Economy, 1947–82*. Karachi: Oxford University Press.

Ali, I. A. (1988). *The Punjab under Imperialism, 1885–1947*. Delhi: Oxford University Press.

Ali, R. (2003). "Understanding Urbanization." In S. A. Zaidi (Ed.), *Continuity and Change: Socio Political and Institutional Dynamics in Pakistan*. Karachi: City Press.

Applied Economic Research Centre (AERC). (1990). "Local Government Administration in Pakistan." Manuscript, Karachi.

Burki, S. J. (1980). *Pakistan under Bhutto: 1971–77*. London: Macmillan.

Callard, K. (1957). *Pakistan: A Political Study*. London: George Allen and Unwin.

Cheema, A., and U. Ali. (2005). "How Rule-Based Is Punjab's Intergovernmental Fiscal Transfer System?" Social Enterprise Development Centre Working Paper, Lahore University of Management Sciences.

Cheema, A., A. I. Khwaja, and A. Qadir. (2005). "Decentralization in Pakistan: Context, Content and Causes." Kennedy School Working Paper RWP05-034, Harvard University, Cambridge, MA.

Cheema, A., and S. K. Mohmand. (2003). "Local Government Reforms in Pakistan: Legitimising Centralization or a Driver for Pro-Poor Change?" Paper written for the Pakistan Drivers of Pro-Poor Change Study conducted by Institute of Development Studies (U.K.), Collective for Social Science Research, Karachi. Department for International Development, United Kingdom.

Gauhar, A. (1996). *Ayub Khan: Pakistan's First Military Ruler*. Lahore: Sang-e-Meel.

Gazdar, H. (1999). "Poverty in Pakistan: A Review." In S. R. Khan (Ed.), *Fifty Years of Pakistan's Economy*. Karachi: Oxford University Press.

Government of Pakistan. (1981). Population Census of Pakistan. Population Census Organization: Statistics Division, Islamabad.

Government of Pakistan. (1998). Population Census of Pakistan. Population Census Organization: Statistics Division, Islamabad.

Haq, M. (1985). Interview. *Overseas Mashriq*, June 27, p. 5.

Hasan, A. (2002). *The Unplanned Revolution*. Karachi: City Press.

Jalal, A. (1995). *Democracy and Authoritarianism in Pakistan: A Comparative and Historical Perspective*. Lahore: Sang-e-Meel.

Local Government Ordinance (LGO). (1979). Lahore: Law Book Land.

Local Government Ordinance (LGO) (2001). *The Punjab Gazette*, 8th October 2001. Government of the Punjab. Law and Parliamentary Affairs Development.

Local Government Plan (LGP). (2000). National Reconstruction Bureau.

Manning, N., D. Porter, J. Charlton, M. Cyan, and Z. Hasnain. (2003). *Devolution in Pakistan: Preparing for Service Delivery Improvements*. Pakistan: World Bank.

Metcalfe, T. R. (1962). "The British and the Moneylender in Nineteenth-Century India." *Journal of Modern History* 34: pp. 390–397.

Nasim, A. (1999). *Local Government Finance in the Punjab*. Lahore: Punjab Municipal Development Fund Company.

Nath, A. (1929). *Development of Local Self-Government in Punjab (1849–1900)*, Lahore: Punjab Government Record Office Publications.

Noman, O. (1988). *Pakistan: Political and Economic History since 1947*. London: Kegan Paul.

Pasha, M. (1998). *Colonial Political Economy: Recruitment and Underdevelopment in the Punjab*. Karachi: Oxford University Press.

Rizvi, S. A. (1976). *Changing Patterns of Local Government in Pakistan*. Karachi: Pakistan Historical Society.

Siddiqui, K. (1992). *Local Government in South Asia*. Dhaka: University Press Limited.

Talbot, I. (1996). "State Society and Identity: The British Punjab, 1875–1937." In G. Singh and I. Talbot (Eds.), *Punjabi Identity: Continuity and Change*. New Delhi: Manohar.

Talbot, I. (1998). *Pakistan: A Modern History*. New York: St. Martin's Press.

Tinker, H. (1968). *The Foundations of Local Self-Government in India, Pakistan and Burma*. New York: Praeger.

Van den Dungen, P. H. (1972). *The Punjab Tradition: Influence and Authority in Nineteenth-Century India*. London: George Allen and Unwin.

Venkatarangaiya, M., and M. Pattabhiram (Eds.). (1969). *Local Government in India: Select Readings*. Bombay: Allied.

Waseem, M. (1994). *Politics and the State in Pakistan*. Islamabad: National Institute of Historical and Cultural Research.

Wilder, A. R. (1999). *The Pakistani Voter: Electoral Politics and Voting Behavior in the Punjab*. Karachi: Oxford University Press.

World Bank. (1996). *Supporting Fiscal Decentralization in Pakistan*. Report No. 15092-PAK. Washington, DC: The World Bank.

World Bank. (1998). *A Framework for Civil Service Reform in Pakistan*. Report No. 18386-PAK. Washington, DC: The World Bank.

World Bank. (2000). *Pakistan Reforming Provincial Finances in the Context of Devolution: An Eight-Point Agenda*. Report No. 21362-PAK. Washington, DC: The World Bank.

Zaidi, S. A. (1999). *Issues in Pakistan's Economy*. Karachi: Oxford University Press.

9

Decentralization in Pakistan: Are Local Governments Likely to Be More Accountable Than Central Governments?

Philip E. Keefer, Ambar Narayan, and Tara Vishwanath

Introduction

Widespread advocacy of decentralization has its roots in discontent over central-government responsiveness to citizens, whether manifested as high rates of corruption, an excessive focus on patronage, or inadequate public-good provision. The record surrounding decentralization, however, is mixed. For example, in two of the most rigorous studies of the public-policy effects of decentralization in developing countries, Faguet (2002) and Azfar, Kähkönen, and Meagher (2000) conclude that public investment by local governments is more progressive and responsive to the poor than central-government investment decisions. Looking at a number of other cases, however, Manor (1999) finds that the effect of decentralization on public-sector performance is far from ensured.

A recent and growing literature on political economy suggests numerous political-market failures that might give rise to government breakdowns (see Keefer and Khemani, 2005). To the extent that decentralization does not fix them, we should not expect decentralization to improve outcomes. Government breakdowns can occur if political and electoral institutions are different at the local level and less conducive to "good government," if voters are less informed about the actions of local politicians, if the horizons of local politicians are more limited, if political competitors in local elections are less able to offer credible promises to voters, or if devolution is simply limited and incomplete. From this literature, one can conclude that local governments will do better than central governments if local electoral and political institutions and local competition for political office hold local governments more tightly accountable to citizens.

These differences between central and local governments have received little attention in the literature on decentralization. We examine these and their implications for the effects of decentralization in Pakistan. Our conclusion, perhaps not surprisingly, is that although decentralization may alleviate some political-market imperfections in Pakistan, it may exacerbate others.

The analysis here does not assess the success of Pakistan's devolution, which was initiated only in 2001. Instead, we argue in the next section of this chapter that the central government indeed exhibited significant, politics-driven policy failures, particularly in the provision of social services. One key manifestation of this failure was the extent to which central-government politicians had incentives to provide narrowly targeted services rather than broadly available public goods. In the following sections, we outline key elements of the Pakistani decentralization and tentatively assess the extent to which they are likely to mitigate the distortions evident in central-government decision making. The analysis suggests that although special-interest influence—driven, for example, by voter ignorance—is likely to be less pronounced in Pakistan, other sources of distortion may be greater in local governments.

Policy Breakdowns in Pakistan: Health and Education

The political-market imperfections that we examine here are those that drive politicians to deny public goods to broad segments of the population to focus instead on rent seeking and on narrow transfers to strictly and politically delimited individuals and groups. Evidence of three kinds suggests that prior to decentralization, elected central governments in Pakistan confronted exaggerated incentives to provide narrow, targeted goods and services at the expense of broader public goods. Policy failures in health and education are one indicator. Explicit documentation of legislator activities is another. A third is evidence from more than one hundred villages that the competition for votes leads to school construction but not improvements in school quality.

Health and education are good barometers of these incentives: where incentives to target are high, broad indicators of health and education access and quality should suffer. Broad access is by definition the opposite of targeting, while quality almost always requires performance improvements in public-sector provision that are difficult to target to

Table 9.1
Regional comparison of infant mortality rate

Country	1992	1995	1997
Bangladesh	85.1	74.1	66
Bhutan	75	67.8	63
India	79	74	71
Maldives	45	37.2	32
Nepal	96	79	79
Pakistan	104	95.6	90
Sri Lanka	17.6	16.5	15.9

Source: World Bank (2003).

specific beneficiaries. In health, Pakistan exhibited far worse infant mortality figures than other countries in the region that were as poor or poorer than Pakistan, as table 9.1 makes clear. Improvements in infant mortality require health-system reforms that are difficult to target to narrow, favored groups. These improvements were not vigorously pursued by central-government decision makers in the 1990s. Anecdotal evidence from various sources suggests that quality characteristics of health facilities were also widely deficient, with considerable evidence of underused facilities. One would expect this, since facility construction is a priority intervention for governments primarily interested in targeting favored populations with benefits.[1]

Universal—that is, untargeted—primary education is another government service that was underprovided in the 1990s. Primary gross enrollment rates changed little in the 1990s. Overall enrollments were low, and they exhibited persistent, large gender, urban-rural, and rich-poor gaps. Primary gross enrollment rates among the top three deciles, by per capita consumption, were around 90 percent, whereas that among the bottom three deciles was around 50 percent. Similarly, in the province of Sindh, only 25 percent of girls living rural areas were enrolled in primary school, compared to 62 percent in its urban areas.[2]

Results from the Pakistan Rural Household Survey facilities survey (2001), reflecting the situation prior to decentralization, provide a stark example of the disjunction between political willingness to provide education quantity (school buildings) and education quality. No classes were held in thirty-four out of the 200 schools surveyed; these were cases of so-called ghost schools.[3] In the schools that were open, close to 20 percent of the teachers were absent, 48 percent and 52 percent lacked basic amenities like drinking water and toilets, respectively, and 77 percent lacked an adequate supply of textbooks. Student enrollment was markedly lower in low-quality schools.

The broad policy record is consistent with political incentives more concerned with targeted than with broad public-good provision. There is also direct evidence from a number of sources that Pakistani legislators were overwhelmingly concerned with supplying targeted resources to constituents rather than high-quality public goods. Wilder (1999), for example, quotes former members of the National Assembly from Punjab as saying: "People now think that the job of an MNA and MPA is to fix their gutters, get their children enrolled in school, arrange for job transfers.... [These tasks] consume your whole day" (p. 196); "Look, we get elected because we are ba asr log [effective people] in our area. People vote for me because they perceive me as someone who can help them.... Somebody's son is a matric fail, and I get him a job as a teacher or a government servant" (p. 204).

This contrasts sharply with legislator activities in other countries. Members of the U.S. Congress, well-known for their incessant efforts to secure reelection, spend fewer than six hours per week directly and personally intervening on behalf of constituents to obtain favors for them or help them solve bureaucratic difficulties.[4] Despite the large political payoff to being able to take credit for constituent services, political incentives in the United States also drive legislators to spend time on larger policy issues that Pakistani legislators abjured.[5]

The final piece of evidence that the incentives of central government politicians in the 1990s were more favorable to education infrastructure than to education quality comes from more detailed analysis of the PRHS (2001) household surveys. As part of PRHS (2001), information about teacher absenteeism and facility quality was collected for around 200 primary schools. Community surveys were conducted for all villages in the sample, yielding information about new schools constructed in the 1990s, elections, political institutions, infrastructure, and demographics. These data show a significant positive association between the construction of boys' schools in the 1990s and indicators of a village's political activity and attractiveness to politicians. They show no such association for indicators of quality (teacher absenteeism or the presence of blackboards, textbooks, or electricity in the schools) (see Keefer and Khemani, 2005).[6]

Taken together, this evidence suggests that elections mattered for central and provincial government decision makers in the 1990s but that electoral competition drove them to increase the quantity of targeted goods and services (school buildings) but not to improve their quality. The question that we explore in the remainder of the chapter is whether devolution in Pakistan is likely to reduce the distortions triggered by competition for political office at the provincial and national levels, first by describing the precise institutional details of devolution in Pakistan and then by systematically assessing the various sources of distortion in political decision making and their presence in the new local governments.

Summarizing the Electoral, Administrative, and Fiscal Details of Devolution in Pakistan

The effects of devolution depend largely on the precise details of its design. The design features relevant to an assessment of the relative incentives of local and central or provincial governments are briefly summarized here (see chapter 8 in this volume for more details). Prior to decentralization, the structure of government in Pakistan was similar to that throughout South Asia and little changed from the legacy of British colonial rule. It divided the country into four administrative tiers—the center, the province, the division, and the district. During most of the 1990s, both central and provincial government were elected and parliamentary. The center-controlled funding and administration.

Administratively, the federal government, through the Public Service Commission, recruited the elite District Management Group (DMG); personnel from the DMG filled 40 to 60 percent of the posts of deputy commissioner in the districts. The remainder were filled by the provincial governments. The deputy commissioner controlled all executive, judicial, and developmental functions in a district, while each sector of local administration (such as education) was managed by the parent provincial line department.

The government of President Musharraf introduced an ambitious plan to devolve administrative and fiscal powers to a series of new local governments: districts or zilas (called "city districts" in the four provincial capitals), tehsils (called "towns" in the four city districts), and union councils. The National Reconstruction Bureau (NRB) implemented the plan over the period 2001 to 2002, holding several waves of local elections from December 2000 to September 2001, leading to elected governments in Pakistan's ninety-six districts (ninety-two districts and four city districts); 307 tehsils and thirty city towns; and 6,022 union councils.[7] The elections were perceived as largely fair and impartial. Participation rates averaged 52.5 percent, ranging from 33 percent in Balochistan to 59 percent in Punjab.

Formal electoral and political institutions are both complicated under Pakistani devolution. Each level of local government in Pakistan has councils, nazims (head of administration), and naib (deputy) nazims. Decision-making authority and control over the bulk of local government resources reside largely with the district government. District nazims are indirectly elected by an electoral college comprised of all union councilors in a district. Similarly, the electoral college for tehsil nazims and naib nazims is comprised of all the union councilors in the tehsil. District councils are composed partially of the union council nazims, who are directly elected in their unions. Women must occupy district council seats amounting to at least 33 percent of the total number of union councils in the district; women are elected in electoral districts defined by the district tehsils. Despite this legal requirement, however, only 17 percent of new union councilors' seats went to women. Peasants (in the countryside) and workers (in the city) comprise another 5 percent of seats, as must minorities. These groups are elected at large in the whole district.

Unions comprise a group of villages and are of approximately equal size; only officials of union governments are elected directly by citizens. Each union council is composed of nineteen members elected directly at large in the union on a nonparty basis. The precise electoral rules (how many votes each voter can cast, for example) are not in the local government ordinance (article 151) and unclear. It appears that each voter in the union receives only one vote and that the top nineteen vote getters win. Twelve seats are reserved for Muslims, of which four are reserved for women; six are reserved for peasants and workers, of which two are reserved for women; and one seat is reserved for minority communities. In addition, each union has a nazim and naib nazim, who are members of the union council but are elected on a joint ticket at large by the whole union.[8]

The Political Economy of Policy Distortion: Will Decentralization Improve Public-Good Provision and Reduce Corruption?

Decentralization should mitigate two obstacles to efficient public-sector performance—divergent public-good preferences among large groups of citizens, and difficulties confronting large groups of citizens seeking to hold public officials accountable for their performance. The actual success of decentralization, however, depends on a number of additional factors. Do the political and electoral rules of local government provide stronger incentives to politicians to provide high-quality public goods and to refrain from corruption? Do local officials have confidence that decentralization will last, so that they are constrained by reelection concerns from maximizing personal rents? Are the conditions of political competition—such as citizen information and the credibility of political promises—more conducive to government accountability at the local level? Are local variations in demand for public goods (such as girls' education) likely to lead to their undesirable underprovision in some jurisdictions after decentralization? Answers to these questions suggest that it is not self-evident that local governments in Pakistan confront stronger incentives to provide high-quality public goods than the central government did in the 1990s.

Devolution—Administrative and Financial—Is Partial

One key characteristic of Pakistani devolution that might limit its influence on outcomes is that it is partial. Provincial authorities continue to exercise significant control over both local administration and local finances.[9] With respect to the first, under devolution the post of district coordinating officer (DCO) replaces the former deputy commissioner. Although DCOs lack many of the legal powers of the deputy commissioner, they still have significant executive and managerial responsibilities. Not the least of these are the authority to prepare the first draft of the district budget and to control district personnel. Though the DCO formally reports to the district nazim, the nazim can only request the transfer of the DCO and initiate the DCO's performance evaluation. However, the transfer goes through only if the provincial government concurs, and the nazim's performance evaluation is valid only if countersigned by the chief secretary and chief minister of the provincial government. Similarly, the ten to twelve executive district officers (responsible for sectors such as education), who formerly reported to the parent-line departments in the provincial government, now report to both the DCO and the nazim. Once again, though, the nazim can only request that the provincial government transfer these officials and provincial governments retain sole authority to appoint them. Moreover, district nazims are prohibited from hiring any "advisors, special assistants, or political secretaries other than support staff allocated to his office from among the officials available in the district" (*SBNP Local Government Ordinance 2001*, article 18(2)).

Devolution is limited with respect to finances, as well. Funds for local government come almost entirely from upper-level governments with strings attached. The formula for provincial allocations and the conditions on those allocations are decided by the Provincial Finance Commission (PFC) and, ultimately, by the provincial governor. The members of the PFC are provincial officers or others nominated by the provincial government; there is no automatic representation of locally elected officials on the PFC. There are substantial variations among PFC recommendations between Sindh, NWFP, and Balochistan, illustrating the discretionary powers of the PFC. In addition, though grants from provincial governments have a need-based component and are based on an index of backwardness (for example in Sindh), the construction of this index is opaque.[10]

Districts rely overwhelmingly on provincial funds for current expenditures (capital expenditures are unfunded). Own funds of district governments in Sindh account for only 1.3 percent of the total revenue, for example.[11] In addition, there are substantial limitations on district-government discretion regarding the use of transfers. Transfers are made into several accounts. The bulk of transfers go to account I, which consists mainly of expenditures on salaries that, in turn, cannot be used for other purposes: district governments have little power to hire and fire. Nonsalary expenditures come out of account IV, which are approximately 10 percent of salary expenditures (account I).[12]

District Nazims Are Powerful and May Face Weaker Electoral Constraints Than the Heads of Provincial and National Governments

An important advantage of decentralization is meant to be the greater ability of voters to hold local decision makers accountable for their actions. Discussions of decentralization usually assume that voters directly elect these decision makers, but district nazims are elected indirectly. Though there is little research on this question, the procedures for electing them may limit their incentives to provide public goods.

The indirect election of the district nazim matters because the nazim is the key politician in local politics. Nazim control over budget policy is the best indicator of this. Within district government, where most local-budget authority resides under devolution, district nazims exercise significant influence. First, the district nazim has proposal power: the district council must consider the budget proposed by the district nazim rather than elaborate its own. Proposal power is not necessarily significant, but, second, district councils have no explicit authority to amend the budgets. Instead, article 112 speaks only of council votes to *approve* the budget submitted by the nazim, even noting in (1) "Provided that the charged expenditure may be discussed but shall not be voted upon by the Councils." Third, council failure to approve any budget leads to zero spending fourteen days after the expiration of the financial year (*SBNP Local Government Ordinance 2001*, article 112(5)). Failure to pass the nazim's budget therefore leaves the council in the position of shutting down government, giving the nazim extra leverage in budget negotiations. Finally, the Local Government Ordinance requires that the naib nazim be the chairperson of the council, but since the naib nazim is elected on the nazim's ticket, this gives the executive substantial authority over the affairs of the legislative body, without corresponding influence (as in a parliamentary system) of the legislative body on the political future of the nazim.

Public-good provision should rise and corruption should drop as a result of devolution to the extent that voters can hold nazims more tightly accountable for their actions than they could elected executives of provincial or national governments, who were the key decision makers predevolution. One determinant of this is whether electoral give nazims greater incentive to provide public goods to all citizens. This may or may not be the case, however.[13]

The district nazim is elected by an electoral college of officials (union councilors) who are themselves elected at large in the unions.[14] The larger the number of voters represented by the union councilors who elect the district nazim, the greater the incentive of the nazim to provide broad public services to satisfy those union councilors and their constituents. A union council candidate is sure to take office if he or she wins one-nineteenth of the total vote. If this were the case for all union councilors, then the district nazim would have an incentive to make decisions that appealed to at least ten-nineteenths of all voters, since the the district nazim requires the support of approximately ten-nineteenths of all union councilors.

However, union councilors could win with considerably less support under many plausible circumstances. In particular, the larger the number of union council candidates and the greater the vote share of the losing candidates, the smaller the vote share of the winning candidates. Moreover, the distribution of votes among winning candidates is unlikely to be uniform. If the top union council candidate receives 50 percent of the vote, other candidates could get into office with much less than one-nineteenth of the total vote in their union. To the extent that the district nazim wins the support of union council candidates who themselves gained office with a small number of votes, the nazim's incentive to provide broad-based public goods accordingly falls.

These incentives need to be compared to those of the executives of provincial or national governments in the 1990s. They took power only if their members of Parliament (MPs) and the MPs of possible coalition partners, each elected in single-member district elections, won a majority of parliamentary seats. To win, a prime minister needed at least the majority of seats in Parliament, and the winner of each seat required at least a plurality of the votes in the constituency but not more than one-half of all the votes. At most, prime ministers therefore required the support of just one-fourth of all voters, mitigating their incentives to supply public goods. The electoral incentives to provide public goods therefore increase under devolution only to the extent that district nazims are forced to seek the support of union councilors who collectively need the support of more than one-fourth of all voters. However, there are many circumstances in which this may not be the case, and the number could fall substantially below one-fourth.

Local Officials May Not Have Longer Policy Horizons Than Central or Provincial Officials

Elected officials with little expectation of standing for reelection are more difficult for voters to hold to account and have shorter horizons. Uncertain horizons, in turn, encourage politicians to seek rents rather than to provide services. However, it is not obvious that horizons of local officials are shorter than those of elected officials prior to devolution. It appears that national and provincial governments were characterized by short horizons in the 1990s, with the threat and reality of expulsion from office a permanent condition. On the other hand, however, it has been evident since the late 1990s that both of the chief political actors of the 1990s, Nawaz Sharif and Benazir Bhutto, intended to return to office. At the same time, the history of decentralization in Pakistan (discussed in chapter 8 in this volume) is replete with reversals and provides compelling reasons for local officials to have short horizons. Apart from historical concerns regarding their tenure, locally elected officials also confront a time-bound constitutional guarantee, such that after six years, and consistent with the 1973 constitution, parent provinces will be able to disband local governments at any time.

There is, then, little reason to believe that local government officials have longer horizons than those of central governments.

Lobbying, Special Interests, and Decentralization in Pakistan

An important source of inefficiency in political decision making is the influence of special interests on politicians. The available, if limited evidence suggests that the role of special interests in national (electoral) politics in Pakistan was significant and vote buying and the growing expense of elections are widely noted (Wilder, 1999, p. 206). Shafqat (1999) suggests that campaign spending rose to $120,000 per parliamentarian in the 1997 elections. In the United Kingdom, with an electoral system that closely resembles Pakistan's, spending per constituency amounted to less than $10,000 in the 1992 elections (Pattie, Johnston, and Fieldhouse, 1995).

Bardhan and Mookherjee (1999) argue that the influence of special interests need not be less under decentralization, however. They develop a model of electoral competition under uncertainty in which, in the style of Grossman-Helpman lobbying models, campaign expenditures from the rich help to persuade uninformed voters. Decentralization is less likely to succeed when the local rich (special interests) are more cohesive, electoral competition is limited, loyalty or ideological biases of voters are significant, voters are uninformed, poor voters are disproportionately uninformed, and, somewhat more ambiguously, uncertainty about the ideological or loyalty biases of voters is greater. In the case of Pakistan, these conditions weigh slightly in favor of decentralization.

First, anecdotal evidence (e.g., Gazdar, 2002) suggests that special interests, whether landowners or family or clan lines (*zaats*), appear to be no more cohesive at the local than national levels. In some rural areas, a single family or landowner is dominant; in those circumstances, decentralization will increase special-interest cohesiveness and reduce public-sector performance. In most areas, however, there are multiple clans and landowners who are often at loggerheads and do not form political alliances; special interests are therefore likely to be divided rather than cohesive in both national and local elections.

Second, the recent local elections were much more competitive than national elections of the 1990s (and than national elections since the 1990s, when none have been held). In the 1990s, it was well understood that military dissatisfaction with the incumbent parties would ensure that the opposition would take power, leading to widespread voter abstention and greater willingness of candidates to buy their way onto the lists of one party and not the other. In the framework of Bardhan and Mookherjee (1999), because electoral outcomes are less certain in local than in national elections in Pakistan, the payoffs to special interests of making payments to candidates in local elections are lower, reducing their influence on candidate positions. Unfortunately, while greater electoral uncertainty reduces the influence of special interests and increases political incentives to provide quality public services, it may also reduce disincentives for politicians to seek rents (act corruptly).[15]

Third, ideological biases of voters are likely to matter more in national than in local elections. Voters in Punjab and in Sindh, the two most populous states in Pakistan, exhibited a large and persistent bias toward either the Muslim League headed by Nawaz Sharif and the People's Party of Benazir Bhutto. Decentralization in this context forces politics to a lower level where intraparty rivalries are more likely to emerge and where pronounced biases toward one or another candidate independent of performance are likely to be attenuated.

The second and third factors suggest reasons for optimism about decentralization in Pakistan, at least insofar as decentralization is expected to improve the quality of public services. Optimism is tempered somewhat by a fourth factor, indirect elections and voter inability to identify which policy makers are responsible for outcomes. Voters do not directly elect key decision makers, and elected local government decision makers have little control over important aspects of policy making and implementation. Poor performance by those officials whom voters can directly elect is therefore difficult to evaluate. In particular, the institutional structure makes it difficult for voters to verify whether poor policy outcomes are related to the failure of their union councilors to select the right district nazim or shirking by the district nazim in spite of the best efforts of the district councils to hold him accountable. This uncertainty loosens electoral accountability and suggests that decentralization might worsen public-sector performance.[16]

Feudalism and the Political Economy of Pakistan

A particular special interest has long been of interest in Pakistan—the landed, even feudal, elite. One traditional view of Pakistani politics has held that feudal landlords, by virtue of their strong control over rural voters and the significant overrepresentation of rural voters in the national and provincial legislatures, exercised disproportionate influence in national-level policy making.[17] Because of their disinterest in the welfare of most citizens, public-good provision declined. If landlord influence was key to policy failures by central government, then decentralization will improve policy performance if local governments are less vulnerable to this influence.

Neither seems to be the case. Landlords seem to have done well in local elections. However, the evidence is weak that their influence is primarily responsible for the policy failures of the 1990s. First, landlords are not a monolithic class and compete vigorously among themselves for political office. Many landlords, including the most feudal, lost their parliamentary seats in the 1990s. Second, anthropological evidence shows that rural inhabitants were less reliant on landowners in the 1990s than in earlier years, reducing the leverage of landowners over the voters in their areas. For example, landlords were less likely to offer support in the event of family illness, since the offspring of traditionally powerful landlord families now spend more time in the city (Beall et al., 1993). Third, land concentration and therefore the influence of landlords seem not to explain the political decisions to build schools or improve school quality (Keefer and Khemani, 2005). Finally, in a careful survey of 125 primary schools in selected rural locales, Gazdar (2002) finds landlord influence to be neither unambiguously pernicious nor sufficient to explain the pervasive breakdown of the educational system that was observed.

The Credibility of Preelectoral Promises and the Benefits of Decentralization in Pakistan

One final characteristic of political competition, the credibility of preelectoral promises of candidates, also influences whether decentralization will improve outcomes. The picture here is, once again, mixed. Political promises are assumed to be credible in Grossman-Helpman style models. However, in Pakistan, as in countries ranging from Bolivia and Indonesia to the Philippines and Bangladesh, political parties project no credible policy stances to voters on issues ranging from education to trade reform. The lack of credibility has a significant negative impact on policy outcomes. At the very least, noncredible challengers find it more difficult to replace even poorly performing incumbents because voters do not believe they will do better.[18]

Keefer and Vlaicu (2005) argue that where parties are not credible, politicians can still rely on their personal reputations for providing goods, jobs, and government access to individuals with whom they have had contact. These relationships with voters are often termed *clientelist*. Such candidates have little incentive, however, to provide public goods that benefit a broad range of the public. Keefer and Khemani (2003) argue that clientelist-based credibility is a key reason for the poor provision of social services.

There is little information on the relative credibility of preelectoral political promises in the recent local elections in Pakistan, though it does not seem to have been a hallmark of these elections. Candidates for local office were either new to the political game or had held national office. In neither case is it possible to argue that they were more credible, and there is some reason to think that their reputations were weaker. In addition, parties were entirely disallowed in the recent local elections. This does not make outcomes worse under decentralization, since national parties of the 1990s were not credible on matters of public policy and broad public-good provision. However, since parties are the most important vehicle for developing policy reputations, their absence at the local level suggests limited prospects for the credibility of preelectoral promises to improve dramatically.

An additional factor detrimental to credible political promises in local political competition is considerable uncertainty about the resources available to the new local governments, the powers that they can exercise, and the process of decision making and the relative strength of the players inside the new governments. Voters cannot distinguish noncompliance caused by shirking with noncompliance caused by their representative's lack of influence over decision making. They are therefore handicapped in their ability to verify compliance with preelectoral promises that are made.

On the positive side, to the extent that credibility in both local and provincial or national elections rests on the personal characteristics of the political competitors and their relationships with individual voters, decentralization leads to the proliferation of elected officials. This might make it more likely that voters will be given a choice between two or more candidates with whom they have a personal history and whose promises they can believe. To the extent that this happens, voters can extract competing, credible offers from candidates, forcing better performance.

Unfortunately, evidence reported in Gazdar (2002) implies that rural voters, at least, do not have multiple patrons and cannot extract competing offers from political candidates. Based on extensive fieldwork in thirteen rural villages throughout Pakistan, he finds that voters are almost always identified with exclusive and well-defined voting blocs, each headed by an influential person (a zaat head, a teacher, a landlord). Defection is rare, making it unlikely that voters have credible relations with multiple potential candidates for local office (that is, belong to multiple voting blocs). This means that political competitors are still likely to compete for the heads of the voting blocs, who in turn may need only to pass on a fraction of the benefits of competition to the voters in the bloc as a condition of maintaining bloc cohesion.

Decentralization and Demand-Side Problems of Social-Service Delivery

All of the foregoing compares the incentives of politicians in local and national governments to conclude that the success of decentralization is far from a foregone conclusion. The effects of demand-side characteristics change with decentralization, too, however. In particular, the ability to achieve such goals as improvements in girls' education may be limited by decentralization to the extent that decentralization provides more scope for cultural or other biases against girls' education to intrude on political decision making.

The evidence suggests little effect of competition for national or provincial legislative offices on the construction of girls' schools in rural areas, though substantial effect on boys' schools. By implication, girls' schools must emerge at the initiative of the provincial and national government executive branches, prompted perhaps by their relationship with foreign donors or a desire to appeal to urban elite or more secular constituencies. Still, nearly half of all girls between ten and twenty years old in Pakistan have never attended school, and this may not reflect failures of political accountability—quite the contrary. When asked, the parents of nearly 40 percent of the girls who have not gone to school indicated that parental or elder disapproval was the main reason. These responses may in fact mask the supply-side problems that are the focus of the analysis here or may reflect more complex parental tradeoffs between the relative costs and benefits of sending their female children to school. The simple explanation, though, seems also the most persuasive: voters in rural Pakistan do not attach a high value to girls' education. From the point of view of elected officials, pushing for expanded access for girls to existing educational facilities is therefore not only of limited political utility but presents real political hazards.

Central-government influence seems to be key in explaining what girls' education there is in many areas of Pakistan. Because of substantial variation across Pakistan, particularly between rural and urban areas, in the demand for girls' education, decentralization may therefore lead to a deterioration of development in those areas where demand is low.

The example of other countries highlights the role of central-government intervention in these cases. In the United States, efforts to persuade states to provide education to African American students in the same facilities as other students eventually required federal intervention, over the objections of the representatives of these states in the national legislature. The parallels with Pakistan are inexact, since African American families were eager to educate their children and frustrated by the lack of access. The key point, though, is that significant local opposition to an education reform did not naturally dissipate as a consequence of local reform efforts but required the intervention of a higher-level government.

Conclusion

The arguments here suggest that the efficacy of decentralization as a remedy for distortion in public policy is contingent on numerous factors, ranging from electoral rules to the credibility of preelectoral promises. The evidence here both explains the mixed results surrounding the adoption of decentralization and identifies concrete characteristics of political competition and decision making that need to be considered in evaluating decentralization and, more especially, in designing it. The analysis of Pakistani decentralization, in light of these factors, suggests that prospects for decentralization can be improved by a number of changes. These include the direct election of district nazims; the deeper embedding of decentralization in the constitution; improving voter information about the actions of local officials and their responsibility for public policies that impinge on voter welfare; and cultivating the credibility of political promises made by political competitors at the local level, such that this credibility does not rest on the personal or clientelist connections of voters with local candidates.

Acknowledgments

We are deeply grateful to Nobuo Yoshida for useful inputs, data analysis, and background research and to Asim Khwaja for insightful and thorough comments on an earlier version. We also wish to thank Nicholas Manning and Hanid Mukhtar for providing information on recent developments in Pakistan's devolution process.

Notes

1. The Pakistan Rural Household Survey (PRHS) (2001) is a nationally representative, multitopic, rural survey covering sixteen districts with a sample size of about 2,800 households distributed among approximately 160 villages. The number of outpatient visits per year per health facility shows a vast difference across thirty-eight basic health units (BHUs): the top three facilities regularly show more than 1,500 visits per month, and the bottom three facilities consistently report 0 visits each month during the year preceding the survey.

2. Pakistan Integrated Household Surveys (PIHS) from the 1990s.

3. These findings from the PRHS, although based on a different sample, are quite similar to findings by Gazdar (2002). The latter found that 14 percent of the 125 schools visited (seventeen schools) had either a building but no school or were reported to be "generally closed."

4. This is the time they spend while in Washington, as opposed to their districts, to make the appropriate comparison with the citations from Pakistan (Johannes, 1983).

5. U.S. legislators have larger staffs, of course. This, however, is reflective of the underlying problem: legislators in Pakistan, driven by a clientelist political environment that is discussed below, need to intervene personally to get credit for providing services. A large staff dilutes their ability to do this.

6. Girls' schools—culturally less preferred in Pakistan—also show no relationship to political factors, as we would expect.

7. The system does not apply to the cantonment (military) areas of towns and cities or to the federally administrated tribal areas (FATA).

8. See chapter 8 in this volume for a comparison of the pre- and postdevolution power of local governments.

9. See chapter 8 in this volume for an analysis of the politics of devolution and its design.

10. The total revenue for current expenditures of the Sindh provincial government can be divided into "divisible pool" (75 percent of total revenue), "nondivisible pool" (14 percent), and "grant from 2.5 percent GST" (11 percent). According to the interim PFC award (Government of Sindh, 2002), 40 percent of the divisible pool should be transferred to the districts based on the *index of backwardness* attached in the PFC award; it also appears implicitly that 75 percent of the grant for 2.5 percent GST are meant to be transferred to districts.

11. PFC Award (2002).

12. PFC Award (2002).

13. Indirect election in Pakistan is fundamentally different than the election of prime ministers by parliaments or of U.S. presidents by an electoral college. Lizzeri and Persico (2001), for example, argue that electoral colleges of the type used to elect the U.S. president concentrate candidate attention on a few swing states, depressing their incentives to

provide broad public goods. Unlike the electors in the electoral college, however, union councilors are not obliged to vote for any particular district nazim candidate.

14. If a nazim or naib nazim ticket does not receive a majority of all votes in the first round, a second round of elections is held in which the ticket obtaining a plurality of votes wins.

15. Uncertainty therefore has mixed effects on public policy, since it also reduces special-interest incentives to peddle influence in lobbying models, as Bardhan and Mookherjee (1999). There is no inconsistency between the models: uncertainty in both cases reduces a candidate's probability of election for any give policy announcement. It therefore devalues both the expected value of the privileges that special interests seek and the value of seeking office.

16. Information about outcomes, however, is less likely to plague decentralization. Voters—even poor voters—are at least as well informed about policy performance at the local level as at the national level as it pertains to the policy issues that have been delegated to local authorities (for example, whether a school has been built or a teacher has been absent). Similarly, low media incentives to report relevant political events, analyzed by Strömberg (2004) may be particularly weak for local government. Certainly, media coverage of local issues is weak in Pakistan and in rural areas practically nonexistent. However, these issues have never been reliably covered in Pakistani media, regardless of the level of government in charge of them.

17. Husain (1999, p. 19) argues more strongly for the pervasive and negative influence of semifeudal landlords on the Pakistani state.

18. Persson and Tabellini (2000, chap. 8) show that noncredible politicians provide a low level of broad public goods, provide no government services or goods targeted to specific voters, and retain substantial rents for themselves. This result is somewhat anomalous because politicians confronting election in most developing countries are desperate to provide narrow, targeted public goods.

References

Azfar, Omer, Satu Kähkönen, and Patrick Meagher. (2000). "Conditions for Effective Decentralized Governance: A Synthesis of Research Findings." Working Paper, IRIS Center, University of Maryland.

Bardhan, Pranab, and Dilip Mookherjee. (1999). "Relative Capture of Local and Central Governments: An Essay in the Political Economy of Decentralization." Working paper, November 30.

Beall, Jo, Nazneen Kanji, Farhana Faruqi, Choudry Mohammed Hussain, and Mushtaq Mirani. (1993). "Social Safety Nets and Social Networks: Their Role in Poverty Alleviation in Pakistan." DFID (formerly ODA), London.

Faguet, Jean-Paul. (2002). "The Determinants of Central vs. Local Government Investment: Institutions and Politics Matter." Working Paper 02-38, Development Studies Institute, London School of Economics.

Gazdar, Haris. (2002). "A Qualitative Survey of Poverty in Rural Pakistan: Methodology, Data and Main Findings. A Background Study for World Bank Pakistan Poverty Assessment 2002." Karachi: Collective for Social Science Research.

Government of Pakistan. (2001). "The SBNP Local Government Ordinance 2001."

Government of Sindh. (2001). "The Sindh Local Government Ordinance 2001." August 6.

Government of Sindh. (2002). *Report and Recommendations of the Provincial Finance Commission (interim)* ("interim PFC award of Sindh").

Husain, Ishrat. (1999). *Pakistan: The Economy of an Elitist State*. Karachi: Oxford University Press.

Johannes, John R. (1983). "Explaining Congressional Casework Styles." *American Journal of Political Science* 27(3): 530–547.

Keefer, Philip, and Stuti Khemani. (2005). "Democracy, Public Expenditures and the Poor." *World Bank Research Observer* 20(1): 1–28.

Keefer, Philip, and Razvan Vlaicu. (2005). "Democracy, Credibility, and Clientelism." World Bank Policy Research Paper 3472, Washington, D.C.

Lizzeri, A., and N. Persico. (2001). "The Provision of Public Goods under Alternative Electoral Incentives." *American Economic Review* 91(1): 225–239.

Manor, James. (1999). *The Political Economy of Democratic Decentralization*. Washington, DC: World Bank.

Pattie, Charles, Ronald Johnston, and Edward Fieldhouse. (1995). "Winning the Local Vote: The Effectiveness of Constituency Campaign Spending in Great Britain, 1983–1992." *American Political Science Review* 89(4): 969–983.

Persson, Torsten, and Guido Tabellini. (2000). *Political Economics: Explaining Public Policy*. Cambridge, MA: MIT Press.

Shafqat, S. (1999). "Democracy in Pakistan: Value Change and Challenges of Institution Building." *Human Development in Asia 1999: The Crisis of Governance*. Karachi: Human Development Center/Oxford: Oxford University Press.

Strömberg, David. (2004). "Mass Media Competition, Political Competition, and Public Policy." *Review of Economic Studies* 71(1): 265–284.

Wilder, Andrew. (1999). *The Pakistani Voter: Electoral Politics and Voting Behavior in the Punjab*. Karachi: Oxford University Press.

World Bank. (2003). Implementation Completion Report: Pakistan Social Action Program Project, Report No. 18043, Poverty Reduction and Economic Management Division, South Asia Region.

10

Decentralization and Local Governance in China's Economic Transition

Justin Yifu Lin, Ran Tao, and Mingxing Liu

Introduction

In any discussion of China's decentralization and local governance, three aspects deserve special attention. First, China is a large country with five levels of government. Below the central government are 31 provincial level units (42 million people on average), 331 prefecture level units (3.7 million people on average), 2,109 counties (580,000 people on average), and 44,741 townships (27,000 people on average). Furthermore, there are about 730,000 more or less self-governed villages in rural areas below the township level (World Bank, 2002). The multilevel nature of Chinese bureaucracy frequently causes confusion when people talk about decentralization and local governance in China, since the level can range from provincial to village.

Second, the fact that China is still a transitional economy in a process of marketization makes the existing literature on China's decentralization somewhat different from the general decentralization literature. Since China used to be a planned economy and most of the economic activities were under center's control in the plan period, the reforms initiated since the late 1970s can be viewed as a process of delegating more decision-making powers in investment approval, firm entry, revenue mobilization, and expenditure responsibilities to lower levels of government and granting more autonomy in production and marketing to state-owned enterprises. As a result, much of the literature on China's decentralization actually dealt with China's economic transition and liberalization (see Qian and Weingast, 1996, as an example), compared to the general literature of decentralization that focuses on the transfer of public functions to lower-level governments.

Third, China is still a party state with all levels of government officials appointed from above by the ruling Communist Party. Unlike many industrializing countries of Africa or Latin America that are often plagued by bureaucracies that lack experience or organizational capacity, the Chinese bureaucracy is an elaborate network that extends to all levels of society, down to the neighborhood and working unit, and exhibits a high degree of discipline by international standards (Parish and White, 1978, 1984). Within each level, an impressive organizational apparatus is able to transmit state policies down to lower-level government agencies step-by-step through several layers of government bureaucracy (Oi, 1995). In the 1990s, grassroot elections took place extensively at the village level, which is not formally a level of government. Therefore, the concepts of constitutional decentralization and political decentralization do not quite fit in the case of China since there are no institutionalized rights of local governments in the central decision-making procedures and no widely accepted genuine elections at and above the township level.

This chapter focuses on a limited number of topics considered essential to an understanding of China's decentralization and local governance by the authors. Considering the multilevel nature of Chinese bureaucracy, we focus on the decentralization and governance issues at local level (county, township, and village levels) and strive to illustrate the structure and evolution of intergovernmental arrangements at higher levels that constitute the institutional background. Since China is still a transitional economy, the Chinese state is still (though to a lesser and lesser extent) involved in some competitive sectors and intervenes in its citzens' social and economic lives on many fronts. The decentralization process in China has been accompanied by institutional changes, such as the granting of more power in nonpublic functions (such as investment approval and entry of nonstate firms) to local governments. Given that the decentralization of nonpublic functions constitutes an important element in China's economic transition and in many cases took place simultaneously with the decentralization of public functions, both dimensions are explored here. Furthermore, the centralized political system has shaped the administrative and fiscal decentralization process and also constitutes the basis for understanding major local-governance issues in China, such as unfunded mandates, farmer's tax burdens, and ineffectiveness in antipoverty programs.

The chapter begins with a review of the centralization-decentralization cycles in the plan period before 1978 and the logic for such cycles. We discuss administrative and fiscal decentralization in

China's market-oriented reforms since the late 1970s; their impacts on economic growth, spatial inequality, and poverty reduction; the recentralization since 1994 and its effect on local public finance and public-goods provision; and based on analyses of China's intergovernmental fiscal and political arrangements, explore two major local governance issues in China—unfunded mandates and ineffectiveness in anti-poverty efforts.

The Centralization-Decentralization Cycle in the Plan Period

The founding of the People's Republic of China in 1949 marked a new era in Chinese history. Government leaders believed that to defend the new socialist system and to keep pace and even overtake Western industrial countries, rapid industrial development, especially the establishment of a complete set of heavy industries, was essential. Learning mainly from the Soviet experiences, the Chinese government began to formulate and implement the first five-year plan, which gave priority to heavy industrial development beginning in 1953.

However, the development of capital-intensive industries would have been extremely costly if the free market had been allowed to operate in a capital-scarce economy. To mobilize resources for such a heavy industrialization, a plan system was established that was characterized by a trinity of a macro-policy environment of distorted prices for products and essential factors of production (such as trained personnel, funds, technologies, and resources), highly centralized planned resource allocation, and a micro-management mechanism in which firms and farmers had no decision-making power (Lin, Fang, and Zhou, 2003).[1] For instance, a commune system was set up in the rural areas in the late 1950s to guarantee a state monopoly on grain procurement. Besides supplying grain at depressed prices, the communes and production brigades were also responsible for mobilizing financial and human resources for local public-good provision (such as water conservancy construction) by organizing farmers for compulsory labor.

Under the plan system, a heavily centralized fiscal system was established. The accounting systems of state-owned enterprises (SOEs) were incorporated directly into the government's budget, and major resources were controlled by the center. The State Planning Commission determined local revenue and expenditure plans on an annual basis, known as unified revenue and unified expenditure (*tongshou tongzhi*). Local governments (at the province, prefecture, county, and commune levels) did not have independent budgets.[2] As to expenditure assignment, the central government was responsible for national defense, economic development (capital spending, R&D, universities, and research institutes), industrial policy, and administration of national institutions such as the judicial system. Responsibility for delivering day-to-day public administration and social services—such as education (except universities), public safety, health care, social security, housing, and other local and urban services—was delegated to local governments.

However, in a country of the size of China, formulating, administrating, coordinating, and monitoring the central plans were time-consuming and became more and more so as the economic system became larger and more complicated. For example, the number of state-owned enterprises (SOEs) subordinated to the central government increased from 2,800 in 1953 to 9,300 in 1957, and the number of items in material allocation under central planning increased from 55 in 1952 to 231 in 1957 (Qian and Weingast, 1996). The classical problem of control and monitoring under information asymmetry emerged soon after the planned system was set up. As the economy grew larger with more projects initiated and enterprises started, the plan system became increasingly unmanageable. To make things worse, a highly centralized planned system inevitably undermined the incentives of local governments when local coordination in industrial development was essential.

Under this background, China initiated its first decentralization within the planned framework by delegating more powers to local governments in 1957. The policies then included (1) delegating nearly all SOEs to local governments, such that the share of industrial output by the enterprises subordinated to the central government shrank from 40 percent to 14 percent of the national total; (2) changing central planning from a national to a provincial basis, with decisions about fixed investment to be made by local governments rather than the central government; and (3) fixing revenue-sharing schemes for five years, and granting local governments some authority over taxes. The share of central revenue decreased from 75 percent to around 50 percent within two years.

Indeed, local incentives responded quickly to decentralization. Local small industries (such as backyard steel mills and coal mines) boomed in this period. This program, however, did not succeed because of serious coordination failures caused by the radical decentralization.

The soft-budget constraint faced by local governments and SOEs soon led to excessive investment expansion and inefficient interregional duplication of production. Recentralization began in 1959, when all large and medium-sized industrial enterprises were again subordinated to the center. However, centralization again brought about the incentive problem and economic stagnation in the 1960s. Thus a second wave of decentralization followed in the early 1970s, when local governments gained more authority over fixed investment and local revenue. Afterwards, a similar but less serious investment boom led to yet another round of recentralization in the mid-1970s.

In retrospect, it is easy to see that decentralization under a plan system was not able to alleviate the inefficiency problem since it could neither improve microefficiency through market discipline nor change the heavy-industry development strategy inconsistent with China's comparative advantage. Under the soft-budget constraints faced by local government and SOEs, a cycle of decentralization leading to disorder, disorder leading to centralization, centralization leading to stagnation, and stagnation leading to decentralization was inevitable.

Decentralization under Market-Oriented Reforms, 1978 to 1993

Low efficiency in the plan system was considered to be a serious problem as early as the 1950s before the first round of decentralization was initiated (Mao, 1956), but not until 1978 were some fundamental reforms undertaken. What was evident to policy makers in the late 1970s was the correlation between production inefficiency of enterprises and communes and lack of stimulus for workers and farmers. That explains why the reforms began with the micromanagement system in the late 1970s in an attempt to improve work incentives. In rural areas, the household-responsibility system (HRS) emerged in 1978. In just a few years, the system became a dominant form of microeconomic organizations in rural areas. In cities, reforms in SOEs were initiated in the early 1980s, centering on power delegation and profit sharing. Such reforms rendered rural households and SOEs de facto residual claimers of their production and thus greatly promoted work incentives.

Administrative and Fiscal Decentralization
Accompanying the microreforms in rural areas and SOEs was a process of administrative and fiscal decentralization, which was deemed

necessary in a large country like China to induce local coordination in market-oriented reforms.

Administrative Decentralization From the administrative perspective, the reform period witnessed a significant strengthening of local governments' role in local economic management, such as investment approval, entry regulation, and resource allocation. A particularly striking example is the opening-up policy initiated in the coastal regions. Starting from 1979, many provinces were allowed to set up their own foreign-trade corporations. From then on, regional experimentation with opening up began, which includes the "one-step-ahead" policies implemented in Guangdong and Fujian in 1978, the establishment of four special economic zones (Shenzhen, Zhuhai, and Shantou, and Xiamen) in 1980, and the declaration of fourteen coastal cities as "coastal open cities" in 1984. Not only did these areas enjoy lower tax rates and a higher share of revenues, but perhaps more important, they enjoyed special institutional and policy environments and gained more authority over local economic development and the establishment of special economic zones and economic-development zones.

Another dimension of administrative decentralization was the delegation of more state-owned enterprises to local governments at the provincial, municipal, and county levels beginning in the early 1980s. By 1985, the state-owned industrial enterprises controlled by the center accounted for only 20 percent of the total industrial output at or above the township level, while provincial and municipal governments controlled 45 percent and county governments 35 percent (Qian and Xu, 1993). With an ownership shift from central to local, local governments were provided with incentives in taxes and profits to step up their effort in revenue collection. At the same time, the spending of the fixed investment for local-government-owned enterprises fell naturally on the shoulders of local government. Since SOEs had provided a wide range of social services (like education, health care, and pension services) to their employees, more local ownership implied that local governments would take primary and final responsibilities for these expenditures.

Fiscal Decentralization The fiscal dimension of decentralization was no less dramatic. In 1980, the intergovernmental fiscal system shifted away from unified revenues and unified expenditures and toward a "cooking in separate kitchens" (*fenzao chifan*) that divided revenue and expenditure responsibilities between the center and the provincial governments.[3] After that, the central-provincial fiscal arrangement experienced further changes, such as the proportional-sharing system in 1982 and the fiscal-contracting system in 1988. In the 1988 fiscal-contracting system, the center negotiated different contracts with each province on revenue remittances to the center and permitted most provincial governments to retain the bulk of new revenues. There were six basic types of sharing schemes in 1988, and they continued through 1993 (Bahl and Wallich, 1992). Besides fixed subsidies from the center (in fourteen provinces), fixed-quota deliveries to the center (in three provinces), fixed sharing with the center (in three provinces), and quota deliveries with a prespecified growth (in two provinces), other provinces adopted either an incremental sharing (a certain share is retained locally up to a quota, and then a higher share is retained in excess of the quota in three provinces) or a sharing up to a limit with growth adjustment (ten provinces retained a share within a specific percentage of revenue from the previous year and then retained all revenues above that quota).

At the lower level, the provinces had substantial flexibility in setting the rules for subordinate levels. Each province specifies the sharing system with its prefectures, the prefecture for its counties, and so on. Expenditure assignments were structured in a similar way: the central government sets the division of expenditure responsibilities between the center and the provinces, and the intermediate layers decide how they share responsibilities with subordinate levels.

Decentralization and Economic Performance, 1978 to 1993
In general, with the decentralization of 1978 to 1993, political powers were still heavily centralized, but local governments began to enjoy more autonomy in local economic management (such as enterprise production and material marketing), to control a larger share of fiscal resources, and at the same time to assume primary responsibilities for local public-goods provision. This implies a very decentralized fiscal-expenditure arrangement in which local government assumed greater responsibility for providing education, health, housing, social security, local infrastructure, and so forth. In the context of marketization reforms (deregulation), the decentralization in this period was associated with significant economic growth as well as mixed performances in spatial inequality and poverty reduction.

Economic Growth and TVE Development Decentralization in this period played an important role in promoting national as well as local economic growth. From 1978 to 1993, China's per capita gross national product (GNP) increased in real terms by around 280 percent. National absolute poverty was reduced by more than 50 percent in the first half of the 1980s, dropping from 17.9 percent of the population in 1982 to 6.1 percent in 1984 (World Bank, 2001). This downward trend corresponds to the growth of real income and real GNP. China also witnessed an across-the-board growth in both coastal and inland regions. Indeed, if each of China's provinces were taken as an economy, about twenty out of the top thirty growth regions in the world in the period would be provinces in China.

Much of the economic growth in the period could be attributed to a spectacular entry and expansion of nonstate enterprises, especially the township and village enterprises (TVEs), which actually have been one of the most distinctive features in China's economic development and transition (Qian and Xu, 1993). Nationally, the output of TVEs grew more than sixfold in real terms between 1985 and 1997, leading China's rapid industrial and overall growth. By 1993, TVEs already accounted for 36 percent of the national industrial output, up from 9 percent in 1978. Within the rural sector, the TVEs accounted for three-quarters of rural industrial output (Che and Qian, 1998).

The rise of TVEs was closely related to administrative and fiscal decentralization from the late 1970s to the mid-1990s. Local governments actively supported market-oriented, nonstate enterprises to expand their revenue base under competition between jurisdictions for getting rich first. With the decollectivization of agricultural production, local governments had to seek further revenue sources, and the fiscal reform that gave higher shares of revenue (TVE tax or profits) to local governments and granted them the rights to use the fiscal surplus paved the way for local governments to support the TVE developments under a better incentive system. The decentralization policies granted local-government officials great autonomy over their economies, including the autonomy to set prices, to make investment with self-raised funds, and to restructure their firms, and to issue licenses to newly established firms.[4] By delimiting better the property rights between governments at different levels, decentralization rendered governments at each level the residual claimant and controller of its own public enterprises.[5]

In the transitional process, local governments at the county, township, and village levels played unique roles in fostering local economic development, especially in supporting the TVEs. In the early to mid-1980s, when the TVEs started their golden period of growth, private entrepreneurs were still uncertain about the directions of central policy regarding private enterprises. Local governments assumed the entrepreneurial role and started rural industrial development.

According to empirical investigations carried out by Byrd and Gelb (1990) and Oi (1995), although most TVEs enjoyed a considerable degree of enterprise autonomy, the community government made strategic decisions in investment and finance, manager selection, and the use of after-tax profits for public expenditure. The community governments usually initiated internal fund raising, either from collective accumulation or from individual contributions to start up the community-owned enterprises. The community governments were also pivotal in securing loans from either the Agricultural Bank of China (ABC) or rural credit cooperatives (RCCs), two major external sources of financing, using the community assets as collateral and providing loan guarantee for TVEs. Using information and contacts that they developed beyond the locality through a government network, local-government officials could usually provide many essential services to local enterprises, such as raw materials and information about new products, technology, and markets for TVE products.[6] Local officials also often tried their best to circumvent government regulations to allow TVEs to receive the maximum tax advantages and exemptions so that more revenues could be kept within the locality to further the competitive advantages of TVEs, and they provided local governments with more funding for local public goods and service provision.

Fiscal Decline and Impacts on Spatial Inequality and Poverty Reduction Though decentralization was correlated to high economic growth in the 1980s, it also led to significant fiscal decline of the state. The total budget revenues fell from 35 percent of GDP in 1978 to below 12 percent in the mid-1990s. This was because the old revenue mechanism became unsustainable as central planning was dismantled. Profitability in industry fell as prices adjusted to market forces, sharply cutting the government revenue intake through state-owned enterprises. The emergence of nonstate enterprises competing for profits also contributed to revenue decline. Since the enterprise reforms required profit-sharing schemes to provide incentives, it reduced revenue flows to the budget, while creating extrabudgetary funds that were managed independently by enterprises.

The decentralization also led to fiscal decline of the center. In most instances, the revenue-sharing contracts between the center and provinces were regressive, since they allowed richer localities to keep a larger portion of collected revenue. The contracting system tended to favor richer localities with more local enterprises since local firms were the richest sources of extrabudgetary or off-budgetary revenue. Taking extrabudgetary revenue into account, poor regions with few local enterprises had to share an even larger proportion of total collected revenue with the center. As similar contracts were made between the provinces and subprovincial units, the bias against poor localities extended to the grassroots levels (World Bank, 2002). As a result, local shares of budget revenue rose steadily from 54 percent of the total government revenue in 1978 to 61 percent in 1988 and rose further to 78 percent in 1993.

With fiscal declines of the state as a whole and the central government, the center's redistributive power was seriously damaged. Fiscal stress and declining central revenues had already led to dwindling intergovernmental transfers and a de facto devolution of responsibilities to local governments. With the introduction of fiscal contracts in 1988, the central government formally ended its responsibility for financing local expenditures. The role of local governments was thereby shifted from providing services to financing them, a decentralization of responsibilities.[7] While these levels of government had always provided such services, they had previously provided them as agents of the central government—that is, the center always subsidized the financial gap when necessary. By the end of the 1980s, fiscal decentralization, which tied budgetary expenditures more closely to local revenues, had created a budgetary crisis in nearly all poor counties that they experienced difficulties even in paying basic salaries (Park, Rozelle, Wong, and Ren, 1996). In these regions, high nondiscretionary outlays for personnel on the government payroll, including local officials, teachers, health workers, and other social-services personnel generally account for well over half of local budgetary revenues. Educational spending, most of which goes for teachers' salaries, often accounts for 40 to 50 percent of local budgetary revenues in poor counties. Poor-county governments had to employ a range of creative mechanisms to cope with their persistent and accumulating fiscal deficits. These mechanisms include deferring wages, borrowing from the budgets of various local-government bureaus, and borrowing against the next year's budgeted fiscal transfers from higher levels of government (Park et al., 1996). Local governments in less developed regions had to cut spending on social development and let individuals share more health-care and education expenses (West and Wong, 1995).

Partly because of the limited redistributive power of the state, especially that of the center, China witnessed an increasing spatial inequality and stagnation in poverty reduction. Spatial inequality began to rise after an initial decline of urban-rural as well as interprovincial inequality from 1978 to the mid-1980s (Chen and Wang, 2001; Kanbur and Zhang, 1999). Such initial decline can be accounted for largely by increased agricultural prices as well as by rapid rural growth in this period. However, when China further decentralized, opened up, and experienced an explosion of trade and foreign direct investment in the mid-1980s, spatial inequality began to rise steadily. The Gini index of provincial per capita income declined from 29.3 percent in 1978 to 25.6 percent in 1984 but then rose to 32.2 percent in 1993 (Kanbur and Zhang, 1999). At the same time, the urban-rural average income ratio declined from 2.87 in 1978 to 1.86 in 1985, then increased to 2.5 by 1993 (SSB, 2004). After the mid-1980s, the poverty rates even increased—reaching 14.7 percent in 1989—and then stagnated, hovering around 10 percent in the early 1990s. This was despite continuous growth in national income and GNP, indicating that in these years the poor did not share the benefits of overall economic growth.

Recentralization since 1994

Fiscal Reform in 1994
As a response to the fiscal decline, the center in 1994 initiated a drastic fiscal reform to raise the central revenue share from around 35 percent of general revenue to 60 percent along with a substantial increase in fiscal transfer. Among a comprehensive package of measures, the centerpiece of 1994 fiscal reform was to introduce the tax-sharing system (*fenshuizhi*), which fundamentally changed the way revenues are shared between the center and the provincial governments. Under the tax-sharing system, taxes were assigned either to the central or local government, with the center having the bulk of the tax revenue, especially the 75 percent of newly created value-added tax (VAT). Local taxes consist mainly of business taxes, personal and enterprises income taxes, and other small taxes such as urban construction, land-use and real estate taxes, and agricultural taxes.

The expenditure responsibilities were nominally unchanged with the subprovincial levels (prefecture, county, and township) still facing the expenditure responsibilities that were delegated to them through the decentralization in the 1980s. While in most other countries social security and welfare are almost always provided by the central government and education and health are often shared responsibilities with the provincial and central governments, in China the county and township levels together provide the bulk of vital public services, including 70 percent of budgetary expenditures for education and 55 to 60 percent of those for health. Cities at the prefecture and county levels account for all local expenditures on unemployment insurance, social security, and welfare (World Bank, 2002). A critical difficulty has arisen in maintaining the social safety net due to large-scale restructuring of China's state-owned sectors since the mid-1990s. Many of the social-service and social-security responsibilities that used to be taken care of by SOEs have now been passed to local governments without corresponding resources being set aside to meet these responsibilities. Many local governments, now insolvent, are in urgent need either of additional transfers or of a further rationalization of the intergovernmental fiscal system.

Not only there is an expenditure structure out of line with international practice, but there also is a serious lack of a clear assignment of responsibilities among different levels of governments below the province. This leads to a high degree of concurrent and overlapping expenditures among the subnational levels in China. In practice, concurrent responsibilities have made it more difficult to identify what level of government should be accountable for the delivery of particular services. Due to the weak bargaining position of lower-level governments under the centralized political system, there has been a tendency of concentration of revenue to upper-level governments and delegation of expenditure responsibilities to lower-level governments. The tendency became increasingly apparent after the 1994 fiscal reform. Provincial governments has tended to squeeze larger shares of revenues from lower-level governments and at the same time assigned more responsibilities to the latter.[8]

The center had originally planned to mobilize fiscal resources to channel more transfers from richer areas to poorer ones, but the promised transfers have not materialized. To satisfy the needs of coastal provinces that generate much of the revenues, lump-sum tax rebates were offered to guarantee them their pre-1994 income. In addition, to permit each province to share in the growth of its lost tax base over time, the center committed to giving back 30 percent of its increased revenue from the newly created value-added tax as well as consumption tax each year. The tax rebates, the largest item in overall transfers, are highly correlated with incomes and disequalizing in nature. The *earmarked grants*, the second-largest item of transfer, have been found to be mildly disequalizing because they were dominated by food and other consumer subsidies that favored urban areas (Wong, 1997). To offset this regressive effect, the government introduced an equalizing (general-purpose) transfer to aid poor regions in 1996. They are rule based and rely on variables such as provincial gross domestic product (GDP), student-teacher ratios, number of civil servants, and population density. However, these transfers have been underfunded since their inception, accounting for just 2 percent of total transfers. For example, in 1998 the central government allocated 2.2 billion yuan to equalization transfers, compared to the estimated fiscal gap of Y.63 billion produced by the formula. What each eligible province received was its estimated fiscal need multiplied by a coefficient of 0.035, which was derived from 2.2 divided by 63.

Impacts of Revenue Centralization

Since the mid-1990s, revenue centralization without corresponding equalizing transfers has been partially responsible for enlarging inequality in both income and public spending across regions. The Gini index of provincial per capita income further rose from 32.2 percent in 1993 to a historical high of 37.2 percent in 2000. Urban-rural average income ratio increased from 2.5 in 1993 to 3 by 2003. The combination of heavy responsibilities and inadequate transfers means that the levels of service provision vary across localities according to levels of local economic development. Among provincial-level units, the ratio of the highest to lowest in per capita budgetary expenditures (net of all transfers) has risen from 6.1 in 1990 to 19.1 in 1999. The coefficient of variation has grown from 0.55 to 0.86, indicating growing dispersion among the provinces (Kanbur and Zhang, 2003).

The current fiscal system leads to highly differentiated local disposable revenues across regions and also a highly heterogeneous level of local public-good provision. In richer regions, local governments, especially those at the county and township levels, are generally able to provide decent public goods and services to residents and businesses since they enjoy higher tax revenues coming from the development of nonagricultural sectors and can draw on additional incomes from the sale of rights to develop local land and from certain profit remittances they receive from TVEs. By contrast, in less developed areas, most in inland China, local revenues must come mainly from agriculture and are much more limited. In the absence of sufficient and dependable equalizing transfers from higher-level governments, local governments in these regions frequently find themselves unable to pay their bills. In some cases, even basic wage payments are delayed for long periods (one year or more), or government employees can get only half of their wages.[9] The so-called hidden deficits also emerged where the budget funds officially recorded as having been allocated to designated spending categories but in fact were diverted (or borrowed) to pay for more pressing needs (wages).

As the higher-level governments shift more expenditure responsibilities to lower levels, local governments, lacking formal taxing autonomy and often finding transfers from higher levels increasingly unreliable, tend to pursue extrabudget revenue expansion energetically to meet expenditure needs (Wong, 1998). Besides local SOE profits and user charges for infrastructure, much of the extrabudget revenue came either from various quasi-fiscal fees levied on local enterprises or from direct illegitimate fee charges on farmers by local governments that have almost total autonomy in levying and spending the fees and operate with virtually no oversight. According to Ahmad, Keping, Thomas, and Raju (2002), the ratio of local off-budget revenues to total local revenues was as high as 40 percent throughout the 1990s.

Heightened pressures on revenue-starved local governments usually led to overinvest in revenue-generating industrial enterprises, bureaucratic predation on enterprise resources, regional protectionism, and the diverting of government attention away from long-term development projects. In many cases, township governments or village organizations were highly indebted due to unsuccessful industrialization efforts. Lack of resources, poor leadership, misuse of funds by local officials, and corruption accounted for most of such failures, which further turned out to increase fee charges on farmers, enlarge income disparities, and cause more rural unrest. For example, in the mid-1990s, many local governments in inland China, driven by budget incentives and TVE development mandates set by upper-level governments (usually the provincial governments), borrowed huge amount of funds from local banks (especially the local branches of the Agricultural Bank of China and the rural credit unions) and initiated a wave of

TVE investment frenzy, which generated huge debt at the township and village levels (Chen, 2003). The average township-level debt is estimated to be Y.4 million across the country (Zhu, 2001). To ensure local tax revenues, some less developed regions took administrative measures to erect barriers against the industrial products of other regions, and in some extreme cases local-government employees were forced to buy locally produced cigarettes before their wages were paid.

Local Governance, Unfunded Mandates, and Poverty Alleviation

Under a centralized political system with extensive expenditure decentralization but little revenue decentralization, local-government officials have tended to be more responsive to the Communist Party and to the higher-level government policies than they are to local needs. These officials are, after all, controlled from above both by tight hierarchical personnel arrangements and by fiscal-transfer arrangements. The problem is further complicated and aggravated by the fact that all levels of government in China are growth-driven and "overtaking" in nature. The performance of individual government officials at every level are evaluated by a series of indicators imposed from above. These indicators usually include a number of economic targets, such as the annual growth achieved in local GDP, the growth of revenue collected and the revenue contributions made to higher levels of the state, and the quantities of foreign investment attracted, as well as various social targets (such as birth control, public security, school enrollments, and so on). Successfully reaching or exceeding the targets set by higher-level governments is decisive for local officials seeking political promotion.[10]

Unfunded Mandates, Local Governance, and Recentralization
When local governments lack autonomy in formal taxation and effective transfer mechanisms are not in place, much of the development mandates imposed from above are underfunded, and local governments have to find their own ways to meet the targets set up by the upper-level government, which leads to serious local-governance issues in China.

In less developed regions where agriculture dominates, farmers are directly taxed in the form of various illegal fees. In our field surveys in some agricultural townships in Jiangsu and Hunan, we find that after the mid-1990s local-government bureaucracies began to expand their staffs quickly to carry out the important but demanding work of collecting explicit taxes from individuals and households throughout their jurisdictions. In such regions, a vicious cycle clearly emerged: local governments had to recruit more staff, both formal (*bianzhi nei*) and informal (*bianzhi wai*), to ensure tax collection; higher tax revenues then had to be used to support the enlarging local bureaucracy; which led, in turn, to even higher tax collections and even larger governments.

In more developed regions where urbanization and industrialization contributed to raising land values, grabbing land from farmers became pervasive. Revenue-hungry city governments have every incentive to expropriate more agricultural land for urban expansion and commercial leases and make a profit since such land revenues fall into the locally controlled extrabudgets. With faster urbanization and stronger regional competition for outside investments in this period, local governments initiated a wave of land requisition and established industrial parks and urban new-development zones.

In response to farmers' complaints and the social unrest caused by excessive tax burdens and abusive land requisition, the center in recent years began to further centralize the fiscal and administrative systems. On the fiscal front, the center has begun to claim a share of the personal and enterprise income taxes that used to belong exclusively to local governments. Since 2000, the central government has also initiated a rural tax reform that aimed to remove all local informal fee charges and make up the shortfalls with fiscal transfers from the center. Facing protests by farmers about the inadequacy of the compensation they receive in land requisition for urban development, the center has begun to centralize decision-making power where converting agricultural land to urban and industrial construction is concerned, with the intention of limiting transgressions in granting arable land-use rights, illicit expropriations of arable land, and actions damaging to arable-land management. Starting in 2005, numerous development zones are required by the center to be removed, and national inspection teams are sent out to ensure progress. A newly promulgated Party document has declared that China intends to establish and implement the most rigorous arable-land-protection system in the world to ensure farmers' rights and national food security (State Council, 2004).

Broadly speaking then, instead of decentralizing controls further, the center has lately sought to centralize fiscal and administrative powers. Considering the social unrests caused by such serious problems in rural taxation and land requisition, it is understandable that the center would choose to implement such policies. But will these new measures bring the desired results? In the absence of free elections and genuine local participation, local governments inevitably lack accountability, and the center has to step in to heavily regulate local government behavior, directly dictating what shall be done and what cannot be done. However, when local governments are deprived of most of their fiscal and administrative autonomy, the only choice for the center must be to keep control in its own hands and provide transfers. These transfers embody central policy intentions, but they entail significant costs in dampening local initiatives to mobilize resources and to cater to local needs and may also easily lead back to the further expansion of local bureaucracy and to rent seeking under the soft-budget constraints created by such transfer mechanisms.

Poverty Reduction and Local Governance
The political and fiscal arrangements in China also lead to a fairly top-down approach in antipoverty policy formation and implementation. The major antipoverty programs in China are all planned from above and reflect political priorities and resource availability rather than locally defined needs or opportunities. Usually they are not designed or implemented on the basis of consultation with intended local beneficiaries. One of the most prevalent complaints heard by farmers in poor areas that have received poverty-alleviation investment funds is that they were not allowed to choose what activities to do and often are forced to participate even when they did not have the time, resources, or know-how to undertake the project. It has been found that when households are given funds, provided with extension assistance, subjected to tight monitoring on their repayment, and offered participation in a sympathetic, supportive group, there is a rapid increase in the household's economic status and increased empowerment of farmers (Rozelle, Zhang, and Huang, 1998).

Under such a system, the center is more willing to use earmarked transfers instead of general-purpose transfers. Given that the center knows that an increase in general-purpose transfers may easily result in local bureaucracy expansion and increasing staff wages other than the public-goods provision that reach to the poor, earmarking the transfer and directing its use to designated purposes become the only alternatives. This also helps to explain why the center, after the 1994 fiscal reform when it began to have more and more flexibility and control over fiscal resources, has not increased its equalizing general-purpose transfer but instead significantly utilized the earmarked transfers. However, dependence on earmarked transfer usually translates into highly political negotiations in transfer allocation. Lack of rule-based formulas and transparency in transfer tends to systematically distort local incentives and draw local governments in poor regions into unhealthy competition for more transfers and political performance that caters to the higher level. In China's case, such earmarked transfers have easily degenerated into poorly targeted patronage-type programs in many regions (Park, Wang, and Wu, 2002).

When the evaluation of poverty is conducted from above, local governments have a natural tendency to focus on projects that can reduce poverty headcounts quickly but ignore the poorest people most in need. Since local officials are evaluated in no small part on the basis of concrete targets (such as the number of poor who have been lifted out of poverty), officials have an incentive to direct the funds to the better-off poor households or to areas with better natural resources so that project costs can be lower and the expected success rate higher. Zhu and Jiang (1996) found that poor county governments usually omit some of the poorest villages in the public-works construction projects based on an evaluation of economic returns. Villages with more favorable economic conditions were more likely to receive support. In the subsidized-loan program, local officials have strong incentives to direct funds toward industrial projects because they might generate more fiscal resources and also because local officials face career evaluations in which TVE output and profit count as major successful performance indicators even if they do not contribute much to poverty alleviation (Murdoch, 2000). All such practices result in significant leakage of benefits away from the poor and consist of a major constraint on the effectiveness of China's antipoverty programs.

Under the current system, there has also been an excessive focus on physical capital development (such as agricultural production and infrastructure construction in antipoverty programs), while investment in human capital (education, labor training, and health) and in capacity building in agriculture, and in social assistance lags far behind. This is not only because this type of investment cannot show an immediate success by raising short-term income growth but also because physical capital and infrastructure investment are more visible and easily regarded as concrete progresses in poverty alleviation. The result is that farmers in poor regions have to pay high education charges and poor health has emerged as a major cause of poverty among vulnerable populations either due to excessive health expenditures or through the loss of labor as a result of illness. According to the World Bank (2002), lack of investment has led to a clear decline in access to health and education and to growing gender disparities in access to basic education in poor regions.

Conclusion

In this chapter, we selectively review some of the key issues of decentralization and local governance in the context of China's economic transition. We argue that the centralization-decentralization cycle is endogenous to the traditional plan system, which featured heavy industrialization. Although decentralization in market-oriented reforms helped to promote economic growth by hardening local budget constraints and promoting local incentives to foster economic growth, it has led to lower central redistributive power and enlarging spatial inequality. Without clear and appropriate intergovernmental expenditures, responsibility division, and equalizing transfer arrangements, the recentralization in 1994 has significantly impaired the local capacity to provide decent public goods and services in less developed regions and brought about serious local-governance issues and social unrest in China.

After the new rural tax reforms were enacted, local governments in agricultural regions lost most of their local tax basis and became increasingly dependent on higher-level government transfers. The problem lies not so much in whether the center can provide sufficient transfers but in whether such gap-filling transfers will discourage local-resource mobilization and give perverse signals of a soft-budget constraint to local governments. If local fiscal authorities are delinked from local government's service-provision responsibilities and functions, then local officials will have scant incentive to effectively provide the needed public goods and services since a higher share of fiscal resources is coming from a transfer that reflects more upper-level policy intentions rather than local needs. On the one hand, a centralized one-party political system has inevitably led to a lack of local-government accountability to local population and widespread corruption. On the other hand, various unfunded development mandates and policies from the center, and the current cadre supervision and monitoring system endogenous to the political system have resulted in distorted local government behavior such as excessive rural taxes and abusive land requisition. If such policy burdens cannot be removed, the alternative can be only further administrative and fiscal centralization that may bring yet more distortions in local government behavior. In the long run, good governance will be the outcome of a more decentralized administrative and fiscal system that includes a sound intergovernmental transfer arrangement, of wider local political participation and competition under free elections, and, ultimately, of stronger factor mobility across regions.

Notes

1. Under the plan system, (1) a macro-policy environment with depressed interest rates, exchange rates, and prices for much demanded goods was the prerequisite for the prioritized development of heavy industries; (2) the planned resource-allocation system was to resolve the contradiction between an aggregated demand that exceeded an aggregated supply under the distorted macro-policy environment and to guarantee resources for heavy industries; and (3) the micro-management institution without any autonomy was implemented to prevent enterprises from corroding profits and state assets by taking advantage of their operation rights (Lin, Fang, and Zhou, 2003).

2. In this system, the center set spending priorities and approved local budgets. Local governments acted as agents of the central government. Policy was set by the central government, including civil-service wage scales, pension and unemployment benefit levels, educational standards, health-care standards, and any other relevant aspects of local budgets. Intergovernment transfers were set at a level equal to the gap between locally collected revenues and permitted local expenditures. This revenue-sharing system was based on extensive negotiation: since neither revenues nor expenditure needs could be perfectly known, central transfers were deliberately set at levels below expenditure needs in an effort to flush out local reserves. In addition, it was also highly redistributive, with sharing rates that varied greatly across regions (World Bank, 2002).

3. Under this system, (1) some fiscal sources were clearly specified as the central government's revenue (including custom duties and revenue remitted by central-government-owned enterprises); (2) other sources (such as the salt tax, agricultural taxes, and the revenue of local-government-owned enterprises) were defined as the local governments' revenues; (3) for large-scale SOEs under dual central- and local-government leadership, those governments shared the industrial and commercial taxes (turnover taxes) with some fixed proportion. The sprit of the rearrangements in 1980 is to preserve incentives for the local governments while guaranteeing the central government's revenues.

4. While in the planning period, state planning seriously limited the autonomy of local governments to generate and retain revenues. Localities were required to turn over all or most of their revenues to upper-level governments. The surplus retained was also subject to higher-level approval before it was used. The upsurge of TVEs in the postreform period is also closely related to the two waves of decentralization before the reform, which led to the rise of some collective enterprises (such as commune and brigade enterprises) in rural areas outside the state plan before the advent of reform.

5. The deregulatory policies from the center to support TVE development was also essential. Since the 1980s, the TVEs have no longer been restricted to the industries that served agriculture (such as producing chemical fertilizer and farm tools), and they were allowed to enter sectors that only SOEs had access to previously. They also no longer used only local resources and could sell beyond local markets. In this period, TVEs in the more labor-intensive light and consumer-goods industries had huge profit margins and short supplies due to the depression of these sectors in the planned system, which prioritized capital-intensive sectors. In addition, much of the TVE production, particularly at earlier stages, required relatively little expertise and start-up costs. However, as competition in both product and financial markets hardened with market deepening since the mid-1990s, local governments began to privatize TVEs and returned to the more "normal" functions of local public-goods provision.

6. According to Oi (1995), the roles played by local governments in product development, market research, and technology acquisition went beyond the usual provision of bureaucratic service and were more like the activities of an entrepreneurial development state. Officials from local science and technology commissions or enterprise management bureaus spent much time and energy to represent local TVEs at higher-level agencies to acquire technology, materials, and funding and sometimes even accompany TVE managers to higher-level bureaus to facilitate access to inputs and services.

7. As a result, local expenditures grew much faster than central expenditures, especially social security expenditures, unemployment insurance, increased pension spending, and increased subsidies for housing and fuel. The share of local expenditure grew from 54 percent in 1978 to 66 percent in 1993 and 64 percent in 1999.

8. According to the World Bank (2002), there was a trend toward an increasing shares of expenditures at the provincial level and a declining share for the county and township levels combined during the period 1994 to 1999.

9. An example is the middle-income coastal province of Hebei. In 1998, wage arrears to schoolteachers reached 155 million yuan, and an additional Y.186 million in arrears emerged in 1999. Although provincial governments raised Y.740 million in recent years to solve the widespread wage arrearage problem in the past several years, the total provincial wage arrears still reached Y.1.29 billion by the end of 2000 (Chen, 2003).

10. Some scholars have vividly described the current arrangement as a "pressure-imposing system" (Rong, Cui, et al., 1998) under which all local-government and party agencies and cadres, from county to village levels, face constant pressures from above to perform according to higher-level policy. As a result, local cadres are enmeshed in attending meetings, writing and reading documents and reports, receiving visitors, and passing various inspections. To meet all their targets, local officials have a tendency to fabricate statistics on economic growth and government revenues, exaggerate farmers' income growth, and underreport rural tax burdens. Either showcase projects (such as the more visible roads or expensive education and health-care facilities) top the local-government agenda, or already excessive local fee charges on farmers are increased yet again to meet financial needs.

References

Ahmad, Ehtisham, Li Keping, Richardson Thomas, and Singh Raju. (2002). "Recentralization in China?" IMF Working Paper wp/02/168.

Bahl, Roy, and Christine Wallich. (1992). "Intergovernmental Fiscal Relations in China." Working Paper WPS 863, Country Economics Department, World Bank.

Bardhan, Pranab. (2002). "Decentralization and Governance in Development." *Journal of Economic Perspectives* 16(4).

Byrd, William, and Gelb Allen. (1990). "Why Industrialize? The Incentives for Rural Community Governments." In William Byrd and Qingsong Lin (Eds.), *China's Rural Industry: Structure, Development, and Reform* (chap. 17). Oxford: Oxford University Press.

Che, Jiahua, and Qian Yingyi. (1998). "Institutional Environment, Community Government, and Corporate Governance: Understanding China's Township-Village Enterprises." *Journal of Law, Economics, and Organization* 14(1): 1–23.

Chen, Xiwen. (2003). *China's County and Township Public Finance and Farmer Income Growth*. Shanxi: Economic Press.

Chen, Shaohua, and Yan Wang. (2001). "China's Growth and Poverty Reduction: Recent Trends between 1990 and 1999." World Bank Policy Research Working Paper No. 2651.

Kanbur, Ravi, and Zhang Xiaobo. (1999). "Which Regional Inequality: The Evolution of Rural-Urban or Coast-Inland Inequality in China?" *Journal of Comparative Economics* 27: 686–701.

Kanbur, Ravi, and Zhang Xiaobo. (2003). "Spatial Inequality in Education and Health Care in China." Discussion Paper No. 4136, Centre for Economic Policy Research.

Lin, Justin Yifu, Cai Fang, and Li Zhou. (2003). *The China Miracle: Development Strategy and Economic Reform*. Hong Kong: Chinese University Press.

Mao Tse-tung. (1956). "On the Ten Major Relationships?" *Selected Works of Mao Tse-tung* (vol. 5, p. 284). Peking: Foreign Languages Press.

Murdoch, Jonathan. (2000). "Reforming Poverty Alleviation Strategy." In Anne Krueger (Ed.), *Economic Policy Reform: The Second Stage*. Chicago: University of Chicago Press.

Oi, Jean. (1995). "The Role of Local State in China's Transitional Economy." *China Quarterly*, no. 144 (Special issue on China's Transitional Economy): 1132–1149.

Parish, William L., and Martin K. Whyte. (1978). *Village and Family in Contemporary China*. Chicago: University of Chicago Press.

Parish, William L., and Martin K. Whyte. (1984). *Urban Life in Contemporary China*. Chicago: University of Chicago Press.

Park, Albert, Scott Rozelle, Christine Wong, and Changqing Ren. (1996). "Distributional Consequences of Reforming Local Public Finance in China." *China Quarterly* 147: 751–778.

Park, Albert, Sangui Wang, and Guobao Wu. (2002). "Regional Poverty Targeting in China." *Journal of Public Economics* 86: 123–153.

Qian, Yingyi, and Barry Weingast. (1996). "China's Transition to Markets: Market-Preserving Federalism, Chinese Style." *Journal of Policy Reform* 1: 149–185.

Qian, Yingyi, and Xu Chenggang. (1993). "Why China's Economic Reforms Differ: The M-Form Hierarchy and Entry/Expansion of the Non-State Sector." *Economics of Transition* 1(2): 135–170.

Rong Jinben, Cui Zhiyuan, et al. (1998). *From a Pressure Imposing System to a Democratic Cooperation System: The Political Reform at County and Township Level* (in Chinese). Beijing: Chinese Press of Translating and Editing.

Rozelle, Scott, Zhang Linxiu, and Huang Jikun. (1998). "China's War on Poverty." Paper prepared for the Conference on Socialism with Chinese Characteristics: China in Transition, Logan, UT.

State Council. (2004). "Policy Directives to Promote Farmers' Income." State Council, Beijing. Feb. 8.

State Statistical Bureau (SSB). (2004). *Chinese Statistical Yearbook 2004*. Beijing: China Statistics Publishing House.

West, Loraine A., and Christine P. W. Wong. (1995). "Fiscal Decentralization and Growing Regional Disparities in Rural China: Some Evidence in the Provision of Social Services." *Oxford Review of Economic Policy* 11(4): 70–84.

Wong, Christine (Ed.). (1997). *Financing Local Government in the People's Republic of China*. Hong Kong: Oxford University Press.

Wong, Christine. (1998). "Fiscal Dualism in China: Gradualist Reform and the Growth of Off-Budget Finance." In Donald Brean (Ed.), *Taxation in Modern China*. New York: Routledge Press.

World Bank. (2001). *China: Overcoming Rural Poverty*. Washington, DC: World Bank.

World Bank. (2002). *China National Development and Sub-national Finance: A Review of Provincial Expenditures*. Washington, DC: World Bank.

Zhu, Ling, and Jiang Zhongyi. (1996). "Public Works and Poverty Alleviation in Rural China." New York: Nova Science.

Zhu, Shouyin. (2001). "Explorations in Reducing Farmer's Burdens: An Analysis of Rural Tax Reform." Chinese University of Hong Kong Working Paper Series. Available at ⟨http://www.usc.cuhk.edu.hk/wk_wzdetails.asp?id=1590⟩.

11 Decentralization in South Africa

Martin Wittenberg

Introduction

Contributions elsewhere in this volume (chapters 7 to 10) show that decentralization can be part of undemocratic regimes' attempts to maintain control. The case of South Africa prior to 1994 exemplifies this process further. Indeed, the apartheid state's intentions were particularly radical—to balkanize the country and government through a set of local proxies.

In response, many of the antiapartheid movements tended to be strongly centralist (McCarthy, 1992). In their view, a strong central state was required to undo the fragmentation wrought by apartheid. How South Africa ended up with a system that according to some calculations (Bahl, 2001) is more decentralized than any comparable one is an interesting story that this chapter intends to sketch out.

I first outline the apartheid system of decentralization to show that this system was highly complicated and had a number of unintended consequences. It created a set of regional and local bureaucracies that tended to be corrupt and coercive and generated severe regional and local financial crises that served as the backdrop against which the new constitution was negotiated. The pressures to incorporate the regional and local interests that had been created led to the particular compromises embodied in the current system, and the logic of that system and some of the countervailing pressures within it are currently unfolding.

In an initial assessment of the successes and failings of this reform process, I note that the current system has notched up some impressive achievements, notably in ensuring that the financial flows are more formula driven and less capricious. However, many of the decentralizing features of the current system are undercut by a centralizing drift in the political system. Indeed, given the dominant position of the ruling party, it is unclear how decentralized the system will continue to be in future.

Perhaps one lesson to be learned from South Africa's experience is that particular forms of decentralization emerge out of particular constellations of social forces but that they in turn create new local and regional interests that affect the future trajectory of that system.

Decentralization in South Africa before 1994

Decentralization in white-ruled South Africa went through three broad periods.[1] In the first, a new unitary state was established from four colonies. Within this state, two systems of governance coexisted—a democratic system for white South Africans with considerable local autonomy and a much more centralized, undemocratic system for black South Africans.[2] Since this system was untenable in the long run, the state embarked on a unique social experiment in the second period. It attempted to partition the country into separate states. This form of decentralization was coercive and led to major fiscal and economic crises in the black parts of this system. In the final period, the state tried to reintegrate the different subsystems through new cross-cutting institutions. This proliferation of structures led to the administrative and fiscal mess that created the need for a new form of decentralization in the democratic era.

The Consolidation of the South African State, 1910 to 1948

The Union of South Africa emerged in 1910 as a merger of four British settler colonies. The state was created as a three-tier system, with elected bodies at all three tiers. The overall nature of the state was unitary rather than federal, but the existence of well-organized regional interests ensured that there was always some element of decentralization. The system is depicted schematically in figure 11.1. Municipalities (the lowest tier) existed only in proclaimed urban areas.

In the rural areas, there was no formal system of local government. Indeed, there were two distinct types of rural areas—privately owned farms and a number of reserves where the land was communally owned. In these areas, control was exercised indirectly, through the local chiefs and headmen. The key functionary of central control was the local magistrate. Outside the reserves, black South Africans were

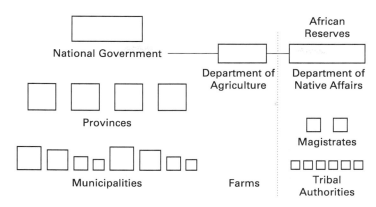

Figure 11.1
The system of decentralization, 1910 to 1948

subject to strong movement controls (the infamous pass laws). Their purpose was, in part, to keep cheap labor pools in the rural areas for farmers and for the employers of migrant labor, such as the mines. Despite these restrictions, increasing numbers of black South Africans found their way into the urban areas, provoking an incipient urban crisis. It also posed the long-term question of how urbanized black South Africans would be politically accommodated.

The Period of Grand Apartheid, 1948 to 1982

The solution proposed by the National Party and implemented vigorously in the decades after 1948 attempted no less than the balkanization of South Africa into separate ethnically pure states. The reserves, which were initially the residual pieces of land that white South Africans could not or would not take over, would become the central pillars of the new political order as eventually independent states. This policy came to be known as *apartheid*.

To accomplish this goal, several objectives had to be accomplished. The reserves had to be spatially consolidated so that the pretense of statehood was plausible. Greater control had to be exercised over the movement and location of black South Africans outside the reserves. Also, a set of interests linked to the reserves had to be created that could be relied on to support the cause of balkanization. Finally, at a micro level, social interactions between individuals of different races and "nations" had to be minimized to reduce miscegenation. National "purity" was necessary to justify separation.

The logic of this program led to a reconfiguration of the system of decentralization. The nascent dualistic system of decentralization that existed in 1948 was elaborated and made vastly more complicated in the next three decades. Broadly speaking, there were three important systems of decentralization. The first one was the system of national government, provinces, and municipalities that applied to white South Africans. This system became progressively more centralized during this period, as national government assumed increasing control, particularly over the lives of black South Africans. It did not trust even white-controlled local authorities to act with the same single-mindedness that characterized the center. The second one was a centralized system of control over the lives of black South Africans outside the reserves (or *homelands* or *Bantustans*). This system attempted to integrate control over movement, access to the labor market, and access to accommodation. The third was the system of governance within the reserves. This could be seen as a remarkable, if warped, attempt at decentralization. These regional structures eventually received all the trappings of independent states: police forces, armies, and foreign diplomats. To ensure that these "states" remained compliant clients, the internal structures were rigged to bolster the regime-friendly elements. Various direct and indirect interventions in the running of these states also occurred. Nevertheless, the handover of power was sufficiently real that capricious outcomes were always a possibility.

To complicate the situation even further, separate systems for coloured South Africans and Indian South Africans were devised. Furthermore, there were always parts of the country that were in limbo—that had been excised from one system and were still in the process of being transferred to another. Many of these *trust areas* remained in limbo for decades. The resulting complicated structure is depicted in figure 11.2.

While this system was intended to divide the majority politically and to keep tight control over the process of urbanization of blacks, it also led to several unintended consequences. One of the consequences was the fiscal crises of the black urban areas. After the townships were removed from the control of the white municipalities, they had to become essentially self-funding. This proved impossible in the long run. The Soweto riots of 1976 brought home to the state the realization that urban blacks could not be wished away and that there was major discontent brewing.

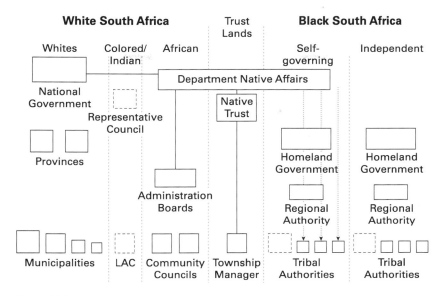

Figure 11.2
Decentralization during grand apartheid, 1948 to 1982

Another consequence was the economic crises in the homelands. The progressive mechanization of farming ensured the extrusion of hundreds of thousands of farm workers from white South Africa. Given the restrictions on urbanization, many of these ended up in the reserves, which placed enormous pressure on the available resources there. The state attempted to entice industry into the reserves, but since few reserves were well located for manufacturing, it had little success in doing so. With little in the way of an economic base, the homelands had a remote chance to ever become viable autonomous states. Instead, they became the repository of the destitute, the unemployed, and the unemployable. Their main function turned out to be social control. This was not a stable equilibrium. Only through vigorous repression was the state able to maintain the façade that independence was supported by the bulk of the population.

Corruption was an unintended by-product of the system, as well. In view of the enormous powers wielded by the bureaucracies dealing with the lives of the black majority, it is hardly surprising that every one of these bureaucracies turned out to be highly corrupt. Officials could be bribed to allow illegal workers to be admitted to the urban areas, employed, or housed. Politically well connected people managed to make fortunes out of trading in properties ahead of changes in their status. Within the Bantustans, most things worked on patronage and corruption.

The Reform and Eventual Collapse of Apartheid, 1982 to 1994

In the aftermath of the 1976 Soweto riots, the state began to reassess its policies. It realized that it needed to find ways of cutting across the existing administrative and spatial frameworks. In particular, it wanted to give additional groups of black people a stake in the system.

The fundamental problem, however, was that simply bringing black faces into governing structures could not resolve the fiscal and economic crises that were fueling popular discontent. The state needed to find ways of redistributing resources from the privileged white system of decentralization to the other systems. Since local white power was fairly well entrenched, the state's solution was twofold: centralize control further (such as by abolishing the elected provincial tier) and create bridging structures that cross-cut the existing administrative systems. Two types of bridging structures were implemented. At the regional level, nine development regions with associated development agencies were created to try to facilitate development across the borders of the homelands (see McCarthy, 1992; Wittenberg and McIntosh, 1992). At the local level, regional services councils were created to provide financial support for developing the urban black townships.

These structures provided yet another layer of complexity to the already complicated picture depicted in figure 11.2. These new cross-cutting structures proved somewhat resilient. They were positioned at levels designed to reintegrate spaces that grand apartheid had tried to cut apart. As such, they provided a convenient starting point from which the postapartheid system of decentralization could be constructed.

Nevertheless, they could not solve the underlying problems of apartheid: the spaces set aside for Africans were simply not economically viable. Partition might have worked if the spatial and economic provisions for it had been less niggardly. The main reason that they were not more generous was that no white community wanted to be sacrificed in the general interest (the NIMBY phenomenon).

Since an equitable partition was never going to be entertained, the primary function of decentralization was always going to be a more coercive one—to maintain control over the black population. Since this control was to be exercised in part indirectly, corruption was an inevitable feature of the system. One of the most pernicious legacies of apartheid, therefore, was endemic corruption in the large regional bureaucracies. Another was the administrative and spatial mess created by segregation.

Decentralization under the Democratic State

The Transformation Process and the Shape of the New System

The national negotiation process occurred against a backdrop of several hard facts. The apartheid state had not been militarily defeated, and hence suitable guarantees had to be given to the incumbents of the central state bureaucracy about their future. The Bantustans had to be reincorporated into the fabric of the country, and its bureaucracies also sought employment guarantees. The townships and periurban areas had to be brought into one system of urban administration. And lastly, the National Party and the representatives of other minority groups were categorically opposed to a strong unitary state, on the assumption that in such a state previously obtained concessions and guarantees would not be easily enforced.

To complicate matters more, at the time of the national negotiations, a number of Bantustan leaders jumped ship and moved to the African National Congress (ANC). The ANC was happy to do deals with them because it strengthened its hands at the negotiations. The cost of these alliances, however, was that the Bantustan bureaucracies had to be given meaningful roles. Furthermore, the ANC did not relish the thought of having to govern with an unsympathetic central civil service. It started to look to some of the Bantustan bureaucracies for credible black bureaucrats.

The Regional Tier In short, the ANC came to feel that a regional dispensation might be one way of reining in the national bureaucracy and buying off the Bantustan leaders. Given the latter purpose, it did not take all that much to converge on the set of development regions as the basis of the new provincial dispensation. The purpose of these regions had been to plan across the boundaries and to do so in a way that resembled economically meaningful entities.

These provinces were given "teeth" by being given considerable functions (particularly in relation to social services) in the new constitution. The ANC insisted that these not be exclusively provincial functions.

Instead, the central government retained overall policy-making and coordinating functions. In this way, South Africa's version of the German system of overlapping jurisdictions came into being.

Elections to the new provinces occurred concurrently with the national elections of 1994. The ANC ended up in control of all provinces except the Western Cape and KwaZulu Natal. In the latter, it ended up in a coalition government with the Inkatha-Freedom Party.

The Local Tier   The transition at the local tier was considerably more protracted, with fundamental changes being made at least until 2000, when the second democratic municipal elections took place. In the first phase of the process, transitional authorities were created through a process that involved bottom-up local negotiations as well as top-down demarcations made by the provincial and national governments. Elections for these transitional authorities were held in 1995 but with a weighted vote, which ensured that minorities had effective vetoes over the decision-making process. The second phase saw the demarcation of new municipalities and new district councils and ended with the municipal elections in 2000. These happened on a fully democratic basis within the new boundaries. The third phase (still underway) saw the reallocation of powers and functions between municipalities, district councils, and new special-purpose utilities.

The New System of Decentralization   The new shape of the system is schematically depicted in figure 11.3. This system differs from the previous one in many respects. The racial basis of the local government system has been removed, and all municipalities now cut across the previous divides. This has led to a certain amount of centralization. This is most evident in the case of the metropolitan councils, where all the preexisting municipalities were disbanded. As a result, a total of 14 million people (32 percent of South Africa's population) live in areas administered by just six councils. Even in the nonmetropolitan areas, the municipalities are generally much larger than they previously were. Indeed, the system was rationalized from roughly 800 "transitional councils" to 231 municipalities. South Africa now has municipalities in all parts of the country, including the farming and tribal-authority areas. In most parts of the country, there is now effectively a four-tier system of governance, with district councils and municipalities making up the lowest two tiers.

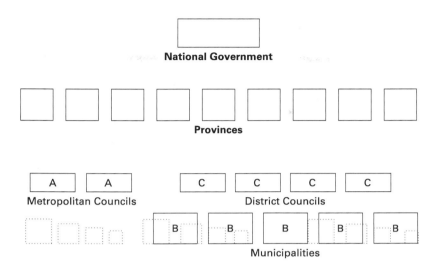

Figure 11.3
Decentralization in democratic South Africa
Note: The previous municipalities are shown with dotted outlines.

It is questionable whether South Africa really needs four tiers, particularly since there are frequently overlapping competencies between them. Relationships, particularly between local councils and district councils, are often far from cordial. Furthermore, the districts can also be uncomfortably close to the provinces in size. This raises the question of why the system evolved in this particular way. There are several reasons.

By the time that the local government system took shape, the ANC was firmly in power nationally and in most of the provinces. Because it was not willing to tolerate the idea of pockets of right-wing resistance being constituted around particular neighborhoods and local authorities, municipalities had to be large enough to ensure that the political power reflected the overall demographics of the area.

There were also good economic and planning reasons for increasing the size of municipalities. Apartheid had geographically cut apart most South African cities. Many black workers ended up in commuter dormitory towns that could be more than 100 kilometers away from the city that they serviced. Administering these areas in an integrated way was seen as essential for beginning to undo the damage done by apartheid. While these new municipalities were relatively large, there were many predominantly rural municipalities that had no preexisting administrations or tax base and consequently had very limited capacity. In this context, some planners felt that considerable power should be vested in a district tier that could then support these fledgling authorities. This, however, created problems in areas where well established municipalities suddenly found a new tier above them that became responsible for certain functions but did not have the capacity to carry them out.

It might have made more sense to do away with the district tier altogether or to have made it a voluntary association of municipalities. To some extent, this tier may owe its continued existence to the fact that preexisting tax bases (the Regional Services Council Levies) accrued to this level.

The Legal Framework

The underpinning of South Africa's decentralization program is provided by the 1996 constitution. This constitution stipulates that there will be three tiers of government and lists the responsibilities of each. The importance of constitutionally providing for these tiers is that central government cannot simply abolish any of them, nor can it unilaterally change the nature of a particular province or municipality. Actions such as the conversion of elected provinces to appointed ones, as happened in 1986, are therefore no longer possible. At least they would require a constitutional amendment, and this in turn would be subject to review by the constitutional court.

The position of provinces is further entrenched by the provision that South Africa's upper house of Parliament, the National Council of Provinces, is elected indirectly by the provincial legislatures. The support of a majority (five) of provinces is required for any legislation to be passed. Constitutional amendments require support from six provinces.

The national constitution also prescribes that provincial and local governments are entitled to an "equitable share" of nationally raised revenue. The constitution does not prescribe what this means, but it does imply that the allocations be made in terms of a formula. Such formulas now exist for both the provincial and the local allocations, although they are currently under review. This is discussed in more detail below.

The guarantor of the integrity of this system is the constitutional court, a body that did not exist previously. Indeed, litigation has been quite active around the system of decentralization. The constitutional court first flexed its muscle when it refused to certify the first version of the new constitution, since it felt that it did not sufficiently embody the agreements reached in the interim constitution. The eventually certified 1996 constitution therefore provided for a slightly stronger role for the provinces.

Litigation has also occurred in relation to the equitable share. The national government was taken to court by the Uthukela district council on the basis that this council did not receive its rightful "institutional capacity grant." The National Treasury argued that in fact districts did not qualify for this particular grant. National government lost the case in the Pietermaritzburg High Court ("District Municipalities," 2002), but took the matter on appeal. Nevertheless, the case was eventually settled out of court, and since then the districts have become eligible for this grant.

The Financial Framework

The current financial framework is markedly different from the previous system. Large-scale financial transfers occurred during the apartheid era to all kinds of subnational structures. These transfers were made completely arbitrarily and could be withheld as a form of discipline over recalcitrant structures. During the period of heightened civil unrest, large transfers were made to areas that had been "pacified." This "oil-spots" strategy ensured that transfers were very unequally distributed.

The current system is much less arbitrary. There are two components—a system that deals with the decentralization of revenues raised nationally and autonomous sources of funds for some of these levels. We deal with these in turn.

The current system of fiscal decentralization is mapped out in the Intergovernmental Fiscal Relations Act of 1997 (National Treasury, 1999, pp. 2.2–2.11). This sets up a set of formal consultative processes that have to occur prior to the tabling of the national budget in Parliament. In essence, the provinces and representatives of the local authorities have to be consulted prior to the tabling of the annual Division of Revenue Act.

The budget must make provision for the following: (1) the vertical split of national revenue between spheres (national, provincial, and local governments), (2) the horizontal split of the provincial equitable share between the provinces, and (3) the horizontal split of the local

Table 11.1
Division of revenue, 1999 and 2000 to 2005 and 2006

	1999/00 Outcome	2000/01 Outcome	2001/02 Outcome	2002/03 Revised	2003/04 Medium-term	2004/05	2005/06
Millions of rupees:							
National	66,385	73,178	87,709	98,853	108,983	117,549	126,323
Provinces	99,465	108,899	121,099	136,919	158,995	175,468	191,590
Equitable	89,094	98,398	107,460	123,457	142,386	155,313	167,556
Conditional	10,370	10,501	13,638	13,462	16,609	20,155	24,033
Local	4,610	5,536	6,516	8,801	12,001	13,249	14,624
Equitable	2,163	2,315	2,607	3,964	6,343	7,078	7,698
Conditional	2,447	3,221	3,909	4,837	5,658	6,171	6,926
Noninterest	**170,460**	**187,613**	**215,324**	**244,573**	**279,979**	**306,266**	**332,536**
Percentage:							
National	38.90%	39.00%	40.70%	40.40%	38.90%	38.40%	38.00%
Provinces	58.40%	58.00%	56.20%	56.00%	56.80%	57.30%	57.60%
Equitable	52.30%	52.40%	49.90%	50.50%	50.90%	50.70%	50.40%
Conditional	6.10%	5.60%	6.30%	5.50%	5.90%	6.60%	7.20%
Local	2.70%	3.00%	3.00%	3.60%	4.30%	4.30%	4.40%
Equitable	1.30%	1.20%	1.20%	1.60%	2.30%	2.30%	2.30%
Conditional	1.40%	1.70%	1.80%	2.00%	2.00%	2.00%	2.10%

Source: National Treasury (2003b, table 1.1, p. 5).

government equitable share between all municipalities (types A, B, and C). I discuss these components in more detail below.

Nationally Raised Revenues: The Vertical Split   The vertical split is not decided on by formula. It is arrived at through the consultative process referred to earlier. Within this process, however, the National Treasury plays a highly influential role, not least since it has a higher level of capacity than most of the other actors involved. Since it is ultimately up to Parliament to pass the Division of Revenue Act, this would seem to give preeminence to the national level.

A cursory look at the figures suggests that there may be some room for concern. As table 11.1 shows, the share of provinces in national revenue has come down over the first four financial years. This trend is budgeted to change. Nevertheless, the comparison between the actual and the budgeted figures can be misleading, since the provinces have in many cases been underspending on their budgets. This is a large cause for concern, since the provinces have crucial responsibilities in the delivery of services. It reflects on the lack of capacity in many of the provincial governments. In short, the trends evident in the table may be less a reflection of increasing national dominance and more a sign of provincial capacity problems.

It is striking how large a portion of the national budget (after dealing with the national debt) is allocated to provinces. This feature has led Bahl to suggest that South Africa is fiscally far more decentralized than one would expect given South Africa's level of development, geographic size, population size, and population homogeneity (Bahl, 2001, p. 3).

Although the equitable-share allocations are unconditional grants (the provinces and local authorities can in theory do with them what they want), in practice there are important constraints. The chief one of these at the provincial level is that the provinces employ much of the bureaucracy, including teachers, doctors, and nurses. Social grants are paid out by provinces. Since salaries of bureaucrats and social welfare benefits are determined nationally, this reduces the scope for maneuvre on the provincial budgets. Nevertheless, the provinces have been reasonably successful in reducing the share of personnel expenditure in the overall budgets over the last few years (National Treasury, 2003b, p. 23).

The provinces therefore now have increasing room for making independent decisions. In a number of cases, they are doing so quite successfully. The Gauteng province, for instance, has created a development arm that is spending large amounts of money on infrastructure projects.

Despite the unconditional nature of the equitable share allocation, the national government tries to encourage spending in particular ways. In the case of the local government equitable share, for instance, part of the grant is designated as a *free basic-services grant*. While the government cannot force municipalities to spend this grant on supplying free basic services to poor people, it is trying to use moral suasion to achieve this objective.

The Provincial Equitable-Share Formula   The allocations to different provinces within the overall provincial share are made in terms of a formula. The formula has various components, as described in the *Budget Review 2003* (National Treasury, 2003a, p. 259). There is an education share, a health share, a social security component, a population share, an infrastructure backlog component, an economic output component, and a component that is split equally among all provinces. Each of these parts is intended to reflect an aspect of provincial competence and funding needs. Since the overall allocation is an unconditional grant to the province, these component allocations are purely indicative. As the *Budget Review* (National Treasury, 2003a, p. 259) notes,

Although the formula has components for education, health and welfare, the share "allocations" are intended as broad indications of relative need and not earmarked allocations. Provincial Executive Committees have discretion regarding the provincial allocations for each function.

The formula is broadly redistributive. Poorer provinces and provinces with poorer infrastructure will tend to get higher allocations.

The Local-Government Equitable-Share Formula A strong redistributive element is also built into the local-government equitable-share formula. The formula was announced in 1998 (National Treasury, 1998) and has evolved since then[3] (for a recent overview, see Reschovsky, 2003). The largest component of the formula (making up about 82 percent of the overall equitable share in the last budget) is a set of grants intended to assist municipalities in providing basic services to low-income households. The formula also provides some limited support for the administrative costs incurred by poorer municipalities.

A more controversial component of the formula is a set of nodal allocations (comprising 3.6 percent of the equitable share) that are targeted to twenty-one particular development nodes announced by the president in 2001. National line departments were also asked to prioritize funding to these areas. In theory, the nodes were identified as places of particular poverty, but the case for this has not been unambiguously established.

As with the provinces, these subcomponents of the overall allocation act purely as guidelines. Municipalities can in practice spend their equitable share more or less how they wish (short of embezzling the funds).

One thing that should be stressed is that the formula has changed in every year since it was first introduced in 1998. First, the local government system itself has changed constantly. Second, a number of allocations that had historically been channeled through national or provincial line departments were progressively incorporated into the overall equitable-share envelope. Third, there have been data changes as new sources of information have become available. To smooth the resulting shocks to the allocations, the existing practice has been to guarantee that every municipality would receive at least 70 percent of the previous year's allocation.

Autonomous Sources of Funds: Levies from the Regional Services Council   The regional services council (RSC) levies are an important source of finance, particularly for district councils. They comprise two taxes: a flat-rate tax on payroll and a flat-rate tax on turnover. A comprehensive assessment of how these taxes operate is given by Bahl and Solomon (2000). They point to the fact that on many dimensions these are not good taxes and note that compliance is quite low. Companies self-assess their liabilities, and the municipalities are not entitled to audit them: "In many ways, the RSC levy more closely resembles a donation than it does a tax" (Bahl and Solomon, 2000, p. 8).

In the opinion of Bahl and Solomon, the low level of the tax currently and the quasi-voluntary payment have ensured that there is no stronger public opposition to this type of tax. Given these problems it is perhaps surprising that total revenue from the RSC levies is as high as it is (4.4 billion rand in 2002/2003).

Property Taxes   The major source of income for local government in the urban areas is from property rates—12.5 billion rand in 2002 to 2003 (National Treasury, 2003b, p. 35). At present, there is no uniform system of valuing or rating property. Historically, different provinces had different rules: in some cases, only land was valued and rated; in other cases, land and improvements were valued and rated. Agricultural land was not valued. Tribal land, since it is held in communal tenure, provides additional problems.

User Charges   A number of white municipalities traditionally made significant profits from their trading accounts, particularly from the reticulation of electricity. At present, the government is proposing to take away the function of electricity reticulation from municipalities and to vest it in regional electricity-distribution utilities. This will have a large and negative impact on local finances. One mooted solution to this is to give municipalities rights to some portion of the profits emanating from these utilities.

While some aspects of local authority operation may have been profitable, a number of others were taking large losses. One problem that

many municipalities have inherited from the conflictual period of the
1980s is a low propensity on the part of many urban residents to pay
their accounts (National Treasury, 2003b, pp. 43–44):

The most recent reports suggest that municipalities have accumulated R. 24.3
billion in outstanding debtor balances or unpaid consumer bills. This accumulation over the recent past represents approximately 10 percent of the total
operating budgets for the last five years.

Bureaucratic Reforms

As the local government system was reshaped, different bureaucracies
had to be melded together in the new municipalities; parts of existing
bureaucracies had to be hived off to new locations; and whole new
bureaucracies had to be created in places where there had never been
proper local authorities.

Parallel to these changes, a number of municipalities embarked on
corporatization exercises. The city of Johannesburg, for instance, created separate service providers to deal with functions such as refuse
collection and electriticy and water reticulation. In a number of vigorously contested cases, municipalities engaged private service providers to run water schemes and the like.

The latter reforms all emanated from the continuing problem of revenue collection. It is hoped that some of these bureaucratic reforms
might improve customer care (and hence satisfaction and willingness
to pay), ensure accurate and timely billings, overhaul the internal systems, and provide more appropriate levels of service.

Monitoring

For the system to work, there have to be appropriate monitoring and
early warning systems in place. In the case of the financial system, the
National Treasury is piloting legislation to ensure that there are appropriate financial controls in each tier of government.

The need for such systems was brought home early in the development of the current intergovernmental system, when there were a
number of crises. The most acute one was in the Eastern Cape government, which in one month was unable to pay pensioners due to over-
spending in other provincial departments. It was technically bankrupt.
It had assumed that the national government would simply step in and
cover all the liabilities. The national government did not do so and
hence the crisis.

As a result, measures were introduced to ensure that properly quali-fied financial managers were employed in all departments that spent significant amounts of money. The Public Finance Management Act of 1999 clarified the role of accounting officers and established sanctions, including civil liability, for such officers (National Treasury, 1999, p. 3.15). Similar legislation was introduced for the municipal tier in the Municipal Finance Management Act of 2003. This act also tries to en-sure that municipal accounts and budgets work in standardized ways.

Another important monitoring mechanism in the current system is the office of the Auditor General. All public bodies are audited by this office. Regrettably, there is cause for concern about the state of local government financial controls. As of September 30, 2002, 5 percent of all municipalities had failed to produce accounts for the 2000 to 2001 fi-nancial year, and 77 percent had failed to produce 2001 to 2002 finan-cial statements (National Treasury, 2003b, p. 46). Furthermore, in a high proportion of cases where audits were performed, the Auditor General gave only a qualified opinion. Among the reasons for the Au-ditor General's reservations were inadequate debtor controls and in-adequate provisions for writing off bad debts.

A different sort of monitoring of the system is performed by the Financial and Fiscal Commission (FFC), a statutory body that makes proposals about the functioning of the intergovernmental system. It does research into what would be appropriate changes to the existing formulas. It also makes recommendations about a variety of issues such as municipal borrowing powers and changes to the electricity dis-tribution system. Furthermore, the round of budget allocations begins with a set of recommendations from the FFC about how the cake should be split. The National Treasury and the Department of Provin-cial and Local Government are required to respond formally to all these proposals. Because the FFC is not directly involved in the alloca-tions process (unlike the Commonwealth Grants Commission in Aus-tralia, for instance), it does not have the direct clout to make its views count. It therefore plays much more the role of a think-tank, raising issues and preparing the ground for initiatives that national govern-ment departments then may eventually take up.

The Political System
Thus far we have looked at how the system of decentralization works at the formal level: the legal framework, financial system, bureaucratic

system, and monitoring mechanisms. The operation of the system in practice is, however, crucially influenced by the dominant position of the African National Congress (ANC) within most parts of the country.

The national legislature and the provincial legislatures are all elected by a proportional representation system. This ensures that representatives within those bodies are elected through the party list and not directly elected. Proportional representation ensures that minority interests are represented in all these bodies, but it also gives enormous power to the people in control of the party list. In particular, it allows the party bosses to "fire" members of Parliament or of the provincial legislatures that do not toe the party line. It is also in general not possible for these elected representatives to defect to another party without losing their seat.

This central-party power has been exercised quite frequently. Virtually every provincial premier (the equivalent of a state governor in the United States) in ANC-controlled provinces has been replaced through central intervention since 1994. In some of these cases, the intervention was designed to settle feuds between factions within the province; in other cases, it dealt with the perception of inadequate governance or local corruption; and in yet other instances, it was supposed that the central power brokers were worried about the emergence of a charismatic regional leader.

At present, it is well understood within the ANC that provincial premiers and mayors all fall under central discipline. The central party can deploy or redeploy people to these positions at will.

Nevertheless, the ANC itself is a quasi-federal body. Regional and local congresses have the power to elect their own political leaders. This can lead to tensions when the regional ANC has one political leader while the provincial premier happens to be a different individual. This means that attempts to centrally control the makeup of the provincial and local executives is always subject to some negotiations with the local political structures.

In the case of municipalities, there is a further constraint in that at least some councilors are elected directly through a ward system. Such councilors cannot be simply redeployed elsewhere.

While the operation of this system ensures that central political control can be tightly exercised over the ANC-controlled provinces and councils, this is not the case when other parties are in government. In this regard, there have been two problematic provinces: the Western Cape was under the control of the opposition Democratic Alliance, while in KwaZulu Natal there was a coalition government between the Inkatha Freedom Party and the ANC.

This has recently changed. A break-up in the Democratic Alliance led to the defection of the National Party component, which entered into alliance and subsequently merged with the ANC. The end result of this process saw the ANC take control of the Western Cape province and of the Cape Town metropolitan council. It also led to the significant weakening of the position of the Inkatha Freedom Party within the KwaZulu Natal legislature. The suspicion is that many of these defections were prompted by the promise of better career prospects. Given the ANC's controlling position at many levels, it is better able to offer rewards to politicians within its fold.

This weakening of the opposition was confirmed in the general election of 2004. The ANC now effectively controls all provinces. What effect this extension of ANC dominance will have on the medium-term development of South Africa's system of decentralization remains to be seen.

Assessment: How Is the System Functioning?

Careful econometric work on how the system is performing still has to be done. There are many difficulties to be confronted in doing this appropriately. First, the 1994 transition was not one from a uniformly centralized to a decentralized system. Instead, it was a change from a coercive decentralized system to a democratic decentralized system (a type C decentralization, in the language of the introduction to this volume). In the field of education, for instance, it involved the rationalization of about seventeen education departments into nine provincial departments. It is difficult to conjecture how a centralized democratic system might have performed.

Second, many other changes happened concurrently. In particular, there was a major restructuring of the South African economy, which became more open as sanctions were lifted and tariffs reduced. Macroeconomic policy was largely conservative. Labor-market policy, on the other hand, strengthened the roles of trade unions and made labor markets less flexible. These macroeconomic changes affected many indicators of well-being within local authorities and provinces.

Finally, there are data problems in comparing outcomes, particularly at the local-authority level. The new municipal boundaries show little continuity with the previous boundaries, including those of the magisterial districts, which were the organizing unit of data collection in the past. Consequently, it is often difficult to monitor changes across the transformation break, since the spatial units to which the information applies have changed.

Given these problems, we present in this section preliminary and impressionistic views.

Poverty Alleviation and Social Spending
One of the biggest changes that has occurred is that poor areas are explicitly targeted through the formula. Poor rural areas, in particular, have been the major beneficiaries of the change in the system. In the past, they received no intergovernmental transfers (except for a limited stipend paid to chiefs) since there was no local government in these areas to speak of. Now they receive substantial funds.

This raises the question of whether the new system of decentralization has had any impact on poverty. The available evidence suggests that democratization has had a significant impact on interracial inequality (Jenkins and Thomas, 2000; Seekings, 2003). The evidence from a panel dataset collected in the province of KwaZulu Natal suggests that there is considerable mobility out of poverty (Cichello, Fields, and Leibbrandt, 2001), although much of this mobility is associated with job losses and gains. More distressingly, the lackluster performance of the South African labor market has, according to some estimates, led to an overall increase in income poverty in the period 1995 to 2000 (Statistics South Africa, 2002). These findings are attenuated by the impacts of state redistribution. In the same period, access by the poor to most basic services has improved (Statistics South Africa, 2002). Indeed, state spending in general is quite successful in reaching the poor. South Africa's remarkable noncontributory social-pension system is but one example of this.

Another study based on the KwaZulu Natal panel study finds that social capital has become a more important determinant of income generation in the postapartheid period than previously (Maluccio, Haddad, and May, 1999). This would be compatible with observing that the new system generates more opportunities for the majority to use their skills and networks.

Underfunded Mandates
One of the stated aims of the current government is to provide "free basic services" to all its citizens, particularly the poor. To this end it increased the equitable-share funding of local government. There is

some doubt, however, whether these funds are completely adequate for carrying out this mandate. This has been the source of persistent complaints by local authorities.

There are other mandates that are probably more onerous. South Africa's Bill of Rights (enforced by the Constitutional Court) provides extensive social and economic rights to its citizens. This has meant, for instance, that eviction of illegal occupiers of land and buildings has become more difficult, since there is now a duty on the state (and in this instance on local authorities) to provide adequate shelter.

The fundamental problem is not so much that the central government is shifting existing functions to a subnational government without the necessary resources but that there are probably not enough resources in the system as a whole to meet all of the needs and backlogs that the current government would like to tackle. Local authorities as the direct service providers feel some of these pressures more directly.

Effectiveness of Poverty Targeting

A question that surfaced early in the development of the system was whether the state had adequate information to permit proper poverty targeting. In fact, the state's information base was very weak. The statistical system prior to 1994 was highly differentiated: reasonably reliable censuses were run in white South Africa, and very little information was available on the rest. The independent homelands were, in fact, missing from the official statistics.

In the process of overhauling the statistical system, the 1996 national census was a key event. Additional socioeconomic information became available through a set of national household surveys, the October Household Surveys and the 1995 Income and Expenditure Survey. The question was whether this information could be used to say anything sensible about the distribution of poverty.

The solution adopted was to use an imputation method (for details, see Alderman et al., 2000). There are some questions about how well this imputation process works (Wittenberg, 2002), but there is little doubt that the current system is much more effective in reaching the poor than the politically and ideologically driven transfers of the past.

Patronage

In the old system of decentralization, transfers from the national government to local areas were driven completely by the preferences of the center. The state concentrated resources either where it wanted to bolster a client or where it wanted to diffuse opposition. The move to formula-driven allocations was an enormous step forward in breaking some of those patronage networks.

There are, however, some new forms of patronage. The nodal allocations seem essentially idiosyncratic. At present, they make up a relatively small part of the transfer system, but there may be pressure to extend it.

Slimming Down the State?
One of the key promises of the new government system was a rationalization of the many bureaucracies that had been created under apartheid. With the creation of the new provinces, some rationalization occurred. This rationalization did not always occur in the most appropriate places (such as the freezing of some health posts). Nevertheless, personnel expenditure (as a percentage of total expenditure) climbed in the period 1997–98 to 1999–00 as a result of some new hires and wage increases (National Treasury, 1999, p. 21). Since then, personnel expenditure has come down sharply (National Treasury, 2003b, p. 23), although total employment in the public service is scheduled to rise to meet greater service-delivery targets (National Treasury, 2003b, p. 183).

The amalgamation of municipalities also led to some degree of rationalization. Nevertheless, personnel expenditure as a proportion of total expenditure has ballooned (National Treasury, 2003b, p. 198). In part, the amalgamation of bureaucracies has frequently led to a ratcheting up of wages and conditions of service to the most favorable level.

At the same time, the consolidation of district municipalities has led to the creation of new bureaucracies. The global effect of this is as yet quite small. Indeed, the six metropolitan councils employ the bulk of all local government employees. As noted above, there is some concern whether the district-council layer will contribute to efficient service delivery or be an obstacle toward it.

In summary, there is as yet little evidence that South Africa's decentralized system is leading to more efficient government. To some extent, it is too early to tell, since the system has been in constant flux and has not yet been allowed to settle down. Furthermore, there would have been inevitable transition and learning costs associated with creating a new system out of the fragmented past. The evidence from the provincial budgets is encouraging in that regard, suggesting that the system may be consolidating properly.

Corruption and Misadministration

South Africa's subnational levels of government have been frequently rocked by allegations of corruption and misadministration. Many of the more spectacular examples have been concentrated in the Mpumalanga provincial administration. In a famous scandal, the province handed over most of its public parks to a private company, the Dolphin Group, without a process of public tender. Subsequently, it was suggested that some members of the local ANC might have benefited. The provincial premier, Matthews Phosa, was eventually removed from office, although corruption charges against him were never proven.

A considerable level of corruption was expected when many of the provinces took over homeland administrations. They were handling large programs, such as pension payments, which by their nature would attract fraudsters. Indeed, there have been several scandals involving ghost pensioners and ghost civil servants who were drawing significant benefits. The attempt to clean up the administrative infrastructure has in some cases created problems of its own. In the case of the Eastern Cape, for instance, about 20,000 legitimate pensioners were taken off the pension list when the government tried to tighten up on fraud. A hearing was organized by the Eastern Cape legislature into the welfare system, which ended up with these damning conclusions ("Welfare Collapses in E Cape," 2000, p. 33):

The report found welfare clerks to be "often drunk"; "do not investigate the queries and problems but just send people from pillar to post"; "poorly informed about policies and often appear to make up their own rules, especially about child-care grants"; and "do not assist if they have paid money to the wrong person and make no attempt to help the correct beneficiaries to obtain their money," even though it was the official's fault.

It is not clear whether a nationally organized bureaucracy would always perform better in these areas.

A different type of corruption can be seen in some areas where there have been blatantly political appointments to bureaucratic positions (see, for instance, "IFP's 'Jobs for Pals' Policy," 2001). This potentially has very negative impacts on the capacity of local authorities to deliver. It might be seen as a form of capture of the local authority by the local political elite. Given that in many very poor areas employment by the local authority is the most lucrative form of income available, this form of capture is perhaps to be expected.

Alignment with Local Needs

One of the arguments adduced in favor of decentralization is that it should lead to a closer congruence between local needs and local-service delivery. One would therefore expect to see at least some variety in the services offered in different parts of the country.

Differences in policies have been noticeable in some areas. For instance, the policies of the Western Cape (while under opposition control) and KwaZulu Natal toward the treatment of AIDS were different than those operating in the ANC-controlled areas. Even though health care is also a provincial competence, it is striking that few of the ANC-controlled provincial health departments dared to steer a different path to the public policy announced by the national minister of health. The sole exception to this was the Gauteng province, where the premier, Mbazima Shilowa, announced that antiretrovirals would be made available in all public hospitals for the purpose of preventing mother-to-child transmission ("Gauteng Saves Babies," 2002). This announcement led to a furious public exchange at the end of which it was announced that Gauteng was not, in fact, breaking ranks with national policy. The program would just be an extension of the prevailing testing regime. It did not change the fact that the drug Nevirapine would be available in all hospitals.

In short, there is some evidence that local concerns can be more effectively addressed in the current decentralized system. Nevertheless, considerable central influence, exercised if necessary through party structures, is very much in evidence.

Unfinished Business

There are certain aspects of the democratic transformation process that still have some way to run. One of the thorniest questions is the position of the chiefs (amakhosi) and of communal land. In particular, in KwaZulu Natal this issue still has the potential to disrupt the operations of local government (see, for instance, "Amakhosi Could Delay Planning," 2002).

In a different way, the success of the decentralization program depends on adequate transparency. The current intergovernmental system is not all that transparent, and the existing local government equitable-share formula is not very transparent at all. Many of the ingredients of the formula (like the poverty counts) are poorly understood by those most closely affected by it. Indeed, there are not many people even within the bureaucracies administering these grants that properly understand how the formulas work.[4] In essence, the integrity of the system depends on a very thin layer of overstretched people in the national bureaucracies. Given the constraints under which they are working, they have done a good job thus far. For the long-run development of the system, however, a proper understanding of how the system works must diffuse downward—not only to the provinces and municipalities but also to the interested ratepayer and resident associations.

One of the key ingredients that is currently missing from the system is a lively and functioning civic movement that can hold local officials to account. South Africa had a lively civic movement during the struggle against apartheid. Unfortunately, the leadership of this movement was either absorbed into the government or went elsewhere. The assumption seems to have been that with the achievement of democracy, many of the local issues would automatically be addressed, but a vigilant community is as necessary to keep a democratic state under control as it was to unseat an undemocratic one.

Conclusion

This chapter has given a broad overview of decentralization as it was under apartheid and as it is currently. Many of the issues confronting the system today have their roots in that past—the capacity problems at the provincial level; the awkward position of districts that are linked to the lower-level municipalities but also in some tension with them; the revenue-raising problems of local authorities. We argued earlier that a given set of institutional arrangements and boundaries creates interests that then have effects on the ability of the system to move to a different set of arrangements.

The challenge facing South Africa is how to ensure that the reforms that have been introduced thus far create interests that will ensure that these reforms are carried through to the end. We have noted that there are many positive signs. The social-service benefits are certainly more widely distributed than ever before. The equitable-share formula, despite possible misgivings about the accuracy of the data, is certainly reaching many more poor areas than would have been the case under other dispensations. A system of legal and financial checks and balances is being created.

Nevertheless, there is also some evidence of a centralizing drift. Some of this is driven by technocratic and efficiency concerns. Some of it, however, seems motivated by a distrust of policy experiments emanating from sources outside the center.

There are undoubtedly cases where central intervention was required to stop large-scale abuses. However, if the benefits of decentralization are to be achieved, then it is essential that a dynamic is created where local interests can play some of that policing function.

Acknowledgments

I would like to thank the editors of this volume and the discussant, Geeta Kingdon, for helpful comments. John Luiz and Stefan Schirmer carefully read the draft paper and provided useful feedback. They are not responsible, however, for any errors that remain.

Notes

1. For a lengthier discussion, see the working-paper version of this document (Wittenberg, 2003).

2. It is impossible to avoid racial terminology when discussing South Africa. The "race groups" according to which society was organized were white South Africans, coloured South Africans (mixed-parentage individuals), Indian South Africans, and black South Africans. The actual classification was even more detailed than this. The term *black* is used ambiguously in South Africa. Some times it is used to refer collectively to coloureds, Indians, and blacks, while at other times it refers more exclusively to blacks. I generally use it in the more exclusive sense, although with some exceptions, where context should make the more extended sense clear.

3. A number of changes to this formula are in the pipeline (National Treasury 2005, app. E). They do not fundamentally affect the picture presented here.

4. This may change with the recently announced revisions to the equitable-share formula.

References

Alderman, Harold, et al. (2000). "Combining Census and Survey Data to Construct a Poverty Map of South Africa." In Statistics South Africa, *Measuring Poverty in South Africa*. Pretoria: Statistics South Africa.

"Amakhosi Could Delay Planning." (2002). *Natal Witness*, February 20, p. 3.

Bahl, Roy. (2001). "Equitable Vertical Sharing and Decentralizing Government Finance in South Africa." Working Paper 01-6, International Studies Program, School of Policy Studies, Georgia State University.

Bahl, Roy, and David Solomon. (2000). "The Regional Services Council Levy: Evaluation and Reform Options." Mimeo.

Cichello, Paul, Gary Fields, and Murray Leibbrandt. (2001). "Are African Workers Getting Ahead? Evidence from KwaZulu-Natal, 1993–1998." *Social Dynamics* 27(1): 120–139.

"District Municipalities Win Case." (2002). *Natal Witness*, February 7.

"Gauteng Saves Babies from Government AIDS Policy." (2002). *Weekly Mail and Guardian*, February 18.

"IFP's 'Jobs for Pals' Policy." (2001). *Natal Witness*, December 7.

Jenkins, Carolyn, and Lynne Thomas. (2000). "The Changing Nature of Inequality in South Africa." Working Paper 203, World Institute for Development Economics Research, United Nations University.

Maluccio, John, Lawrence Haddad, and Julian May. (1999). "Social Capital and Income Generation in South Africa, 1993–1998." Discussion Paper 71, Food Consumption and Nutrition Division, IFPRI, Washington, DC.

McCarthy, Jeff. (1992). "Local and Regional Government: From Rigidity to Crisis to Flux." In David M. Smith (Ed.), *The Apartheid City and Beyond: Urbanization and Social Change in South Africa* (pp. 25–36). London: Routledge.

National Treasury. (1998). *The Introduction of an Equitable Share of Nationally Raised Revenue for Local Government*. Pretoria: National Treasury, Republic of South Africa.

National Treasury. (1999). *Intergovernmental Fiscal Review 1999*. Pretoria: National Treasury, Republic of South Africa.

National Treasury. (2003a). *Budget Review 2003*. Pretoria: National Treasury, Republic of South Africa.

National Treasury. (2003b). *Intergovernmental Fiscal Review 2003*. Pretoria: National Treasury, Republic of South Africa.

National Treasury. (2005). *Budget Review 2005*. Pretoria: National Treasury, Republic of South Africa.

Reschovsky, Andrew. (2003). "Intergovernmental Transfers: The Equitable Share." In Roy Bahl and Paul Smoke (Eds.), *Restructuring Local Government Finance in Developing Countries: Lessons from South Africa* (pp. 173–235). Cheltenham, UK: Edward Elgar.

Seekings, Jeremy. (2003). "The Reproduction of Disadvantage and Inequality in Post-apartheid South Africa." Paper presented at the North Eastern Workshop on Southern Africa, University of Vermont, Burlington.

Statistics South Africa. (2002). *Earning and Spending in South Africa: Selected Findings and Comparison from the Income and Expenditure Surveys of October 1995 and October 2000*. Pretoria: Statistics South Africa.

"Welfare Collapses in E Cape." (2000). *Weekly Mail and Guardian*, June 9, p. 33.

Wittenberg, Martin. (2002). "Comments on Measuring Poverty for the Purposes of Allocating the Local Government Equitable Share." Mimeo.

Wittenberg, Martin. (2003). "Decentralization in South Africa." Policy Paper, Econometric Research Southern Africa.

Wittenberg, Martin, and Alastair McIntosh. (1992). "Decentralization in South Africa: Regional Power or Local Development?" Local Government Policy Project, University of the Western Cape.

List of Contributors

Omar Azfar
IRIS Center
University of Maryland,
College Park

Gianpaolo Baiocchi
University of Massachusetts,
Amherst

Pranab Bardhan
Department of Economics
University of California,
Berkeley

Shubham Chaudhuri
World Bank, Washington, DC

Ali Cheema
Department of Economics
Lahore University of
Management Sciences (LUMS)

Jean-Paul Faguet
Development Studies Institute
and STICERD
London School of Economics

Bert Hofman
World Bank, Beijing, China

Kai Kaiser
World Bank, Washington, DC

Philip E. Keefer
World Bank, Washington, DC

Asim Ijaz Khwaja
John F. Kennedy School of
Government
Harvard University
Cambridge, MA

Justin Yifu Lin
China Center for Economic
Research
Peking University

Mingxing Liu
School of Government
Peking University

Jeffrey Livingston
Department of Economics
Bentley College
Waltham, Massachusetts

Patrick Meagher
IRIS Center
University of Maryland, College
Park

Dilip Mookherjee
Department of Economics
Boston University

Ambar Narayan
World Bank, Washington, DC

Adnan Qadir
Pakistan Administrative Staff
College
Lahore, Pakistan

Ran Tao
Institute for Chinese Studies
University of Oxford

Tara Vishwanath
World Bank, Washington, DC

Martin Wittenberg
School of Economics
University of Cape Town

Index